DISCARDED

C0-GMW-156

Practical Guide to Intranet Client-Server Applications Using the Web

Norman E. Smith

Wordware Publishing, Inc.

[redacted]

Library of Congress Cataloging-in-Publication Data

Smith, Norman E. (Norman Earl), 1952-
Practical guide to intranet client-server applications using the Web / Norman E. Smith.
p. cm.
Includes index.
ISBN 1-55622-549-0 (pbk.)
1. Intranets (Computer networks). 2. Client-server computing. 3. World Wide Web (Information retrieval system) I. Title.
TK5105.875.I6S58 1997
005.2'76—dc21

97-20680
CIP

Copyright © 1998, Wordware Publishing, Inc.

All Rights Reserved

2320 Los Rios Boulevard
Plano, Texas 75074

No part of this book may be reproduced in any form or by any means without permission in writing from Wordware Publishing, Inc.

Printed in the United States of America

ISBN 1-55622-549-0
10 9 8 7 6 5 4 3 2 1
9706

Product names mentioned are used for identification purposes only and may be trademarks of their respective companies.

All inquiries for volume purchases of this book should be addressed to Wordware Publishing, Inc., at the above address. Telephone inquiries may be made by calling:

(972) 423-0090

[redacted]

Contents Summary

Table of Contents

Chapter 1

About This Book

Introduction

Client-server computing means many things to many people. Generally, client-server computing means an application that has a client portion that runs on the user's local computer, whether a PC, Macintosh, or workstation, and a server portion that runs on a larger host computer such as a Unix-based server or mainframe computer. Client-server applications are most often database-centric. This book examines client-server applications that are intranet based. Intranet applications use World Wide Web (WWW) technologies on local networks.

I recently read an editorial about client-server computing that likened "dog years" to "client-server years." The implication was client-server is evolving at a very fast pace. It seems that every couple of days another client-server related product announces a major new feature or upgrade. Just about every software package on the planet is adding Web support or at least HTML as an output option.

Java is maturing. The "visual" languages continue to add functionality into their base or kernel code to support such things as database access that only a year ago required a third-party function library. Two-year-old client-server books don't even mention some of today's hottest buzzwords.

So how can *Practical Guide to Intranet Client-Server Applications Using the Web* not be out of date by the time it is written and published? The long answer is read the book to find out. The short answer is by concentrating on a small segment of client-server known as Web-based intranets. The techniques and approaches presented throughout this book emphasize *practical*. Open solutions that work as well today as they will next year or the year after. Even as commercial packages for automatically developing Web-based client-server applications proliferate, there will always be a need to provide custom client-server solutions. The generic Web-based approach presented in this book illustrates techniques that you can use effectively for many client-server applications.

Developing client-server applications using Web-based tools instead of traditional proprietary tools, such as PowerBuilder or Delphi, is under consideration in many companies with the explosion of the Web. There are many advantages to a Web-based approach. Some tools are inexpensive compared to proprietary tools, rapid development of both prototype and production systems, and the wide choice of commercial packages that support HTML output. This book takes a look at choosing the tools. It also identifies exactly what is involved with developing an intra/internet application including several case studies with complete source code.

This book examines client-server intranet applications. This should be of interest to you if you care about client-server computing on the Web. Programmers faced with developing Web intranet applications and managers who need to make informed decisions about using a Web-based or traditional client-server approach for intranet applications will both find much useful information here.

Hardware aspects of client-server computing are not addressed in this book. Selecting platforms for clients and servers as well as the network hardware considerations are beyond the scope of this book. Web-based clients and servers exist for most modern computers. With a little care in application design, the client and server platforms used for Web-based client-server applications do not matter. Other considerations such as the database server for the system will drive hardware selection.

Appendices at the end of the book present related information.

Client-Server Approaches

Many approaches to implementing client-server applications exist. There are "thin" clients with "fat" servers, and "fat" clients with various weight servers. There are two-tier, three-tier, and multi-tier approaches. Each is discussed in more detail in later chapters.

The thin versus fat clients and servers is really another way of saying how the application processing is partitioned between the client and the server. Thin clients typically do little application processing and primarily handle the user interface. Fat clients contain some amount of the application specific processing such as field validation or connecting to the database. There is an infinite variation on degrees of thinness. The thinner the client, the larger the portion of the application that must reside in the server.

Client-server applications are often described in terms of "tiers." Tiers may refer to hardware or software. People generally mean software tiers. Tiers describe the partitioning of the application between the client and server. Experts have identified many possible tiers, although two-tier and three-tier are the most common. Two-tier is a client tier and a server tier. Three-tier is a client tier, an application processing tier, and a server (usually database) tier.

Vocabulary

At a distance, client-server applications do not appear overly complex. There is a client. There is a server. The client supplies the user interface and the server supplies the data. Looking any deeper reveals client-server computing is not simple and is in fact complex. At the conceptual level, there is a whole new vocabulary, abbreviations, and buzzwords to deal with.

Many of the terms listed here have obtained buzzword status. Everyone uses the latest buzzwords and few understand them. Client-server is definitely in that category.

The remainder of this section lists and defines a few of the major client-server terms.

API	Application Program Interface
Client	The portion of an application that interacts with the user.
CORBA	Common Object Request Broker Architecture
DBMS	Database Management Systems
GUI	Graphical User Interface
Internet	Networking based on the Internet protocols first evolved in Unix such as TCP/IP. Internet has evolved to mean the worldwide computer network that started as the ARPAnet and is publicly accessible. Internet tools are typically FTP, telnet, and WWW-based browsers and servers.
Intranet	Networking based on the Internet protocols, generally using WWW-based tools. The primary difference between internet and intranet networks is an intranet is generally protected from public access, often by a network firewall.
LAN	Local Area Network
Middleware	Frequently termed the glue in client-server applications. Middleware usually provides the communications interface between the client and the server.
NFS	Network File System
Object Oriented	A software development methodology where data is modeled as "objects" and procedures that operate upon the data are called "methods."
ODBC	Open Database Connectivity
OLE	Object Linking and Embedding
RAD	Rapid Application Development
RPC	Remote Procedure Call
Server	The portion of an application that supplies information and services requested by a client. A single server generally services multiple clients.
SQL	Structured Query Language
SSL	Secure Socket Layer
Thick Client	A client that performs much of the application processing.
Thick Server	A server, usually paired with a thin client, that performs most of the application processing.

Thin Client A client that performs little actual application processing beyond handling the user interface. The user interface is some sort of GUI such as X-Windows or Presentation Manager.

Thin Server A server, usually paired with a thick client, that performs little of the application processing.

Tier A distinction of various abstractions of an application. Tiers may be logical, representing software work divisions or hardware distribution.

Writing Style and Organization

Each chapter covers a single topic. It consists of an introduction to the topic. Examples are presented where appropriate. The introduction serves as a formal definition of the topic to be covered. A chapter may include other sections necessary to fully explain the given topic.

The case studies generally present versions of the filter in more than one language. Discussions may apply to all language versions or to a single language version.

Identifiers and reserved words are set in italic type.

Two-key combinations are a combination of a shift key and a letter. The shift keys are Alt, Ctrl, and Shift. For example, "Press Ctrl-C to exit" means press the "C" key while holding the Ctrl key down. The word "Press" indicates a key or key combination should be pressed to continue.

Coding Style

The coding style used in this book favors clarity in the code used in the examples. The coding style of many C programmers combines statements where possible. For example, the typical way of testing the length of a string for 9 is:

```
if(strlen(xxx)==9){ ... }
```

The same code following coding style in this book is:

```
len = strlen(xxx);
if(len == 9){
        ...
}
```

The code contains few descriptive comments. Sections of code are marked off that are referred to in the descriptions in the text. Since new concepts are being presented, the readability of the code is more important than absolute program efficiency in the examples. The examples are illustrative and the sample programs may or may not be robust enough for real world production use.

Chapter 2

2

Client-Server Computing

Introduction

This chapter discusses "what is client-server computing." It briefly covers client-server computing history. The "tier" architectures are discussed. Popular client-server tools such as Borland's Delphi are briefly discussed.

What Is Client-Server Computing?

Client-server is a relatively new computing term that means different things to different people. The generally accepted, high level definition is an application, usually database centric, that is divided into a client portion to handle the user interface, data validation, and error checking and a server that responds to client requests for data and resources.

When client-server first became hot, file server vendors touted their systems as the server to PC clients. The application could be any program that accessed files on the server. Today few people would consider this client-server computing; remote file access is simply part of a LAN and its services.

Today client-server generally implies an application with a client portion and a server portion. The client performs one or more of the following processing:

- User interface
- Command interpretation

- Data entry
- Data validation
- Online help
- Error recovery

The server:

- Responds to client requests
- Services multiple clients
- Performs functionally related operations
- Handles contention and record locking
- Manipulates shared data
- May manage shared resources

The server is generally passive, waiting for client requests to service. The following figure illustrates the server's relationship with clients at a conceptual level. One server generally handles multiple clients.

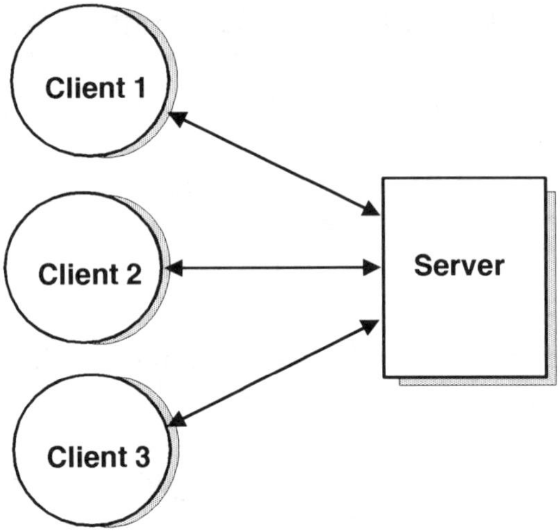

A Server Handles Multiple Clients

User Interface

The client handles user interaction. This includes screen handling or a Graphical User Interface (GUI) in today's PC-based client computers. Display windows, mouse, and keyboard all fall into the user interface category of processing. Display window processing may include multimedia functions if the application has multimedia portions.

Command Interpretation

Client applications that include any sort of scripting capability obviously must include command interpretation capabilities. Many client applications must be able to interpret parameters and execute procedures when buttons are pressed or hyperlinks selected. This can be considered command interpretation.

Data Entry

Virtually all client-server applications do some sort of data entry. Data entry is not just filling in field values in a form but any data input required by the application. This may be as simple as entering an e-mail address or entering a search string. Processing is necessary each time data is entered.

Data Validation

After data has been entered on a form, it generally requires some initial validation. Validation may range from making sure required fields contain some data to date checks to content validation. Validation here refers to any checks that can be performed totally within the client portion of the application.

Online Help

Most of today's interactive applications include some form of interactive help. Windows applications usually include Windows Help files and may offer context sensitive help. HTML, PDF, Envoy, or other electronic document files along with their associated viewers may be offered as well. The main point is these all run in the client and not the server.

Error Recovery

There are many forms of error recovery a client-server application might be required to perform. There may be data errors, communications errors, hardware failures, or any number of other errors that must be handled properly.

Server Types

There are many types of servers. Most client-server applications are database centric, so most people mean database server when the term "server" is used. Typical server types are:

- Database
- File
- Compute
- Display

One characteristic that most servers have in common is they run under multitasking operating systems. Otherwise, multitasking must be built into the server application to allow more than one client to be handled at a time.

Database Server

A database server is exactly what it sounds like. It is a server that waits for retrieval requests and other commands from clients, then acts upon the specified database. The database server is also frequently termed a database engine. Oracle, SQL-Server, Informix, and SyBase are popular database servers that are frequently used in client-server applications.

File Server

A file server provides transparent file access to a client. File server vendors were among the first to use the term client-server. Typical low-end file servers are PCs running Novell NetWare, OS/2, or Windows NT. Midrange file servers are often Unix systems providing access via NFS. Mainframes are the ultimate in terms of speed and storage capacity. The client typically accesses files on the file server as if mounted as a local disk. The application on the client should never know the difference.

Compute Server

Compute servers are special purpose from a software standpoint. They exist to perform some computationally/resource intensive operation. Oftentimes, dedicated or special purpose hardware is used for compute servers.

Display Server

The display server is very system specific. The most obvious example is the X-Windows server, which generally runs only on Unix workstations.

Client-Server History

In the beginning, there was no client-server computing. A dumb terminal was connected to a host computer using a dedicated communications line such as RS-232 or 20Ma loop. Later RS-422 was also used. The dumb terminal provided the user with a keyboard and screen. The screen had character cell-based capabilities; the cursor could be addressed, but characters were in the terminal's ROM. All of the application ran as a single unit within the host. This computing model is often termed monolithic computing. You might also think of this as one-tier computing.

The first client-server applications generally passed large amounts of data between client and server. Later two-tier and most three-tier applications have migrated to a message passing scheme that allows the network connection to remain open a minimum amount of time as well as generally pass smaller amounts of data at any one time. Needless to say, the choice of data or message passing affects the network load. The differences may not be noticed on a lightly loaded network with few users but may be crippling as more users are added.

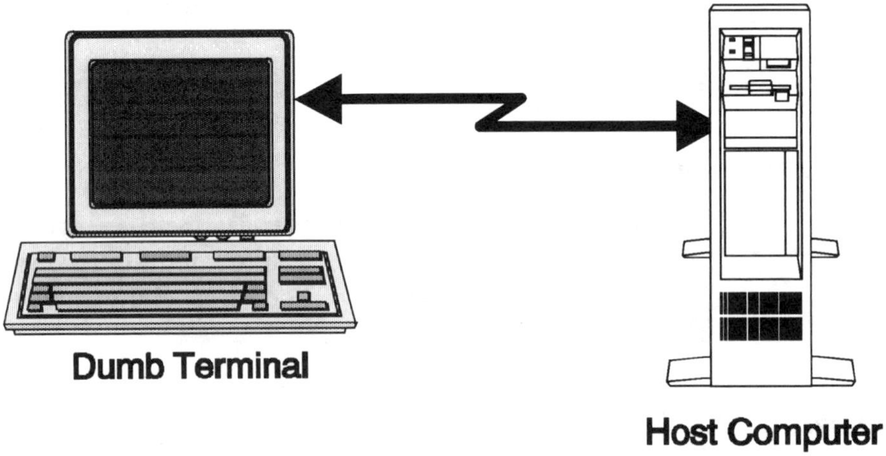

Monolithic Computing Model

Two-Tier Client-Server Computing

The first-generation client-server applications were generally implemented in two logical tiers. This model of computing often has two tiers of hardware as well. This is not the case when the client and server both run on the same computer. Two-tier client-server divides the application into two distinct parts (the tiers) where one portion runs on the client computer and a separate portion runs on the server. Keep in mind that the client and server code should not care nor even know whether they are running on the same computer or not. Thus, the application is divided across the client and the server.

The amount of the application logic that runs in a client or server determines whether it is "thin" or "fat." Thin implies that little application processing is present and fat implies that a large portion of the application logic is present. There are varying degrees of thin and fat. A thin client usually handles very little application logic and mainly exists to handle user interaction via a GUI. Thin clients are attractive when the client computer, usually older PCs, have limited performance. PCs that are 386 or low-end 486 based are typical of this type client hardware. There just aren't enough MIPS to handle a GUI, communications, and a significant portion of the application processing.

Two-tier client-server has shown to be more difficult to develop and maintain than originally expected. Two-tier applications often do not scale well. As an application grows in both complexity and number of users, additional servers or a new division of processing between the client and server may require major rewrites of two-tier applications. Also, client-server tools took time to mature. Today, a number of database and tool vendors supply development packages that support two-tier client-server application development. Visual Basic, Delphi, and PowerBuilder are current examples of this type of tool. Most of these client-server tools are in the process of migrating toward three-tier support with each release.

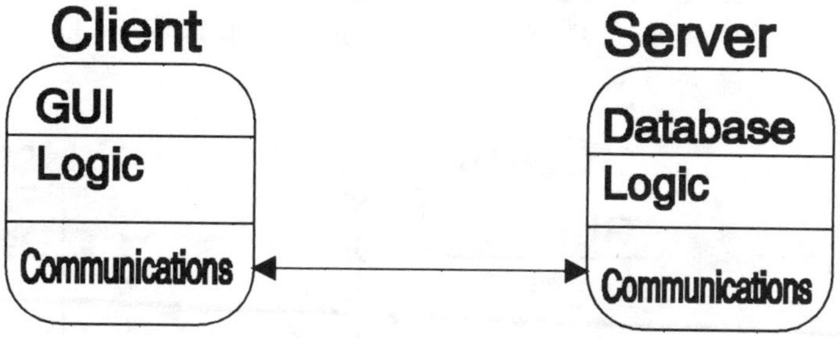

Two-Tier Client-Server Model

Middleware

Middleware is a term used to describe the communications "glue" between the client and server. The client portion of the application usually interfaces with the middleware via an API. The middleware then handles communications with the server. It eliminates the need for the application and, just as importantly, the application programmer from having to deal with the complexity of interfacing directly with the low level operating system or hardware to communicate with the server.

Generic middleware handles communications using a very generalized approach that can be used for any type of application. There is usually a like piece of software on the host computer to handle client communications and interface with the server software. Examples of generic middleware include:

- TCP/IP
- DCE
- NetBIOS
- Named pipes
- LAN Manager

Specific middleware is a level up from generic middleware. It handles communications for a specific class of server such as database or mail or web. Examples include ODBC for database servers, SNMP for mail servers, and SSL for web servers. Middleware at this level may run "on top of" a generic middleware protocol. HTTP running on top of TCP/IP is typical of this.

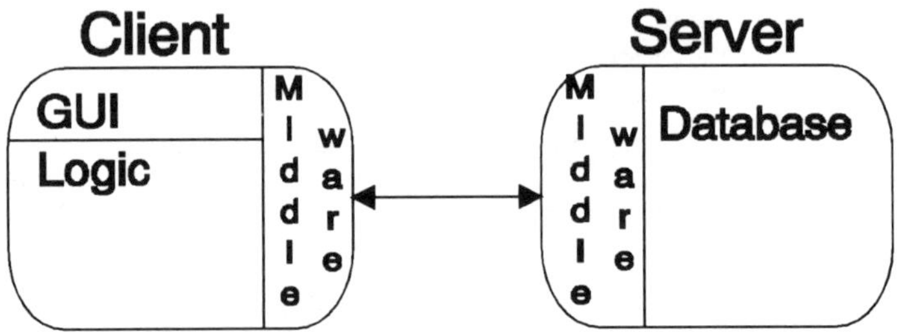

Middleware Model

Three-Tier Client-Server Computing

The latest form of client-server computing to evolve is three-tier. Some people also use multiple tier to generically include any approach that uses more than two logical tiers.

There are several approaches for multi-tier client-server development today. The most obvious one is continuing to use two-tier tools for the client side GUI and processing. A second approach that may gain popularity, especially for large projects, is an integrated client-server development tool such as TI's IEF. A third approach uses a two-tier front end such as Visual Basic or PowerBuilder along with an integrated back end development package that generates the server application code and database connection.

A primary difference between two- and three-tier applications is the extra software layer on the server. Where two-tier applications tend to either put the logic in the client and pass records (data) to the database (fat client model) or pass data to the database where stored procedures and triggers implement the application logic (thin client model), three-tier applications tend to pass messages between the client and server portions of the application code. The server portion performs the application logic, then sends transactions to the database. The application logic is usually called "Business Rules" in the client-server community.

The third tier adds some complexity because it is an additional piece of code to develop. The tools and programming languages used for the server code depends a great deal on the server platform. Visual Basic is not appropriate for the application tier on a Sun Sparc Server. A Unix server probably dictates C or C++ while an Intel-based server running Windows NT may also use Delphi for the application tier effectively. In short, there is no single answer for which language to use for the server portion of a client-server application as long as you don't force the server development to use the same programming language as the client when it's not appropriate.

The server portion of the three-tier architecture adds somewhat to the overall complexity of the application. There are definite benefits to a three-tier client-server approach however. These include:

- Scalability
- Generally lower network traffic
- Flexibility

The scalability is improved because the server code and the database are separate; they may start out on a single host computer and later be separated. Multiple application servers may talk to one central database or one application server may still serve the clients while accessing multiple databases as the system scales up. The three-tier modularity makes rearranging the pieces much easier than in the two-tier client-server model.

Lower network traffic stems from passing small messages around the application rather than whole data records.

Flexibility is gained because the client, server, and database systems may each be replaced without affecting the other pieces, provided the interfaces do not also change. For example, changing the database from SyBase to Oracle only affects the server portion of the application, not the client. Rewriting a Visual Basic client in Delphi has no effect on the rest of the application, provided the interface between client and server code is met.

Many of today's commercial database-centric applications, including SAP's R/3, use the three-tiered client-server model in order to obtain scalability and flexibility. Web-based intranet applications are also generally three-tier client-server applications.

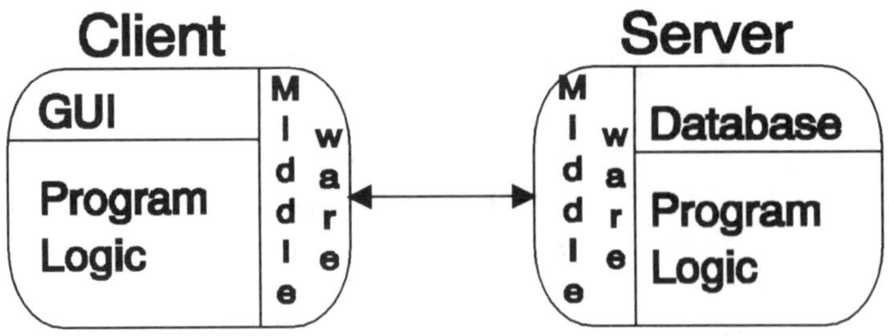

Three-Tier Client-Server Model

Popular Client-Server Tools

There is a large selection of client-server development tools available in today's computer marketplace. The following table takes a very quick look at several of the most popular non-Web tools. What most of these tools have in common is they are generally optimized for developing two-tier applications.

Language	*Description*
Borland Delphi	Delphi is an object-oriented "Rapid Application Development" tool. The programming language is based on Borland's Object Pascal and generates native code for the PC. The development environment is "visual," capitalizing on the ideas first used in Visual Basic. Both native database and ODBC drivers are provided.
Visual Basic	Visual Basic is the original visual programming language. It provides the tools to build client applications. Version 4 can access databases via ODBC. The single largest complaint about Visual Basic applications is lack of speed because it is interpreted. Version 5 should be out by the time this book is published. It is supposed to provide a native compiler among the enhancements.
PowerBuilder	PowerBuilder is a tool for developing GUI front ends to database applications. It is one of the oldest client building tools. PowerBuilder has cross platform capabilities including Windows 95, Windows NT on Intel and Alpha, Solaris (Unix), and Macintosh clients and starting with Version 5 has a Netscape plug-in. ODBC and native drivers are available for Oracle, Sybase System 11, Informix, SQL Server 6, and DB2.

Language	*Description*
C/C++	The old standby client-server languages are C and C++. The latest PC C/C++ compilers such as Microsoft Visual C++ and Borland C++ provide a visual programming environment for client development along the lines of Visual Basic. Communications and database capabilities are provided via subroutine libraries. Before the addition of visual client building, tools such as PowerBuilder held a clear development advantage.
Developer/2000	Developer/2000 is a client-server development tool produced by Oracle. It includes modules for designing and developing data entry forms and generating reports from an Oracle database.
Access	Access is Microsoft's personal SQL-based database product. Because it has ODBC capabilities built in, Access is often used as a front-end client to other SQL database systems such as Oracle and Sybase.
Other Languages	Several other programming languages, mostly object oriented, such as Smalltalk and Eiffel have been successfully used for client-server development. Any language that can access object libraries may be used effectively.

Summary

Client-server computing is many things to many people. It is a buzzword. It is also an approach to scalable computing applications. A number of generalizations can be made about client-server applications:

- They provide cooperative software processes.
- It does not matter whether client and server run on the same computer or not.
- Most common application is networked database.
- Significant work takes place in both the client and the server.

- The client generally requests and consumes information or services supplied by the server.
- The server supplies requested information or service to the client.
- The client is proactive.
- The server is reactive.
- The client handles interaction with the user.
- Client-server applications hide the server and network from the user.

Successful client-server applications require a clear management vision of where the application is going and what it takes to get there. It also requires a great deal of upfront work, even more than normal software development projects.

Whole books have been written on the information covered in this chapter. The information presented here is intended to show the breadth of client-server computing while the rest of the book covers one specific area, Web-based applications, in detail.

Chapter 3

Traditional Client-Server Versus Web-Based Approach

3

Introduction

This chapter compares and contrasts traditional and Web-based client-server development. Traditional client-server here means following a non-Web development methodology where there is client development, server development, and possibly multiple application tiers. There are many choices, so many that making a rational decision may seem impossible.

Traditional Client-Server Approach

The "traditional" client-server application is database centric. Most client-server development tools are oriented in that direction. So, let's start at the top. The basic client-server model can be depicted as:

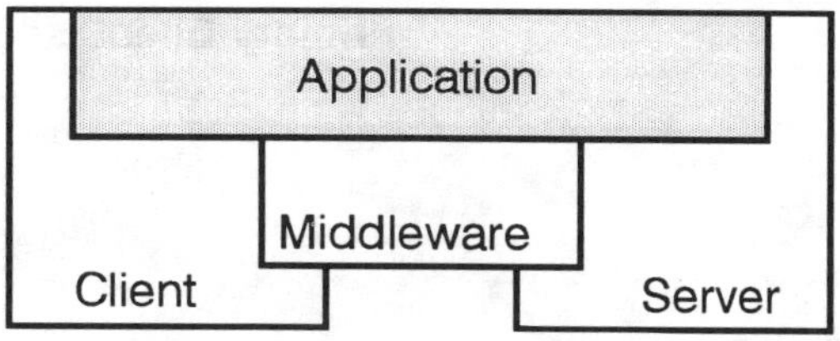

Basic Client-Server Model

This diagram is used as a starting point for discussions in this section.

Client-server development requires a great deal of upfront planning and analysis; even more than normal software development projects. There are many issues and decisions that must be made either prior to starting development or as part of the initial analysis phase. Several client issues should be addressed at this point, including:

- Hardware platform
- Implementation language
- DLLs
- Thin or fat
- Deployment

The Client

The following illustration depicts the primary client issues to consider.

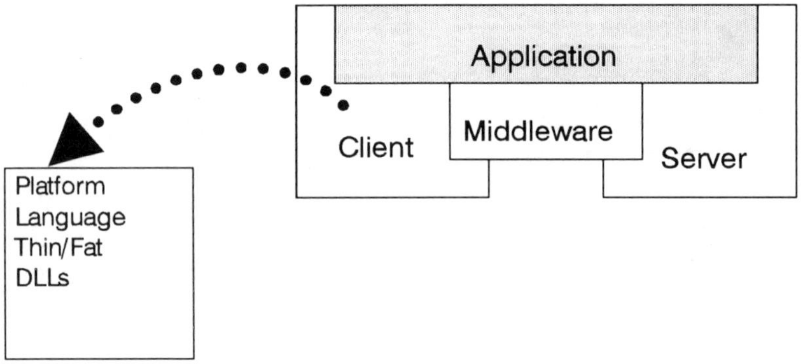

Primary Client Issues

Hardware Platform

The hardware/software for the client is a chicken and egg question. In some cases, the software will determine the client hardware, and in others, the hardware selection influences the software. Two primary hardware considerations are processing power (MIPS) and network bandwidth.

In today's computing world, consider a 100mz Pentium with 16MB of memory and ethernet a minimum Intel-based client configuration for normal users. Developers need high-end machines such as 200mz Pentium Pros with 32 or 64MB of memory, large (2GB+) hard drives, and large (17 inch or larger) monitors. Fast developer systems usually pay for themselves several times over during the course of a project. Recycling existing computers for clients is often done, especially at the start of a project. Resist the temptation to use 386-based PCs or 68k-based Macintoshes. In general, they just don't have the necessary speed or hardware resources. Hindering users with slow client hardware will only make users frustrated and raise resistance level to the new system.

Several tools, such as PowerBuilder, are multi-platform and can work in mixed client environments. Multi-platform tools may allow the hardware decision to be driven by considerations other than just the hardware required by a particular software development package. The most common solution is simply selecting the client hardware based on the current organizational infrastructure. Organizations that use PCs will probably choose PC-based clients, while Macintosh- or workstation-based shops are likely to stick with the client hardware they know best.

Implementation Language

The choice of client implementation language or tool is likely to strongly influence hardware selection. It is also a relatively complex issue that must be weighed by the developer organization. Factors include:

- Developer experience
- Tool cost, both for developer license and training
- Hardware
- Software selected for other portions of the system
- Whether the client will be thin or thick

Project vision also comes into play to a certain extent as well. Visual Basic might be chosen for a relatively small, minimal functionality system with limited growth potential. If you know up front that the client is a starting point that eventually will expand to every desktop in the organization, then a more robust and faster compiled language such as Delphi or Visual C++ might fill the bill in the long run better.

Developer experience should also enter into the language selection equation. Never choose a language that no developers have any experience with. Even one experienced developer will significantly shorten the learning curve for the whole staff. Plan on training when a new programming language or tool is used.

One last point on choosing a client implementation language; choosing a language or tool ties you to that vendor for the life of the project. Choosing Visual Basic means dealing, either directly or indirectly, with Microsoft. Choosing PowerBuilder ties you to Powersoft, etc.

DLLs

Dynamic Link Libraries (DLLs) issues only apply when the client is Windows (either Windows 3.1, Windows For Workgroups, Windows 95, or Windows NT). The proliferation of system DLLs over the past few years has made DLL selection an important issue in the client selection equation.

DLLs typically contain generic system libraries, such as the Visual Basic runtime module. Application programs generally distribute the DLLs they need to run. Frequently distributed DLLs include:

- Visual Basic runtime
- ODBC drivers
- Winsock
- Graphics conversion library
- Application modules

The problem is one of configuration management and user support. Assume a user's PC functions properly. Suppose a new package is loaded with a newer ODBC driver. The updated DLL overwrites the existing ODBC driver used by another program. Now, some of the old applications no longer work because of DLL differences. DLLs often are not completely backward compatible. Applications may work in conjunction with a DLL bug and often do not work when the bug is corrected in the driver. There also may be subtle differences between driver DLLs from different vendors which may also affect an application.

There is not a great deal that can be done about the multiple DLL version problem beyond being aware the potential for problems exists. The knowledge will provide some hope of identifying such a problem when it happens. Working with vendors is often necessary to solve DLL incompatibility problems. Keeping Windows applications up to date tends to minimize this type of problem.

Thin or Fat

The thin or fat client issue keeps surfacing. The decision must be made early on because it influences tool selection. The thinner the client, the less critical speed and memory considerations become. Rapid application development (RAD) is often traded for performance. Interpreted Visual Basic falls into this category of tool. (Visual Basic 5.0, with code compilation, should be available by the time this is published.)

The fatter the client, the more critical speed and memory usage become. The tradeoffs of RAD and performance swing in favor of performance. Client-server tools are evolving to provide both RAD and performance.

Factors that affect the thin versus fat client quesion include:

- The client hardware; low-end client hardware points to thin client software
- The network; a heavily loaded network favors the fat client

Whatever the client makeup, it is important to at least plan the approach up front so the client decisions can be factored into other development decisions.

Deployment

Thinking about application deployment may seem strange during initial planning, but is very important especially when a large number of users are involved:

- How much installation is required?
- How are updates handled?
- Is there a standard client hardware configuration and what is it?
- What is the standard client software configuration?
- Are there known DLL incompatibilities?
- Can client installation be staggered?

The list of development related questions goes on and on.

Automated client installation is practical. Many installation utilities are available today that can be used for any size application. Another possibility to consider is network installation. Fat clients may also require control or table files that require frequent update. Again, knowing the client makeup plan up front can prevent much pain later during application development.

Summary

The point is not necessarily to answer every development question up front. Some of the answers will be obvious; some are tough. Asking the question makes people think about the issues. Some issues about other project areas may have different solutions when deployment issues are considered than when the issues are totally ignored.

The Server

Server issues are depicted in the following illustration:

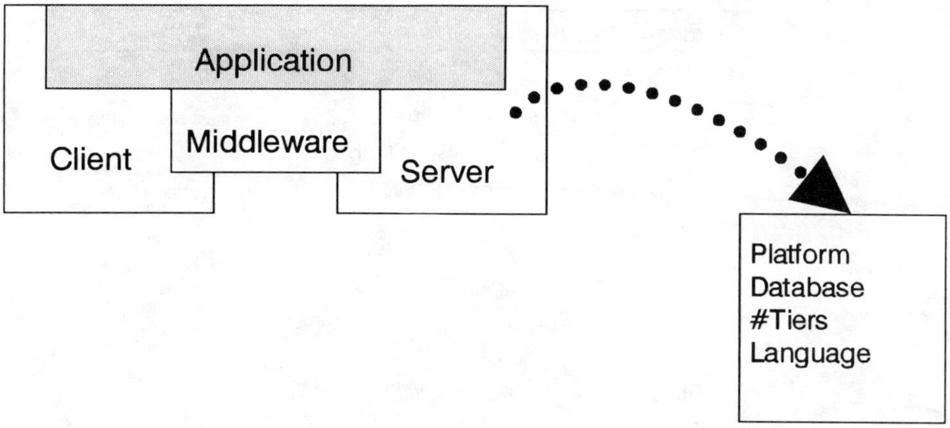

Server Issues

Hardware Platform

In some ways, the server hardware platform is easy. The rule of thumb is "get the fastest processor, with the most memory and largest disks that you can afford." There are many factors in the actual selections that are similar to the client selection factors.

The OS and database choice must go hand in hand with the hardware choice. The OS must be multitasking. Other multitasking OSs (all are multiuser as well), including DEC OpenVMS, IBM MVS and OS/400, also make good choices in some cases. Other PC operating systems suitable for some applications are IBM OS/2 and Novell NetWare. Today's two most prominent server OSs are Unix and Windows NT. Both are robust and capable. The following table summarizes the hardware platform availability for Unix and NT:

Hardware Platform	Unix	NT
Intel PC	Solaris 86	X
	Linux	
	SCO Unix	
	UnixWare	
Sun Sparc	Solaris	
	Linux	
Dec Alpha	DEC Unix	X
	Linux	
HP RISC	HP/UX	
MIPS RISC		X[1]
Power PC	IBM AIX	X[2]
	Linux	

(1) Support being phased out by Microsoft

(2) Under development

There is one very big difference between desktop computers and server computers. That is I/O bandwidth. Unix vendors seem much more aware of this than their PC counterparts with one or two exceptions. Don't get caught in the trap of using a desktop computer as a server. Applications tend to run fine in the beginning on a desktop computer masquerading as a server. Eventually, performance will suffer as the system load increases.

Desktop disk space expansion is generally more limited to two IDE drives, while server computers usually have SCSI controllers which can control up to eight disk drives.

Memory is another area that often comes up lacking in desktop computers used for servers. On the desktop, 32MB of memory seems like unlimited real estate. In a server, 128MB or 256MB of memory is often fully utilized.

Database

The database selection goes hand in hand with the hardware choice. You can't run Microsoft SQL Server on Solaris for example. Keep in mind that even though a vendor's database may run on several platforms, each vendor generally supports one platform better than others. The following table summarizes the hardware platforms supported by the major relational database servers:

Database	Unix	NT
Oracle	X	X
Informix	X	
Sybase	X	
SQL Server		X
Open Ingres	X	

The database manager must be able to interface with the communications middleware or provide a mechanism to be called by other programs in the system.

The client approach and number of implementation tiers also relate here. Choosing a thin client and two tiers adds the requirement that the database server support some sort of stored procedure mechanism or other programming capability with which to implement the business rules.

Tiers

The number of logical tiers planned for the system is an important decision too. There are several decisions associated with choosing a traditional two-tier or a three-tier approach. This decision should be made in conjunction with choosing the client approach. A thin client implies that much of the application processing will be done on the server, either as a third tier or as a fat server.

A two-tier system means choosing tools for the client as well as the server and, more than likely, choosing a middleware package. This question ties back to the client because the server side of the middleware equation must be compatible with the client side middleware. The system is not going to function very well if the client middleware is ODBC and the database server does not support ODBC.

A three-tier system adds the decision for implementing the third tier, where the business rules will be encoded. A third tier adds a second choice to make in the language category: the implementation language for the third tier. This is mentioned here because the business rules tier usually runs on a server.

Language

The programming language for the server may very well not be the same one used for the client. This is especially true if the client is a PC and the server is a Unix platform. The client side may be Delphi or Visual Basic, neither of which run on Unix systems. The base language on the server side is probably going to be C/C++ or a vendor proprietary language supported by the database server.

The number of tiers also comes into play. A two-tiered application may use an SQL-based language built into the database server. For example, PL/SQL in Oracle. A three-tiered application is much more likely to require a traditional language (C/C++) unless a three-tier specific package is used to implement the business rules.

Middleware

Middleware issues are identified in the following diagram:

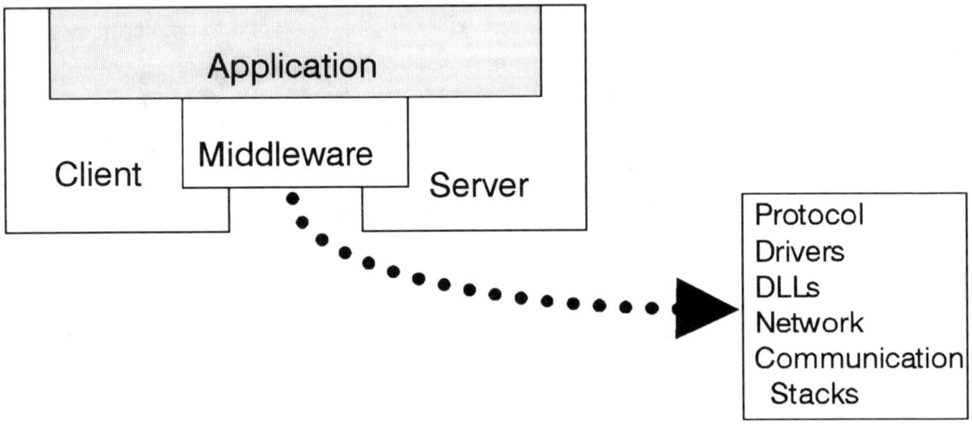

Middleware Issues

Protocol

The communications protocol selected must be compatible with the remainder of the system. The protocol here implies both the low level transport protocol such as TCP/IP and the higher level ODBC, HTTP, etc. TCP/IP has evolved as the de facto standard for most mixed platform environments.

The middleware higher level protocol requires a conscious decision because it affects performance. ODBC is fairly generic; that is, most database systems and middleware support it. However, many middleware packages such as PowerBuilder and Delphi also support faster native links to several popular database servers.

Drivers

ODBC device drivers come in several flavors as well. First, ODBC has evolved over time. There is a basic Level 1 functionality and a more advanced ODBC Level 2 capability. Not all ODBC drivers support Level 2 operations. Windows 3.1 required third-party ODBC drivers. Windows 95 drivers are included with several Microsoft products including compilers and the Access database.

DLLs

DLL selection was also discussed under the deployment section above. DLLs should be kept as generic as possible, for example using VBRUN30.DLL. It is likely there is little known about the exact third-party DLLs that will be used at the beginning of the project and is therefore not critical beyond being aware all of the DLLs required for client operation will have to be included with the software distribution.

Network

Most of the time the physical network already exists within the organization, and there is little to consider beyond making sure that the software is compatible with the physical hardware and communication lines.

Communication Stacks

The communication stacks are a generic term given to the network drivers. The term stack implies that multiple logical connections or sessions are made to the network. This item is listed mainly as a reminder that compatibility must be maintained or the client and server will not communicate. Winsock and Novel IPX are examples of communication stacks.

Alternative Approaches

There are a number of client-server development approaches that are considered alternatives to the traditional development approach. The first approach is using a completely integrated client-server development package. The idea is to describe the business rules and the package generates the client and server portion of the system. This approach will probably become more common as the packages mature.

The most common alternative approach to traditional client-server development is a Web-based intranet application. The choices described in the previous sections are a little different because many of the decisions are implicit in choosing the Web approach. The remainder of this section discusses the same upfront planning decisions that apply to Web client-server applications.

Web Client

Most of the client issues have predefined answers. The hardware platform can be almost any computer. There are even Web browsers that work with character cell dumb terminals. As this is written, there are two dominant PC-based browsers, Netscape Navigator and Microsoft Internet Explorer. The implication is hardware choice is not a big issue as long as the browser supports the features required by the application. The following diagram shows the client issues in Web-based client-server applications:

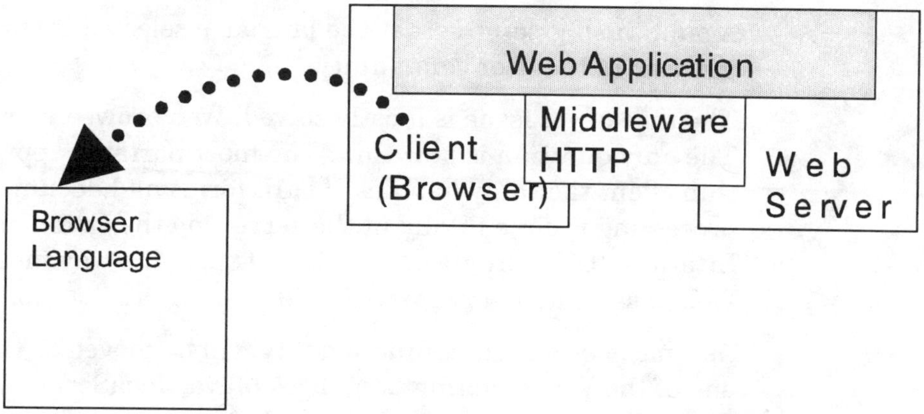

Client Issues in Web-based Client-Server Applications

The main Web client issue is your user community must use a browser that supports whatever features that the application depends on. For example, early browsers did not support uploading files from the PC to the server, while the latest do. If the application requires the client to be able to upload files, then that becomes one of the specifications for user browser selection.

The language choice is also fairly restricted. Some of the choices are presently limited by the browser. The following table summarizes language choices for Web-based clients:

Browser	*Language*
Netscape Navigator	Java
	JavaScript
Microsoft Internet Explorer	Java
	JScript[1]
	VBScript
Hot Java	Java
NCSA Mosaic	None
Other Browser	Unknown

(1) Jscript is Microsoft's JavaScript implementation. Support is added in Internet Explorer 3.01 and later.

Again, the big point is that the language selected is supported by the browser in the user community.

The thin or fat issue is mostly solved. Web browsers are thin clients. The only question is how thin. The most portable approach is a very thin client that only handles HTML forms and documents. The processing is done totally in the server via the Common Gateway Interface (CGI) program interface. This is the way most of today's Web-based client-server applications are built.

As time goes on, more functionality will be moved to the client via one of the Web scripting languages (Java, JavaScript, VBScript, and Active-X). The languages all have different origins:

- Java is a development of Sun Microsystems.
- JavaScript is a simplified form of Java developed by Netscape. Microsoft JavaScript implementation is called Jscript. Jscript is included with Internet Explorer starting with Version 3.01 and later.
- Active-X is a Microsoft invention. Compiled "controls" are downloaded from the server and executed on the client.
- VBScript is also a Microsoft language. It is comparable with JavaScript in capabilities.

I see two issues with Web scripting languages at the present time, maturity and security.

Maturity and security are closely related. Java and JavaScript are both designed for Internet scripting. Both take security seriously. Some holes have been found in Java and corrected. Java's security should continue to improve as the language implementations mature.

Java

Java is an invention of Sun Microsystems as an internet enabled programming language. Java is an object oriented language which resembles C++ but without some of the C++ baggage. Most notably missing are pointers and multiple inheritance. Java defines a "virtual machine" that executes compiled Java byte code. The Java virtual machine is implemented in the browser, making Java byte code programs platform independent.

Java applications may be developed as stand-alone applications or as applets. Java applets are small bits of code that are downloaded and executed by the browser as needed. A simple Java applet example is:


```
import java.awt.*;
import java.applet.*;

public class Applet1 extends Applet {
void button1_Clicked(Event event) {
button1.requestFocus();
click_num = click_num + 1;
textField1.setText("Clicked:" + click_num);
}

int click_num;
char string[];

void Applet1_MouseDown(Event event) {
// to do: place event handler code here.

button1.enable(!button1.isEnabled());
}

public void init() {
super.init();

click_num = 0;

//{{INIT_CONTROLS
setLayout(null);
addNotify();
resize(426,266);
button1 = new java.awt.Button("Count Clicks");
button1.reshape(140,98,87,26);
add(button1);
textField1 = new java.awt.TextField();
textField1.setText("Clicked: 0");
textField1.reshape(140,150,119,23);
add(textField1);
//}}
```

```
}

public boolean handleEvent(Event event) {
if (event.target == this &&
event.id == Event.MOUSE_DOWN) {
Applet1_MouseDown(event);
}
if (event.target == button1 &&
event.id == Event.ACTION_EVENT) {
button1_Clicked(event);
}
return super.handleEvent(event);
}

//{{DECLARE_CONTROLS
java.awt.Button button1;
java.awt.TextField textField1;
//}}
}
```

This applet counts the number of times the mouse button is clicked while the cursor is on the button labeled "Count Clicks." This applet was developed using Symantec's Visual Cafe. The corresponding HTML code that executes the applet is:

```
<HTML>
<HEAD>
<TITLE>JAVA Applet Example</TITLE>
</HEAD>
<BODY>
<FORM>
<APPLET CODE="Applet1.class" WIDTH=430 HEIGHT=270></APPLET>
</FORM>
</BODY>
</HTML>
```

The following table identifies the Java compilers/development packages available as this is written:

Java Compiler	Vendor	Platform
Java SDK	JavaSoft	Solaris
		Windows 95
		Windows NT
Visual Cafe	Symantec	Windows 95
		Windows NT
		Macintosh
Cafe	Symantec	Windows 95
		Windows NT
J++	Microsoft	Windows 95
		Windows NT
JBuilder	Borland	Windows 95
		Windows NT
Jfactory	Rogue Wave	Windows 95
		Windows NT
Roaster	Natural Intelligence	Macintosh

JavaScript

JavaScript is an extremely cut down Java implementation with predefined browser classes and methods. File I/O is basically left out of the language, making JavaScript programs relatively safe from viruses. The maturity issue applies to JavaScript too; its language specification is evolving. Major changes between JavaScript as implemented in Netscape Navigator 2.0 and 3.0 broke much JavaScript that worked with Navigator 2.0. Netscape has submitted the JavaScript specifications to a standards body for approval. The new JavaScript standard is likely to incorporate the current JavaScript and additions based on Microsoft's JavaScript implementation.

As JavaScript implementations mature along with the language specification, there is a definite place for JavaScript in the Web-based application arena.

JavaScript was developed by Netscape to add scripting to Navigator. JavaScript is based on Sun's Java-Lite or Mocha version of Java.

Though JavaScript was first included in a browser by Netscape, Microsoft has since included JavaScript support in Internet Explorer in the form of JScript.

There are incompatibilities between JavaScript and Jscript because Netscape did not make the JavaScript specification public initially. Microsoft reverse engineered JavaScript and implemented it as Jscript. The net effect is that both JavaScript and Jscript are difficult to justify for production applications unless your user community all uses Netscape or Internet Explorer. The first browser release after the JavaScript specification is approved will probably cure most if not all of the compatibility problems.

JavaScript source code is embedded in the HTML document within the <SCRIPT> tag. The closing </SCRIPT> tag is required and source is often included in HTML comments so browsers that do not support JavaScript will not display the code. An example of JavaScript code is:

```
<HTML>
<HEAD>
<TITLE>JavaScript Applet Example</TITLE>
<SCRIPT LANGUAGE="JavaScript">
var ClkCount = 0;
function CountClicks(){
var text;

ClkCount = ClkCount + 1;
text = "Clicked "+ClkCount+" times";
window.status = text;
}
</SCRIPT>
</HEAD>
<BODY>
<FORM>
<INPUT TYPE="BUTTON" NAME="LOOK"
VALUE="COUNT CLICKS" onclick="CountClicks()">
</FORM>
</BODY>
</HTML>
```

This script counts the number of times the mouse button is clicked while the cursor is on the button labeled "Count Clicks."

JavaScript has the potential to simplify CGI-based Web applications by performing generic field validation in the client. JavaScript code can also be dynamically created on the server, which opens the door for some sophisticated dynamic applications.

VBScript and Active-X

VBScript and Active-X are Microsoft's response to Java and JavaScript. Active-X controls have severe security problems. Active-X controls are compiled and work via Windows OLE. Therefore, an Active-X application has complete access to the client machine. There is no provision for security, at least not as this book is being written. An example Active-X page that demonstrates the potential problems is at http://www.halcyon.com/mclain/ActiveX/Exploder/welcome.html. This page contains an Active-X control that shuts down your machine. Several third-party developers are developing Netscape Navigator plug-ins to support Active-X.

Not only is there potential abuse from executing downloaded code as with other Web scripting, but it's much easier for someone to write destructive Active-X controls. The potential security risks using Active-X for production applications with client access to the Internet are enormous.

VBScript code is implemented by embedding Visual Basic code in <SCRIPT> tags. The following HTML document illustrates the Active-X code to count the number of times the "Count Clicks" button is clicked:

```
<HTML>
<HEAD>
<TITLE>JavaScript Applet Example</TITLE>
<SCRIPT LANGUAGE="VBScript">
Dim ClkCount
call init_count()

sub CountClicks
ClkCount = ClkCount + 1
```

```
MsgBox = "Clicked " & ClkCount & " times";
TxtLinkDescription.Value = "xxx";
end sub
sub init_count
ClkCount = 0;
end sub
</SCRIPT>
</HEAD>
<BODY>
<FORM>
<INPUT TYPE="BUTTON" NAME="CountClicks"
VALUE="Count Clicks">
</FORM>
</BODY>
</HTML>
```

Summary

Web-based client-server applications are generally much simpler to implement. Many of the choices necessary with a traditional implementation go away because they just don't apply.

Web Server

A Web-based server also predefines answers to many of the server issues identified in previous sections just as many of the client questions are answered by choosing the Web client. It also raises a few different ones. Multiple web servers (both commercial and free) are available for most server platforms. The server questions boil down to a general selection. Items to consider are:

- Security
- Commercial or free
- Other features

The following figure depicts Web server issues:

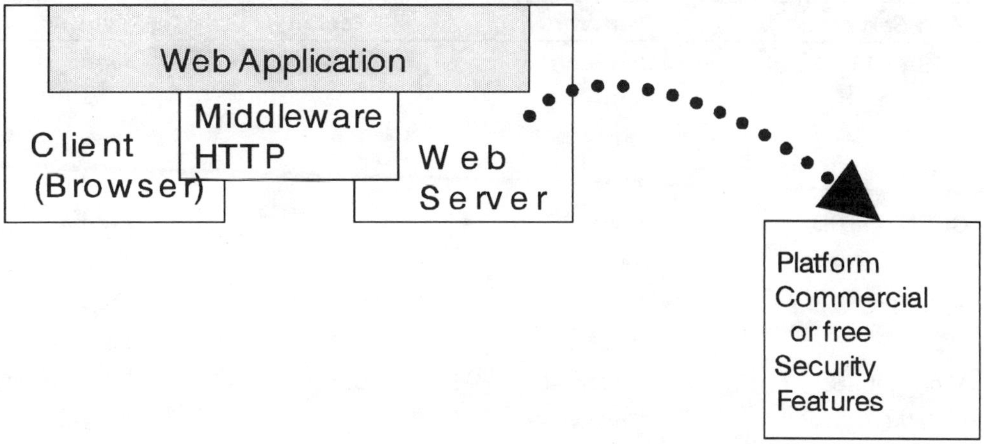

Web Server Issues

If security is an issue and the application requires some security features, the client and server must both support the same security features, such as Secure Socket Layer (SSL). Otherwise no security is in force.

The choice of commercial or free is mostly personal. The first Web servers were all free. Many Web sites are still powered by descendants of these servers. Commercial Web servers have support and features that may not be supported by the free servers. Many sites start out with a free Web server and later move to one of the commercial servers as requirements change.

A large added value provided by commercial Web servers is usually features. For example, the Netscape Commerce Server has built in e-mail facilities as well as secure HTML Form transmission with Netscape Navigator browsers.

The server hardware platform narrows the Web server choice somewhat. The following table lists popular Web servers and the platform each runs on:

Web Server	*Platform*	*Security*	*Type*
NCSA HTTPD	Unix		Free
	VMS		Free
	MAC		Free
	Other		
CERN HTTPD	Unix		Free
	VMS		Free
Apache	Unix	SSL	Free
	Linux	SSL	Free
Microsoft IIS	Windows NT	SSL	Free with NT 4.0
EMWAC	Windows 95		Free
	Windows NT		Free
Oracle Web Server	Unix		Commercial
WebSite 1.1	Windows 95	SSL	Commercial[1]
	Windows NT	SSL	Commercial
WebSite Pro	Windows 95	SSL	Commercial
	Windows NT	SSL	Commercial
Folkweb	Windows 95		Shareware
	Windows NT		Shareware
MacHTTP/WebStar	Macintosh		Commercial
Purveyor	Netware		Commercial[1]
	Windows 95		Commercial[1]
	Windows 95		Commercial[1]
Netscape Netsite	Unix		Commercial[1]
	Windows 95		Commercial[1]
	Windows NT		Commercial[1]
Netscape Commerce Server	Unix	SSL	Commercial
	Windows NT	SSL	Commercial

(1) Free version available for trial.

This is a long list of products, but it is by no means exhaustive.

Summary

This discussion of upfront planning and the decisions that need to be addressed reinforces the added complexity of implementing a client-server application compared to a traditional single user application.

The choices that you make in upfront planning all have a great impact in the overall direction of project development. It should be clear by now that all of these decisions are intertwined. None can be made in a vacuum nor ignored.

Chapter 4

Web-Based Client-Server Computing

Introduction

The details of the Web approach to client-server applications are addressed in this chapter. There are advantages and disadvantages to a Web client-server applications approach just as there are with any approach. Both advantages and disadvantages are discussed. Web-based applications imply intranet or Internet applications.

Inter/Intranet Applications

Internet applications are applications that use World Wide Web (WWW) technologies and are accessible via the Internet. Intranet applications are applications that use WWW technologies and are accessible via private, internal networks. Another general difference is information versus application. Internet-based pages generally provide public access to information. Intranet applications generally are interactive applications that update internal databases.

The following diagram shows Web-based client-server model:

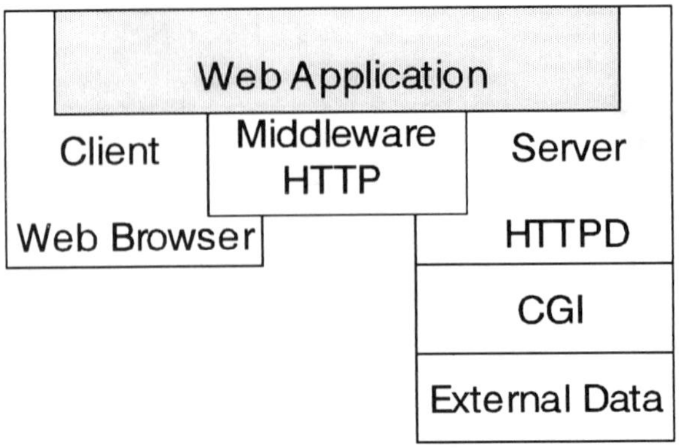

Web-Based Client-Server Model

The basic model is very similar to the one presented in previous chapters. The remainder of this section discusses the client, middleware, and server topics.

Client

The client of a Web-based application is a Web browser. There are many Web browsers. Netscape Navigator and Microsoft Internet Explorer have over 90 percent of the browser market and generally drive the market in terms of features. Both can be downloaded from the Internet and often are installed on most new PCs at the factory. Other browsers are not covered for this reason in this book. The following table lists Web browsers:

Browser	Platform	Availability
Netscape Navigator	Windows 3.1 Windows 95 Windows NT Macintosh Various Unix	http://home.netscape.com
Microsoft Internet Explorer	Windows 95 Windows NT Macintosh[1]	http://www.microsoft.com

Browser	Platform	Availability
NCSA Mosaic	Windows 3.1 Windows 95 Macintosh Various Unix	http://www.ncsa.uiuc.edu
Hot Java	Windows 95 Solaris	http://www.javasoft.com
Spyglass Mosaic[2]	Windows 3.1 Windows 95 Macintosh	http://www.spyglass.com
Spyglass Red Baron	Linux	http://www.redhat.com
Quarterdeck	Windows 95[3]	http://www.quarterdeck.com
Lynx	Unix VMS Amiga MS-DOS	ftp://ftp2.cc.ukans.edu/pub/Lynx http://www.fweb.edu/dir/Lynx
Arena	Linux	http://www.w3.org
Spry	Windows 3.1	http://www.spry.com

(1) Under development

(2) Available as part of the *Internet In A Box* product

(3) Included as part of the *Procomm* product

The original graphical Web browser is NCSA's Mosaic. NCSA is the National Center for Supercomputer Applications and is part of the University of Illinois, Champaign. NCSA Mosaic is largely responsible for the explosion of the Web! Netscape was started by members of the original Mosaic development team. For a short time, the browser competition was between Mosaic and Navigator. Spyglass obtained the commercial rights to Mosaic and has included versions in several networking products. Lynx is sort of the odd man out in the early browser skirmishes. It was designed as a text-only browser for people using VT-100 and compatible terminals on Unix and VMS systems. There were also versions of Lynx for MS-DOS and the Amiga. As graphical Web pages took over, Lynx largely lost its appeal and the originators, the University of Kansas, have dropped development. Hot Java is JavaSoft's Web browser built to demonstrate Java before the language was accepted by Netscape and

Microsoft. All of the early browsers still work for simple Web pages but generally do not handle the latest HTML 3.2 tags nor the scripting languages well if at all.

Internet Explorer has burst onto the scene to give Netscape Navigator serious competition. The first couple of Internet Explorer (IE) versions took a back seat to Navigator. However, Version 3.0 of each are roughly equal although each supports some features the other does not.

Middleware

The middleware picture is relatively clear with a Web-based application. The basic networking protocol is HTTP, generally running on top of TCP/IP. There are a couple of variations in HTTP for security: S-HTTP and SSL. Browsers and servers support one or the other so there is little control over which you use other than through browser and server selection.

S-HTTP stands for Secure HTTP. It was the initial proposal for secure transactions on the Web. S-HTTP was never widely adapted, but information can be obtained at http://www.commerce.net.

Secure Socket Layer (SSL) was the Netscape response to the slow development of the S-HTTP standard. Netscape implemented its own approach rather than waiting for S-HTTP. Today, most browsers and servers support SSL.

Client middleware for Web-based applications is an Internet Socket driver. The Winsock network drivers in Windows 3.1, Windows 95, and Windows NT supply that functionality for PC clients. Some clients are starting to implement ODBC, either directly or via Java or Active-X. Some additional requirements may be necessary to support client side ODBC, depending on the client software and application approach (thin or thick) used. Overall, the middleware issue is much simpler with Web-based applications than with traditional client-server approaches.

Server

The Web server is the second major part of a Web-based application. There are a number of choices for Web servers. Platform, features, support, and security are the primary considerations. These are all discussed in Chapter 3.

Approximately half a dozen servers account for 75 percent of all Web sites on the Internet. These are:

- Apache—Unix/Linux
- CERN—Unix
- Microsoft IIS—NT
- NCSA—Unix
- Netscape—All versions
- WebSite—Windows 95/NT

The list is in alphabetical order, although Apache is the number one web server. Check http://www.netcraft.co.uk for the latest listing. The following list identifies Web servers along with a Web availability.

Web Server	Platform	Availability
NCSA HTTPD	Unix, VMS, Macintosh, Other	http://www.ncsa.uiuc.edu
CERN HTTPD	Unix, VMS	http://www.w3.org
Apache	Unix, Linux	http://www.apache.org
Microsoft IIS	Windows NT	http://www.microsoft.com
EMWAC	Windows NT	http://emwac.ed.ac.uk
Oracle Web Server	Unix	http://www.oracle.com
MacHTTP/WebStar	Macintosh	http://www.starnine.com
WebSite 1.1	Windows 95, Windows NT	http://www.ora.com
WebSite Pro	Windows 95, Windows NT	http://www.ora.com
Folkweb	Windows 95, Windows NT	
Purveyor	Windows 95, Windows NT, Netware	http://www.process.com
Netscape Netsite	Unix, Windows 95, Windows NT	http://home.netscape.com
Netscape Commerce Server	Unix, Windows 95, Unix NT	http://home.netscape.com

Characteristics

Web-based client-server applications have several high level characteristics:

- Browser provides the GUI
- Stateless system
- Fat server
- Thin client
- Three tiers

GUI

One of the primary reasons that Web-based applications enjoy quicker development cycles and usually cost significantly less than traditional client-server applications is that the browser supplies a tested GUI with a textual (HTML) interface.

Think about all of the work involved in designing, developing, and testing the front-end GUI. Even with the current crop of visual development tools, it is a lot of work! Each change to the GUI in a typical client-server application requires updating the form, recompiling the associated programs, and testing the changes. Once a change is tested, it must then be distributed to the user community. From a software development standpoint, the steps necessary to properly perform this type of change is fairly involved and therefore expensive.

Contrast that with the same change to a Web-based application. First of all, the change to form may simply be editing a text file and testing a matter of loading the page in the browser. Deployment is automatic; the user gets the updated screen automatically when the page is accessed next.

The time saved in testing and deployment is a major Web application advantage.

Stateless

By default, Web applications are stateless. That is, the server does not keep a connection from one client action to the next. Each client request is essentially a login, transaction, logout. A traditional client-server application requires the user to establish a session, perform as many transactions as needed, then explicitly terminate the session. The net effect is the server can easily retain information about the current "state" of the client such as access rights, the contents of fields on a form, etc. A stateless system requires that each transaction be autonomous; the server knows nothing about the state of the client previous to the start of this transaction.

A stateless client-server application simplifies two issues: anonymous login and not having explicit logoff. The lack of knowledge about the client state by the server has an unwanted side effect of complicating the server code to compensate. For example when a form is submitted, the server has no way of knowing what data may be on the form or whether this is the first time the form has been submitted. The server program must process the transaction as the first submission every time. If an error is detected, the entire form must be passed back to the client instead of just the error information.

There are ways to get around the problems caused by lack of state. These include:

- Passing the full client state on every transaction
- Saving state on the server via a "cookie"
- Using Java/JavaScript to open a data stream to the server

The simplest and most portable way of preserving state in an application is passing full state information. The basic CGI mechanism and HTML form capabilities combine to make this practical. This approach will be illustrated in one of the case studies.

Cookies are a Netscape invention to store state on the server and are used in many "shopping cart" applications. Cookies effectively minimize the state information that must be continuously passed between the browser and server. The state information is stored on the client until requested by the server.

One of the primary reasons for saving state is accessing database information. Java includes a JDBC or Java DataBase Connectivity class that can be used to open a connection between the client and the database server via ODBC. This allows the client application to log into the database once and perform multiple transactions. The time of a database login is saved and network traffic minimized by passing only data being manipulated as opposed to all of the data on the form every time a transaction is initiated.

Fat Server/Thin Client

Up until recently, the only choice for a Web-based client-server application was a very thin client that displayed HTML with forms for the user to enter data into and a very fat server application that performed 100 percent of the application. That is rapidly changing with the advent of Web centric programming languages including Java, JavaScript, and VBScript. The very thin client/very fat server requires a fairly large amount of data transfer with no interaction as the user enters data. All of the data entered on the form is sent to the server when the "submit" button is clicked. If an error occurs, all of the data must be sent back to the client with the appropriate error messages. In other words, the whole form must be processed as one unit.

The very fat client is not likely in a Web application. However, the first step toward adding a little weight to a Web client is one of the "script" languages, either JavaScript or VBScript. Both are ideal for high level data validation in the client such as:

- Range checks
- Checking for presence of required fields
- Context sensitive help
- Validating reasonable combination of selections
- Date validation

These may not seem like very big items, but they can:

- Significantly reduce network traffic
- Reduce complexity of the server code

- Reduce size of the server code
- Increase responsiveness of the application

The closest thing to a fat Web client is an application that makes heavy use of Java. Java is a much more powerful programming language than either JavaScript or VBScript. Java applets can access network resources such as opening a communications socket to another computer and essentially keeping a session open for more than a single transaction. Corel has already demonstrated a prototype word processor written in Java that runs over the Internet, so the potential for very sophisticated applications is there.

Three Tiers

Web applications are generally three-tier client-server applications. There is the client (tier one), the CGI interface to a processing program (tier two), and a database server (tier three) such as Oracle, assuming a database application. The communications server or middleware is taken care of by the Web browser and server via the HTTP protocol. The application is made up of an HTML form for display on the client, a CGI program or script to process the form on the server, and a database server accessed by the CGI program to supply the data.

How a Web Application Works

There are several facets to a Web application including:

- Communications between client and server
- How HTML plays on the client
- CGI interface and processing layer on the server

The following sections discuss each of these areas.

Web Communications

A Web-based application starts execution at the browser. The following diagram illustrates a typical HTTP session between the Web browser and the Web server:

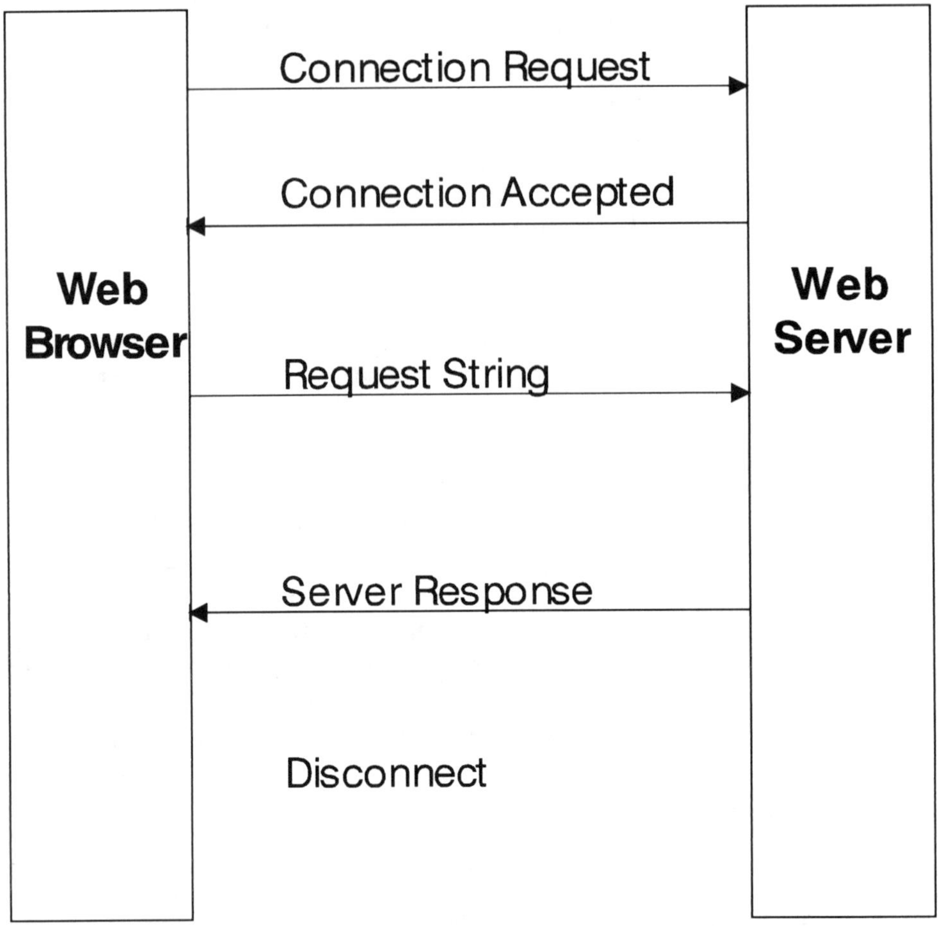

Typical Browser/Server Network Session

The diagram is somewhat oversimplified but paints an accurate picture of what happens. The client requests a TCP connection to the server computer. When the server accepts the connection, the client sends a request string. This request string may be a document name, a CGI program with arguments, or any of several MIME messages. The server processes the request and writes the resulting response back to the browser. Either the browser or the server may break the connection. The server breaks the connection when the complete response has been sent. The client breaks the connection when the user clicks the "stop" button in the browser. Both client and server implement time-outs to prevent the connection being locked open.

HTML on the Client

Think of HTML as the formatting language of the Web. HTML has an SGML heritage, which means HTML documents are ASCII with tags for marking various document structure such as headings, paragraphs, or lists. There has been much debate, both within the Web and SGML communities, about whether or not the other is relevant. The Web community said that SGML is not needed for HTML because browsers accept HTML markup that cannot be processed as SGML. The SGML community said HTML is not real SGML because HTML markup is format oriented rather than structure oriented as "good" SGML should be, and most HTML documents will not pass SGML parsing. Actually both sides were wrong to a certain extent.

HTML Versus SGML

SGML, or Standard Generalized Markup Language, is a standard for defining markup languages. It is ISO Standard 8879:1986 and has met wide acceptance in both government and industry where information reuse and long document lives make SGML a good investment. An SGML approach consists of several pieces including:

- SGML declaration
- Document Type Definition (DTD)
- Document instances

The SGML declaration defines such things as the character set used, the length of tag names, and whether or not end tags may be optional. Most sites have a single SGML declaration file that all SGML tools use.

The Document Type Definition defines the element names, document structure, abbreviations, and which end tags are optional. Document structure is the order of elements, which elements are required, and element grouping. DTDs exist for most versions of HTML. Check *http://www.w3.org* for HTML DTDs. There are a number of publicly available DTDs in addition to HTML that are in wide use. *http://www.sgmlopen.org* is a good starting point to learn more about SGML.

I say both sides were wrong because there are advantages of treating HTML as an SGML application. First, SGML tools work just as well on HTML documents as with any other SGML document provided the HTML DTD is available. There are a number of free or inexpensive SGML tools that are available including SGMLS/NSGMLS which are free validating parsers and an add-on to GNU Emacs called PSGML for structured editing within Emacs. Corel WordPerfect 7 includes SGML editing tools. Corel just doesn't mention it. The SGML tools are not installed as part of the standard WordPerfect 7 install; the SGML option must be selected from the custom installation. Several SGML tools, including SoftQuad's HoTMetaL and InContext's Spider HTML editors, are based on their respective full-blown SGML editors.

The following table illustrates the difference between HTML that is not SGML (the unstructured column) and HTML that is SGML compliant (the structured column):

Unstructured HTML	*Structured HTML*
	<HTML>
	<HEAD>
	<TITLE>DocTitle</TITLE>
	</HEAD>
	<BODY>
<H2>Header	<H1>Header</H1>
<P>The text just goes here.	<P>The text just goes here.
This is a para, followed by	This is a para, followed by
a list:	a list:
	<UL>
<LI>List item 1	<LI>List item 1
<LI>Let's make <H3>BIG	<LI>Let's make <B>bold
text</H3>	text</B>

Unstructured HTML	Structured HTML
<LI>List item 3	<LI>List item 3
	</UL>
<H1>Another Header	<H1>Another Header
<P>Moretext...	<P>Moretext...
	</BODY>
	</HTML>

The significant thing to notice in the figure is that the structured version is relatively easy to automate further processing. For example, generating a Table of Contents automatically is practical with the structured version because you can count on the heading tags (<H1>, <H2>, <H3>, etc.) to be section headers. Hyperlinks can be created automatically in the Table of Contents as well. The unstructured version on the left will produce an incorrect Table of Contents that must be corrected by hand. (If you are interested in this sort of HTML manipulation, check out my *Practical Guide to SGML Filters*, ISBN 1-55622-511-3 published by Wordware for the details.) The consistency of HTML as SGML documents makes both manipulating and reusing HTML documents practical.

HTML and the Client

HTML provides the basic capabilities for generating a user interface for data entry via tables and forms. HTML tables provide the mechanism for presenting a formatted display and HTML forms for creating the input boxes, radio buttons, and check boxes of a typical database-centric client-server application.

Where Web browsers and HTML fall down is interaction. The basic data entry is handled automatically by the browser, but interaction and field validation are not part of the recipe. When a form's data is submitted to the server, the contents of the entire form are passed. The server performs all of the processing, including validation, of that data. When an error is detected, the entire form is sent back to the browser for correction. The effects of this are:

- Network traffic is increased because the entire form data may be passed between the client and server multiple times to complete a transaction.
- There is not immediate feedback to the user about errors.
- The program on the server side has to be more complex because of the added error processing that must be performed.

The following illustration is a typical, although simple, data entry form. The form has a header, a couple of data entry fields, including a description and input box, and buttons. The processing, other than typing in data and submitting the data typed into the form, has to be performed on the server via a CGI script. Let's look at the form:

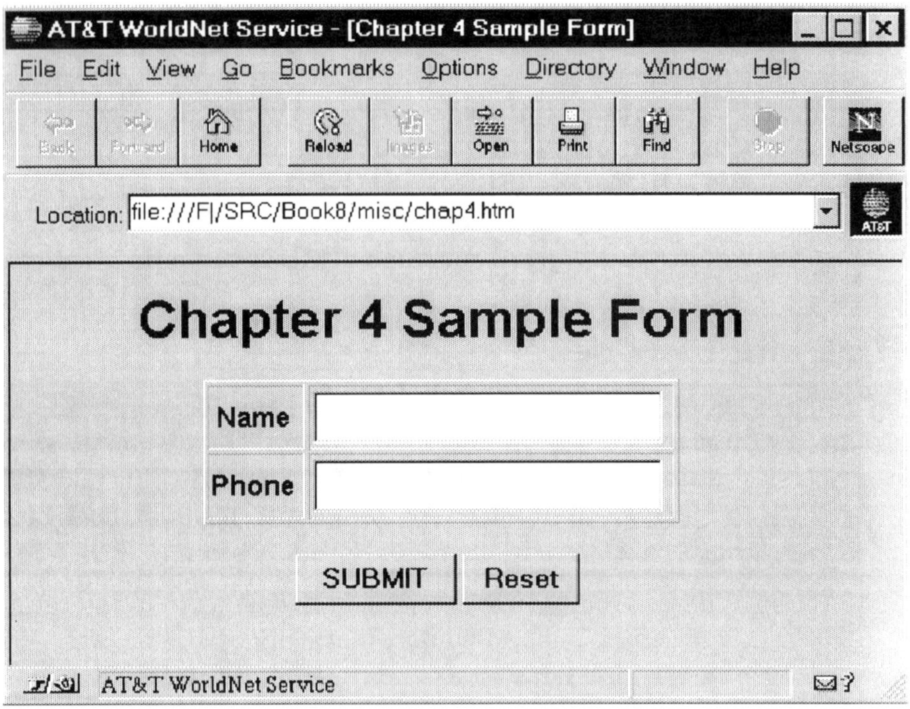

CGI and Processing

The interface between the Web server and the server processing is Common Gateway Interface, or CGI. Basically CGI provides a way for the Web server to run an external program and pass information from the client. CGI is discussed in detail in Chapter 6.

The CGI processing is often called a script because Perl, which is a scripting language, performs the CGI processing. However, any programming language that can access host environment variables or read/write from STDIN/STDOUT can be used effectively. Interpretive languages such as Perl are most often used due to the interactive nature of CGI programming. The compile and link times for compiled languages seriously affect productivity when developing a CGI application. Since a CGI script/program is passed information from the browser, the business rules are encapsulated at this point. CGI programming is not overly complex once you learn the secrets.

Advantages of Web-Based Client-Server Applications

The primary advantages of Web-based client-server applications can be summarized in the phrase "cheap and fast development." A general statement can be made about the cost and capabilities of Web-based client-server applications versus traditional client-server applications which is illustrated by the following figure:

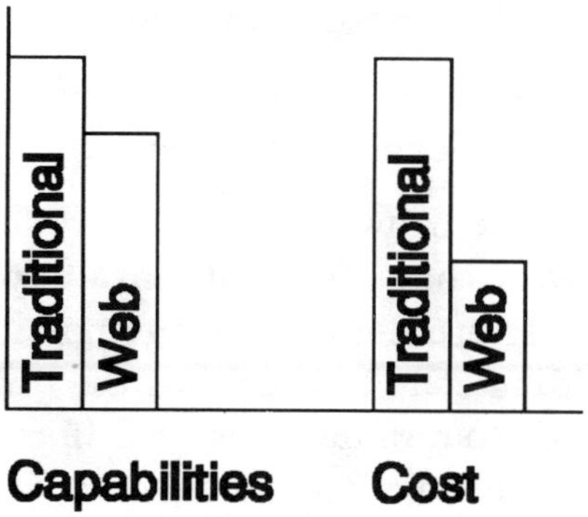

Traditional Versus Web Applications

The overall Web paradigm is driven by the simplicity of interaction with the browser. The effect is that a Web-based application has a more limited range of capabilities than a PowerBuilder or Delphi application. For generic CGI-only applications, one of the trade-offs is the inability to perform any processing on the client beyond collecting data. This is changing with the maturation of client side languages like Java and JavaScript.

The cost of developing a Web-based client-server application is also significantly less than traditional client-server development. So there is a trade-off between capability and cost. The bottom line is if you can live with the limitations of a Web-based application, then it is a very attractive option.

Lesser advantages of Web-based application development include:

- Minimal development resources required
- Availability of commercial development environments
- Works well in heterogenous computing situations
- A very open solution

Web-based application development requires minimal development resources. A minimum development environment is generally provided by the host system that the Web server runs on, especially if the host is a Unix system. The needed items are:

- The client Web browser
- The CGI scripting language
- File access to the host computer
- General development tools

The client Web browser is necessary for testing. Be sure to use the same browser that users will have to prevent feature differences from causing problems later. Supporting multiple browsers often means adding code to check for the browser and having browser specific code to handle browser differences. This is not a good situation because of the added complexity and support required. In any case, use what the user uses. The scripting language must be available, obviously. Testing is limited without access to the Web server because of the interactive nature of the application. Therefore, developers need access to the Web server computer to place HTML and CGI programs on for testing. General programming tools such as text and HTML editors are necessary as well.

Availability of commercial development environments is already happening. Commercial Java packages such as Symantec Cafe/Visual Cafe, Microsoft J++, and Borland JBuilder have been released and are maturing rapidly. Several third-party packages are available via the Web to automate generic CGI applications. There is even a PowerBuilder plug-in for Netscape. In addition, many commercial packages have HTML output as options. All of these trends added together point to an acceptance of Web-based applications.

Web-based applications work well in heterogenous computing situations. The primary reason is the generic browser interface in the form of HTML. The client Web browser does not matter as long as it supports whatever HTML features are used by the application. Therefore, Web-based client-server applications provide a very open solution.

Disadvantages of Web-Based Client-Server Applications

Most things have pluses and minuses and Web-based applications are no exception. The disadvantages also vary slightly depending on whether or not a client side programming language is used. In general the disadvantages are:

- Application speed sensitive to many variables
- Network traffic less than optimal
- Limited client side processing

Web-based applications are affected by more variables than non-Web client-server applications, especially when server processing is via CGI. The CGI mechanism is generic because it executes external programs. That means under a heavy load, a lot of new operating system processes are started and shut down. This system overhead varies widely among operating systems.

Another variable that affects speed is the database server. Picture a fairly large system where the Web server is on one computer and the database server is on a different computer. The stateless mode typical of Web-based applications means multiple logons to the database are possible per transaction unless much care is taken during design. This gets back to the limited client side processing in the Web browser.

The disadvantages are heavily outweighed by the advantages for many applications.

Summary

Web-based client-server applications are generally simpler, faster, and less expensive to develop than traditional client-server applications. There are a few disadvantages that must be weighed before choosing the Web approach. If the application can fit within the Web framework limitations, then the Web approach should be considered.

Chapter 5

Basic Web Software

Introduction

This chapter examines the basic software necessary to implement Web-based client-server applications. There is more to a Web application than just a server and browser. The building blocks are:

- Web server
- Browser
- HTML
- Computer Gateway Interface (CGI)
- Graphics
- Document conversion
- Other

Most of these have been discussed at some point in previous chapters. Hopefully, another look is worthwhile!

Web Server

One of the cornerstones of Web client-server applications is the Web server. The purpose of the Web server is responding to HTTP requests from the browser. The CERN server was the first Web server. As the WWW took off in popularity after the release of NCSA Mosaic, NCSA also implemented a server. These two servers, both of which are free, accounted for the majority of the Web servers through the first couple of years of WWW popularity. Eventually commercial servers appeared with added features, such as enhanced security, and largely replaced the NCSA and CERN Web servers for commercial sites. Many of the commercial servers are based on the code base from one or the other of the two original servers.

There is one notable exception. The Apache server is currently the most widely used Web server on the Internet. It is the exception because it is not commercial. Apache is NCSA based with the addition of the Secure Socket Layer (SSL) protocol for data encryption and many speed enhancements. Apache's appeal is based on features, speed, and the fact that it is available on most Unix platforms including Linux. Linux equates to an inexpensive Unix on a PC platform. The Linux/Apache combination makes it possible for companies to set up a very capable Web server for minimal cost. Its biggest disadvantages are not being commercial and only running on Unix platforms (some people do not think this is a disadvantage).

Commercial Web Servers

There are several popular commercial Web servers including:

- Netscape Netsite and Commerce Server
- Microsoft IIS
- O'Reilly WebSite and WebSite Pro

A more complete list is presented in the previous chapter. There are other very functional Web servers available. Don't limit yourself to the few mentioned here. What these servers all have in common is they are intended for high volume environments running on top-of-the-line computers.

Personal Web Servers

Another category of Web server that is often ignored is the "personal" Web server. There are several Web servers that are at home on your local personal computer including:

- O'Reilly WebSite
- Microsoft Personal Web Server
- ENWAC

What these Web servers have in common is they comfortably fit and run on smaller desktop PCs. Each runs on Windows 95. Personal Web servers open up the possibility of small, local applications such as program documentation or a front end to $\TeX$.

Web Server Hints

A Web server can be a wonderful thing to behold but only when it works. There are differences in the details of just about every Web server. For example, the filename may vary for specifying the access control to the server. Details of specific features may vary from one Web server to another. The message is "read the installation instructions" for your particular Web server and follow them!

A misconception is that a network connection is necessary to run a Web server. That is not true. The server is limited without a network connection, but a connection is not necessary. A personal Web server may run local to one particular computer without any network connection. A local Web server can perform useful work including:

- Acting as a Web development station
- Accessing local HTML documents
- Running local programs/applications

Put some thought into how to structure the directories that make up the server! Most Web servers expect to find HTML pages in a directory tree that starts with *httpd/htdocs* and CGI in *cgi-bin*. The exact directory locations are usually parameters somewhere in the server setup. (However, there are conventions that by following will make your life easier.) Don't be afraid to organize HTML pages into a directory structure under *htdocs*. As the site grows, structure in the directory layout may save your sanity.

Web Browser

The second cornerstone is the Web browser which functions as the client. The most popular browsers today are Netscape Navigator and Microsoft Internet Explorer. Both are inexpensive or free and frequently come preloaded on new PCs. Navigator currently runs on more platforms than Internet Explorer. There are some differences in the exact features each supports, but in general they are comparable.

Previous chapters covered issues related to browser selection. One last time, pick your browser and implement to it! While they are more or less equal, Navigator and Explorer are not always compatible, especially when used as clients in a client-server environment! JavaScript and JScript are not 100 percent compatible and probably won't be until the JavaScript standard is approved. Internet Explorer also includes VBScript while Navigator does not. The different capabilities of the two should influence your decision.

Feature	*Netscape Navigator*	*Internet Explorer*
Java	◆	◆
JavaScript	◆	
JScript		◆
VBScript		◆
Active-X	■	◆
Tables	◆	◆
Forms	◆	◆
Windows 3.1	◆	
Windows 95	◆	◆
Unix	◆	
Macintosh	◆	●

■ Third party add on
◆ Yes
● Under development

The availability of multiple high quality Web browsers is a good thing. The competition implies that both will continue to evolve and improve. The most important factor is not which browser but choosing the browser with the features you need.

HTML

HTML, or Hyper Text Markup Language, is one of the simplifying components of Web applications. It is an ASCII-based markup language. HTML is an SGML (Standard Generalized Markup Language) application which means that there is an HTML DTD (Document Type Definition). Actually, there are several. The current HTML DTD is 3.2. The significant versions are:

- 2.0
- 3.0
- 3.2

HTML 2.0 was the first HTML DTD officially published by W3C (http://www.w3c.org). It added Forms to the basic HTML tag set. HTML 2.0 opened up the Web to client-server computing because data could be entered and passed back to the server and processed via CGI scripts.

Version 3.0 added Tables. Presentation could be spruced up using tables. A combination of Forms and Tables allows professional-looking data entry screens.

HTML 3.2 is the current HTML specification as this is being written. It adds <SCRIPT> and <STYLE> to support client side scripting languages and style sheets respectively.

The details of how HTML fits into Web applications development are covered in Chapter 7.

Computer Gateway Interface

The Computer Gateway Interface (CGI) is at the heart of most Web applications. CGI is the interface that allows the Web server to execute external programs and pass parameters from the browser. The Web server executes an external program, usually referred to as a CGI script, when the file requested is in the *cgi-bin* directory or a subdirectory under it. The external program is executed as a stand-alone program. The script in "CGI script" comes from the fact that most programs are in scripting languages such as Perl or one of the

Unix shells. A CGI script can be written in almost any programming language.

There are two ways for information to be passed from the browser to the script: GET or POST. The METHOD attribute on the <FORM> tag specifies whether the server passes information via GET or POST.

The GET method passes the "CGI string" from the browser by setting the environment variable QUERY_STRING. POST specifies that the string is passed via STDIN. The environment variable REQUEST_METHOD indicates whether the HTML form specified GET or POST. There are cases when a CGI script may get information via GET sometimes and POST other times so this is important information. The following Perl code segment demonstrates checking REQUEST_METHOD:

```
if($ENV{'REQUEST_METHOD'} eq "GET"){
        print "Calling page used GET method\n";
}else{
        if($ENV{'REQUEST_METHOD'} eq "POST"){
                print "Calling page used POST method\n";
        }
}
```

The CGI string has a specific format that must be decoded before use. The general form is:

```
NAME1=VALUE1&NAME2=VALUE2
```

This example shows most CGI string features. Each field on the HTML form is included. In the example, two fields are specified, NAME1 and NAME2. The "&" character separates the fields. The "=" separates the name from the value. There are a couple more characters that have special meaning in a CGI string, + and %. A more complete example is:

```
FULLNAME=Norman+E.+Smith&JOB=Author&SPECIAL=%27
```

The "+" is the place holder for a blank and the "%" takes the next two numeric digits as the numeric value in hexadecimal of a character.

The general method for parsing a CGI string is a multistep process:

1. Split the original string into fields at each "&".
2. Split each field into name and value at the "=".
3. Substitute a blank for each + in the value.
4. Convert each %xx to the character.

Thus, the example breaks down this way:

1. The fields are:

FULLNAME=Norman+E.+Smith
JOB=Author
SPECIAL=%27

2. The fields break down as:

FIELD NAME	VALUE
FULLNAME	Norman+E.+Smith
JOB	Author
SPECIAL	%27

3. Next, substitute blanks for +:

FIELD NAME	VALUE
FULLNAME	Norman E. Smith
JOB	Author
SPECIAL	%27

4. Finally, convert hex characters to their ASCII values:

FIELD NAME	VALUE
FULLNAME	Norman E. Smith
JOB	Author
SPECIAL	'

The following Perl subroutine takes a CGI string and parses the various pieces into an associative array that is very convenient to use later in the program:

```
sub parse_cgi{
        my $CGIstring;
        my $i;
        my $key;
        my $val;

        $CGIstring = $_[0];
                #
                # Split fields into an array
                #
        @CGI = split(/&/,$CGIstring);
                #
                # For each field in the CGI string,
                #
        foreach $i (0 .. $#CGI)
        {
                        #
                        # Substitute blank for +
                        #
                $CGI[$i] =~ s/\+/ /g;
                        #
                        # Extract field name and value
                        #
                ($key,$val) = split(/=/,$CGI[$i],2);
                        #
                        # Convert hex to character
                        #
                $key =~ s/%(..)/pack("c",hex($1))/ge;
                $val =~ s/%(..)/pack("c",hex($1))/ge;
                        #
                        # Store value in CGI associative array
                        # with field name as the key.
                        #
                $CGI{$key} = $val;
        }
}
```

The Perl code covers basic CGI string parsing; it requires some additional code to handle things like duplicate field names and such. *parse_cgi* expects a string argument which is the CGI string and builds the %CGI global associative array with the original field name as the key value and the value as the entry value in the array. After calling *parse_cgi*, the FULLNAME value can be accessed as $CGI{'FULLNAME'} in the Perl program. $CGI{'FULLNAME'} contains "Norman E. Smith" assuming that the example CGI string was the argument to *parse_cgi*.

Graphics

One area that has not been mentioned thus far is graphics. No self-respecting Web page does not include at least a few graphics. Graphics is not an area given much attention in this book. A deep understanding of Web graphics is not necessary to build applications described in this book. A basic knowledge of how to use them in Web applications is. The relative areas of interest include:

- Creating graphic images
- Image maps
- Other graphic formats

Creating Graphic Images

Web graphics today are mostly GIF format bitmap images. Most browsers support JPG images as well. The PNG graphic format is supposed to eventually replace GIF as the standard Web image format. There are a large number of commercial and shareware packages for creating graphics suitable for browser display. Corel even has a whole line of Web related graphics packages. Some graphics packages specifically aimed at Web applications include:

- PaintShop Pro
- Lview Professional
- Corel Web Designer
- Corel Web.Graphics
- Macromedia Backstage

The general rule of thumb that there is a fine line between a pleasing graphical page and one that takes too long to load also applies to intranet applications.

Image Maps

Web browsers support a feature called image maps. It is a mechanism to tie portions of a graphic to a URL. In the early days, all image maps were server side. Basically the client recorded the XY coordinates of a mouse click and sent the coordinates back to the server. The server looked the information up in a table file that mapped image, coordinate, and URL and then returned the page pointed to by the URL. This worked amazingly well, even though constructing and maintaining the image maps were tedious and complicated. What's worse is that NCSA- and CERN-based Web servers use different formats for the image map files.

The HTML file contains an <HREF> tag that points to the server image map file:

```
<HTML>
...
<A HREF="/cgi-bin/imagemap/example"><IMG SRC="example.gif"></A>
...
</HTML>
```

The cgi-bin/imagemap/example file for an NCSA-based Web server contains something like:

```
default /example/example.html
rect /example/example1.html 0,0 50,50
rect /example/example2.html 51,0 100,100
```

The *default* line provides a link if the mouse click is outside the specified areas but on the image. The *rect* lines each define a rectangle. The filename is the URL to retrieve when the mouse click is within the rectangle defined by the upper left (0,0) and lower right corner (50,50). The shape may be a rectangle, a circle, or a polygon.

The latest browsers support client side image maps. The <AREA> element contains the same basic information that the server side image maps require. It is more convenient and much easier to maintain because access to the server is not required.

The following example illustrates the <AREA> client side approach. Let's look at a Web page with a simple image:

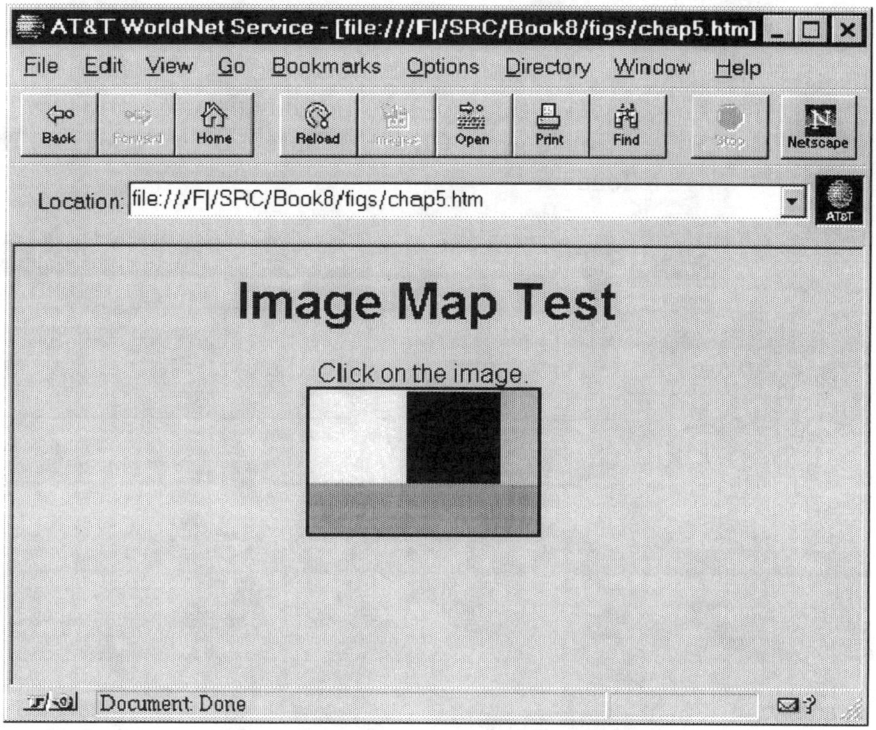

There are four colored boxes in the image. The left box is yellow, the middle box blue, the right box green, and the bottom box pink. This image could just as easily be a navigation graphic. The HTML page contains a client side image map. Chap5.htm is:

```
<HTML>
<BODY>
<CENTER>
<H1>Image Map Test</H1>
<P>
Click on the image.
<BR>
<MAP NAME="chap5-1">
```

```
<AREA SHAPE=RECT COORDS="0,0,66,64" HREF=yellow.htm>
<AREA SHAPE=RECT COORDS="68,0,126,64" HREF=blue.htm>
<AREA SHAPE=default HREF=none.htm>
</MAP>
<IMG SRC="chap5-1.gif" USEMAP="#chap5-1">
</BODY>
</HTML>
```

The <AREA> tags specify the coordinates and HTML URLs to load for each image area. Click the blue box (middle) and the blue.htm page is loaded:

The contents of blue.htm are:

```
<HTML>
<BODY>
<CENTER>
<H1>Image Map Test</H1>
<P>
You clicked on the Blue box.
<BR>
</BODY>
</HTML>
```

When the yellow box is clicked (left), the yellow.htm page is loaded:

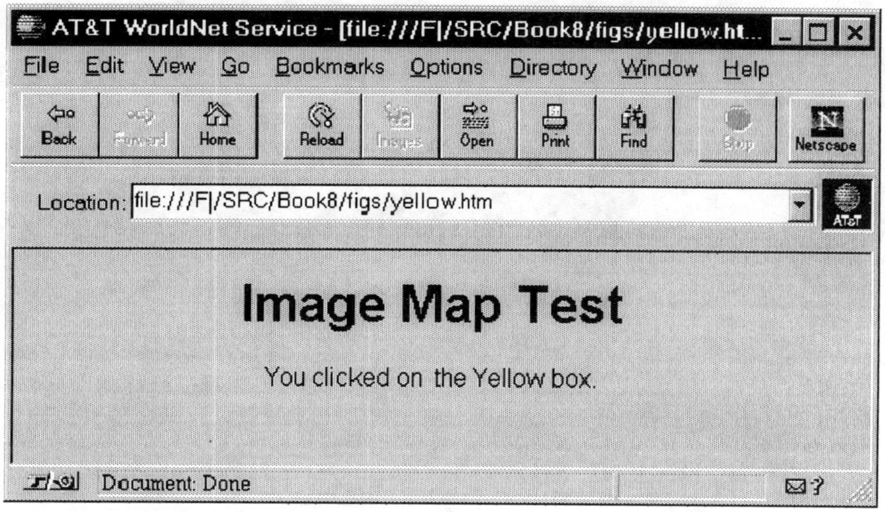

The HTML for yellow.htm is:

```
<HTML>
<TITLE>YELLOW.HTM</TITLE>
<BODY>
<CENTER>
<H1>Image Map Test</H1>
<P>
You clicked on the Yellow box.
<BR>
</BODY>
</HTML>
```

Clicking on any other area of the image loads none.htm:

The HTML for none.htm is:

```
<HTML>
<BODY>
<CENTER>
<H1>Image Map Test</H1>
<P>
You clicked on neither the Yellow nor the Blue box.
<BR>
</BODY>
</HTML>
```

The whole point of this example is illustrating the ease of using client side image maps for menu bars and such in Web applications.

Other Graphic Formats

Tiff format images are relevant to Web applications even though the Web browsers do not directly support displaying Tiff images. Many organizations have warehouses (or at least it seems to be warehouses) of paper documents. There are many reasons for this ranging from statutory to historic to proprietary information. There are good reasons for scanning these documents including lack of the original electronic files and the need for a nonmodifiable form, which may be considered a "record copy." Scanning paper documents is a good solution to these problems. Scanners generally produce Tiff format images.

The implications for a Web site is the necessity of handling Tiff images of full text documents. It is possible for a Web client-server application to handle Tiff images. There are several things to be aware of:

- Conversion to GIF
- Full text searching
- Restricting access

As usual, each new area of consideration presents multiple solutions.

Conversion to GIF/JPG/PNG

Numerous packages exist to convert between graphics formats. Most graphics packages support saving images to one of the formats supported by the current crop of browsers. This is not much help when there are 500,000 images to convert; the process must be automated. There are several issues associated with the graphic automated conversion:

- Convert or not
- Selecting a conversion package
- When the conversion takes place

The first question is whether or not to convert at all. The following table summarizes the factors that influence conversion decisions:

Convert	*Condition*
No	1. A relatively small user community 2. A Tiff viewer browser plug-in is available
Yes	1. A relatively small number of document images
Batch	1. A large number of document images
On Demand	1. Large user community 2. Dynamic or large number of document images

Before discussing each convert option, I should point out that keeping the Tiff files is almost a necessity. There are several reasons for this. First, many packages, whether graphics or OCR or computer output microfiche, accept Tiff. Some will only accept Tiff files. Therefore, Tiff is an important image format even though Web browsers do not handle it directly.

The **No** option requires minimal server resources but requires the user community have extra software in the form of a Tiff viewer. There are a couple of free Tiff viewers available on the Internet. Building your own Tiff viewer is also practical. There are a number of commercial image processing libraries and stand-alone image conversion programs available with some cross platform portability. Two that I have used successfully are the AccuSoft Image library and Image Alchemy.

Conversion may be done either interactively or batch. This also depends on several things including server type and conversion software. A Unix server can easily perform conversion as a batch operation. This is partly because of the available software, and partly because it is convenient to automate the process 100 percent. The 100 percent automation of a major processing function is important in today's business environment.

A Windows NT server implies an interactive conversion. NT has two problems for batch image conversion. First, it is designed as a file server and has limited batch processing capability compared to more traditional host operating systems such as Unix or VMS. Second, most NT software is written for interactive use. There is little that can be done if the conversion program assumes a person sitting at the keyboard.

A final option is on-demand Tiff to GIF conversion. This is an attractive option when there are a large number of documents and the user community is large, such as the public. Tiff images can be converted to GIF on the fly on a SPARC Server in two to three seconds. Caching and "look ahead" conversion can hide the conversion time completely after the first page assuming that the user looks at the page at all. Disk space requirements are minimized because only the currently active pages are stored in both formats.

Full Text Searching

The graphic format comes into play for full text searching of document images. The general approach is to OCR the document images for use as an index. Virtually all OCR packages use Tiff images, which is another reason for keeping the Tiff images of scanned documents. Scanning systems generally put each page into a separate file. This makes creating indexes to individual pages relatively easy. Text databases, such as OpenText or WAIS, can be set up so searches of the text OCRed index returns pointers to the image files.

Document Conversion

An area of Web application development that is important but often hidden in the shadows is document conversion. Document conversion is especially important when the application provides access to full text documents as part of the Web content. There are several options, as usual. There are books devoted to the subject of document conversion. (See *Practical Guide to SGML Filters*, ISBN 1-55622-511-3, published by Wordware Publishing, Inc.) The options include:

- Convert to HTML
- Convert to SGML
- Convert to PDF
- Provide document in original word processor format

Conversion to HTML is sometimes easy and sometimes hard. Most of today's word processors support an "export to HTML" option for creating HTML files from the original word processor document. Corel's WordPerfect also includes a default set of styles that map well to HTML. The net effect is documents that use the default styles, which include several levels of header and bullet lists, convert to HTML, and typically require little if any cleanup.

There are also several word processor to HTML/SGML converters available including HTML Transit and TagWrite. Some of the commercial HTML editors, including SoftQuad's HoTMetaL Pro 3.0 and InContext's Spider, also include conversion from word processors via the Windows clipboard. All told, there are a lot of options to convert documents into HTML.

PDF is Adobe's Portable Document Format. It is appropriate when the original page's format is more important than the content. There are just a few ways to convert documents into PDF:

- Print PostScript to a file, then use Adobe Distiller to convert the PostScript into PDF.
- Use Adobe Capture to scan documents or convert Tiff images into PDF. The result is logically Tiff wrapped in PDF.
- High-end desktop publishing systems are beginning to support "publish as PDF" options.

There are a number of problems with PDF from an information processing standpoint in my opinion. PDF is essentially a write-only format. Once a document is converted to PDF, it can be viewed with Acrobat Reader or printed. That's all! All of the Adobe PDF related tools are interactive, which effectively prevents automation of processing.

Other

The "other" category covers a lot of territory. There is the network, the programming language used for various pieces of the application, and various technology questions in this category at a minimum.

Any program that outputs HTML also falls into this category. Many programs already generate HTML and the number increases rapidly. HTML capability is appropriate for any product that produces paper because it can be treated as "just another output format." This trend makes it easier and easier to put full text content on the Web and into Web applications.

Summary

There are many parts to a Web-based client-server application. Some, such as the client browser and server, are visible. Others have a much less visible but important role such as document conversion. The trick is not ignoring any piece, whether visible or not.

Chapter 6

How a Web-Based Application Works

Introduction

This chapter introduces some of the details of how a Web-based client-server application works. The general program design and implementation are discussed along with a simple example. Hints on how to approach design at the detail level are included along with the CGI interface examples, and other related areas are also covered.

A Quick Example

One area in which Web applications can be effectively used is to provide a GUI-based front end for existing command line applications. The example presented here is a simple implementation of that idea. An application I call File View is the example presented here as the vehicle for discussion. It opens a user specified file and writes it to the browser. Three HTML pages and two Perl CGI scripts implement File View.

The File View application is intended as an intranet-only application! It is a good application to run via a "personal web server," that is a PC-based Web server running locally on the PC with no outside access. File View is implemented using the O'Reilly WebSite 1.1 Web server for Windows 95 and DOS-based Perl as a "personal" Web application. WebSite is NOT connected to the Internet and runs locally for this application. This combination of running a PC-based Web server not connected to a network takes all security considerations out of the application mix. Basically, the entire machine is accessible to the application.

There are many ways to implement the equivalent of File View. The platform, using a client side scripting language, using additional HTML features such as frames and tables, and the screen design are all variables in designing the application. The choices made for this example are:

- ➤ Generic CGI/Perl
- ➤ Multiple HTML pages
- ➤ No client side scripting
- ➤ State passed between the browser and server
- ➤ Security ignored

This combination makes a good illustration of what goes on in a Web-based client-server application.

1. Load **fileview.htm** into the browser:

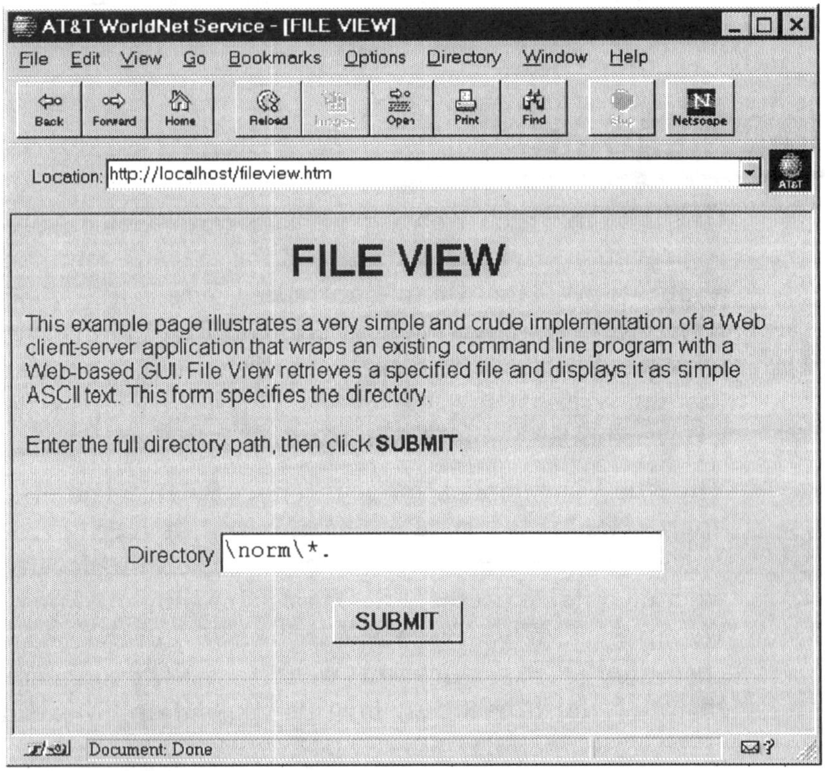

2. Enter a valid file specification. The file specification listed above is valid on my PC. The Perl program used here is not industrial strength. Either enter a plain directory specification or a directory specification with a file specification. The Perl script expects a "*" in the filename string.
3. Clicking the **SUBMIT** button sends the directory specification to the Web server along with the name of the CGI script to run. The Web server executes the script and passes the script's output back to the browser resulting in a list of filenames. The following figure shows a typical file list screen:

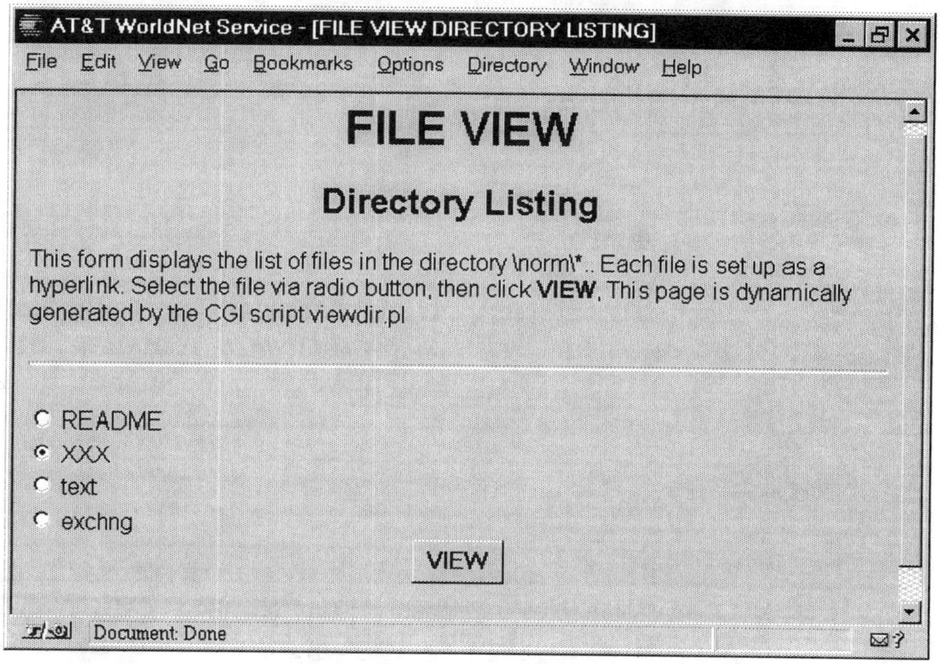

4. Select the file to view by clicking its radio button. Then, clicking the **VIEW** button sends the filename and full directory path to the server along with the CGI script name to execute. The CGI Perl script opens the file and writes the file contents to STDOUT. The Web server intercepts STDOUT and passes the data stream to the browser, displaying the file.

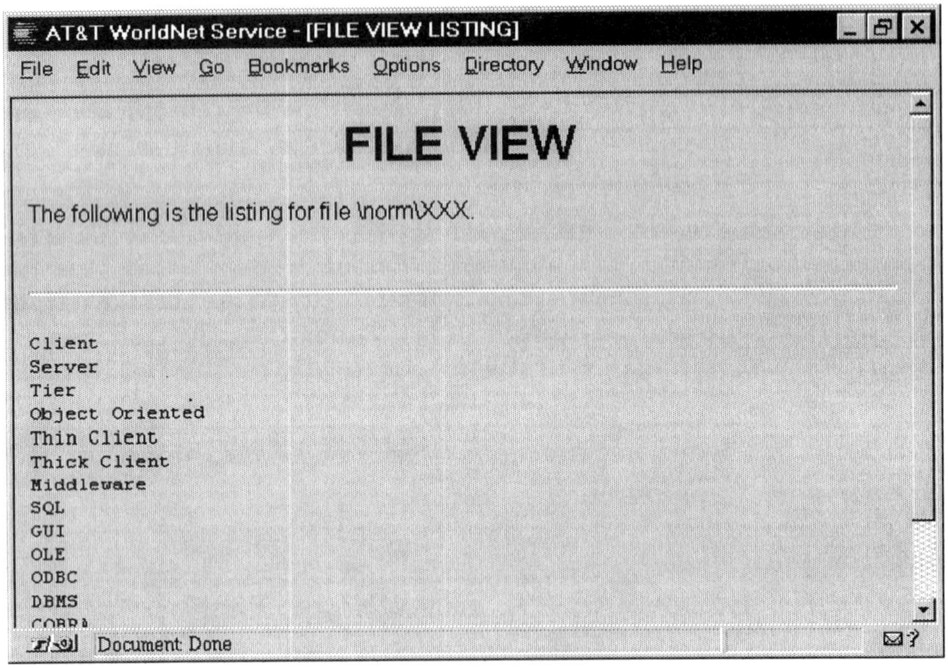

The file display script is simple-minded and makes no provision for processing binary files. Now that we've seen the example demonstrated, it's time to move on to the application design.

File View Design

The File View application is fairly generic, primarily using only the CGI interface to a Perl script and simple HTML. A successful application starts by identifying the requirements. The high level requirements for File View are:

- Provide a page for the user to enter a directory specification
- Provide a page with the files that meet the directory specifications for the user to select the file to view
- Output the contents of the selected file on a page
- Include the directory and filename information on the view page

Much more detailed requirements are necessary for a "real" application. Requirements describe the "whats" of a system. They must be testable and verifiable. Requirements are a measurable indication of when an application is finished.

Three HTML pages and two CGI scripts are necessary to implement File View. Traditional data flow diagrams (DFDs) do not adequately describe the flow of a Web-based system. The following data flow diagram reflects my evolution and represents the flow of the Web-based application:

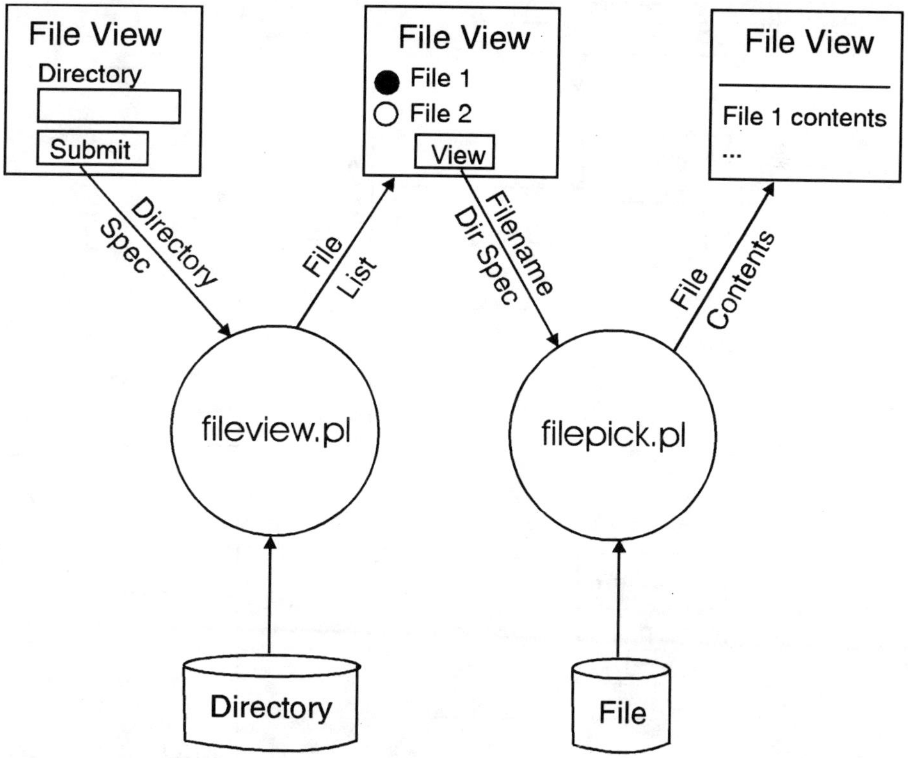

Data Flow Diagram Reflecting the Flow of the Web-Based Application

Notice the DFD lines start from the HTML buttons. Typical real world Web applications have multiple buttons or links. Each button/link represents a different execution path and must be identified accordingly.

Implementation Details

The detailed interaction between the browser and server for File View is shown in the following figure:

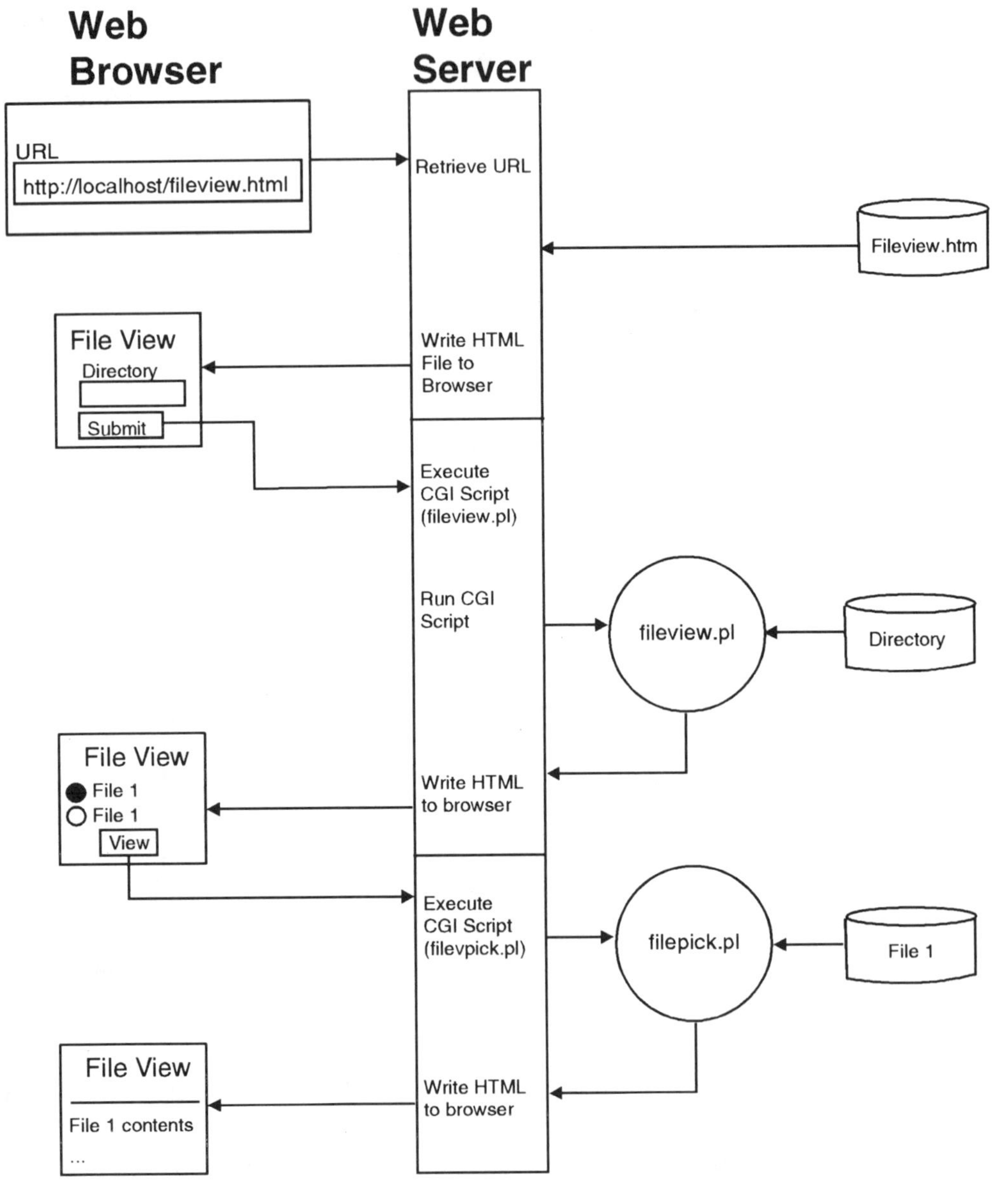

File View Interaction Between the Browser and Server

The lines in the Web server box represent the transaction boundary. Three transactions occur in a typical File View session.

The File View application consists of one static HTML file, fileview.htm, and two Perl Scripts, fileview.pl and filepick.pl. The remaining two HTML pages are dynamically created based on data from the previous page.

Two techniques for dynamic HTML page generation are illustrated. The first uses an HTML template file. The fixed portion of the HTML page is generated by copying the template file to STDOUT in a script. The file directory page is created using the template file filepick.htm. The second technique is simply creating the entire HTML page in the script. The file listing page is completely generated by filepick.pl.

NOTE: As a general rule, use HTML template files when the same HTML contents are used on multiple pages. Generate the HTML completely dynamically for extremely complicated or volatile pages.

Development of File View was done using WebSite 1.1 as the server on Windows 95. WebSite is ideal for personal Web applications like File View. It is easy to install, runs reasonably fast, and supports several CGI modes including:

- MS-DOS CGI
- Windows CGI
- Standard CGI

The MS-DOS CGI is used for 16-bit CGI programs. It requires an MS-DOS batch file to execute each script and passes STDIN via a temporary file. The Windows CGI interface executes 32-bit CGI scripts. These are generally Windows specific programs written in Visual Basic or Visual C++. The Standard CGI interface works with the Korn shell included on one of the Windows NT CDs or special versions of Perl. Pointers to examples of all three CGI interfaces are included in the WebSite distribution.

I chose the MS-DOS CGI interface for this example. Perl 4.036 for DOS was already installed on my PC, so chalk the decision up to laziness. The disadvantages of the MS-DOS CGI interface are closely aligned with differences between MS-DOS and Unix. Executing a Perl script on Unix is a matter of making the first line of the script be:

```
#!/usr/local/bin/perl
```

to tell the Unix shell to execute Perl and feed it the remainder of the script file as a program. The second step in Unix is changing the file protection of the script to eXecute. Use the *chmod* command to change file protection. MS-DOS has no equivalent and must use a batch file to execute the 16-bit Perl script. Thus there is a batch file for each Perl script when using the MS-DOS CGI interface:

Batch File	Executes
fileview.bat	fileview.pl
filepick.bat	filepick.pl

The contents of fileview.bat are:

```
set of=%OUTPUT_FILE%
echo Content--type: text/HTML >%of%
echo. >>%of%
if NOT "%1"==""  echo "%1" "%2" "%3" "%4" "%5" "%6" "%7" "%8" >
      \website\cgi--dos\temp
c:\bin\perl c:\website\cgi--dos\fileview.pl %of%  >>%of%
```

The contents of filepick.bat are:

```
set of=%OUTPUT_FILE%
echo Content--type: text/HTML >%of%
echo. >>%of%
if NOT "%1"==""  echo "%1" "%2" "%3" "%4" "%5" "%6" "%7" "%8" >
      \website\cgi--dos\temp
c:\bin\perl c:\website\cgi--dos\filepick.pl %of%  >>%of%
```

The batch files are not necessary when running File View on a Unix server or one of the other WebSite CGI interface options. Other

Windows 95/Windows NT Web servers may have their own CGI interface quirks for 16-bit scripts.

The user starts File View by entering the application's URL into the browser's location box and presses Enter. The URL is processed by the server and the HTML page, fileview.htm, written back to the browser.

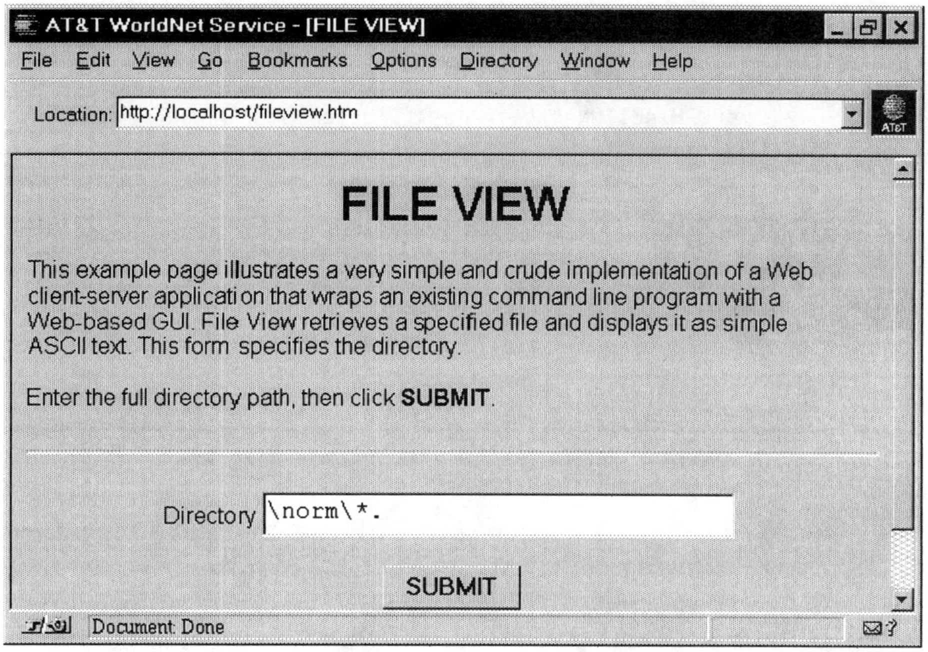

The user enters a full directory specification and clicks on SUBMIT to launch fileview.pl. The data input box is specified in an HTML form. The following listing shows the HTML for the File View page:

```
<!DOCTYPE HTML PUBLIC "--//IETF//DTD HTML 3.0//EN//" [] >
<HTML>
<HEAD>
<TITLE>FILE VIEW</TITLE>
</HEAD><BODY>
<BODYTEXT>
<H1 ALIGN="CENTER">FILE VIEW</H1>
```

```
<P>
This example page illustrates a very simple and crude implementation
of a Web client-server application that wraps an existing command
line program with a Web-based GUI. File View retrieves a specified
file and displays it as simple ASCII text. This form specifies the
directory:
</P><P>
Enter the full directory path, then click <B>SUBMIT</B>.
</P>
<HR>
<CENTER>
<FORM ACTION="/cgi--dos/fileview.bat" METHOD="POST">
Directory
<INPUT TYPE="TEXT" NAME="DIR" SIZE="32" MAXLENGTH="256">
<P>
</P>
<INPUT TYPE="SUBMIT" VALUE="SUBMIT">
<BR>
</FORM><HR>
</BODYTEXT>
</BODY>
</HTML>
```

The HTML form begins with the <FORM> tag and ends with the close tag </FORM>. <FORM> requires several attributes, specifically ACTION (ACTION="/cgi--dos/fileview.bat") and METHOD (METHOD="POST") to provide the server with information about the CGI script to execute when the form is submitted. The ACTION attribute specifies the CGI script name and location on the server and METHOD tells the script whether the CGI string is passed as an environment variable (GET) or STDIN (POST).

The first <INPUT> element, *<INPUT TYPE="TEXT" NAME="DIR" SIZE="32" MAXLENGTH="256">*, generates the text input box for the directory path. The TYPE attribute specifies the type of input, text in this case. NAME specifies the name portion of the CGI string. Thus, the CGI string will be "DIR=value." Where value is the text typed into the text box. The second <INPUT> element, *<INPUT TYPE="SUBMIT" VALUE="SUBMIT">*, defines the "SUBMIT" button.

Clicking SUBMIT sends the form information to the server with a CGI string of:

```
/cgi-dos/fileview.bat?DIR=%5Cnorm%5C*.
```

The server executes fileview.bat and passes the CGI string via STDIN because the <FORM> METHOD is *POST*. This CGI string also illustrates two WebSite MS-DOS CGI interface-specific items. First, the directory is cgi-dos while standard CGI uses cgi-bin. The second is that a batch file, fileview.bat, is executed instead of a script directly. The code for fileview.pl is:


```
#!/usr/local/bin/perl
#
# FILE: fileview.pl
#
# Fields coming back via CGI are:
#      DIR    -- Full path directory spec
#

$WebSite = 1;

if($WebSite == 1){
       $file    = $ARGV[0];
       ($file)  = split(/\./,$file);
       $file   .= ".inp";

       open(PAR,$file);
       $CGIparams = <PAR>;
       close(PAR);
}else{
       print "Content--type: text/HTML\n\n";
       $LEN = $ENV{'CONTENT_LENGTH'};
       read(STDIN,$CGIparams,$LEN);
}
&parse_CGI("$CGIparams");
       #
       # Make sure a directory path was entered
       #
if($CGI{'DIR'} eq ""){
       &print_HTML("c:\\website\\htdocs\\template\\fileerr1.htm");
}else{
```

```
        &process_form();
}
exit;
#######################+----------------------+
#                       | parse_CGI |
#                       +----------------------+
sub parse_CGI{
        local($CGIstring);
        local($i);
        local($key);
        local($val);

        $CGIstring = $_[0];
                #
                # Split fields into an array
                #
        @CGI = split(/&/,$CGIstring);
                #
                # For each field in the CGI string,
                #
        foreach $i (0 .. $#CGI)       {
                        #
                        # Substitute blank for +
                        #
                $CGI[$i] =~ s/\+/ /g;
                        #
                        # Extract field name and value
                        #
                ($key,$val) = split(/=/,$CGI[$i],2);
                        #
                        # Convert hex to character
                        #
                $key =~ s/%(..)/pack("c",hex($1))/ge;
                $val =~ s/%(..)/pack("c",hex($1))/ge;
                        #
                        # Store value in CGI associative array
                        # with field name as the key.
                        #
                $CGI{$key} = $val;
        }
}
```

```
#######################+---------------------------+
#                      | process_form |
#                      +---------------------------+
sub process_form{
       if($CGI{'DIR'} eq ""){
&print_HTML ("c:\\website\\htdocs\\template\\fileerr1.htm");
              return;
       }
              #
              # Display template of fixed portion, the rest
              # is dynamically generated.
              #
       &print_HTML("c:\\website\\htdocs\\template\\filepick.htm");
print "<INPUT TYPE=\"HIDDEN\" NAME=\"DIR\"";
       print " VALUE=\"$CGI{'DIR'}\">\n";

       open(FILES,"dir /b $CGI{'DIR'} |");
       while(<FILES>){
              chop;
              $file = $_;
              if($file eq "." || $file eq ".."){ next; }
              print "<INPUT TYPE=\"RADIO\" NAME=\"FILE\"";
              print " VALUE=\"$file\">$file\n";
              print "<BR>\n";
       }
       close(FILES);
       print "<CENTER>\n";
       print "<INPUT TYPE=\"SUBMIT\" VALUE=\"VIEW\"><BR>\n";
       print "</FORM><HR>\n";
       print "</BODYTEXT>\n";
       print "</BODY>\n";
       print "</HTML>\n";
       return;
}
#######################+-----------------------+
#                      | print_HTML |
#                      +-----------------------+
sub print_HTML{
       open(HTML,"$_[0]");
       while(<HTML>){
```

```
                s/\$DIR/$CGI{'DIR'}/e;
                print "$_";
        }
        close(HTML);
}
```

The following HTML display is generated by fileview.pl:

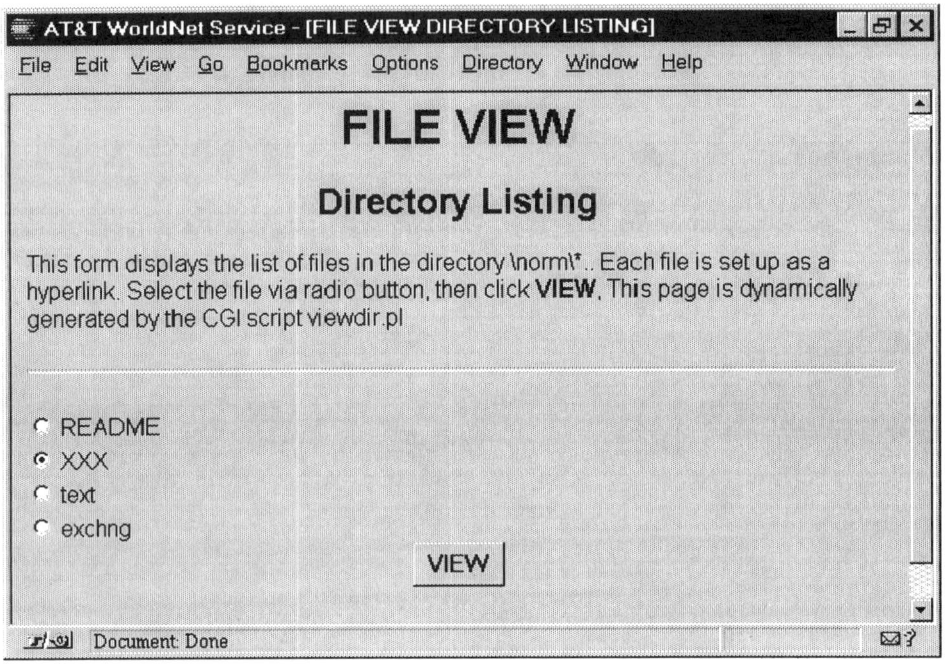

The HTML is dynamically created, as mentioned above, so there is no HTML file that corresponds directly to the screen. The generated HTML for this screen is:

```
<!DOCTYPE HTML PUBLIC "--//IETF//DTD HTML 3.0//EN" []>
<HTML>
<!----FILEPICK.HTM---->
<HEAD>
<TITLE>FILE VIEW DIRECTORY LISTING</TITLE>
```

```
</HEAD>
<BODY>
<BODYTEXT>
<H1 ALIGN="CENTER">FILE VIEW</H1>
<H2 ALIGN="CENTER">Directory Listing</H2>
<P>
This form displays the list of files in the directory \norm\*.. Each
file is set up as a hyperlink. Select the file via radio button, then
click <B>VIEW</B>, This page is dynamically generated by the CGI
script viewdir.pl
</P>
<HR>
<FORM ACTION="/cgi--dos/filepick.bat" METHOD="POST">
<INPUT TYPE="HIDDEN" NAME="DIR" VALUE="\norm\*.">
<INPUT TYPE="RADIO" NAME="FILE" VALUE="README">README
<BR>
<INPUT TYPE="RADIO" NAME="FILE" VALUE="XXX">XXX
<BR>
<INPUT TYPE="RADIO" NAME="FILE" VALUE="text">text
<BR>
<INPUT TYPE="RADIO" NAME="FILE" VALUE="exchng">exchng
<BR>
<CENTER>
<INPUT TYPE="SUBMIT" VALUE="VIEW"><BR>
</FORM><HR>
</BODYTEXT>
</BODY>
</HTML>
```

You may ask "How did he get the HTML if there is no HTML file?" Simply select VIEW->Document Source to view the document in the built-in browser source window. The text can be selected by highlighting the text and pressing Ctrl-C to copy the text to the Windows clipboard. Then paste the text into a text editor or word processor.

6

NOTE: Dynamically created HTML can be captured by:

1. Selecting View->Document Source from the browser menu
2. Highlighting, then selecting the text
3. Pressing **Ctrl-C** to copy the selected text to the clip board
4. Opening an editor or word processor and pasting the contents

NOTE: Select an editor helper application from the options menu and the text for the HTML page will be inserted into that editor when View->Document Source is clicked.

Manipulating the generated HTML file is often a good way to find and correct HTML coding errors during development.

Examine the <FORM> element in the HTML file from filepick.pl listed above. It illustrates additional form features including hidden fields and radio buttons.

Hidden fields are very important in CGI programming. They provide the means for one script to pass values to the next script. The directory path is passed from fileview.pl as a hidden field:

```
<INPUT TYPE="HIDDEN" NAME="DIR" VALUE="\norm\*.">
```

Hidden fields effectively emulate the user typing text into a text box. The data is passed to the next CGI program when the submit button is clicked.

The second form feature on this page is the radio button. Radio buttons allow selection of one of a group of options. Radio buttons are used in the File View application to select a file to view. The following list shows the HTML code that produces the file selection radio buttons on the Directory Listing Page:

```
<INPUT TYPE="RADIO" NAME="FILE" VALUE="README">README
<INPUT TYPE="RADIO" NAME="FILE" VALUE="XXX">XXX
<INPUT TYPE="RADIO" NAME="FILE" VALUE="text">text
<INPUT TYPE="RADIO" NAME="FILE" VALUE="exchng">exchng
```

Radio buttons are grouped by name. For the example, the button name is "FILE." Only one of the four FILE radio buttons may be selected at any one time. The value here is the filename to view. The CGI string for this set of radio buttons when XXX is selected is:

```
FILE=XXX
```

where "FILE" is the NAME attribute value and "XXX" is the VALUE attribute for the currently selected radio button. A default radio button may be specified by including the CHECKED attribute on the button to select. The following line illustrates the CHECKED attribute usage.


```
<INPUT TYPE="RADIO" NAME="FILE" VALUE="XXX" CHECKED>XXX
```

Other form features will be covered as they are used.

The CGI string:

```
cgi-dos/filepick.bat?DIR=%5Cnorm%5C*.&FILE=XXX
```

is sent to the server causing filepick.pl to execute. (Remember that WebSite MS-DOS CGI executes a batch file, which executes the Perl script.) The CGI string supplies the information needed to locate and open the file. The full path filename is constructed by:

- Splitting the directory path on '\'
- Removing the last split segment if the filename contains an '*'
- Appending the filename to the remainder of the directory path

The Perl code for filepick.pl is:

```
#!/usr/local/bin/perl
#
# FILE: filepick.pl
#
# Fields coming back via CGI are:
```

```
#       FILE -- file to view
#       DIR  -- Directory path
#
$WebSite = 1;

if($WebSite == 1){
        $file    = $ARGV[0];
        ($file)  = split(/\./,$file);
        $file   .= ".inp";

        open(PAR,$file);
        $CGIparams = <PAR>;
        close(PAR);
}else{
        print "Content--type: text/HTML\n\n";
        $LEN = $ENV{'CONTENT_LENGTH'};
        read(STDIN,$CGIparams,$LEN);
}
&parse_CGI("$CGIparams");

if($CGI{'DIR'} eq ""){
        &print_HTML("c:\\website\\htdocs\\template\\fileerr1.htm");
}else{
        &process_form();
}
exit;
########################+----------------------+
#                       | parse_CGI |
#                       +----------------------+
sub parse_CGI{
        local($CGIstring);
        local($i);
        local($key);
        local($val);

        $CGIstring = $_[0];
                #
                # Split fields into an array
                #
        @CGI = split(/&/,$CGIstring);
                #
                # For each field in the CGI string,
                #
```

```
        foreach $i (0 .. $#CGI)      {
                        #
                        # Substitute blank for +
                        #
                $CGI[$i] =~ s/\+/ /g;
                        #
                        # Extract field name and value
                        #
                ($key,$val) = split(/=/,$CGI[$i],2);
                        #
                        # Convert hex to character
                        #
                $key =~ s/%(..)/pack("c",hex($1))/ge;
                $val =~ s/%(..)/pack("c",hex($1))/ge;
                        #
                        # Store value in CGI associative array
                        # with field name as the key.
                        #
                $CGI{$key} = $val;
        }
}
########################+---------------------------+
#                       | process_form |
#                       +---------------------------+
sub process_form{
        $file  = &fix_file();

        print "<HTML>\n";
        print "<HEAD>\n";
        print "<TITLE>FILE VIEW LISTING</TITLE>\n";
        print "</HEAD>\n";
        print "<BODY>\n";
        print "<BODYTEXT>\n";
        print "<H1 ALIGN=\"CENTER\">FILE VIEW</H1>\n";
        print "<P>\n";
        print "The following is the listing for file $file.\n";
        print "</P>\n";
        print "<BR><HR>\n";
        print "<PRE>\n";

        open(FILE,"$file");
        while(<FILE>){
                print "$_";
```

```
        }
        close(FILES);

        print "</PRE>\n";
        print "</BODYTEXT>\n";
        print "</BODY>\n";
        print "</HTML>\n";
        return;
}
########################+-----------------------+
#                       | print_HTML |
#                       +-----------------------+
sub print_HTML{
        open(HTML,"$_[0]");
        while(<HTML>){
                print "$_";
        }
        close(HTML);
}
########################+--------------------+
#                       | fix_file |
#                       +--------------------+
sub fix_file{
        local(@files);

        $dir_string = $CGI{'DIR'};
        if($dir_string =~ /\*/){
                @files = split(/\\/,$dir_string);
                $dir_string = "";
                for($i=0;$i<$#files;$i++){
                        $dir_string .= "$files[$i]\\";
                }
                $file  ="$dir_string$CGI{'FILE'}";
        }else{
                $dir_string =~ s/\\$//;
                $file  ="$dir_string\\$CGI{'FILE'}";
        }
        return $file;
}
```

The following HTML page is generated by filepick.pl:

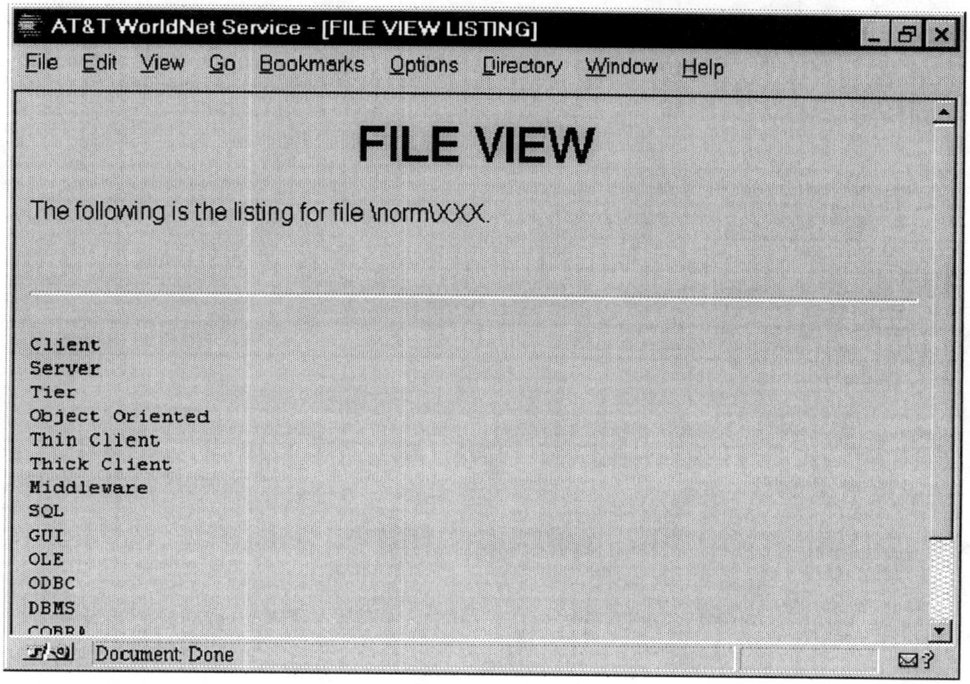

The HTML that generates the page is totally generated within filepick.pl. The HTML for the view page is:

```
<HTML>
<HEAD>
<TITLE>FILE VIEW LISTING</TITLE>
</HEAD>
<BODY>
<BODYTEXT>
<H1 ALIGN="CENTER">FILE VIEW</H1>
<P>
The following is the listing for file \norm\XXX.
</P>
<BR><HR>
<PRE>
Client
Server
Tier
Object Oriented
Thin Client
```

```
Thick Client
Middleware
SQL
GUI
OLE
ODBC
DBMS
CORBA
Thin Server
Thick Server
</PRE>
</BODYTEXT>
</BODY>
</HTML>
```

There are a couple of conditions that are not included in the code that are necessary for a real production level application. There is little error checking. Additional errors that could be tested for include:

- Blank values for the data input fields
- Invalid directory paths
- Only view ASCII files automatically

You get the idea.

Summary

There you have a simple but complete Web-based intranet application. The File View application illustrates many of the aspects of a generic CGI application using Perl as the scripting language. The multiple screens show passing data along the processing stream. File View is also typical of wrapping legacy applications in a Web GUI. The later chapters and case studies go into the areas covered here in more depth and detail.

Chapter 7

HTML Background

Introduction

HTML, or Hyper Text Markup Language, is one of the simplifying components of Web-based applications. It is an ASCII-based markup language. This chapter takes a quick look at HTML background.

HTML History

HTML is a markup language conceived originally as a way for physicists to format shared electronic documents at CERN in Geneva, Switzerland. The HTTP protocol, the first Web server, and a line oriented Web browser were developed. In 1993 NCSA (National Center for Supercomputing Applications) released the first GUI Mosaic Web browser and the World Wide Web exploded! The rest, as they say, is history.

HTML has evolved over the years. The early days of the Web were hectic. Your browser had to be updated almost daily to keep up with the latest HTML tag additions. NCSA Mosaic initially was king of the browsers; everyone else tried to keep up with Mosaic. One of the things NCSA did right with Mosaic was provide multiplatform support from the very beginning.

Several Mosaic developers left NCSA to found Netscape. The browser battles quickly switched to Mosaic versus Navigator. Netscape initially added new tag after new tag in an effort to keep ahead of Mosaic and succeeded. Today's browser battle is Netscape versus Microsoft Internet Explorer.

A side effect of the “browser wars” is the explosion of HTML elements. The initial Mosaic supported a small number, probably a couple of dozen elements. The latest HTML specification has well over a hundred. Even this is not enough as several nonbrowser products add elements for their own use. For example, *Cold Fusion* by Allaire uses several proprietary tags to specify database queries within HTML documents.

The evolution of HTML has resulted in several versions of HTML over the years. The most significant HTML versions are:

- 2.0
- 3.0
- 3.2

Even though the original HTML tag concept borrowed from the idea of generic markup from SGML there was no SGML DTD for a long period of time. DTDs were published for the three HTML versions listed above by World Wide Web Consortium (W3C or W3 Consortium) (www.w3.org).

Prior to HTML 2.0, a couple of unofficial HTML DTDs circulated around the net thanks to Dan Connolly. In fact, very early on I used generic SGML tools to process HTML using one of these DTDs. I started with the unofficial HTML DTD and added elements as each version of Mosaic was released to reflect the current tag set. The SGML-based HTML editors, SoftQuad’s HoTMetaL and InContext’s Spider, still supply multiple DTDs to handle the variations. The official DTDs were a great step toward standardization.

HTML 2.0

HTML 2.0 was the first HTML DTD officially published by the W3 Consortium. It added Forms to the basic HTML tag set. HTML 2.0 opened up the Web to client-server computing because data could be entered on a form and passed back to the server and processed via CGI scripts.

HTML 3.0

Version 3.0's biggest enhancement was the addition of Tables. Presentation of information was greatly enhanced by HTML tables. Combining forms and tables are an excellent way to generate pleasing HTML data entry pages. Frames also appeared in HTML 3.0.

HTML 3.2

Version 3.2 changes are primarily to support client side scripting languages such as Java, JavaScript, and VBScript and style sheets. Both changes mirror important WWW changes.

HTML and SGML

HTML is an SGML application which means that there is an HTML DTD. Actually, there are several, including one for each major HTML version. The current HTML DTD is 3.2.

Most of you will wonder what the big deal is with SGML and why you should care. The single biggest reason is automation potential. HTML treated as SGML is much more structured, as illustrated by the "unstructured versus structured" discussion in Chapter 4. In other words, there is a wonderful consistency to valid SGML documents. Transformations become much simpler and automatable. The importance of data consistency cannot be appreciated until you have had to convert a hundred or a thousand documents for use on the Web today. In fact, whole books have been devoted to the subject. (See *Practical Guide to SGML Filters*, ISBN 1-55622-511-3, also published by Wordware Publishing, Inc.)

Some examples of HTML transformations that are relatively straightforward with HTML/SGML documents are:

- Generating a Table of Contents
- Splitting a large document into smaller chunks
- Creating structural hyperlinks from section to section

Automating each of these processes is difficult and error prone at best with non-SGML compliant HTML.

Another advantage of treating HTML as SGML is using general purpose SGML tools for data manipulation. HTML-only tools are adequate most of the time. However, they are a dead end and limited to processing only HTML. SGML tools generally scale much better. They can also be used for more complicated applications such as preparing data for CD-ROM for example. The next time a few new tags are added to HTML, your HTML tools must be updated to take advantage of them. SGML tools, on the other hand, may be upgraded by simply using the updated DTD.

SGML compliant basically means that an HTML document follows the rules defined by the Document Type Definition. There are two ways to verify compliance. The first is editing the document with an SGML editor using the HTML DTD. The down side of this is most full-blown SGML editors are fairly expensive. Corel's WordPerfect is an exception. It is less than $100 (early 1997) if you qualify for its very liberal upgrade. There is also an SGML mode available for GNU Emacs. Inexpensive HTML alternatives based on full-blown SGML editors are available and include SoftQuad's HoTMetaL and InContext's Spider. There are also rumors of one or two of the first generation HTML-only editors adding syntax checking in their next release.

The second alternative for validating SGML compliance of HTML documents is parsing the documents with an SGML validating parser. Parsing HTML documents is relatively simple once you find out all the secrets.

SGML Parsing

Parsing an HTML document with an SGML parser requires these things:

- An SGML parser
- An HTML DTD
- The HTML document

Several free SGML validating parsers are available from the Internet including:

Parser	Availability	Comments
ARC-SGML	ftp.ifi.uio.no in /pub/SGML/ARC-SGML	One of the first SGML parsers, written by Charles Goldfarb who is known as the father of SGML.
NSGMLS	ftp.jclark.com in /pub/SP/msdos	NSGMLS was written by James Clark as a demo application of his SP SGML parser toolkit. It has all of the features of SGMLS plus some.
SGMLS	ftp.jclark.com ftp.ifi.uio.no in /pub/SGML/SGMLS	Based on ARC-SGML with many significant enhancements by James Clark.
YASP	ftp.ifi.uio.no in /pub/SGML/YASP	

SGMLS/NSGMLS are both commercial grade SGML parsers, and in fact both have been included in commercial packages. Both produce a very easy to process output file format called ESIS.

The examples here all use SGMLS. SGMLS is included with the CD in this book. There are currently three HTML DTDs generally available on the Web, HTML 2.0, HTML 3.0, and HTML 3.2. Each is included in an appendix.

Now for the details. These examples use the following files:

- SGMLS.EXE as the parser
- HTML.DTD for the DTD
- Either UNSTRUCT.HTM or STRUCT.HTM for the document

The HTML documents are the two HTML snippets from the unstructured versus structured document discussion in Chapter 4. The example also assumes that all of the files are in the same directory and that we are running on an MD-DOS PC.

First, we'll parse UNSTRUCT.HTM to illustrate parsing a non-compliant HTML document. Here are the contents of UNSTRUCT.HTM:

```
<H2>Header
<P>The text just goes here.
This is a para, followed by
a list:

<LI>List item 1
```

```
<LI>Let's make <H3>BIG text</H3>
<LI>List item 3

<H1>Another Header
<P>More text...
```

Type:

```
C:\NORM>sgmls -sg html32.dtd unstruct.htm
```

and press Enter to parse the document. The -s flag suppresses the ESIS output stream and -g tells SGMLS to use element names in error messages. SGMLS produces the following output:

```
C:\norm>sgmls -sg default.dec html.dtd unstruct.htm
sgmls: SGML error at unstruct.htm, line 2 at ">":
       H2 end-tag implied by P start-tag; not minimizable
       Element structure: HTML
sgmls: SGML error at unstruct.htm, line 6 at ">":
       Out-of-context LI start-tag ended HTML document element
       (and parse)
```

The first error, at line 2, is flagged because the <H2> element is defined in the DTD as requiring an end tag. The <P> start tag before the end of the <H2> triggered the error. The second error is the <LI> tag without a start of list element such as <UL> or <OL>. At that point parsing stopped. There are other errors later in the document that will be detected after these errors are corrected.

The second example performs the same processing on STRUCT.HTM. The listing of STRUCT.HTML is:

```
<HTML>
<HEAD>
<TITLE>DocTitle</TITLE>
</HEAD>
<BODY>
<H1>Header</H1>
<P>The text just goes here.
This is a para, followed by
a list:
```

```
<UL>
<LI>List item 1
<LI>Let's make <B>bold text</B>
<LI>List item 3
</UL>
<H1>Another Header</H1>
<P>Moretext...
</BODY>
</HTML>
```

Type the following line and press Enter to begin parsing.

```
C:\norm>sgmls -sg default.dec html.dtd struct.htm
```

The result is:

```
C:\norm>
```

which means no errors were detected.

The final SGMLS run shows the ESIS output from parsing STRUCT.HTM with just the -g flag:

```
C:\norm>sgmls -sg default.dec html.dtd struct.htm
(HTML
(HEAD
(TITLE
-DocTitle
)TITLE
)HEAD
-\n
(BODY
(H1
-Header
)H1
-\n
(P
)P
-The text just goes here.\nThis is a para, followed by \na list:\n
ACOMPACT IMPLIED
(UL
(LI
```

```
)LI
-List item 1\n
(LI
)LI
-Let's make
(B
-bold text
)B
-\n
(LI
)LI
-List item 3
)UL
-\n
(H1
-Another Header
)H1
-\n
(P
)P
-Moretext...
)BODY
)HTML
C
```

As you can see, the format is relatively easy to process. *Practical Guide to SGML Filters* includes both AWK and Perl examples of processing ESIS files along with detailed descriptions of the format.

Non-SGML Parsing

For completeness, the next two examples use an HTML specific validator called Web-Lint for validation on UNSTRUCT.HTM and STRUCT.HTM. Web-Lint is a Perl script available from ftp://ftp.khoral.com/pub/weblint/weblint-1.016.zip. Another HTML validation package called HTMLCHEK is also available.

The following listing shows Web-Lint execution and results for UNSTRUCT.HTM:

```
C:\norm\tmp>perl weblint unstruct.htm
DOS/4GW Professional Protected Mode Run-time  Version 1.97
Copyright (c) Rational Systems, Inc. 1990-1994
unstruct.htm(1): outer tags should be <HTML> .. </HTML>.
unstruct.htm(6): illegal context for <LI> - must appear in
<DIR|MENU|OL|UL> element.
unstruct.htm(7): illegal context for <LI> - must appear in
<DIR|MENU|OL|UL> element.
unstruct.htm(8): illegal context for <LI> - must appear in
<DIR|MENU|OL|UL> element.
unstruct.htm(0): no closing </H2> seen for <H2> on line 1.
unstruct.htm(0): no closing </H1> seen for <H1> on line 10.
unstruct.htm(-): expected tag(s) not seen: HEAD TITLE BODY
```

Here is the run of Weblint on STRUCT.HTM:

```
C:\norm\tmp>perl weblint struct.htm
DOS/4GW Professional Protected Mode Run-time  Version 1.97
Copyright (c) Rational Systems, Inc. 1990-1994
C:\norm\tmp>
```


Your results will vary slightly from this listing because the "DOS/4GW" messages are produced by the MS-DOS Perl 4.036 implementation used to run the test.

SGML Tools for HTML

There are a number of SGML tools that work well with HTML. There are structured editors, parsers, translators, text retrieval engines, and viewers. The following table lists representative SGML tools that work well with HTML:

Type	Package	Vendor	Web Site	Platform
Editors	Author/Edit	SoftQuad	www.sq.com	Windows, MacIntosh, Unix
	InContext 2.1	InContext Systems	www.incontext.com	Windows 95
	WordPerfect 7	Corel	www.corel.com	Windows 95, Windows NT
	Adept Editor	Arbortext	www.arbortext.com	Windows 95, Windows NT, Unix

Type	Package	Vendor	Web Site	Platform
Desktop Publishing Systems	Ventura 7	Corel	www.corel.com	Windows 95, Windows NT
	Adept Publisher	ArborText, Inc.	www.arbortext.com	Windows 95, Windows NT, Unix
	FrameMaker+ SGML	Adobe	www.adobe.com or www.frame.com	Windows 95, Windows NT, Unix
	Interleaf	Interleaf Corp.	www.interleaf.com	Windows 95, Windows NT, Unix
Parsers and Translators	OmniMark	OmniMark Technologies, Inc.	www.omnimark.com	Windows 95, Windows NT, Unix, Macintosh
	SGMLS, NSGMLS, SP	James Clark	www.jclark.com	MS-DOS, Windows 95, Windows NT, Unix, Macintosh, VMS
	SGML-C	SGML Systems	www.dircon.co.uk/sgml	Windows 95, Windows NT
Text Search Engines	LiveLink 7	OpenText Corp.	www.opentext.com	Windows 95, Windows NT, Unix
SGML Document Viewers	Panorama Pro	SoftQuad	www.sq.com	Windows 95, Windows NT
	Dynatext	Electronic Book Technologies	www.ebtm	MS-DOS, Windows 95, Windows NT, Unix

This list is by no means complete but does list most of the major players. There are also a number of Web sites with SGML pointers:

- www.sgmlopen.org
- www.sil.org
- ftp.ifi.uio.no/pub/SGML
- www.falch.no/people/pepper/sgmltool/products.htm

Also check out the vendor home pages listed in the previous table.

Document Conversion

Document conversion is another subject that may have no direct application in a Web application. However, eventually you will probably run into some document conversion on applications that handle full text.

Document conversion is the process of converting documents from one format to another. This is covered in conjunction with SGML because SGML is a format-neutral document representation. Documents authored using SGML structured editors are the least expensive to convert because the documents are very structured. Conversion to almost any format from PDF to HTML is not difficult.

Document conversion is also much simplified by the latest generation of word processors and DTP packages where a "Publish to HTML" option is included. Documents in large volume must be converted in an automated manner. When you have 10,000 documents to convert to the Web, having a person sitting at the keyboard converting from word processor to HTML format is too expensive. That is where automated document conversion becomes critical. Check out *Practical Guide To SGML Filters* (ISBN 1-55622-511-3 also published by Wordware Publishing), which covers document conversion in much detail.

Summary

There is a lot to HTML when you look below the surface. It is a markup language with some roots in SGML. HTML has evolved rapidly over the past few years progressing to the current HTML 3.2 specification. Many tools exist for processing HTML including HTML specific tools, SGML tools that work well with compliant or structured HTML, and general purpose tools such as Perl and AWK that also have their place in the HTML world.

Chapter 8

Basic HTML

Introduction

This chapter hits the high points of what I consider basic HTML. There is a surprisingly little knowledge base required to effectively code HTML documents. There is a tag structure defined by the HTML DTD that must be followed. The general structure for an HTML document is:

```
<HTML>
<!-- This is a comment -->
<HEAD>
  <TITLE>Document Title</TITLE>
</HEAD>
<BODY>
  <H1>First Level Heading</H1>
    <P>Paragraph
    <H2>Second Level Heading</H2>
      <P>Another Paragraph
      <UL> <!-- A bullet list -->
        <LI>List item 1
        <LI>List item 2
      </UL>
      <H3>Third Level Heading</H3>
  <H1>Second First Level Heading</H1>
</BODY>
</HTML>
```

Loading this example into the Netscape Navigator browser produces the following display:

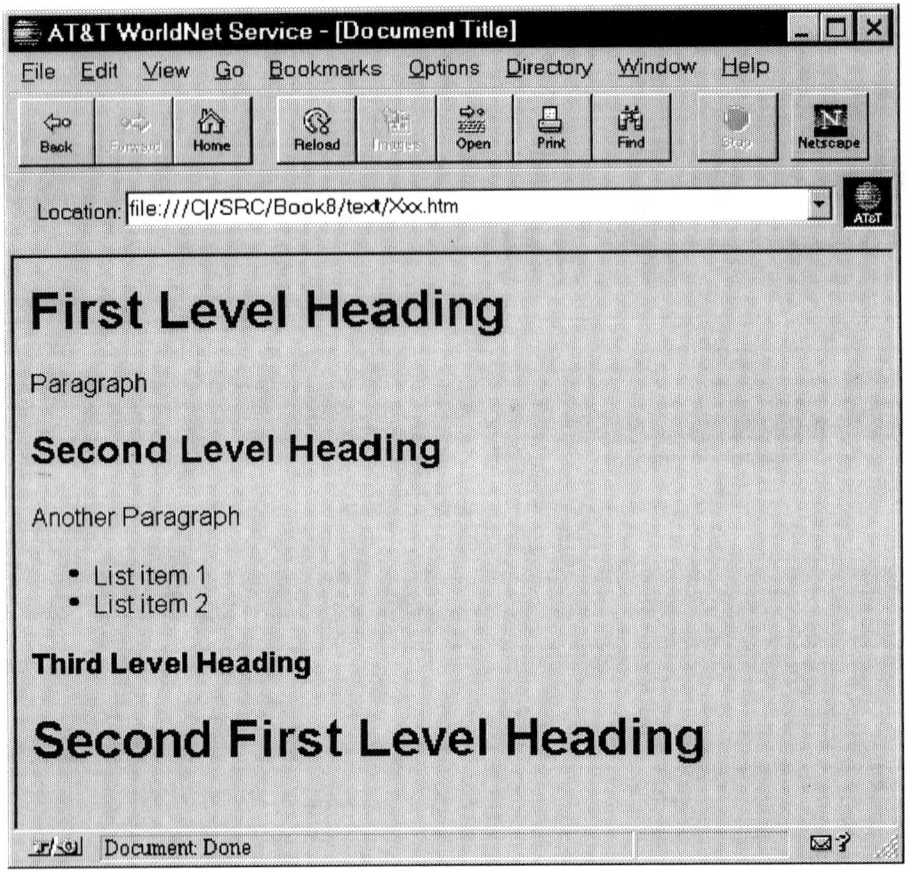

Six levels of heading are supported. This is not inclusive of all the elements that are defined in HTML, just a very basic set to get anyone started. The following table lists what I consider to be a list of basic HTML tags and their use.

Element	*End Tag Required*	*Description*
A	Yes	Hyperlink Anchor. It may specify either a destination or link depending on which attribute is used. The attributes are: *NAME* Specify the name of a hyperlink destination. *HREF* Hyperlink reference

Element	*End Tag Required*	*Description*
ADDRESS	Yes	Generally used to specify information, such as e-mail address of the document's author. Most browsers render <ADDRESS> in italics.
B	Yes	Bold the text enclosed between <B> and </B>. <STRONG> may also be used to produce bold text.
BASEFONT	No	Specify the default size for the font currently in use. The text size is specified via the *SIZE* attribute.
BLINK	Yes	The text between <BLINK> and </BLINK> blinks. Most people find blinking text very annoying.
BLOCKQUOTE	Yes	This element is used for long sections of quoted text.
BODY	No	Mark the start of the body portion of an HTML document.
BR	No	Break the current line at the tag.
CENTER	No	All text after the <CENTER> tag is centered until either a </CENTER> tag or the end of the document is encountered.
COMMENT	Yes	An HTML comment starts with <!-- and ends with -->. The browser skips anything between, providing a way to place descriptive comments in the document or to comment out portions.
DD	Yes	<DD> stands for Dictionary Definition. It is part of a Definition List (<DL>) element. <DD> generally contains the definition of an entry and the <DT> contains the term.
DIVn	No	HTML 3.0 and later provide <DIV1> through <DIV6> as wrapper tags for <H1> through <H6>.
DL	Yes	This element starts a Dictionary List. Each entry contains a <DT> and <DD> pair for each term/definition. For example: <DL> <DT>Term 1 <DD>Definition 1 <DT>Term 2 <DD>Definition 2 </DL> Note that DL modifies the current margins.
DT	No	The <DT> tag marks a Dictionary Term in a <DL> list.
EM	Yes	Text between <EM> and </EM> is "emphasized." Text is generally rendered as italics. You may also use the <I> to obtain italics text.

Element	*End Tag Required*	*Description*
FONT	Yes	Changes the font size and color of text between <FONT> and </FONT> tags.
HEAD	No	<HEAD> encloses the header portion of a document. Such things as title and JavaScript commands are generally included in the header.
Hn	Yes	The Header 1 through Header 6 elements mark heading text for a section of an HTML document. <H1> is typically used at the chapter level for example.
HR	No	<HR> produces a horizontal rule the width of the browser screen.
HTML	No	An entire HTML document is enclosed in <HTML> and </HTML>.
I	Yes	This element produces italics text between <I> and </I>.
IMG	No	This element inserts an image into an HTML document. <IMG> causes a bit mapped image in either GIF, JPG, or PNG format to be displayed in the browser. The only required attribute is *SRC*, which specifies the URL of the image file.
LI	No	<LI> is a list item of either an unordered bullet list (<UL>) or an ordered numeric list (<OL>).
MAP	No	Specifies a client side image map. An image map associates portions of a graphic image to a hyperlink.
OL	Yes	An ordered list is specified by <OL>. Each list item (<LI>) is formatted with a digit or alphabetic counter. <OL> <LI>One <LI>TWO </OL>
PRE	Yes	Preformatted text is displayed with embedded white space in the HTML document preserved. The text is enclosed in <PRE> and </PRE> elements and is generally rendered in a fixed width font.
STRIKE	Yes	Causes a "strike out" line to be printed through the text enclosed in <STRIKE> and </STRIKE>.
STRONG	Yes	<STRONG> is a synonym for producing bold text.
SUB	Yes	Text enclosed in a SUB element is displayed as subscripted text.
SUP	Yes	Text enclosed in a SUP element is displayed as superscripted text.

Element	End Tag Required	Description
TITLE	No	The title element occurs in the <HEAD> portion of the document. The text between <TITLE> and </TITLE> is usually displayed on the title bar at the top of the browser window.
UL	Yes	An unordered list (<UL>) is actually what most people call a bullet list. Each list item (<LI>) element is rendered with a bullet character at the left margin.

This list is not all inclusive!

One additional element in the basic element list that should be explained in some detail is Anchor. The tag for an Anchor is <A>. Anchor is used in two ways, one to mark a location within a document and the second references a document or location. The difference is in the attributes. Specifying a *NAME* attribute means the destination for a hyperlink reference. For example, the following Anchor marks the word **destination** as a hyperlink destination:

```
<P> This is a <A NAME="LOC1">destination</A> within
a paragraph.
```

The hyperlink form of Anchor uses the *HREF* attribute to specify the hyperlink to jump to. The hyperlink may be either a document location on the Web, commonly called a URL, or a location within the current document.

The *HREF* that references LOC1 within the same document is:

```
<A HREF="#LOC1">Jump to "destination"</A>
```

The **#** in the *HREF* attribute tells the browser the link destination, LOC1 in this case, is a specific location in the current document. An *HREF* without a **#** is interpreted as the URL of a specific document:

```
<A HREF="http://www.wordware.com/page1.html">Jump to
"destination"</A>
```

A specific location with an external document can be specified by combining the two forms:

```
<A HREF="http://www.wordware.com/page1.html#LOC1">Jump to
"destination"</A>
```

The following illustration shows the relationship of the hyperlinks:

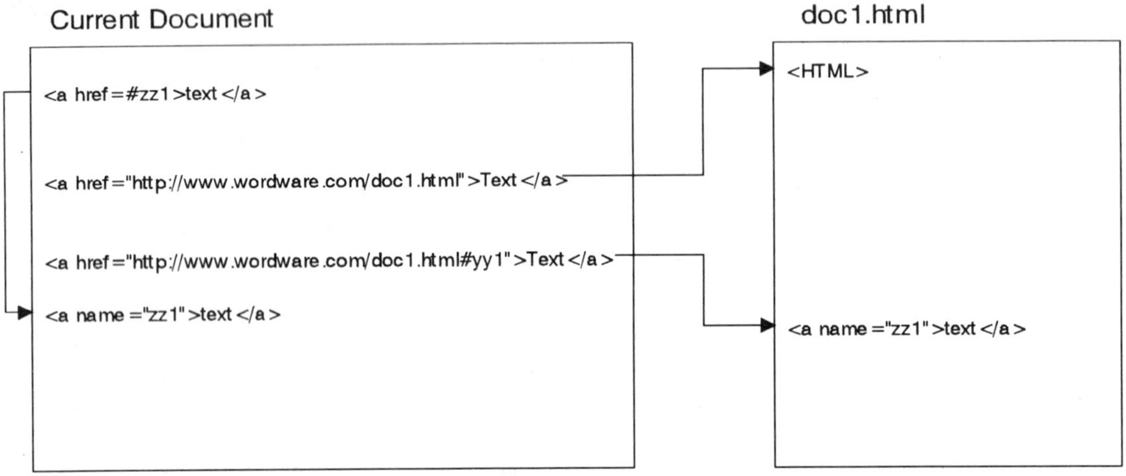

Hyperlinks Relationships

Markup Rules

There are some rules about tag names. The following list summarizes the primary usage rules:

- Element names are enclosed in <..> to form start tags
- Element end tags are the element name enclosed in </..>
- Some elements require end tags
- Elements may have attribute name/value pairs between the name and the closing ">".
- Tags are not case sensitive

The tag name, both start and end, is enclosed in <>. End tags are marked with a "/" after the opening "<". Thus, <HTML> is the tag for opening and </HTML> the tag for closing the HTML element.

Elements may have what look like parameters, such as:

```
<H1 ALIGN="CENTER">
```

The correct name for an element's "parameters" is *attribute*. The attribute is named *ALIGN* and its value is *CENTER*.

URLs

A URL (Universal Resource Locator) is a multipart way of specifying the document location on the Web. For our purposes, a URL consists of four parts:

- Protocol
- Server internet address
- Server port number
- Target resource

A URL can specify any protocol supported by both the client and the server. The common protocols handled by Web browsers include:

HTTP	HyperText Transfer Protocol
FTP	File Transfer Protocol
Gopher	Precursor to the Web
WAIS	Wide Area Information System
File	Local file
NNTP	Network News Transfer Protocol
SMTP	Simple Mail Transfer Protocol
TELNET	Interactive terminal session

The first two are the most common.

The protocol is separated from the server by "://". The server address may be three words separated by '.' (pronounced DOT) or four groups of three digits separated by '.'. Examples of each server address are:

```
www.wordware.com
198.95.249.77
```

The number forms the actual IP (Internet Protocol) address. The name form is translated into the numeric form behind the scenes by a DNS (Domain Name Server). The DNS also supplies routing information for the network packets. The server name is broken down as follows:

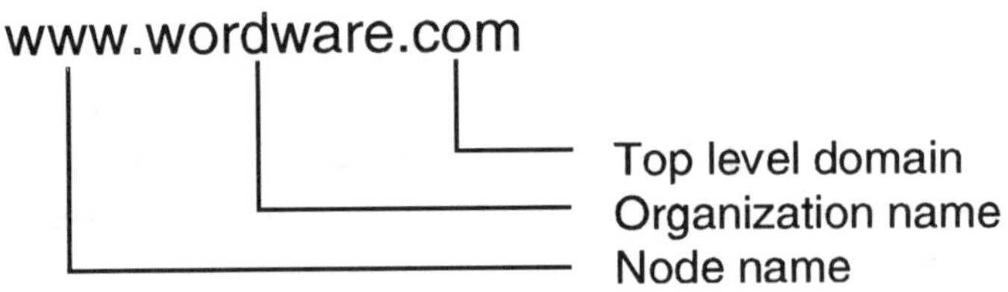

The top level domain name may be one of the following:

.com	Commercial company
.edu	Educational institutions
.gov	U.S. government agencies, nonmilitary
.mil	U.S. Military
.net	Internet service provider
.org	Nonprofit organization

In addition, each country outside the United States has its own top level domain assigned. For example:

.ca	Canada
.uk	United Kingdom
.fr	France

The next portion of the URL, the port number, is optional if the standard port number for that protocol is used. Some standard port numbers are:

80	HTTP
70	Gopher
21	FTP
443	Secure HTTP

When specified, the port number is separated from the server address with a ':'.

The final portion of the URL is the target resource. It is not called "target document" because the resource may be a lot more than just a document. A target resource may be a CGI script to execute for example. The resource is a file path and filename. The separator ':' is optional and generally not used.

The following diagram puts all of the URL pieces together:

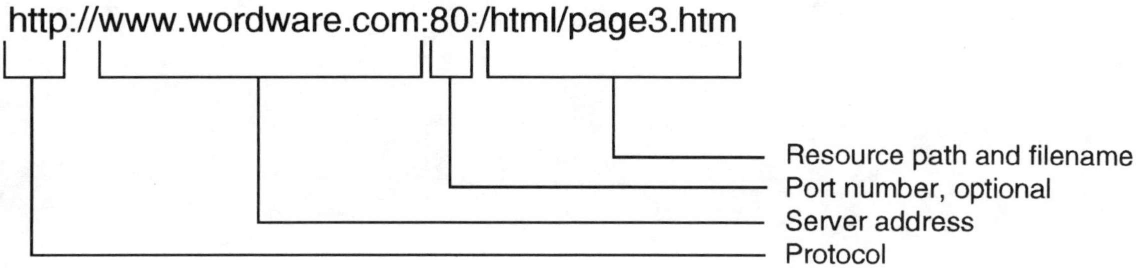

From the Web client-server application point of view, a URL may be either an HTML document, a CGI script, or a Java applet.

Summary

The basic coding of HTML documents can be accomplished using the elements presented in this chapter. The only problem from the point of view of developing Web applications is basic HTML markup provides no means of specifying data entry. Another layer of HTML, forms, is required for that. Forms are covered in the next chapter.

Chapter 9

HTML Forms

Introduction

HTML forms are the basis for Web client-server capabilities. Forms are the client side GUI mechanism while the CGI script is the server side in a Web-based client-server application. The five form elements listed below enable building of HTML data input forms:

Element	*End Tag Required*	*Description*
FORM	Yes	Start a form.
INPUT	Yes	Specify type of form input to accept from the user.
OPTION	Yes	An entry in a <SELECT> list.
SELECT	Yes	A pick list or drop down selection list.
TEXTAREA	Yes	A free form text input box.

Form objects include:

- Text entry boxes
- Radio buttons
- Check boxes
- Pick lists
- Drop down menus
- Multiline, scrollable text areas
- Password boxes

This list should sound familiar if you have used any of the client-server development packages such as Delphi or PowerBuilder.

The general structure of an HTML form is:

```
<FORM>
  <INPUT>
  <SELECT>
    <OPTION>
    ...
  </SELECT>
  <TEXTAREA>
</FORM>
```

The order of elements is not important, but the structure and end elements are! <OPTION> can occur only within <SELECT>.

This simple set of elements creates the application GUI. The secret is in the element attributes. A detailed form example follows the group of tables identifying the attributes for each element.

<FORM>

<FORM> requires an end tag and has several attributes including:

Attribute	*Values*	*Description*
METHOD ◆		*METHOD* describes the method by which the form data is to be accessed by the CGI script. The METHOD specified on the form must match the METHOD used by the CGI script.
	GET	Specifies data be passed from the form to the CGI script via the QUERY_STRING environment variable.
	POST	Specifies the form data be passed to the CGI script using STDIN.
ACTION ◆		Specifies the CGI script to execute when the form is submitted. The CGI script is specified as a URL.
ENCTYPE		Specifies a MIME encoding type. Used for uploading a file to the server.

◆ Required attribute.

A typical form element is:

```
<FORM ACTION="/cgi-bin/perlscript.pl" METHOD="POST">
...
</FORM>
```

<INPUT>

<INPUT> requires an end tag and has several attributes including:

Attribute	Value	Description
TYPE		This attribute specifies the type of input box being defined.
	TEXT	Defines a text box. Also specifies *NAME*, *SIZE*, *MAXLENGTH*, and optionally an initial *VALUE* and *ALIGN*.
	RADIO	Defines a radio button. Also requires *NAME* and *VALUE* with *CHECKED* and *ALIGN* optional.
	PASSWORD	Defines a password box. Requires *NAME*.
	CHECKBOX	Defines a check box. *NAME, ALIGN,* and *VALUE* are required.
	SUBMIT	Specifies the form submit button. The *VALUE* attribute specifies the text for the button.
	RESET	Specifies a button that clears the form back to its default values. The *VALUE* attribute specifies the text for the button.
	HIDDEN	Defines a hidden field. The value is passed to the CGI as if typed into a text box. *NAME* and *VALUE* are required.
	IMAGE	Specifies an image to click on to submit the form instead of the HTML submit button. Specify the image to display via the *SRC* attribute.
ALIGN		This attribute specifies where to align the box currently being defined. The *ALIGN* attribute may be used with any input object.
	TOP	Aligns the object at the top.
	MIDDLE	Aligns the object in the middle.
	BOTTOM	Aligns the object at the bottom.
	LEFT	Left justifies the object within the field.
	RIGHT	Right aligns the object within the field.
	CENTER	Centers the object within the field.
CHECKED		Marks the current input object as selected. *CHECKED* is used with radio buttons and check boxes.

Attribute	Value	Description
MAXLENGTH		Specifies the maximum number of characters an input object may contain. It is typically used with *TEXT*, *PASSWORD*, and *TEXTAREA*.
NAME ◆		Specifies the name of the input object being defined.
SRC		Specifies the URL for the location of the image used by the *IMAGE* attribute in a Submit button definition.
SIZE		The size, in characters, of the input windows for *TEXT* and *TEXTAREA* objects.
VALUE		Specifies the default value for *TEXT* and *TEXTAREA*, the value returned for *RADIO* and *CHECKBOX*, and the text for *SUBMIT* and *RESET*.

◆ Required attribute.

There is much interplay between the <INPUT> attributes. The best way to discuss the interaction is demonstrating the creation of each type of input. The input type is specified by the *TYPE* attribute. The remaining <INPUT> attributes define the characteristics of the GUI object (*TYPE*).

Text Boxes

The TEXT form object has four required attributes in addition to *TYPE*. *NAME* is required to associate a value with for CGI processing. *SIZE* is the number of characters in the text entry box rendered on the screen. The example below shows a text entry box of 32 characters. *MAXLENGTH* is the maximum number of characters allowed in this text box. Text will scroll left and right to accommodate the characters past 32. A default value is specified with the *VALUE* attribute. If no data is entered in the box, the default value will be used.

The following lines contain a typical definition for a text box:

> This is a Text Box. <INPUT TYPE="TEXT" NAME="text1"
> SIZE="32" MAXLENGTH="80" VALUE="Default Value">

Netscape produces the following text box from the above <INPUT> example:

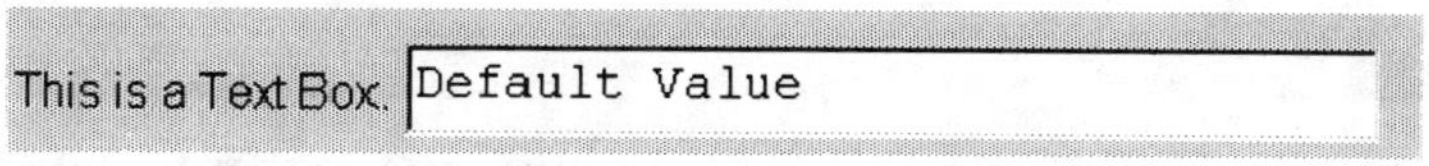

The *NAME* value along with the *VALUE* are passed to the CGI script when the Submit button is clicked, in the form:

NAMEVALUE=VALUE

Thus in the example, the following is sent to the CGI script for this text box:

text1=Default Value

This general format is used to associate form object names with a value, either data input or from a *VALUE* attribute. The term "NAME=VALUE pair" is used to reference this data representation for the remainder of this book.

Radio Buttons

Radio buttons are associated by the value of the *NAME* attribute. Radio buttons with the same *NAME* value are mutually exclusive; only one button in a button group may be selected at any one time. Selecting another radio button in the group deselects the first selection. The following HTML code produces a three button group:

```
This is a 'checked' radio button.
<INPUT TYPE="RADIO" NAME="RAD" VALUE="button1" CHECKED="CHECKED">
Button 2
<INPUT TYPE="RADIO" NAME="RAD" VALUE="button2" ALIGN="TOP">
Button 3
<INPUT TYPE="RADIO" NAME="RAD" VALUE="button3" ALIGN="TOP">
```

This example produces:

The value passed to the CGI script in this case is:

```
RAD=button1
```

Check Boxes

Check boxes are similar to radio buttons, except each box may be checked. Check boxes are not grouped. Each must have a unique name and value. For example, the HTML code for a check box that is checked by default is:

```
This is a 'checked' check box.
<INPUT TYPE="CHECKBOX" NAME="CBOX1" VALUE="cbox1" CHECKED="CHECKED">
```

It produces:

The NAME=VALUE pair is passed to the CGI program when the box is checked. Nothing is passed when the box is not checked.

Password Boxes

A password box is a special text box intended for entry of passwords. Text typed into a password box is echoed as "*". The HTML code for a password box is:

```
This is a password field.
<INPUT TYPE="PASSWORD" NAME="PASS" SIZE="8" MAXLENGTH="32">
```

The display produced is:

The value entered in the password box is returned to the CGI script as a NAME=VALUE pair. *NAME* is the only required attribute. *SIZE*, *MAXLENGTH*, and *ALIGN* are optional. This password example returns:

```
PASS=TESTING
```

when "TESTING" is typed into the password box by the user. The value is not encrypted in any way. Therefore, the password box only keeps prying eyes from seeing the value. Using secure sockets (SSL) to pass forms that transmit password boxes is a good idea.

Submit Button

The submit button kicks form processing off. The contents of the form are sent to the server for processing. The CGI script that runs is specified in the *ACTION* attribute of the <FORM> element. Every form must have at least one submit button. The following HTML generates a submit button:

```
<INPUT TYPE="SUBMIT" VALUE="Submit Button">
```

The following display is generated:

VALUE is the lone required attribute. The contents of *VALUE* are displayed in the button. *ALIGN* and *NAME* are optional.

HINT: Every form must have at least one Submit Button. A form may have multiple Submit Buttons. The same CGI script is run regardless of which button is clicked. Each button returns a NAME=VALUE pair that the CGI script must examine to determine which Submit Button was clicked.

Reset Button

The reset button clears the fields of the form and sets any defaults specified by the various *VALUE* attributes. An example reset button HTML code is:

```
This is a Reset button.
<INPUT TYPE="RESET">
```

This example generates the following browser display.

No attributes are required. Several are optional:

NAME	Allowed but not used
VALUE	The text on the button if specified
ALIGN	Specifies alignment of button with surrounding text

If *VALUE* is not specified, "Reset" is used as the default button text.

Hidden Fields

Hidden fields are a critical part of the overall HTML form capability. Hidden fields are used to carry information from one CGI script to the next CGI script. The following HTML code illustrates a hidden field:

```
A hidden field is here.
<INPUT TYPE="HIDDEN" NAME="HIDDEN1" VALUE="hidden">
```

There is no display created for hidden fields. A hidden field will send a NAME=VALUE pair to the CGI script when the submit button is clicked. The value sent to the CGI script in this case is:

```
HIDDEN1=hidden
```

HINT: There are two choices for passing data or "state" between CGI scripts, hidden fields, and cookies. Hidden fields generally require a little more code but do not leave any residual data on users' systems the way cookies often do.

HINT: JavaScript can read the values specified in hidden fields. Hidden fields are a convenient way to pass parameters to JavaScript code on a browser page, which in turn has potential code savings in the CGI script.

Pick Lists

Pick lists are useful when one or more of a set list of values is valid. Pick lists are displayed as a scrollable box of values. Clicking a particular list item selects that item for the NAME=VALUE pair. The HTML for a simple three item pick list is:

```
This is a pick list.
<SELECT NAME="pick1" size=3>
<OPTION SELECTED VALUE="pick1">Pick item 1</OPTION>
<OPTION VALUE="pick2">Pick item 2</OPTION>
<OPTION VALUE="pick3">Pick item 3</OPTION>
</SELECT>
```


The following display is generated:

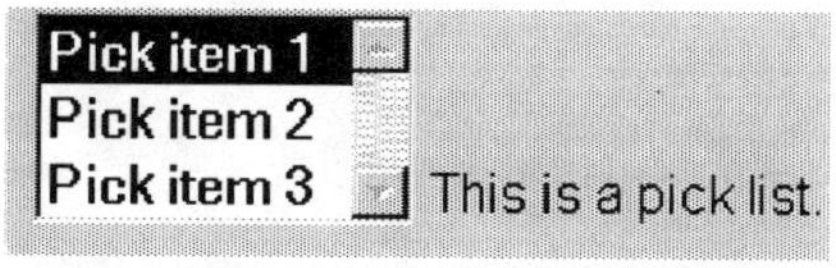

The end tag for <SELECT> is required. <SELECT> uses two attributes, *NAME* and *SIZE*. *NAME* is the name portion of the NAME=VALUE pair and *SIZE* is the number of lines to display in the list. The value of *SIZE* must be at least two.

Each of the <OPTION> elements specifies the text displayed for the item as well as the *VALUE* returned when the item is selected, and whether the default state is *SELECTED*.

Pull Down Lists

Pull down lists are a special case of a pick list. The same <SELECT><OPTION>...</SELECT> structure is used. The only difference is the *SIZE* attribute is either "1" or left off of the <SELECT> tag. The following is the HTML code for a pull down list:

```
A pull down list.
<SELECT NAME="pick2">
<OPTION VALUE="pull1">Pull down 1</OPTION>
<OPTION VALUE="pull2">Pull down 2</OPTION>
<OPTION VALUE="pull3">Pull down 3</OPTION>
</SELECT>
```

This example produces the following browser display:

There is no default selection specified in this example, although one is allowed by specifying the *SELECTED* attribute on one of the <OPTION> elements.

<SELECT>

Pick lists and pull down lists are comprised of two elements, <SELECT> and <OPTION>. The structure is:

```
<SELECT>
 <OPTION>
 <OPTION>
 ...
</SELECT>
```

<SELECT> marks the beginning of either a pull down list or a pick list. The attribute usage for <SELECT> is summarized in the following table:

Attribute	Value	Description
MULTIPLE		Specifies the *MULTIPLE* attribute to allow multiple list items to be selected. No value is necessary.
NAME ◆		The name value for the list.
SIZE		Leaving the SIZE attribute off or specifying a value of "1" creates a pull down list. Values of "2" or greater generates a pick list.

◆ Required attribute.

<OPTION>

The <OPTION> element can occur only within the <SELECT> element and specifies each item in the list. The attributes of <OPTION> are listed in the next table:

Attribute	Value	Description
SELECTED		Specifying *SELECTED* on an <OPTION> element causes that item to be selected by default.
VALUE		The value portion of the NAME=VALUE pair returns to the CGI script when this item is selected.

<TEXTAREA>

A textarea box is a text box with more than one line text which automatically includes scroll bars. The following HTML produces a textarea box three lines high and 32 columns wide:

```
<TEXTAREA NAME="text1" ROWS="3" COLS="32"></TEXTAREA>
This is a text box.
```

Netscape Navigator renders this example as:

The text typed in the textarea box is returned in a NAME=VALUE pair to the CGI script. The following table identifies the attributes used with <TEXTAREA>:

Attribute	*Value*	*Description*
COLS		The number of columns to display
NAME		The name for this object
ROWS		The number of line or rows to display
LANG		The language
ALIGN		Alignment
VALUE		Specifies an initial value
WRAP		Specifies how the text will be wrapped within the text box.
	VIRTUAL	Wrapping takes place on screen but not in the text transmitted to the CGI script
	PHYSICAL	Line wrapping is preserved in the transmitted text just as it is on the screen.
	OFF	The default, no automatic wrapping

Textarea boxes can be used to simulate a simple text editor.

A Complete Form

Now that we have covered each of the HTML GUI data entry objects that can be defined in a form, this section shows a simple form with one example of each form object.

The following HTML document contains an example form that has one of "everything":

```
<!DOCTYPE HTML PUBLIC "-//IETF//DTD HTML 3.0//EN//" [] >
<HTML>
<HEAD>
<TITLE>Sample Form 1</TITLE>
</HEAD>
<BODY>
<BODYTEXT>
<P>
This is a sample HTML Form with one of everything...
</P>
<FORM ACTION="/cgi-bin/test.pl" METHOD="POST">
This is a Text Box.
<INPUT TYPE="TEXT" NAME="MYTEXT" VALUE="Default Value"
SIZE="32" MAXLENGTH="80" ALIGN="TOP">
<BR>
This is a 'checked' check box.
<INPUT TYPE="CHECKBOX" NAME="CBOX1" VALUE="cbox1" CHECKED="CHECKED"
ALIGN="TOP">
<BR>
This is a File upload box
<INPUT TYPE="FILE" NAME="FILE1">
<BR>
A hidden field is here.
<INPUT TYPE="HIDDEN" NAME="HIDDEN1" VALUE="hidden">
<BR>
This is a password field.
<INPUT TYPE="PASSWORD" NAME="PASS" SIZE="8" MAXLENGTH="32">
<BR>
This is a 'checked' radio button.
<INPUT TYPE="RADIO" NAME="RAD" VALUE="button1" CHECKED="CHECKED">
Button 2<INPUT TYPE="RADIO" NAME="RAD" VALUE="button2">
Button 3<INPUT TYPE="RADIO" NAME="RAD" VALUE="button3">
<BR>
This is a Reset button.
<INPUT TYPE="RESET" ALIGN="TOP">
<BR>
This is the Submit button that kicks it all off.
<INPUT TYPE="SUBMIT" VALUE="Submit Button" ALIGN="TOP">
<BR>
<TEXTAREA LANG="en.us" NAME="text1" ROWS="3" COLS="32"> </TEXTAREA>
This is a text box.
<BR>
<SELECT NAME="pick1" size=3>
```

9

```
<OPTION SELECTED="SELECTED" VALUE="pick1">Pick item 1</OPTION>
<OPTION VALUE="pick2">Pick item 2</OPTION>
<OPTION VALUE="pick3">Pick item 3</OPTION>
</SELECT>
This is a pick list.
<SELECT NAME="pick2">
<OPTION VALUE="pull1">Pull down 1</OPTION>
<OPTION VALUE="pull2">Pull down 2</OPTION>
<OPTION VALUE="pull3">Pull down 3</OPTION>
</SELECT>
A pull down list.
<BR>
</FORM>
</BODY>
</HTML>
```

This HTML file generates the following display in Netscape Navigator:

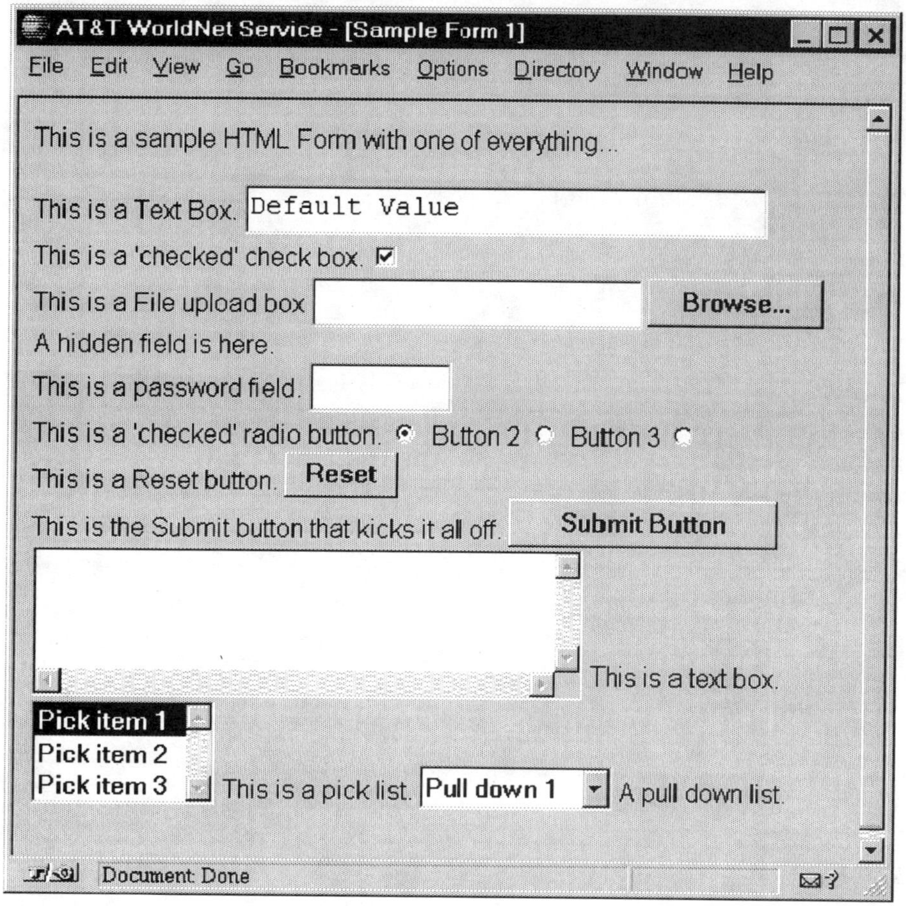

9

Summary

HTML forms are the basis for Web-based client-server applications. They provide the basic user interface elements for building data entry applications. Without forms, the Web would be limited to content delivery.

Chapter 10

HTML Tables, Frames, and Scripting

Introduction

This chapter covers several advanced areas that are an important part of Web-based application capabilities. These areas include:

- Tables
- Frames
- Scripting language support

Each of these areas is covered individually in this chapter.

Tables

HTML tables first appeared in HTML 3.0. HTML tables are relatively simple compared to some table strategies developed in other SGML DTDs. Even so, they define enough functionality to be very useful for both presentation and in defining data entry forms. The basic table structure is:

```
<TABLE>
  <CAPTION>
  <TR>
    <TH>
    <TD>
```

```
  </TR>
  ...
</TABLE>
```

The elements that make up HTML tables are summarized in the following table:

Element	*End Tag Required*	*Description*
CAPTION	Yes	The text for the table caption
TABLE	Yes	Define a table
TD	No	"Table Data," a cell in other words
TH	No	"Table Header," text is bolded
TR	No	"Table Row," a collection of <TH> and/or <TD> elements

Tables do not lend themselves to detailed discussions of individual elements as HTML forms did. Therefore, the approach for describing tables is identifying the attributes for each element, then a couple of example tables.

<CAPTION>

The <CAPTION> element is optional but if used must be the first element within the <TABLE>. The only attribute used is *ALIGN* with a value of either "TOP" or "BOTTOM."

<TABLE>

The <TABLE> element wraps a table definition. A table starts with the opening <TABLE> tag and continues until a matching </TABLE> tag is encountered. The attributes associated with a table are summarized below:

Attribute	*Value*	*Description*
ALIGN	LEFT| RIGHT| CENTER	Specifies alignment of entire table
WIDTH	# pixels or %	Width of screen in either pixels or %

Attribute	Value	Description
BORDER	# pixels	The number of pixels for the border width
CELLSPACING	# pixels	Specifies amount of spacing between cells in pixels
CELLPADDING	# pixels	Specifies the amount of cell padding in pixels

Not specifying *BORDER* generates a borderless table. *CELLSPACING* and *CELLPADDING* are rarely specified in hand crafted tables but are often used by packages such as Microsoft FrontPage in an effort to duplicate WYSIWYG document format. None of the <TABLE> attributes are required.

<TR>

A table row is the basic unit of the table. Its attributes are:

Attribute	Value	Description
ALIGN		Specifies horizontal alignment
	LEFT	Left justifies the table
	CENTER	Centers the table
	RIGHT	Right justifies the table
VALIGN		Specifies vertical alignment
	TOP	Top justifies
	BOTTOM	Bottom justifies

A table row may contain one or more <TH> and <TD> elements. <TH> and <TD> may be in any order.

<TH> and <TD>

The attributes for both types of table cells are identical. Their attributes are summarized in the following table:

Attribute	Value	Description
ALIGN		Specifies cell alignment within the column
	LEFT	Left justifies the text of this cell

Attribute	Value	Description
	CENTER	Centers the text of this cell
	RIGHT	Right justifies the text in this cell
WIDTH	# pixels or %	Sets the width of the cell in pixels or %
BORDER	# pixels	Specifies the number of pixels for the table border
CELLSPACING	# pixels	Specifies the number of pixels between cell columns
CELLPADDING	# pixels	Specifies the number of pixels to add at the end of the cell
COLSPAN		Specifies the number of columns that this cell should span

Leave out the *BORDER* attribute for a table with no borders. The display algorithm in the browser determines the column width, usually based on the size of the longest entry in the column and the number of columns in the table to figure out the width of each column unless *WIDTH* is specified.

Now for a quick example. The tables in this chapter can easily be duplicated as HTML tables. The following HTML segment contains the *ALIGN* and *WIDTH* attribute entries from the previous table:

```
<HTML>
<HEAD>
<TITLE>Table Cell Attribute Table</TITLE>
</HEAD>
<BODY>
<TABLE WIDTH="100%" BORDER>
<TR>
  <TH ALIGN="CENTER">ATTRIBUTE</TH>
  <TH ALIGN="CENTER">VALUE</TH>
  <TH ALIGN="CENTER">DESCRIPTION</TH>
</TR>
<TR>
  <TH>ALIGN</TH>
  <TD></TD>
  <TD>Specifies cell alignment within the column</TD>
</TR>
<TR>
  <TH></TH>
```

```
  <TD>LEFT</TD>
  <TD>Left justify the text of this cell</TD>
</TR>
<TR>
  <TH></TH>
  <TD>CENTER</TD>
  <TD>Center the text of this cell</TD>
</TR>
<TR>
  <TH></TH>
  <TD>RIGHT</TD>
  <TD>Right justify the text in this cell</TD>
</TR>
<TR>
  <TH>WIDTH</TH>
  <TD></TD>
  <TD>Set the width of the cell in pixels or %</TD>
</TR>
</TABLE>
</BODY>
</HTML>
```


The indentation of <TH> and <TD> elements is not necessary. I do it for readability. The HTML display created by Netscape Navigator is not quite as nice as the one typeset above, but is still passable. The table display is:

ATTRIBUTE	VALUE	DESCRIPTION
ALIGN		Specifies cell alignment within the column
	LEFT	Left justify the text of this cell
	CENTER	Center the text of this cell
	RIGHT	Right justify the text in this cell
WIDTH		Set the width of the cell in pixels cr %

This table is relatively simple. The following table example illustrates both spanning columns and nested tables:

```
<!DOCTYPE HTML PUBLIC "--//IETF//DTD HTML 3.0//EN//" [] >
<HTML>
```

```
<HEAD>
<TITLE>Table Example 2</TITLE>
</HEAD>
<BODY>
<P>This page contains a table within a table...</P>
<TABLE BORDER="BORDER">
<CAPTION>This table has a caption</CAPTION>
<TR>
  <TH>Column 1</TH>
  <TH>Column 2</TH>
  <TH>Column 3</TH>
</TR>
<TR>
  <TD COLSPAN="2">row2,col1, It spans col 2</TD>
  <TD>row2,col3</TD>
</TR>
<TR>
  <TD>row3,col1</TD>
  <TD>row3,col2</TD>
  <TD>row3,col3</TD>
</TR>
<TR>
  <TD><TABLE BORDER="BORDER">
    <TR>
      <TH>Table within a table</TH>
      <TD>tab2,row1,col2</TD>
    </TR>
    <TR>
      <TD>tab2,row2,col1</TD>
      <TD>tab2,row2,col2</TD>
    </TR>
    </TABLE>
  </TD>
<TD>tab1,row4,col2</TD>
<TD>tab1,row4,col3</TD>
</TR>
</TABLE>
</BODY>
</HTML>
```

The following display is produced by the previous HTML:

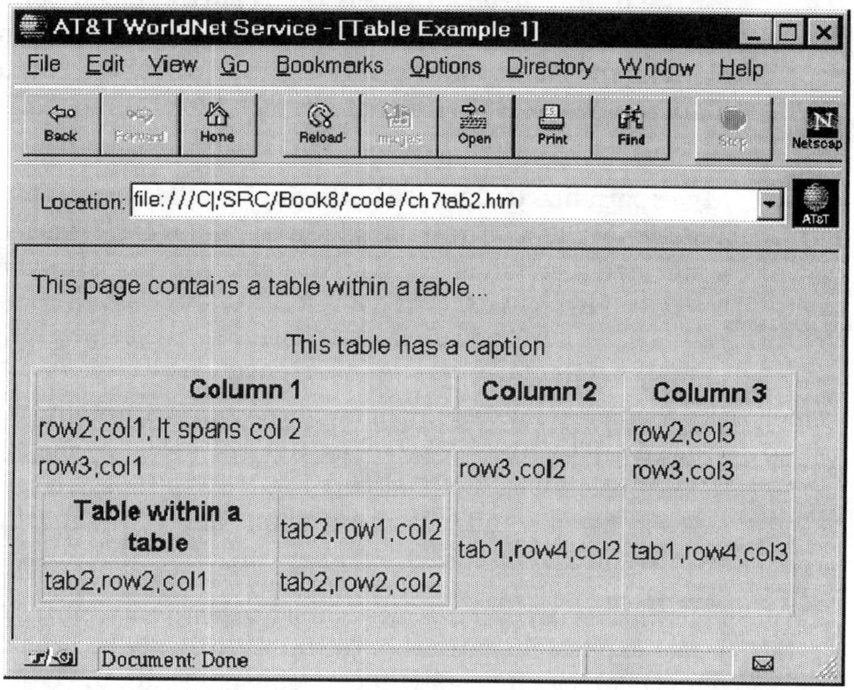

This table illustrates the flexibility of HTML tables. HTML tables are relatively simple once you see how they work. I remember thinking tables were not such a big deal when they first came out. Now, I wonder how the Web world ever got along without them.

ASIDE NOTE:

Bear with me for one final thought on tables. The HTML table code in the example is straightforward and easy to follow. As an exercise, duplicate the above HTML table in any software package you have that generates HTML output, such as FrontPage, WordPerfect 7, Word, or Ventura Publisher 7. Save/export/publish the table to HTML and see the difference. The trend for HTML output from sophisticated WYSIWYG packages is to create an HTML page that looks exactly as the printed page.

This is no trivial task for the software developer and very convenient for the user. The down side is the HTML typically produced is complicated. For example, table columns are often generated with % column widths down to single digits to duplicate column spacing. This generated HTML is not intended for human consumption, and sometimes I wonder if it is meant for browser consumption either.

My experience to date is that today's HTML publishing tools are functional but not quite ready to be taken for granted. A colleague generated a group of HTML data entry forms using one of the current (early 1997) WYSIWYG HTML "publishing tools" to generate the HTML. It took him two full days to generate the HTML forms. I felt like it was an afternoon's work by hand. Then the forms would display in one browser but not another. When viewed on a Unix workstation, the last column was not quite right. The solution was hand editing the HTML files produced by the publishing tool and taking out about half of the markup. The forms worked on all the target browsers just fine after simplifying the HTML.

I also expect this situation to change quickly as products mature. The HTML generated will probably continue to be excessive and unreadable, but interoperability among browsers will improve.

HINT: Tables may nest at almost any point. A table cell may contain most "text" elements.

Forms and Tables

HTML forms are powerful and HTML tables are great for formatting. When combined, they add a lot to the GUI presentation of data entry forms. Let's look at a simple example data entry form. The problem statement is:

> Develop an HTML form for entering a user's address and phone number. The fields are Name, Company, Street Address, City, State, Zip Code, and Phone. The form data is sent to a Perl script named address.pl.

The following HTML code implements this data entry screen using just HTML form capabilities.

```
<!DOCTYPE HTML PUBLIC "-//IETF//DTD HTML 3.0//EN//" [] >
<HTML>
<HEAD>
<TITLE>Data Entry Form Without Tables</TITLE>
</HEAD>
<BODY>
<H1 ALIGN="CENTER">USER INFO ENTRY</H1>
<P>
This data entry form uses HTML Forms without tables. It is functional
but not pleasing with the text boxes snaking down the screen.
</P>
<FORM ACTION="sample1.pl">
User Name<INPUT TYPE="TEXT" NAME="UNAME" VALUE="Enter Name Here"
SIZE="32" MAXLENGTH="80"><BR>
Address<INPUT TYPE="TEXT" NAME="ADDR" VALUE="Enter Address Here"
SIZE="45" MAXLENGTH="80"><BR>
<INPUT TYPE="TEXT" NAME="ADDR2" SIZE="45" MAXLENGTH="80"
ALIGN="TOP"><BR>
City<INPUT TYPE="TEXT" NAME="CITY" VALUE="Enter City Here" SIZE="40"
MAXLENGTH="80"><BR>
State<INPUT TYPE="TEXT" NAME="STATE" SIZE="2" MAXLENGTH="80">
Zip<INPUT TYPE="TEXT" NAME="ZIP" SIZE="9" MAXLENGTH="12"><BR>
Phone<INPUT TYPE="TEXT" NAME="PHONE" VALUE="555-555-5555" SIZE="12"
MAXLENGTH="12">
</FORM>
</BODY>
</HTML>
```

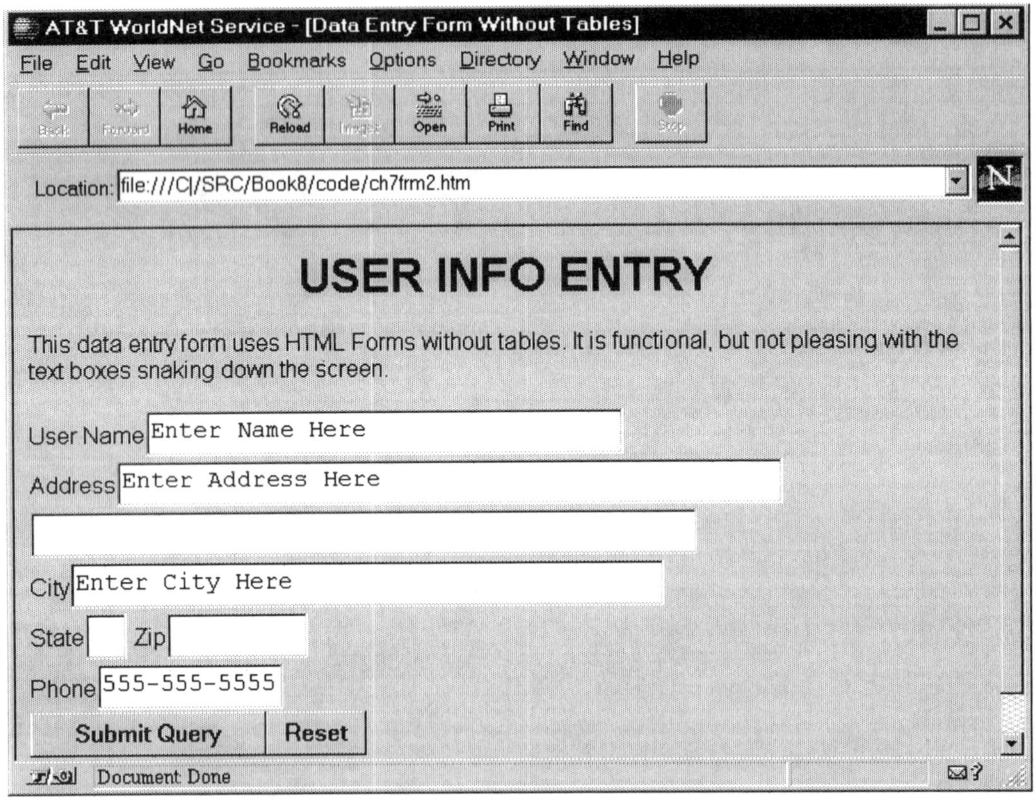

This screen is functional but ugly. Now here is the same data entry screen combining forms and tables:

```
<!DOCTYPE HTML PUBLIC "-//IETF//DTD HTML 3.0//EN//" [] >
<HTML>
<HEAD>
<TITLE>Data Entry Form With Tables</TITLE>
</HEAD>
<BODY>
<H1 ALIGN="CENTER">USER INFO ENTRY</H1>
<P>
This data entry form uses HTML Forms with tables. It is functional,
pleasing, and professional looking.
</P>
```

```
<FORM ACTION="sample1.pl">
<TABLE BORDER WIDTH="550">
<TR>
  <TH>User Name</TH>
  <TD><INPUT TYPE="TEXT" NAME="UNAME" VALUE="Enter Name
       Here" SIZE="32" MAXLENGTH="80">
</TR>
<TR>
  <TH>Address</TH>
  <TD><INPUT TYPE="TEXT" NAME="ADDR" VALUE="Enter Address
       Here" SIZE="45" MAXLENGTH="80">
</TR>
<TR>
  <TH>
  <TH ALIGN="LEFT"><INPUT TYPE="TEXT" NAME="ADDR2" SIZE="45"
       MAXLENGTH="80">
</TR>
<TR>
  <TD COLSPAN=2>
    <TABLE>
    <TR WIDTH="500">
      <TH WIDTH="30">City</TH>
      <TD WIDTH="330"><INPUT TYPE="TEXT" NAME="CITY"
       VALUE="Enter City Here" SIZE="40" MAXLENGTH="80">
      <TH WIDTH="50">State</TH>
      <TD WIDTH="70"><INPUT TYPE="TEXT" NAME="STATE"
       SIZE="2" MAXLENGTH="80">
    </TR>
  </TABLE>
</TR>
<TR>
  <TD COLSPAN=2>
    <TABLE>
      <TR width=500>
        <TH WIDTH="30">Zip</TH>
        <TD WIDTH="330"><INPUT TYPE="TEXT" NAME="ZIP"
         SIZE="9" MAXLENGTH="12">
        <TH WIDTH="50">Phone</TH>
        <TD WIDTH="70"><INPUT TYPE="TEXT" NAME="PHONE"
         VALUE="555-555-5555" SIZE="12" MAXLENGTH="12">
      </TR>
    </TABLE>
</TR>
```

10

```
<TR>
  <TD COLSPAN=2 ALIGN="CENTER">
    <INPUT TYPE="SUBMIT" VALUE="Submit">
    <INPUT TYPE="RESET">
  </TD>
</TR>
</TABLE>
</FORM>
</BODY>
</HTML>
```

HINT: There are a couple of tricks in this example file. There are nested tables in order to get four columns on part of the form and two on other parts. Specifying pixel widths of the various parts is done to make columns match up. Browsers don't all handle the "tricks" equally. Use such tricks only when they work on the browser used by your user community. Otherwise, there will be a lot of unhappy users.

The example file not only nests tables but also specifies table and column widths in order to make fields line up properly. The current browsers do not handle this "manual intervention" identically. The number of pixels was determined by trial and error. You can usually get pretty close by remembering that typical PC monitors are 72DPI (dots per inch) and try to keep screen widths the size that your user community uses.

Let's look at the two rows, the City/State row and the Zip Code/Phone Number row, that contain odd-sized columns:

```
<TR>
  <TD COLSPAN=2>
    <TABLE>
    <TR WIDTH="500">
      <TH WIDTH="30">City</TH>
      <TD WIDTH="330"><INPUT TYPE="TEXT" NAME="CITY"
       VALUE="Enter City Here" SIZE="40" MAXLENGTH="80">
      <TH WIDTH="50">State</TH>
```

```
        <TD WIDTH="70"><INPUT TYPE="TEXT" NAME="STATE"
         SIZE="2" MAXLENGTH="80">
      </TR>
    </TABLE>
</TR>
<TR>
  <TD COLSPAN=2>
    <TABLE>
      <TR width=500>
        <TH WIDTH="30">Zip</TH>
        <TD WIDTH="330"><INPUT TYPE="TEXT" NAME="ZIP"
         SIZE="9" MAXLENGTH="12">
        <TH WIDTH="50">Phone</TH>
        <TD WIDTH="70"><INPUT TYPE="TEXT" NAME="PHONE"
         VALUE="555-555-5555" SIZE="12" MAXLENGTH="12">
      </TR>
    </TABLE>
</TR>
```

There are logically four columns:

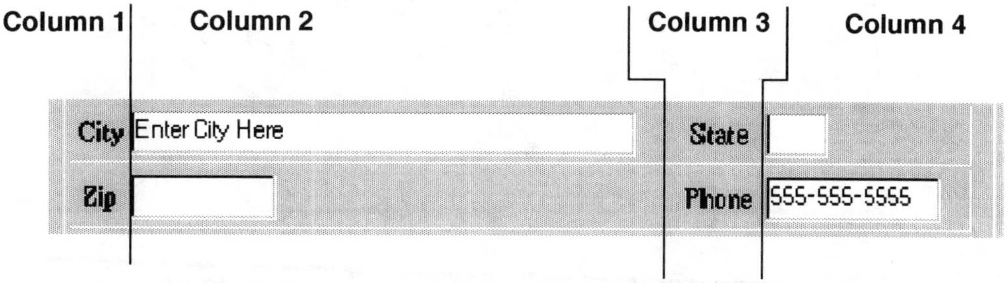

The rest of the form is two columns. The key is making sure that you use the same column widths for all the columns even though multiple tables might be defined, as they are here. The first column is 30 pixels wide, the second is 330 pixels, the third is 50 pixels, and the fourth 70 pixels wide.

Filling in the text boxes with instructions is helpful in some cases and annoying in others. Let common sense guide these decisions.

The following is the data entry form with tables displayed in Microsoft Internet Explorer 3.0:

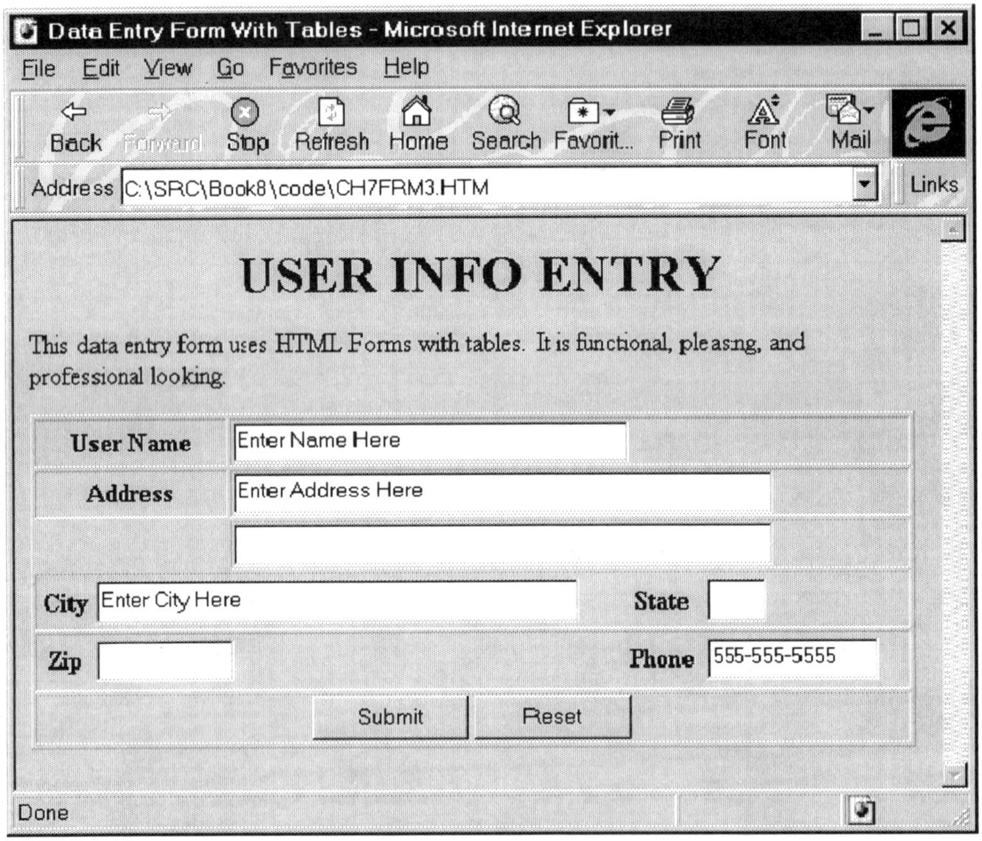

The same HTML file displayed in Netscape Navigator 2.01:

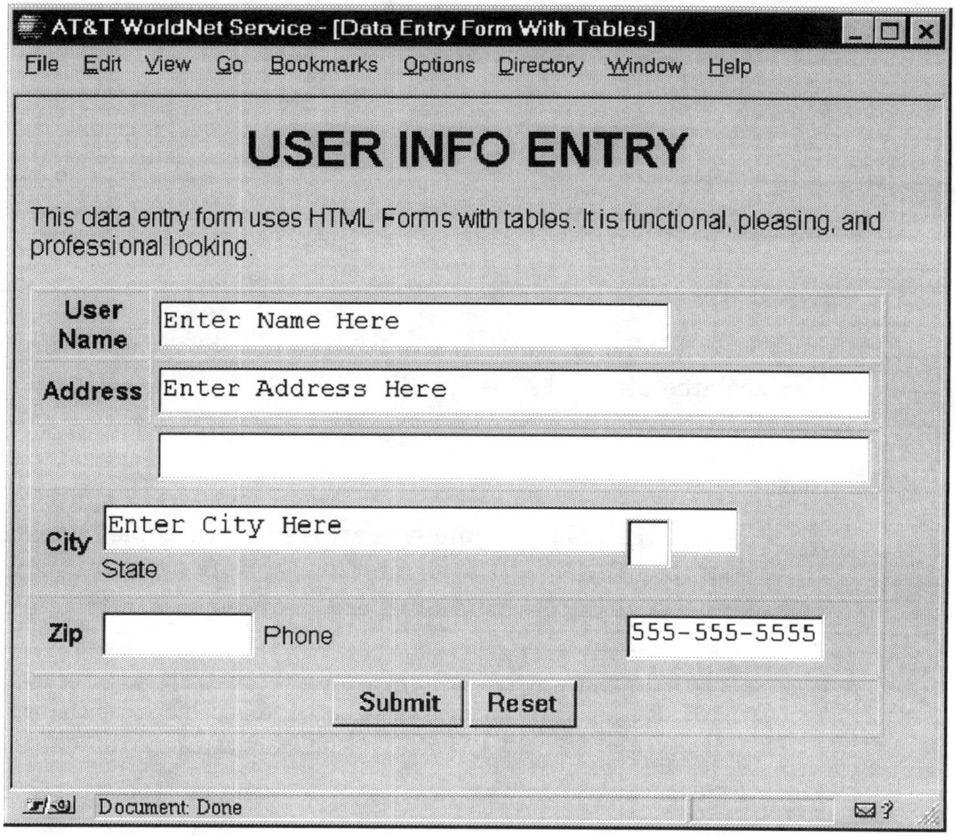

Both screens are included to reinforce testing of all HTML pages in every browser the user community may use.

The combination of HTML forms and tables used together generate pleasing data entry screens.

Scripting Languages

HTML supports the various Web scripting languages with the elements discussed in this section. The following table lists the scripting related tags:

Element	End Tag Required	Description
APPLET	Yes	Specifies a Java applet to execute.
EMBED	No	Specifies a browser plug-in.
PARAM	No	Specifies a parameter value for a Java applet.
SCRIPT	Yes	Marks a section of scripting language code. Several languages may be supported depending on the browser.

The following sections identify the attributes used for the scripting related elements.

<APPLET>

The <APPLET> element specifies a Java applet to execute. Use separate <APPLET> elements to specify each Java applet in a page. The <APPLET> attributes are summarized in the following table:

Attribute	Value	Description
CODE ◆	URL	The applet class filename
CODEBASE	URL	The base directory for the Java code files
HEIGHT ◆	# pixels	The height of the Java window in pixels
NAME		The name of the applet
SRC	URL	The directory containing the applet
WIDTH ◆	# pixels	Width of the Java window in pixels
ALTCODE	Text	Text to display if Java is not used
BASE	URL	The Java base directory

◆ Required

Most commercial Java compilers, such as Microsoft J++ and Symantec Visual Cafe, generate a skeleton HTML file for testing applets that can be used as an example for specifying the applet in the final HTML file.

<PARAM>

The <PARAM> element specifies parameters to pass to Java applets. A <PARAM> element only contains two attributes, both of which are required. The attributes are:

Attribute	Value	Description
NAME ◆		Name of the parameter
VALUE ◆		Parameter value

◆ Required

The following HTML code specifies an applet named Applet1 with a parameter named STRING:

```
<HTML>
<HEAD><TITLE>JAVA Applet Example</TITLE></HEAD>
<BODY>
<FORM>
<APPLET CODE="Applet1.class" WIDTH=430 HEIGHT=270>
<PARAM NAME="STRING" VALUE="Just Testing">
</APPLET>
</FORM>
</BODY>
</HTML>
```


Notice that the parameters are placed before the end applet tag, </APPLET>. This approach allows parameters to be explicitly associated with a particular applet without having to include the applet name attribute in every parameter element.

<EMBED>

The <EMBED> element specifies a browser plug-in such as Adobe Acrobat or Macromedia Shockwave. The attributes are:

Attribute	Value	Description
SRC	URL	Address of the plug-in
WIDTH	#pixels	Width of plug-in window
HEIGHT	#pixels	Height of plug-in window
AUTOSTART	TRUE| FALSE	Automatically starts plug-in on startup
CONTROLS	CONSOLE| SMALLCONSOLE	Specifies the size of the control console for multimedia plug-ins
LOOP	TRUE|FALSE	Specifies whether or not to automatically restart the plug-in at the end of normal execution

<SCRIPT>

The <SCRIPT> element marks a section of code and identifies the scripting language in an HTML document. The attributes used by <SCRIPT> are:

Attribute	Value	Description
LANGUAGE		Specifies the scripting language
	JAVASCRIPT	JavaScript code
	VBScript	VBScript code
	JScript	Jscript
SRC	A URL	The location of the HTML document containing the script code, if specified.

HINT: Enclose the script within HTML comments to hide script code from browsers that do not support scripting languages. HTML comments start with <!-- and end with -->.

The following HTML file includes JavaScript code to perform simple validation on a data entry form:

```
<SCRIPT LANGUAGE="JAVASCRIPT">
function validate(){
        if(document.logon.USER.value == ""){
          alert("Username blank!");
          return false;
        }
        if(document.logon.PASS.value == ""){
          alert("Password blank!");
          return false;
        }
        return true;
}
</SCRIPT>
```

The code basically makes sure that the Username and Password fields contain some text.

Frames

HTML frames implement a technique for dividing the browser display into separately addressable windows with a different document in each. Frames are an important addition to HTML from a user interface perspective. The browser screen can easily be divided into navigation and content areas that allow the user to move around the system without constantly having to back up and reload pages.

Consider a document divided into multiple HTML files. There is a Table of Contents file and one file for each chapter in the document. See the following figure:

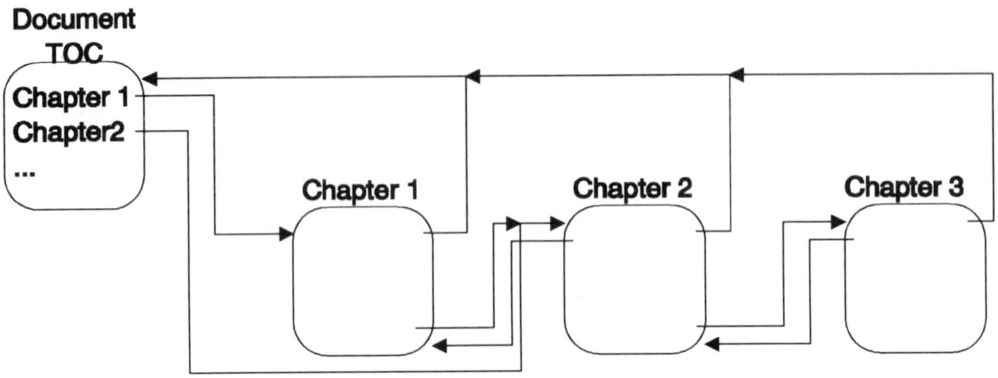

The user enters the document through the Table of Contents, which usually contains the equivalent of a title page and other "front matter" content for the document. The user clicks the hyperlink for Chapter 1. Assume another link at the end of the Chapter 1 file for the HTML file containing Chapter 2. Document access is linear for the most part outside the Table of Contents.

Now, assume the user is in the middle of Chapter 1 and decides the desired information is really in Chapter 3 instead. The user has a couple of navigation choices at this point. The first is following the document chapter chain sequentially to Chapter 3. More than likely, the user will scroll to the nearest Table of Contents link and jump back to the Table of Contents file, then to Chapter 3. Good HTML coding dictates a Table of Contents link at every section heading.

This document structure is convenient to build in an automated process with a "compliant" HTML document and rates "OK" from a user interface point of view. Up until frames were added to HTML 3, this was about the best document structure you could come up with.

Now, let's examine the same document navigation scenario using frames. We'll use two frames, a small one on the left for the Table of Contents and the current chapter in the main window on the right. This is depicted in the following illustration:

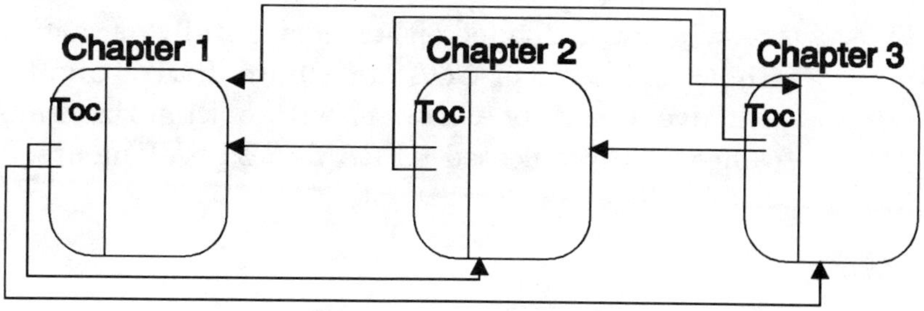

Assume the same scenario from the first example. The user decides in the middle of Chapter 1 the information is really in Chapter 3. Chapter 3 is accessed directly by clicking on the Chapter 3 link in the Table of Contents frame. All in all, the frame-based document is a much better user interface than the traditional HTML treatment of linking back to a Table of Contents file.

The following table identifies the frame related HTML elements:

Element	*End Tag Required*	*Description*
FRAME	No	Specifies the characteristics of a single frame within a frame set.
FRAMESET	Yes	Specifies a set of frames within the current window. Frame sets may nest.
NOFRAME	Yes	Specifies the text to display when the browser does not support frames.

The following sections identify the attributes used with the frame elements.

<FRAMESET>

A <FRAMESET> element divides the current browser window into multiple frames.

Attribute	*Value*	*Description*
COLS ◆	pixels, %, or *	Divide the current browser window into columnar frames.
ROWS ◆	pixels, %, or *	Divide the current browser window into horizontal frames.

◆ Mutually exclusive

The window is divided either horizontally or vertically by specifying either the *ROWS* or *COLS* attribute. *ROWS* and *COLS* are mutually exclusive. Creating a browser with both horizontal and vertical frames requires nested <FRAMESET> elements.

<FRAME>

The <FRAME> element specifies the characteristics of a single frame. You must specify a <FRAME> for each frame created.

Attribute	Value	Description
SRC	URL	URL of frame contents
NAME		Name of the frame
SCROLLING	YES|NO| AUTO	Specifies whether or not scrolling is allowed
NORESIZE		Does not allow resizing of the frame when specified.
MARGINWIDTH	# pixels	Number of pixels for left and right border.
MARGINHEIGHT	# pixels	Number of pixels for top and bottom border.

The following screen dump shows a browser screen with three frames.

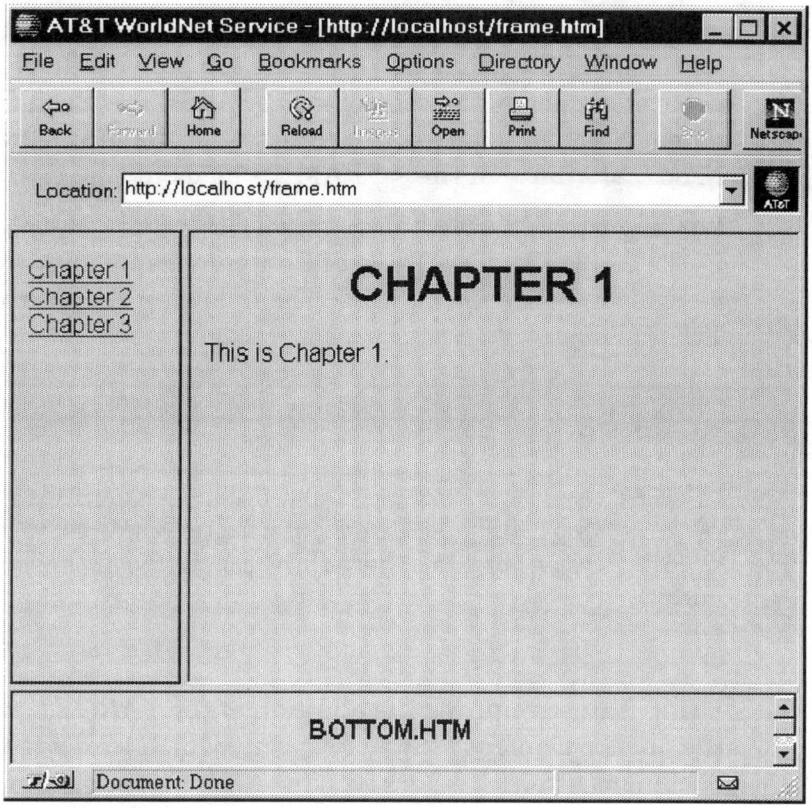

The layout is basically the one described in the frame discussions at the beginning of this section. Generating this display requires a minimum of four HTML files. One for the overall document, which defines the frames and document, and one for each frame panel. FRAME.HTM is the main HTML file:

```
<HTML>
<FRAMESET ROWS="*,55">  <!-- Create bottom and top panels -->
 <FRAMESET COLS="120,*"><!-- Create TOC and Main panels within top -->
  <FRAME SRC="toc.htm" NAME="toc"> <!-- Populate TOC panel -->
  <FRAME SRC="chap1.htm" NAME="main"> <!-- Populate MAIN panel -->
 </FRAMESET>
  <FRAME SRC="bottom.htm" NAME="bottom"> <!-- Populate bottom panel -->
</FRAMESET>
</HTML>
```

The browser is divided into two horizontal panels by the first <FRAMESET> element. Then the top panel is divided into two vertical panels by the second <FRAMESET>. Each frame is given a name, which is required to address a specific frame by specifying the *NAME* attribute in the <FRAME> element.

Loading FRAME.HTM also loads TOC.HTM, CHAP1.HTM, and BOTTOM.HTM. The Table of Contents frame allows direct navigation between chapters. The following HTML code is TOC.HTM:

```
<HTML>
<!--toc.htm-->
<BODY>
<A HREF="chap1.htm" TARGET="main">Chapter 1</A><BR>
<A HREF="chap2.htm" TARGET="main">Chapter 2</A><BR>
<A HREF="chap3.htm" TARGET="main">Chapter 3</A><BR>
</BODY>
</HTML>
```

Using frames requires the addition of the *TARGET* attribute with the anchor element (<A>) to specify which frame to load the linked document into.

HINT: CGI scripts can be specified in both the <FRAME> *SRC* attribute and the <A> *HREF* attribute because both are URLs. Few examples exist of using a CGI script with frames, but it works well. This is a big implication because content can be dynamically generated using CGI scripts instead of static HTML files to populate frames.

Frames are yet another piece of developing Web-based applications that appears complicated at first glance, but are relatively simple once you scratch the surface.

Summary

Advanced HTML is advanced in the sense that much of it is geared toward more advanced online presentation rather than simply specifying text pages. HTML has grown from what was termed "Six tag SGML" at an SGML conference several years ago into a complex markup language with well over a hundred elements. Browsers that support the advanced features described in this chapter can be used to build very effective user interfaces to both full text documents and many other types of online applications.

Chapter 11

Alternative Web Development Approaches

Introduction

There are many alternative approaches available for today's Web developers in addition to simply using HTML forms and Perl CGI scripts. Forms and Perl scripts are still important. However, there are additional choices that supplement your development options. There are even packages that attempt to replace HTML forms and CGI scripting completely. This chapter takes a look at alternative approaches to Web development.

Any field with as much energy expended on it as the Web is bound to have a wide variety of development options. There are so many choices and niches that the options are hard to categorize simply. The categories used for this discussion are:

- Web languages
- Publishing tools
- Database tools
- Other

Web Languages

Perl is the traditional Web language for server side processing. There are good reasons for Perl's popularity even though almost any modern programming language may be used. There are also a few well known languages which have obtained buzzword status such as Java, JavaScript, and VBScript. These are mostly client side languages at present. Both Java and JavaScript can potentially be used for both. There are a few lesser known languages like Netscape's Livewire and Developer 2000 from Oracle that are potentially important as well.

I believe the biggest bang for the buck comes not from attempting to replace HTML forms and CGI scripts completely but from combinations of languages. I can envision Web applications using three or four different languages to get the optimum mix. There are still enough variations among browsers that language choices are somewhat dictated by the browser used by the user community. The server also affects language choices occasionally.

A productive combination today is Perl on the server side and JavaScript on the client. Let's look at a quick example before getting into the individual language discussions. Suppose that an application accesses sensitive information. Most systems, Web-based or not, have a logon screen where the user enters a valid user name and password to gain system access. A typical HTML page for logon is:

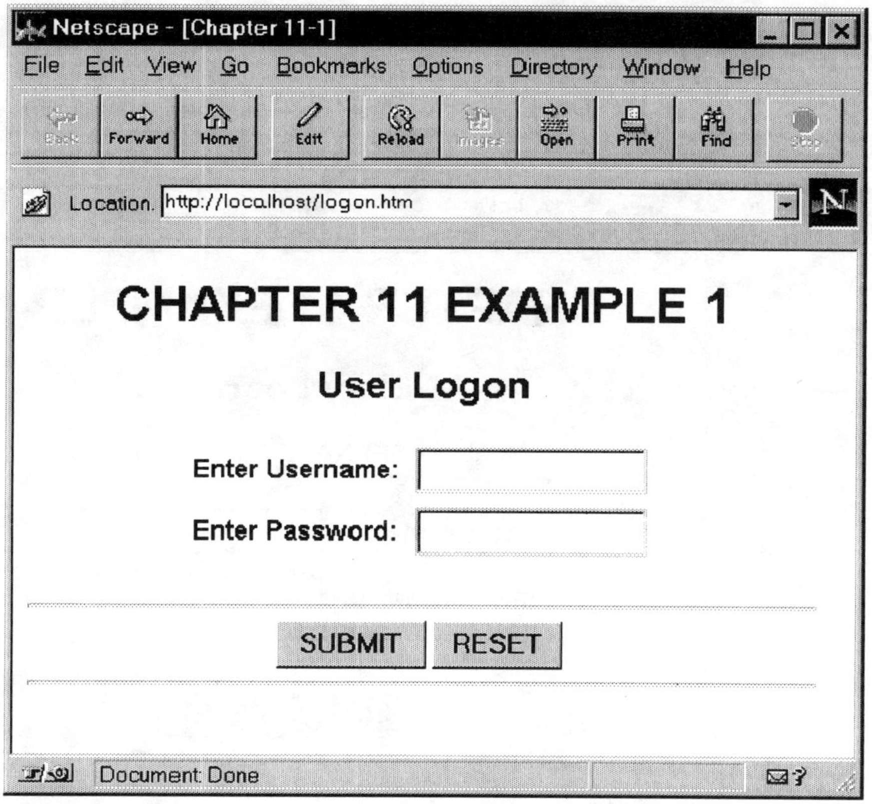

The Perl-only version must perform the following actions:

- Verify that the user name is not blank
- Verify that password is not blank
- Look up user name and password
- If either does not match, repaint the original screen with the appropriate error message
- Paint the next page when no errors are detected

This processing is not overly complex but is messy because there is just no good way to display error messages on the original form. The code complexity increase is much faster than linear as fields are added, especially when valid values may vary as options change. Error text must be inserted on the page. This example will insert the error message on the fly. Here is the logon page after an error:

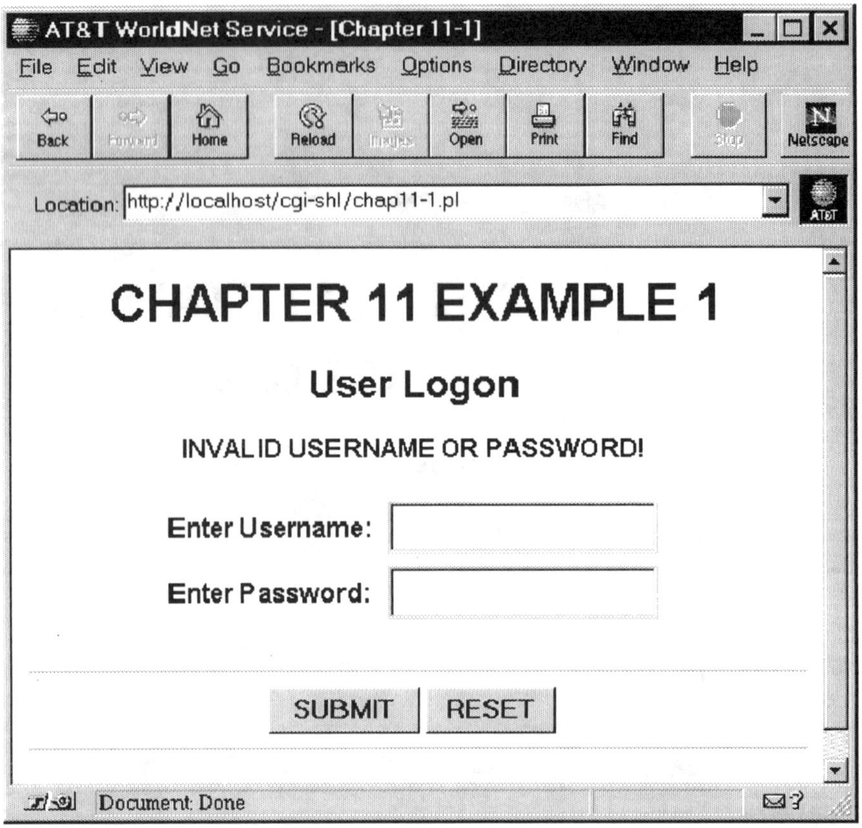

The display is typical of many of today's intranet applications. Here is the HTML code for processing the logon screen using strictly a CGI Perl script:

```
<HTML>
<!--chap11-1.htm-->
<!--02/21/97-->
<HEAD>
<TITLE>Chapter 11-1</TITLE>
</HEAD>
<BODY onLoad="CheckErrorFlag()" BGCOLOR="#FFFFFF">
<CENTER>
<H1 ALIGN="CENTER">CHAPTER 11 EXAMPLE 1</H1>
<H2 ALIGN="CENTER">User Logon</H2>
<!-- error -->
<FORM NAME="logon" ACTION="/cgi-shl/chap11-1.pl" METHOD="POST">
<TABLE>
```

```
<TR>
  <TH>Enter Username:
  <TD><INPUT TYPE="TEXT" SIZE="16" NAME="USER">
</TR>
<TR>
  <TH>Enter Password:
  <TD><INPUT TYPE="PASSWORD" SIZE="16" NAME="PASS">
</TR>
</TABLE>
<BR><HR>
<INPUT TYPE="SUBMIT" VALUE="SUBMIT">
<INPUT TYPE="RESET" VALUE="RESET">
<BR><HR>
</FORM>
</BODY>
</HTML>
```

Notice the comment line (<-- error -->) before the <FORM> tag. It is there for one reason. It provides a convenient place to substitute in an error message. The Perl CGI Script, chap11-1.pl is:

```
#!/usr/local/bin/perl
############################################################
# FILE: CHAP11-1.PL
################### vars.inc################################
$TOOL_DIR     = "c:\\website\\cgi-shl";
$PASS_DIR     = "c:\\website\\cgi-shl";
$HTML_DIR     = "c:\\website\\htdocs";
$TEMPLATE_DIR = "c:\\website\\htdocs\\template";
################## end vars.inc ###########################

       #
       # Global stuff
       #
$error  = "";

&parse_cgi(); # Get data passed in from the HTML form
       #
       # Validate that there is data in the input fields
       #
if($QS{'USER'} eq ""){
       $error = "<B>Username is blank!</B>";
```

```
        &invalid_user();
        exit;
}
if($QS{'PASS'} eq ""){
        $error = "<B>Password is blank!</B>";
        &invalid_user();
        exit;
}
        #
        # Build parameter string to pass to look up
        #
$user_pw = "$QS{'USER'}:$QS{'PASS'}:";
        #
        # Load password file into memory
        #
open(PWD,"$PASS_DIR\\passwd")
              || die "Can't open Password file!\n";
while(<PWD>){
        chop;
        push(@data,$_);
}
close(PWD);
        #
        # search the password for name and password
        #
$success = 0;
foreach $passwd (@data){
        if($passwd =~ /^$user_pw/){
                $success = 1;
                &successful_logon($passwd);
                last;
        }
}
if($success == 0){
        $error = "<B>INVALID USERNAME OR PASSWORD!</B>";
        &invalid_user();      # No data means logon failed.
}
exit;
########################+------------------+
#                       | successful_logon |
#                       +------------------+
sub successful_logon{
        #
```

```
        # Extract fields from the database into @db
        # The @db field order is:
        # username:password:userid:GID:fullname:homedir:shell
        #
        @db   = split(/:/,$_[0]);

        print "Content-type:  text/html\n\n";
        print "<HTML>\n";
        print "<HEAD>\n";
        print "<TITLE>Successful logon</TITLE>\n";
        print "</HEAD>\n";
        print "<BODY BGCOLOR=\"#FFFFFF\">\n";
        print "<H1 ALIGN=\"CENTER\">SUCCESSFUL LOGON</H1>\n";
        print "<P>\n";
        print "Congratulations $db[4], ";
        print " You successfully logged on...\n";
        print "</BODY>\n";
        print "</HTML>\n";
        return;
}
#######################+--------------+
#                      | invalid_user |
#                      +--------------+
sub invalid_user{
        print "Content-type:  text/html\n\n";
        open (HTML,"$HTML_DIR\\chap11-1.htm")
                || die "Can't open logonhtml\n";

        while(<HTML>){
                s/<!-- error -->/$error/e;
                print "$_";
        }
        close(HTML);

        return;
}
#######################+-----------+
#                      | parse_cgi |
#                      +-----------+
sub parse_cgi{
        local($i);
        local($key);
        local($val);
```

```
        local($QString);

        if($ENV{'REQUEST_METHOD'} eq "GET"){
                $QString = $ENV{'QUERY_STRING'};
        }else{
                $LEN = $ENV{'CONTENT_LENGTH'};
                read(STDIN,$QString,$LEN);
        }

        @QS = split(/&/,$QString);

        foreach $i (0 .. $#QS){
                $QS[$i] =~ s/\+/ /g;
                ($key,$val) = split(/=/,$QS[$i],2);


                $key =~ s/%(..)/pack("c",hex($1))/ge;
                $val =~ s/%(..)/pack("c",hex($1))/ge;

                $QS{$key} .= "\0" if (defined($QS{$key}));
                $QS{$key} .= $val;
        }
}
```

HINT: The directory paths for files should always be specified as constants at the beginning of the program. It makes reconfiguring the application, either because the Web server is upgraded or the directory structure changes, much easier and less error prone.

Now let's examine the same page, except it combines JavaScript client side processing for form validation and Perl for server side processing. The page has the identical look and feel of the original. The difference is JavaScript code to make sure the user name and password fields are not empty. The HTML code for chap11-2.html is:

```
<HTML>
<!--chap11-2.html-->
<!--02/21/97-->
<HEAD>
<SCRIPT LANGUAGE="JAVASCRIPT">
function validate(){
        if(document.logon.USER.value == ""){
                alert("Username blank!");
                return false;
        }
        if(document.logon.PASS.value == ""){
                alert("Password blank!");
                return false;
        }
        return true;
}
function CheckErrorFlag(){
        if(document.logon.ErrorFlag.value != "0"){
                alert("Login failed. Invalid User Name or Password!");
        }
}
</SCRIPT>
<TITLE>Chapter 11-2</TITLE>
</HEAD>
<BODY onLoad="CheckErrorFlag()" BGCOLOR="#FFFFFF">
<CENTER>
<H1 ALIGN="CENTER">CHAPTER 11 EXAMPLE 1</H1>
<H2 ALIGN="CENTER">User Logon</H2>
<FORM NAME="logon" ACTION="/cgi-shl/chap11-2.pl"
   METHOD="POST" onSubmit="return validate();">
<INPUT TYPE="HIDDEN" NAME="ErrorFlag" VALUE="0">
<TABLE>
<TR>
  <TH>Enter Username:
  <TD><INPUT TYPE="TEXT" SIZE="16" NAME="USER">
</TR>
<TR>
  <TH>Enter Password:
  <TD><INPUT TYPE="PASSWORD" SIZE="16" NAME="PASS">
</TR>
</TABLE>
```

```
<BR><HR>
<INPUT TYPE="SUBMIT" VALUE="SUBMIT">
<INPUT TYPE="RESET" VALUE="RESET">
<BR><HR>
</FORM>
</BODY>
</HTML>
```

There are two items of significance in this HTML file, the JavaScript code and the ERROR hidden field. The JavaScript code executes when the Submit button is clicked. It pops up an "Alert" box when either field is blank:

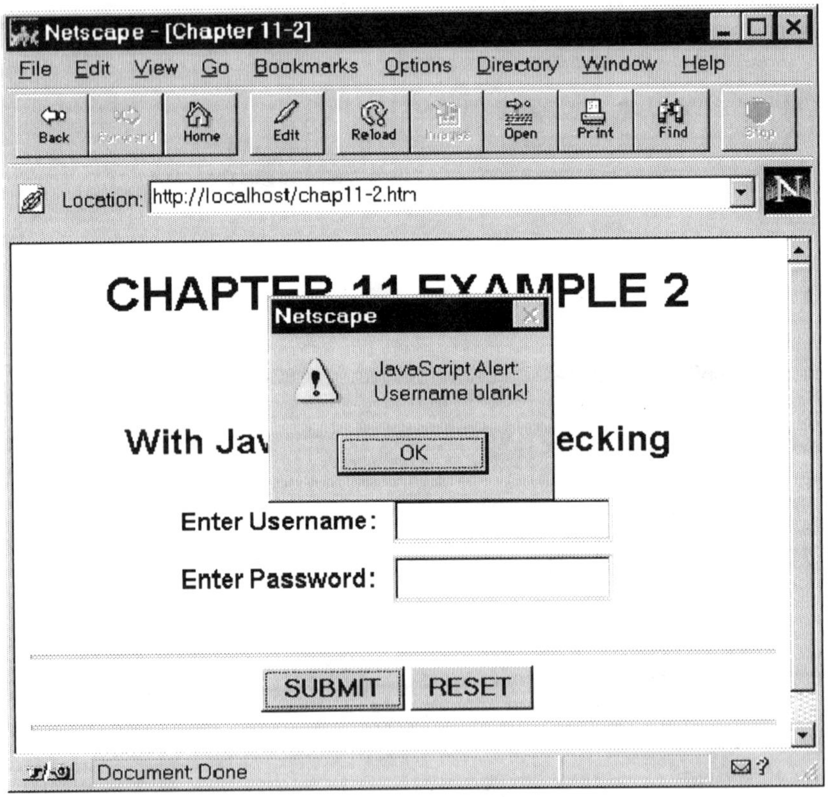

The Submit does not actually execute until the JavaScript code validation is passed. The Perl code for chap11-2.pl is:

```
#!/usr/local/bin/perl
############################################################
# FILE: CHAP11-2.PL
################## vars.inc ###############################
$TOOL_DIR     = "c:\\website\\cgi-shl";
$PASS_DIR     = "c:\\website\\cgi-shl";
$HTML_DIR     = "c:\\website\\htdocs";
$TEMPLATE_DIR = "c:\\website\\htdocs\\template";
################## end vars.inc ###########################
        #
        # Global stuff
        #
$error  = "";

&parse_cgi();          # Get data passed in from the HTML form
        #
        # Build parameter string to pass to look up
        #
$user_pw = "$QS{'USER'}:$QS{'PASS'}:";
        #
        # Load password file into memory
        #
open(PWD,"$PASS_DIR\\passwd") || die "Can't open Password file!\n";
while(<PWD>){
       chop;
       push(@data,$_);
}
close(PWD);
       #
       # search the password for name and password
       #
$success = 0;
foreach $passwd (@data){
       if($passwd =~ /^$user_pw/){
              $success = 1;
              &successful_logon($passwd);
              last;
       }
}
if($success == 0){
       $error = "<B>INVALID USERNAME OR PASSWORD!</B>";
       &invalid_user();      # No data means logon failed.
}
```

11

```
exit;
########################+------------------+
#                       | successful_logon |
#                       +------------------+
sub successful_logon{
              #
              # Extract fields from the database into @db
              # The @db field order is:
       # username:password:userid:GID:fullname:homedir:shell
       @db   = split(/:/,$_[0]);

       print "Content-type:  text/html\n\n";
       print "<HTML>\n";
       print "<HEAD>\n";
       print "<TITLE>Successful logon</TITLE>\n";
       print "</HEAD>\n";
       print "<BODY BGCOLOR=\"#FFFFFF\">\n";
       print "<H1 ALIGN=\"CENTER\">SUCCESSFUL LOGON</H1>\n";
       print "<P>\n";
       print "Congratulations $db[4], ";
       print "You successfully logged on...\n";
       print "</BODY>\n";
       print "</HTML>\n";
       return;
}
########################+--------------+
#                       | invalid_user |
#                       +--------------+
sub invalid_user{
       print "Content-type:  text/html\n\n";
       open (HTML,"$HTML_DIR\\chap11-2.htm")
              || die "Can't open chap11-2.htm\n";

       while(<HTML>){
              s/NAME=\"ErrorFlag\" VALUE=\"0\"/ NAME=\"ErrorFlag\"
VALUE=\"1\"/;
              print "$_";
       }
       close(HTML);

       return;
}
```

```
########################+-----------+
#                       | parse_cgi |
#                       +-----------+
sub parse_cgi{
        local($i);
        local($key);
        local($val);
        local($QString);

        if($ENV{'REQUEST_METHOD'} eq "GET"){
                $QString = $ENV{'QUERY_STRING'};
        }else{
                $LEN = $ENV{'CONTENT_LENGTH'};
                read(STDIN,$QString,$LEN);
        }

        @QS = split(/&/,$QString);

        foreach $i (0 .. $#QS){
                $QS[$i] =~ s/\+/ /g;
                ($key,$val) = split(/=/,$QS[$i],2);

                $key =~ s/%(..)/pack("c",hex($1))/ge;
                $val =~ s/%(..)/pack("c",hex($1))/ge;

                $QS{$key} .= "\0" if (defined($QS{$key}));
                $QS{$key} .= $val;
        }
}
```


The primary difference in the Perl code is less error checking. The following actions are performed by chap11-2.pl:

- Look up user name and password
- If either does not match, repaint the original screen with the appropriate error message
- Paint the next page when no errors are detected

On startup, the JavaScript code checks the value of ERROR and displays an error box when ERROR is 1. The following screen shows the error dialog box:

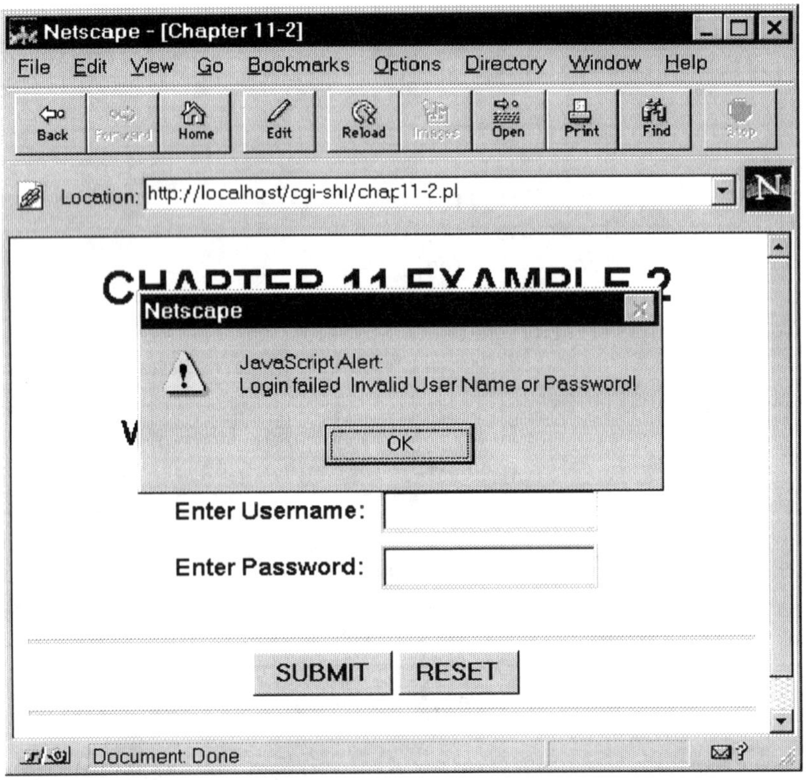

The logic for the application is split across the client and server. The net effect is a simplification of the overall application.

The developer must keep track of the split processing for savings to be realized from the split logic and code simplification. Tools and procedures that record where the processing takes place are necessary. Data flow diagrams that map HTML pages as executable programs and adding extra comments in server code specifying where processing is performed is critical.

Java

Java has obtained buzzword status in a very short time. In other words, people who have no clue about what Java can do or is appropriate for spout off claims that are not practical. This is often true even among programmers. Part of the confusion comes from the fact that Java programs may be either applets or stand-alone. It's easy to confuse the capabilities of the two.

Java is used primarily to "spice up" HTML pages at the present time (early 1997). Applets that do animation or retrieve pages from the host are easy to write. Stand-alone Java programs that do data entry are also easy to write. The Java programs not easy to write combine its stand-alone capabilities (easy screen and therefore database form programming) and the HTML page. Java access to HTML form data is extremely limited. Calling Java from JavaScript and JavaScript from Java is very limited at present. Only a couple of limited examples are available on the Internet. The other way to get Java fully into an application is to write the entire client side in Java. This is possible but more work than most people will do because it is essentially building a custom browser.

JavaScript

JavaScript has already been discussed in this book. I mention it again here to describe the large number of JavaScript versions in use today. Java has overshadowed JavaScript since its inception. However, JavaScript has quietly become an important cog in intranet application development. In spite of the incompatibility among the versions, it has proved capable in improving both user interaction and developer productivity.

HINT: You must be able to specify or at least know which browser the user community uses when making the decision to use JavaScript in an application.

The following table summarizes the different JavaScript versions currently in use:

JavaScript Version	Package	Client-Server	Comment
JavaScript 1.0	Navigator 2.02	C	First JavaScript released
JavaScript 1.1	Navigator 3.01	C	Many enhancements
	LiveWire	S	Server-side JavaScript
	LiveWire Pro	S	
JavaScript 1.2	Communicator 4.0	C	Some time in 1997

JavaScript Version	Package	Client-Server	Comment
JScript 1.0	Internet Explorer	C	Clone of JavaScript 1.0
	IIS 3.0	S	Server-side Jscript, NT only
JBuilder	InterBuilder	S	Borland, NT only, C/S version includes NetScape Fast Track Web Server

HINT: A diverse browser audience generally means using a "lowest common denominator" JavaScript feature set. The latest browser generally allows the developer to take advantage of advanced JavaScript features.

The biggest single impediment to JavaScript acceptance is the incompatibility among versions. Netscape recently supplied European Computer Manufacturers Association (ECMA) with its JavaScript specifications for standardization. The working group includes representatives from Microsoft (Internet Explorer), Borland (InterBuilder), and Netscape. Hopefully, a JavaScript standard will promote compatibility.

When JavaScript is properly used, it can add a great deal of interactivity to the application, simplify the overall application code, and increase developer productivity.

VBScript

VBScript is the Microsoft answer to JavaScript. It mirrors many JavaScript features including many objects. VBScript's primary advantage is its Basic lineage, which translates to a shorter learning curve for programmers already fluent in Visual Basic. The down side is the only implementation of VBScript is Internet Explorer. VBScript is proprietary and its use should be considered suspect in light of more open alternatives (such as JavaScript) including Microsoft's own JScript.

OmniMark

OmniMark is classified as a translating SGML parser and generally not thought of as a Web client-server language. OmniMark, especially Version 3, makes a lot of sense in a few specific cases for server side processing. Sites with a large SGML content base should consider OmniMark. It is an ideal transformation engine for translating SGML content into HTML on the fly.

Version 3 adds a critical feature that makes it practical for Web applications. Version 3 programs can process multiple SGML document instances in a single invocation. Each document may use a different DTD. Prior OmniMark versions could process only a single document per run. The net effect is setting up an "SGML server" to process requests for SGML data which becomes relatively easy in the Web application environment.

Publishing Tools

There are a wide variety of commercial tools that try to fit in the overall scheme of intranet client-server development. These fall into two major categories: screen development tools and content preparation. Examples of screen development tools include:

- Microsoft FrontPage
- Lotus Domino
- Adobe PageMill
- O'Reilly PolyForms

The publishing tools include:

- Corel Ventura 7
- Corel WordPerfect 7
- Microsoft Word
- Adobe Pagemaker

The development tools often have some capability to produce "Web ready" applications by generating the client side HTML and server side code of some sort to process the form. The publishing tools are oriented toward providing full, formatted documents for Web delivery.

Database Tools

Almost every database package from AskSam to ZyIndex have tools to search and display results via the Web. Typical of these packages are:

- AskSam Web Publisher
- LiveLink 7 from OpenText
- Oracle 7
- Informix
- Data Web from Empress Software

This list is only a sample; it is difficult to find a database management system that does not include Web hooks.

Database tool vendors are also well represented in the Web arena. Some of the better known tool vendors with Web capabilities are:

- Oracle Developer 2000
- Borland Interbuilder
- PowerBuilder
- Cold Fusion

These packages often follow the visual approach to generating HTML forms, then generate the code to process the form data. Interbuilder generates server side JavaScript to process the form data for example. Most also include some amount of ODBC connectivity and some even include a Web server.

Other

There are many other Web enabled packages that do not fit into any of the above categories. Chances are if you are using a client-server package, it already has some sort of Web capabilities built in.

Summary

There are many ways to approach Web-based client-server development. While this book concentrates on fairly generic HTML forms with the occasional JavaScript thrown in on the client side and CGI Perl scripts on the server side, there is a growing number of packages that automate much of the Web application development process. The number of alternative tools continues to grow and mature.

Chapter 12

Typical Applications

Introduction

My first thoughts on "typical Web" applications were limiting. The obvious answer is database applications, because HTML forms are a natural for any sort of data entry application. A few days later, I wanted to let some coworkers use an SGML application I had written for my own use. The application used some existing programs with complicated command line interfaces. My desire to have others use the application without a lot of training or forcing them to learn yet another set of arcane programs brought up a second application class that begs for a Web front end, any application with a command line interface. That covers a lot of ground. This chapter touches on command line versus graphical user interfaces and identifies a number of applications that benefit from a Web front end. Most are intranet applications but could just as well be internet based.

Web Front Ends: Why?

Before getting into typical Web application, the side issue of command line interfaces versus GUI is an important one to visit. Addressing it pretty well answers the questions of why do Web front ends. Contrary to popular PC opinion, every application does not have to be a GUI-based application. Microsoft has made it difficult not to develop GUI applications over the past few years. Don't get me wrong, many applications should have a Graphical User

Interface (GUI). Applications that are obvious GUI candidates include:

- Word processors
- Desktop publishing packages
- Graphics programs
- E-mail clients
- Data entry applications

Any application that requires a user sitting at the keyboard to perform work should have a GUI front end. The advantages of graphical user interfaces are:

- Lower training costs
- Ease of use

Users like GUI applications. They are generally easy to learn and use. The knowledge required to get started with a GUI word processor is simply a general knowledge of how GUIs work (how to pull down a menu button, for example). After that, it's a matter of memorizing mouse clicks and maybe a secret key sequence or two. This ease of use translates into the lower training and support costs listed above. GUI applications' ease of use is illustrated by the fact that most current GUI-based applications come with little or no printed documentation.

There are disadvantages to GUI applications as well:

- Increased development cost
- Cannot be run as part of a batch process
- Require a user at the keyboard
- Functionally limited to what is built in

The disadvantages have little to do with usability. These comments especially apply to applications that don't require user interaction. Even with today's visual programming tools, developing GUI applications is much more expensive than developing command line equivalents.

A reality in today's production computer centers is that there are fewer and fewer staff while the amount of work continues to increase. The only way to keep up is automating as many procedures as possible. In other words, the batch process is alive and well in the real computing world. A typical application in this environment might extract data from a database, manipulate the data in some fashion, generate a report, e-mail the report to all department heads, generate and install a Web version of the report, typeset the document, and print 20 copies. Completely automating this process is highly desirable so labor costs are removed from the process.

Automating a complicated process as described above frequently means using programs in ways never envisioned by their developers. Applications with command line interfaces can often be combined in building block fashion to get the work done.

GUI-based applications range from difficult to impossible to run in a processing stream. If the GUI developer did not include a capability you need in a pull down menu, then you are out of luck. Most users don't appreciate this.

SIDEBAR

Let me illustrate the distinction between the two program interfaces with an example. Adobe produces an excellent scanning and OCR program called Capture. Capture was proposed as the program to OCR a thousand documents for a pilot project. The developers met with representatives from the user community to review the requirements. The OCRed text was to be used to build full text search indexes to the scanned pages. The OCR step was a one-time effort for a pilot project leading to a production system. The estimated volume was 15,000 documents averaging 100 pages per year. Bottom line is this process is too expensive with a person at the keyboard.

The user was sure that Capture "worked in batch mode" and plans were made accordingly. The batch mode is called "Watch." It turned out that most of the interactive options were not active in watch mode. Luckily the Capture developers left enough functionality in watch mode that individual pages could be fed from a Sun server to the PC running Capture via a network drive. Capture was used to OCR the documents for the pilot using the "watch" mode with the Sun controlling the process. The pilot developers were lucky!

Web-Based Applications

Good Web-based application candidates are those applications that benefit from a GUI front end. That means any application where user interaction is necessary. Two areas that are likely to bear fruit for Web applications are data entry and command line applications.

Data Entry

Data entry applications that update databases are prime candidates. Any database with a command line interface, such as SQLPlus in Oracle 7, or the CGI programming language has an ODBC feature that can be used with relatively little pain. One of the case studies later in this book is a data entry application.

HTML forms with JavaScript along with CGI Perl scripts provide the minimum tool set for building data entry applications. The resulting application has the benefits of an easy to use GUI and the benefits of less expensive command line application development.

I have arrived at several rules of thumb for Web data entry applications over the years:

Axiom	*Comment*
Don't get too fancy	There are limitations in HTML. Trying to make a form look exactly like an existing piece of paper is more trouble than it's worth and not likely to be pleasing.
Access the database only when necessary	Command line database operations typically log into the database, perform one or more operations, then exit. A form that requires a dozen database accesses is likely to be noticeably slower than the same application with two or three accesses.
Use JavaScript for simple form validation	I have done data entry applications that are both pure CGI and a combination of CGI and JavaScript. The combination simplifies the server side code significantly and in many cases runs faster.
One HTML form, one database table	This is a matter of partitioning the application. Updating a single table in one data entry form helps performance by minimizing the number of database accesses necessary to perform a transaction.

Axiom	*Comment*
Create HTML forms dynamically	Any data entry application is likely to display a form in several similar ways. For example: View—Data values only with no editing Add—Blank values maybe with default values Edit—Edit an existing form Restricted Edit—Edit only some fields There are many variations. Use HTML and script templates to create forms and database update scripts on the fly.

A second type of database application is data retrieval. On the Web, this often means searching full text databases instead of relational databases. The complexity of search forms may be as simple as entering a single word or phrase or as complex as Boolean operators applied to multiple fields in any order. There is no reason complex search results or even reports can't be created on the fly.

The final thought on database applications is, put the same care into the design of the HTML user interface that would be put into a PowerBuilder or Delphi application. Even though the Web development is much simpler to develop, a well thought out form flow is just as important as with any client-server application.

Command Line Applications

Any program with a command line interface that requires some user interaction can be wrapped in a Web front end. Legacy applications are also good candidates. Any time a number of operations are performed in the same order every time, think Web front end. A program that has a number of arguments, especially ones that must be run four or five times to get the right combination of arguments, should trigger "Web front end" thoughts. There are probably hundreds or thousands of programs that fit this description for programmers and computer operators. One of the case studies examines this type of Web application.

Command line programs run via a Web front end are a little harder to visualize. Assume that a report data is extracted from a database, typeset via TEX, and printed automatically. There are several steps involved, each using information from the previous step.

Traditionally, this would be a batch file. The problem is the command line syntax for entering the database query is complicated and error prone. A Web form that collects the database query then runs each of the steps in succession would make the application more robust, because the chances of the database query parameters being specified incorrectly is minimized.

This type of application is a natural for Perl, which is a Unix command language along with its great text processing capabilities. So, the HTML form collects the information, and the Perl CGI script builds the series of command lines to execute to perform the job. It's not complicated and very effective!

Summary

Many applications can be updated to a graphical user interface by simply adding a Web front end. The resources necessary to add a Web front end to a command line interface program is significantly less than rewriting the program to add a GUI.

Chapter 13

Case Studies Introduction

Introduction

The remainder of this book consists of case studies illustrating intranet applications development. This chapter provides a brief overview of each case study, describes the general approach to the case study development, and identifies the tools used in the development process.

Case Studies

The case studies are designed to apply to the areas covered previously in the book. Two scenarios were considered: doing a large number of stand-alone cases to illustrate specific points, and a few larger cases that illustrate the overall system approach and could be implemented as complete applications. The latter approach of a few larger case studies was chosen. The larger case studies allow the same ground to be covered as the smaller, more pointed case studies. Covering the application level of implementation adds elements of Web system design but does not explicitly call out individual areas. With that, the case studies are:

- CGI calculators
- Putting a wrapper on a command line application
- A data entry application

Each case study is presented in its own chapter. At least one complete solution is provided with alternatives identified. Some of the alternatives also include partial code.

CGI Calculators

Web calculators are a dime a dozen. The calculators presented here are different than most. Several are included:

- A four-function RPN calculator using a CGI interface
- A simple formula calculator using a Perl CGI program
- A simple formula calculator using JavaScript completely in the browser

The calculators do not implement a Windows type calculator on purpose. Tons of them are available on the Web already. [Note: There are pointers to 35 JavaScript calculators at http://www.earthweb.net/pages/Gamelan.related.javascript.jsutil.html.]

The calculator examples illustrate the basics of putting together a Web application. They also attempt to show one of the hard things about Web design: There are almost too many choices.

The CGI four-function RPN calculator is 100 percent generic CGI executing a Perl script to compute each value. The CGI simple formula calculator is also completely CGI based. It uses Perl's ability to execute code generated at runtime. The JavaScript formula calculator provides the same functionality as the Perl version using JavaScript's eval() function.

Command Line Application

This case study covers one of the primary intranet Web application classes. The example puts a Web front end on a command line application, GNU's RCS. Revision Control System (RCS) is a configuration management package distributed by the Free Software Foundation. RCS is available on a variety of platforms including Unix and MS-DOS. There is at least one commercial product, MKS Source Integrity, based on RCS. RCS is a very powerful but arcane package that begs for a GUI front end.

Data Entry Application

The second primary intranet application category is database applications. This case study presents an image catalog database. It demonstrates the finer points of data entry development using Web tools. The "database" part is file based. The changes necessary to make it run with Oracle are discussed. The images are Web viewable GIF and JPEG images.

General Approach

The general approach to the case studies is to present the problem, discuss alternative approaches, present the design, and then the implementation. Each case study chapter contains the following main sections:

- Introduction
- Problem Statement
- Approach
- Tools Used
- Design
- Implementation
- Summary

The Introduction section contains a general introduction to the case study. The Problem Statement is a short statement of what the application does. The Approach section describes the overall approach chosen for the implementation. The Tools Used section identifies the tools, such as programming language and Web server used in developing this application. The Design section presents the design of the application. Most of the case studies require multiple programs/screens to implement. The Implementation section presents the code with discussions. Alternatives are discussed where appropriate. Finally, the Summary section summarizes the approach and areas covered in the study.

Tools

Any discussion of tools with a programmer quickly takes on a religious tone. This is especially true in the areas of operating systems, text editors, and programming languages. I am no different in this respect than any other programmer. I have my favorites and strong opinions. Without getting on my soap box and without offending anyone, let me say that I don't believe that any single operating system or programming language can provide an optimum solution for any large organization. I tend to make the following generalizations (this is the programmer in me talking) if given the choice. PCs make good word processors and OK platforms for development (either locally or networked to a server). High-end PCs with Novell NetWare, IBM OS/2, or Microsoft Windows/NT Server make good file and print servers. Unix workstations provide excellent development environments. Unix servers make great Web and database servers and mission critical application that involves networking. IBM mainframes are for secure and robust applications that require massive amounts of I/O. Your generalizations probably don't agree with mine. The point is that there are many types of systems that excel in different areas.

I attempt to use a variety of tools for developing the case study applications because one size does not fit all (as pointed out in the previous paragraph). The following table summarizes the main tools used in developing the case studies.

Tool	*Windows 95*	*Linux*
Hardware	166mz Pentium with 32MB memory, Microsoft Windows 95 www.microsoft.com	166mz Pentium with 32MB memory, Red Hat 4.0 Linux, www.redhat.com
Web Server	O'Reilly WebSite 1.1 www.ora.com ILAR FolkWeb www.ilar.com	Apache
Programming Language	Perl 4.036 Perl 5 JavaScript	Perl 5 JavaScript

Tool	*Windows 95*	*Linux*
Browser	Netscape Navigator home.netscape.com Internet Explorer www.microsoft.com	Netscape Navigator
SGML Parser	SGMLS ftp://ftp.ifi.uio.no in /pub/SGML/SGMLS	SGMLS
HTML Editor	InContext Spider www.incontext.com	
Text Edtior	Jed space.mit.edu in ftp://space.mit.edu in /pub/davis/jed/	Jed

The tools used were largely a function of my home development platform. Most packages that run under Windows 95 also run under Windows NT and the Linux packages are all available under other current Unix systems.

Summary

The goal of each case study is to provide a framework with which to apply the information presented up to this point. This chapter identifies the case studies and describes the approach followed in the case study chapters.

Chapter 14

Case Study 1: CGI Calculators

Introduction

Up to this point, a great deal of background information of building client-server applications using Web tools has presented. This chapter begins the case studies that demonstrate the process through practical examples. The overall approach for developing Web applications is generic CGI, because CGI works today and will work tomorrow while other Web technologies mature.

This first case study examines three relatively simple, one-screen programs. These are three calculators. Examples that touch all the bases of developing CGI applications are the goal of this case study.

Problem Statement

Write three Web-based calculators. The goal is illustrating CGI processing, so a calculator with buttons is not appropriate because there is not client side processing. Many Web calculators based on JavaScript and Java already exist and developing yet another does not contribute to the understanding of developing Web-based client-server Web CGI applications.

Approach

The first calculator is a completely CGI-based Reverse Polish Notation (RPN) four-function calculator. It touches most of the areas of CGI:

- Forms
- Tables
- Perl CGI script
- HTML template files

The user types a number into a box, then clicks a radio button to specify the operation. The program runs, then passes the result back to the screen by dynamically modifying a template file. Here is the basic user interface:

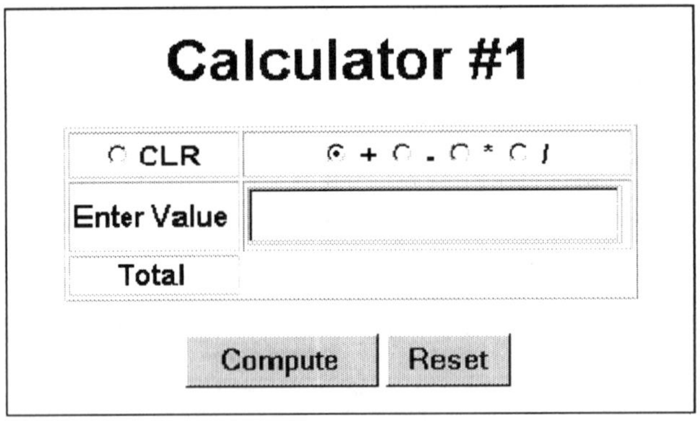

The second calculator is also CGI based. The new areas covered include:

- Dynamically generated HTML
- Using an advanced Perl capability

The difference is the calculator accepts an expression to calculate. The expression is evaluated as runtime-created dynamic code. This calculator also includes most of the features of the first calculator. Its basic user interface is:

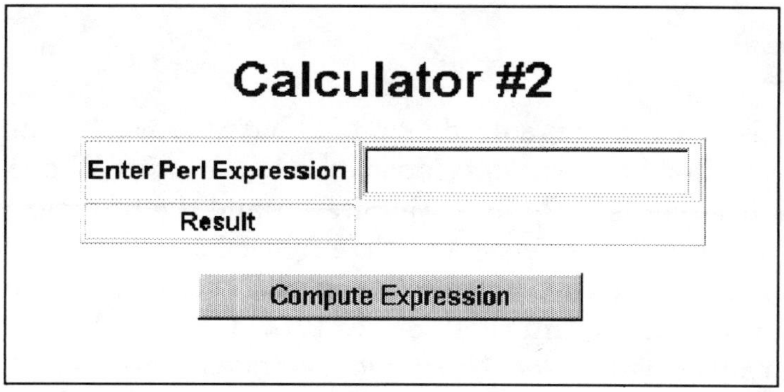

The third calculator breaks the rules given in Problem Statement because it is totally implemented in JavaScript. This is done on purpose to illustrate there is more than one way to implement most Web applications, and the choices you make have a large impact on performance. Early in the book, there were discussions about making development decisions. The difference in performance between calculator 2 and calculator 3 show the effects of design choices. The user interface is virtually identical to the previous calculator:

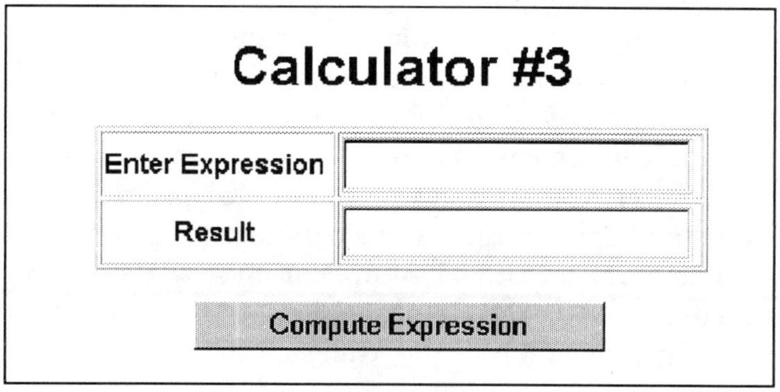

The three calculators provide several approaches to solving essentially the same problem. The main areas of Web development are covered.

Tools Used

This case study is solved using PC-based tools. The implementation presented here was developed on a PC running Windows 95. The Web server is O'Reilly's WebSite 1.1 and the browser is Netscape Navigator 2.01. WebSite was configured as a local server with no connection to the Internet. Internet Explorer insists on connecting to your dial-up Internet Service Provider (ISP) before it will bring up a page with a local host address (http://localhost/...). Internet Explorer was not used in development for this case study, for this reason, even though all three calculators work.

WebSite does not include any version of Perl with its distribution, which is the only shortcoming I have discovered so far. Luckily, there is a hyperlink in its demo page that points to both a Windows 95/NT version of Perl 4 and a Perl 5 that can be configured to work with WebSite. Be forewarned that reading the Perl readme file and following its installation instructions is necessary. I wasted a couple of evenings trying to get Perl working before I gave up and read the instructions.

The biggest incompatibility with WebSite and Unix-based Web servers from a CGI programming standpoint is the CGI directory structure. Most Web servers use /cgi-bin for CGI scripts/programs. WebSite has three CGI directories depending on what type of program is being run. There is cgi-dos to run 16-bit MS-DOS programs, cgi-shl for running 32-bit CGI programs such as Perl scripts, and cgi-win for native Windows programs. All of the scripts here run from cgi-shl. The implication is some minor adjustments in hyperlinks and Perl code probably need to be made when running the applications on another Web server.

I had originally intended to use FolkWeb for developing this case study. However, my demo copy had expired. My schedule did not allow time to order a full copy. I have a very good impression of FolkWeb after using it for one or two of the examples earlier in the book. Installation was straightforward. It includes a Perl in the installation. Thus developers coming from a CGI background can get started instantly.

The HTML is so short I did not use an HTML editor for this case study.

Design

The design of each of the three calculator applications is addressed individually in the following sections.

Calculator 1

The initial part of any design process is identifying the requirements for the application. The high level requirements for the Calculator 1 application are:

- Provide an RPN four-function calculator
- Make it completely CGI
- The calculator may be called initially with no arguments
- Apply the value entered by the user to the previous value using the operator (+,–,*,/) specified

Based on these requirements, we can make some initial design decisions about the application, such as:

- Use Perl for the implementation language
- Use HTML forms for data input
- Use an HTML template file
- Use HTML tables to provide a pleasing user interface
- Assign filenames

The first calculator consists of an HTML template file and a Perl script from a file standpoint. The processing is encapsulated in a Web page and a CGI script. This can be confusing when trying to create a mental picture of the application. Two data flow diagrams (DFD) provide two perspectives on the program operation. The first shows the I/O that the programmer has to deal with directly, which is the traditional use of a DFD:

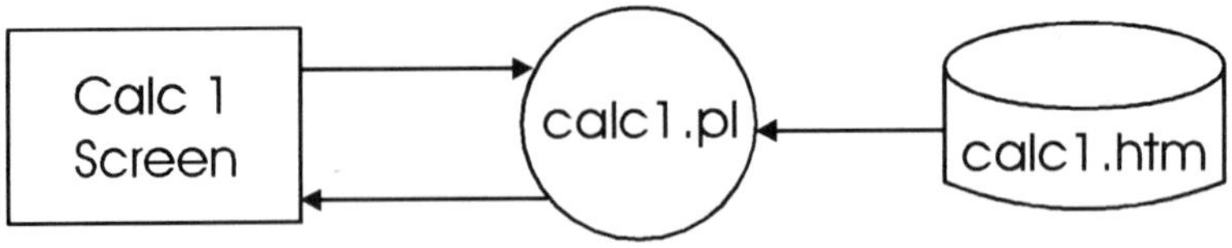

The Perl program, calc1.pl, is called via a hyperlink, either from another screen or from the user clicking the Submit button. Calc1.pl processes the request, then copies calc1.htm back to STDOUT. Writing to STDOUT effectively writes to the browser screen. This diagram does not show the sequence of events possible from the screen or include the Web server. The items not shown contribute to hiding the complete operation of the application.

The second DFD for the first calculator improves somewhat:

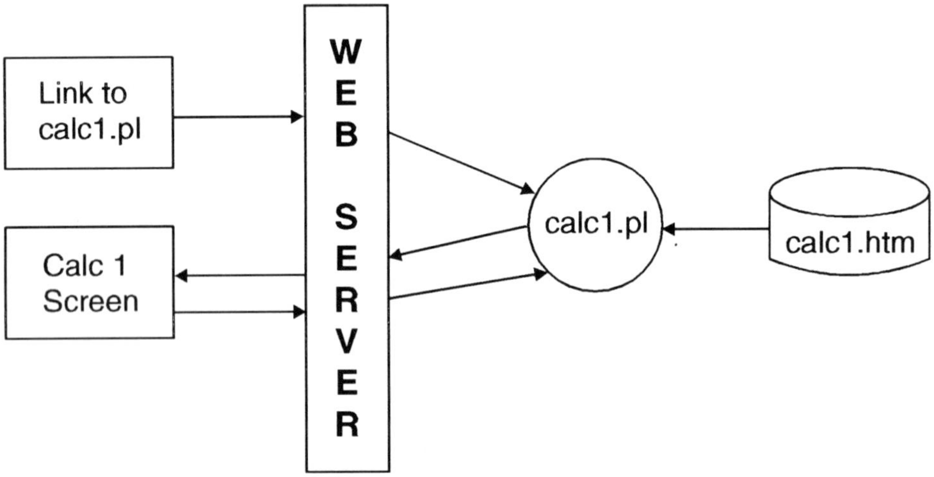

This second DFD is better because it shows the Web server and a possible sequence of events. However, it still does not show data exchanged between the browser and the Perl CGI program. Let's try a third DFD:

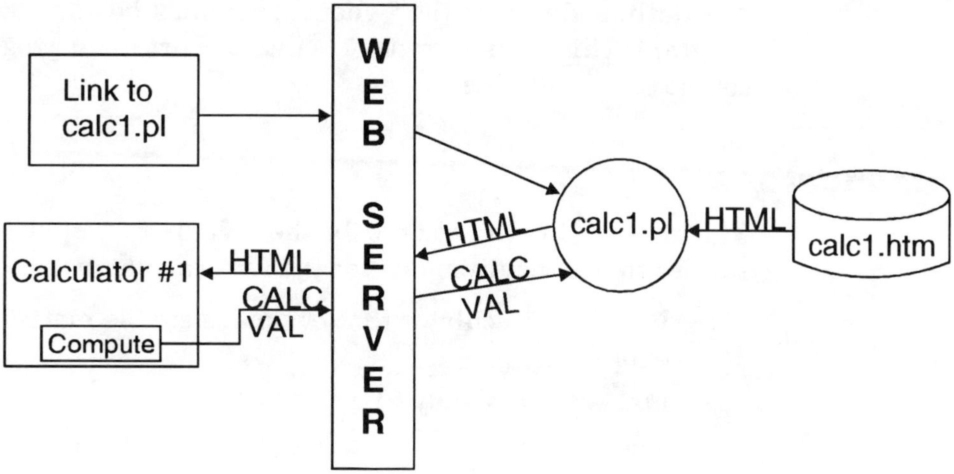

This is the preferred data flow. It shows all of the pieces, whether programming is required or not, the Web server for example. This DFD also shows the sequence of actions that occur for the application. There are two additions from the previous data flow, the button on the screen and the information passed among the components.

The high level design is mapped by the DFD. The lower level details are influenced by the requirements. The design decisions also contribute to the overall design. The final piece is mapping out the details of calc1.pl. I tend to think in outlines, whether writing books or writing programs. For this reason, I use a processing outline rather than traditional pseudo code.

```
BEGIN calc1.pl
       Get CGI arguments
       if(arguments passed)
              Calculate new value based on operator
              Copy calc1.htm to STDOUT passing new value
       else
              Copy calc1.htm to STDOUT with no value
       Endif
END calc1.pl
```

The outline identifies the "whats" that must be done by the program. This outline translates into a short main program plus a couple of subroutines.

Calculator 2

The high level requirements for the Calculator 2 application are very similar to the requirements for the first calculator:

- Provide a calculator that evaluates simple mathematical expressions
- Make it completely CGI
- The calculator may be called initially with no arguments
- Compute the expression entered by the user

The initial design decisions for Calculator 2 are:

- Use Perl for the implementation language
- Use HTML forms for data input
- Dynamically generate the HTML in the Perl program
- Use HTML tables to provide a pleasing user interface
- Assign filenames

The data flow diagram that describes calculator 2 is:

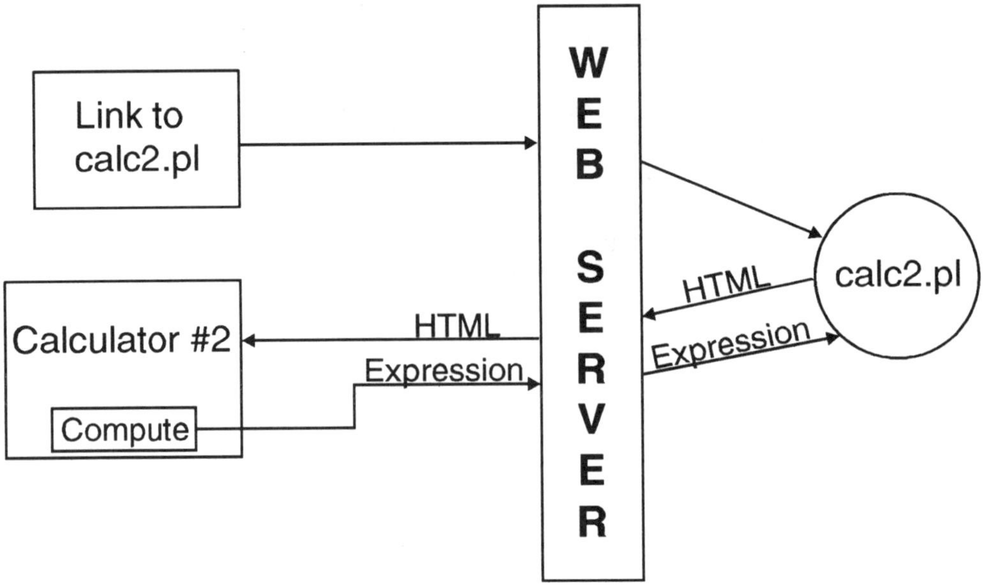

As you can see, Calculator 1 and Calculator 2 are very similar at this design level. Here is the processing outline for calc2.pl:

```
BEGIN calc2.pl
       Get CGI arguments
       if(arguments passed)
              Evaluate the expression
              Generate HTML code to STDOUT passing new value
       else
              Generate HTML code to STDOUT with no value
       Endif
END calc2.pl
```

The pseudo code outline is not down to the absolute lowest detailed level. The level of detail included in pseudo code must describe the operation of the program at the level the programmer understands everything that the program does. Pseudo code at this level is appropriate for an experienced Web developer.

Calculator 3

The third calculator is a little strange compared to the other two from the design standpoint, because the processing all takes place in the browser. The high level requirements for the Calculator 3 application are a subset to those in Calculator 2:

- Provide a calculator that evaluates simple mathematical expressions
- Implement the calculator in JavaScript
- Compute the expression entered by the user

The initial design decisions for Calculator 3 are:

- Use JavaScript for the implementation language
- Use HTML forms for data input
- Calculate the expression value in the browser
- Use HTML tables to provide a pleasing user interface
- Assign filenames

The data flow diagram that describes Calculator 3 is:

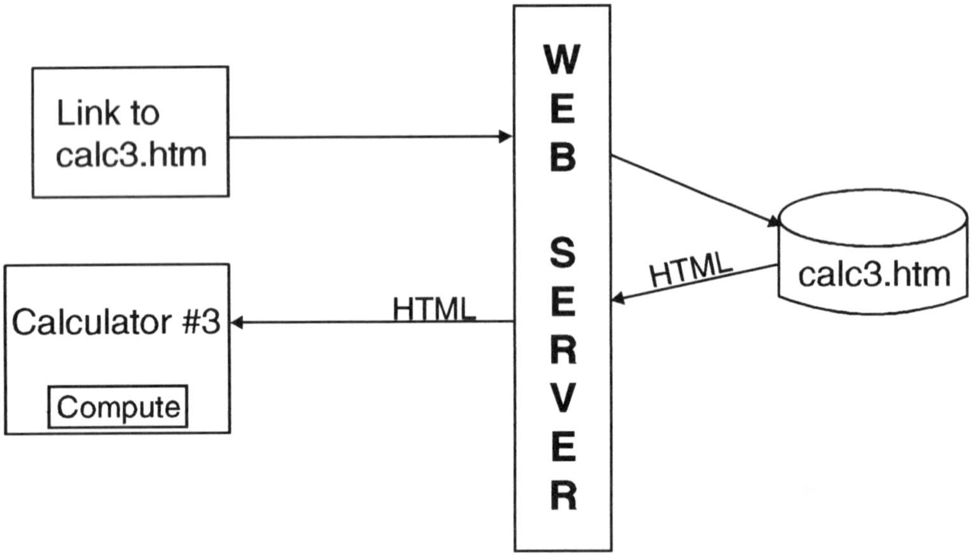

A Web application that runs completely in the browser is rare. Applications with some client processing is more and more common, and your design notation must accommodate that processing representation.

Implementation

This section presents the implementation of the three calculator designs described above. Each is discussed separately.

Calculator 1

The implementation of Calculator 1 is spread across several areas. There is the HTML page, the Perl CGI script, and the HTML file. The HTML file is a template in this case. All of the pieces must work in concert for the application to function properly.

The HTML is a template file in this case. The difference between simply using an HTML file in a hyperlink and using it as a template is actually slight. The template is intended to be accessed by a CGI script, not directly from a hyperlink. The template file generally contains either a partial HTML file or "markers" within the file that allow values to be substituted in at runtime. The HTML template file, calc1.htm in this case, contains markers ($TOTAL and $VALUE) for the results of the calculation. The contents of calc1.htm are:

```
<HTML>
<HEAD><TITLE>Calculator #1</TITLE>
</HEAD>
<BODY BGCOLOR="#FFFFFF">
<H1 ALIGN="CENTER">Calculator #1</H1>
<P>
<CENTER>
<FORM METHOD="POST" ACTION ="/cgi-shl/calc1.pl">
<INPUT TYPE="HIDDEN" NAME="TOTAL" VALUE="$TOTAL">
<TABLE BORDER>
<TR>
<TH>
<INPUT TYPE=RADIO NAME="CALC" VALUE="CLR">CLR
<TH>
<INPUT TYPE=RADIO NAME="CALC" VALUE="+" CHECKED>+
<INPUT TYPE=RADIO NAME="CALC" VALUE="-">-
<INPUT TYPE=RADIO NAME="CALC" VALUE="*">*
<INPUT TYPE=RADIO NAME="CALC" VALUE="/">/
<TR COLSPAN=2>
  <TH>Enter Value
  <TD>
    <INPUT ALIGN=RIGHT TYPE="TEXT" NAME="VAL" VALUE="$VALUE">
</TR>
<TR COLSPAN=2>
  <TH>Total
  <TD ALIGN=RIGHT>$TOTAL
</TR>
</TABLE>
<P>
<INPUT TYPE="SUBMIT" NAME="CALC1" VALUE="Compute">
<INPUT TYPE="RESET">
</FORM>
<HR>
This simple calculator is RPN. Enter a value and an operation
and click "Compute."
</BODY>
</HTML>
```

14

I use markers that are valid Perl variable names. That is why they all start with a "$." This makes it easy to visually find markers in the HTML file. In this file, the script searches for $TOTAL and $VALUE, then substitutes the current value for each before writing the HTML code to the browser.

HINT: HTML template files can be used in conjunction with dynamically generated HTML. A typical combination use is generating a report from a database. The heading and footer of the report can each be in separate template files. The detail portion of the page is dynamically created using values retrieved from the database.
A second combined use is where multiple pages have the same basic heading, but different bodies. Use a template file for the header and dynamically generate the body.

The code for calc1.pl is relatively straightforward. There is a short "main" section followed by several subroutines. The code is:

```
#!/usr/local/bin/perl
##########################################################
# FILE: CALC-1.PL
# Fields coming back from the HTML form are:
#       CALC    - The operation
#       VAL     - Value user entered

$TEMPLATE_DIR = "c:\\website\\htdocs\\template";

&parse_cgi(); # Get data passed in from the logon.html form

if($QS{'VAL'} eq ""){
        &display_new_form();
}else{
        &process_form();
}
exit;
```

```
#######################+------------------+
#                      | display_new_form |
#                      +------------------+
sub display_new_form{

        print "Content-type: text/html\n\n";

        open(HTML,"$TEMPLATE_DIR\\calc1.htm");
        while(<HTML>){
                s/\$TOTAL/$TOTAL/eg;
                s/\$VALUE/$VALUE/eg;
#               s/\$VALUE//eg;
                print "$_";
        }
}
#######################+--------------+
#                      | process_form |
#                      +--------------+
sub process_form{
        local($val);
        local($op);

        $VALUE = int($QS{'VAL'});
        $op    = $QS{'CALC'};
        $TOTAL = int($QS{'TOTAL'});
        if($op eq "="){
                $TOTAL = $VALUE;
        }else{
                if($op eq "CLR"){
                        $TOTAL = "00";
                }else{
                        eval("\$TOTAL = $TOTAL $op $VALUE");
                }
        }
        $VALUE = "";
        &display_new_form();
}
#######################+-----------+
#                      | parse_cgi |
#                      +-----------+
```

14

```
sub parse_cgi{
        local($i);
        local($key);
        local($val);
        local($QString);

        if($ENV{'REQUEST_METHOD'} eq "GET"){
                $QString = $ENV{'QUERY_STRING'};
        }else{
                $QString = "";
                $LEN     = $ENV{'CONTENT_LENGTH'};
                read(STDIN,$QString,$LEN);
        }

        @QS = split(/&/,$QString);

        foreach $i (0 .. $#QS){
                $QS[$i] =~ s/\+/ /g;
                ($key,$val) = split(/=/,$QS[$i],2);

                $key =~ s/%(..)/pack("c",hex($1))/ge;
                $val =~ s/%(..)/pack("c",hex($1))/ge;

                $QS{$key} .= "\0" if (defined($QS{$key}));
                $QS{$key} .= $val;
        }
}
```

There are several items that need to be pointed out in the code. The use of a variable to contain file paths is a habit developers should acquire. The line here is:

```
$TEMPLATE_DIR = "c:\\website\\htdocs\\template";
```

This simple convention will save much maintenance time and effort the first time the application is restructured.

HINT: When developing a system, the path variables should be put into a separate file and included in each program. Then only one file has to be changed when a file location changes.

The second item of significance is the call to *&parse_cgi()*. This subroutine or its equivalent must be in every CGI script. Its purpose is decoding the CGI string. The details of processing CGI strings is covered in Chapter 5. *&parse_cgi()* is also a prime candidate to put in a separate file and include in each program in the application. *&parse_cgi()* also automatically handles the difference between getting the CGI string via GET or POST methods. There are times when the same CGI script will be called with GET one time and POST another.

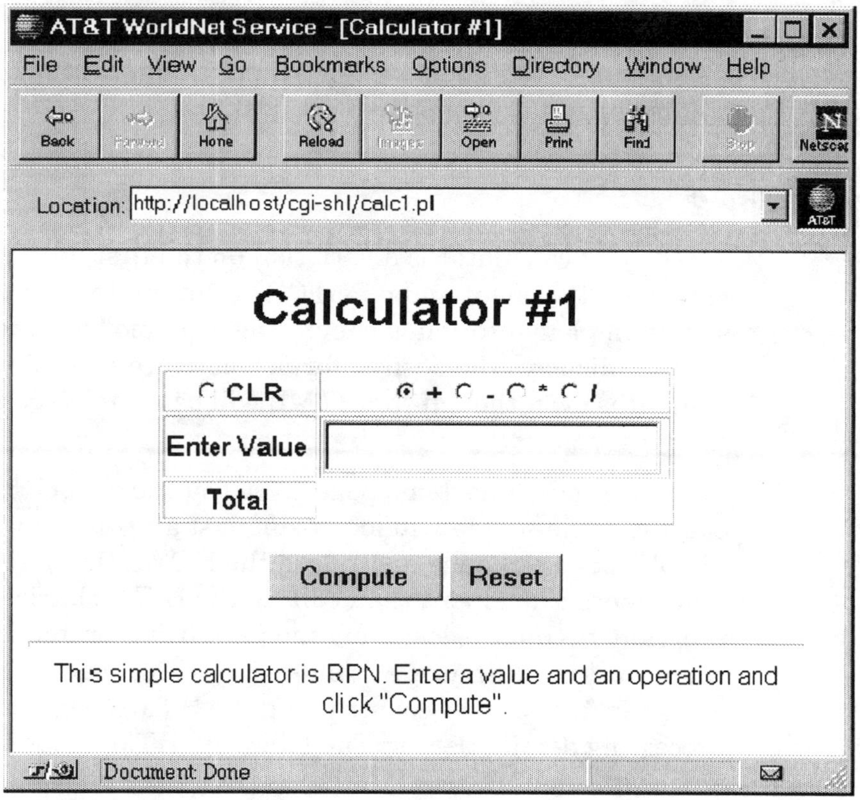

The calculator application operation is relatively straightforward:

1. The user enters a number in the dialog box, clicks one of the four operator (+,–,*,/) radio buttons, then clicks Submit.
2. The browser sends the form data, VAL and CALC, via the CGI string to the Web server specifying the program /cgi-bin/calc1.pl be run.
3. The Web server executes calc1.pl passing the CGI string via POST because POST was specified in the **<FORM>** element.
4. Calc1.pl executes, performing the calculation.
5. Calc1.pl opens the template file, c:\website\htdocs\template\calc1.htm, and writes the contents back to the browser while substituting the result of the operation for the **$TOTAL** marker.
6. The browser receives the HTML code from the server and paints the screen.
7. The browser then waits for the next user action.

Calculator 1 is a simple CGI-only application that illustrates several points about developing Web applications.

Calculator 2

The second calculator is a variation on the first. Both are made up of HTML on the client and a Perl CGI script on the server. The first step in implementation is generating a "demo" or "sample" HTML file that displays the desired form. There are several reasons for doing this even though the HTML will be completely generated by the program.

First, a stand-alone demo page gives you the chance to work out the exact way the screen will look using just an editor and a browser. Simply make a change and reload the HTML file to test. This is much more convenient than editing the HTML buried in a Perl program. Second, redesigning the page from scratch is much easier when working with just a stand-alone HTML page. Third, the coding will go faster because constructing the HTML page tends to make processing details clearer. The following HTML code is the stand-alone version of the HTML that is generated by calc2.pl:

```
<HTML>
<HEAD><TITLE>Calculator #2</TITLE>
</HEAD>
<BODY BGCOLOR="#FFFFFF">
<H1 ALIGN="CENTER">Calculator #2</H1>
<P>
<CENTER>
<FORM METHOD="POST" ACTION ="/cgi-shl/calc2.pl">
<TABLE BORDER>
<TR>
  <TH>Enter Perl Expression
  <TD><INPUT ALIGN="RIGHT" TYPE="TEXT" NAME="EXPR">
</TR>
<TR>
  <TH>Result
  <TD ALIGN="RIGHT">$TOTAL
</TR>
</TABLE>
<P>
<INPUT TYPE="SUBMIT" NAME="CALC2" VALUE="Compute Expression">
</FORM>
</BODY>
</HTML>
```

Keep a screen print to use as a reference and the HTML file to save retyping the HTML when you are finished testing the page.

HINT: Always write a demo stand-alone version of dynamic pages before adding the code to a script. This allows tweaking the page to get the exact presentation before committing it to code.

Notice that I included the substitution markers in the stand-alone HTML. That also serves as an aid during the coding process.

HINT: Save the stand-alone HTML file for coding. Substitute \$ for $ (except for the markers if you use $ in marker names) and \" for ". Insert *print* " at the start of the line and *\n";* at the end of each line. The result will be ready to drop into the Perl program.

The code for calc2.pl is:

```
#!/usr/local/bin/perl
##############################################################
# FILE: calc2.pl
# Fields coming back are:
#       EXPR    - The expression to calculate
#       TOTAL   - The result of the previous calcualtion

$TEMPLATE_DIR = "c:\\website\\htdocs\\template";

&parse_cgi(); # Get data passed in from the logon.html form

if($QS{'EXPR'} eq ""){
       &display_new_form();
}else{
       &process_form();
}
exit;
########################+-------------------+
#                       | display_new_form |
#                       +-------------------+
sub display_new_form{

       print "Content-type: text/html\n\n";

       print "<HTML>\n";
       print "<HEAD><TITLE>Calculator #2</TITLE>\n";
       print "</HEAD>\n";
       print "<BODY BGCOLOR=\"#FFFFFF\">\n";
       print "<H1 ALIGN=\"CENTER\">Calculator #2</H1>\n";
       print "<P>\n";
       print "<CENTER>\n";
       print "<FORM METHOD=\"POST\" ";
```

```
        print " ACTION =\"/cgi-shl/calc2.pl\">\n";
        print "<TABLE BORDER>\n";
        print "<TR>\n";
        print "  <TH>Enter Perl Expression\n";
        print "  <TD><INPUT ALIGN=\"RIGHT\" TYPE=\"TEXT\"";
        print " NAME=\"EXPR\">\n";
        print "</TR>\n";
        print "<TR>\n";
        print "  <TH>Result\n";
        print "  <TD ALIGN=\"RIGHT\">$TOTAL\n";
        print "</TR>\n";
        print "</TABLE>\n";
        print "<P>\n";
        print "<INPUT TYPE=\"SUBMIT\" NAME=\"CALC2\" ";
        print " VALUE=\"Compute Expression\">\n";
        print "</FORM>\n";
        print "</BODY>\n";
        print "</HTML>\n";

}
#######################+--------------+
#                      | process_form |
#                      +--------------+
sub process_form{
        local($expr);

        $expr    = $QS{'EXPR'};
#       $expr    =~ s/\$/\\$/g;
        if($expr =~ /=/){
                ($TOTAL,$the_rest) = split(/=/,$expr);
                eval("\$TOTAL = $the_rest");
        }else{
                eval("\$TOTAL = $expr");
        }
        &display_new_form();
}
#######################+-----------+
#                      | parse_cgi |
#                      +-----------+
sub parse_cgi{
        local($i);
        local($key);
        local($val);
```

14

```
        local($QString);

        if($ENV{'REQUEST_METHOD'} eq "GET"){
                $QString = $ENV{'QUERY_STRING'};
        }else{
                $QString = "";
                $LEN     = $ENV{'CONTENT_LENGTH'};
                read(STDIN,$QString,$LEN);
        }

        @QS = split(/&/,$QString);

        foreach $i (0 .. $#QS){
                $QS[$i] =~ s/\+/ /g;
                ($key,$val) = split(/=/,$QS[$i],2);

                $key =~ s/%(..)/pack("c",hex($1))/ge;
                $val =~ s/%(..)/pack("c",hex($1))/ge;

                $QS{$key} .= "\0" if (defined($QS{$key}));
                $QS{$key} .= $val;
        }
}
```

There are two major differences between the code for calc1.pl and calc2.pl. One is the entire HTML code is embedded in the Perl program in calc2.pl and read from a template file in calc1.pl. Secondly, the way calc2.pl performs the calculation is by evaluating the expression passed from the user; calc1.pl executes only the single operation specified by the user. The program structure is identical other than that.

The screen generated by calc2.pl is:

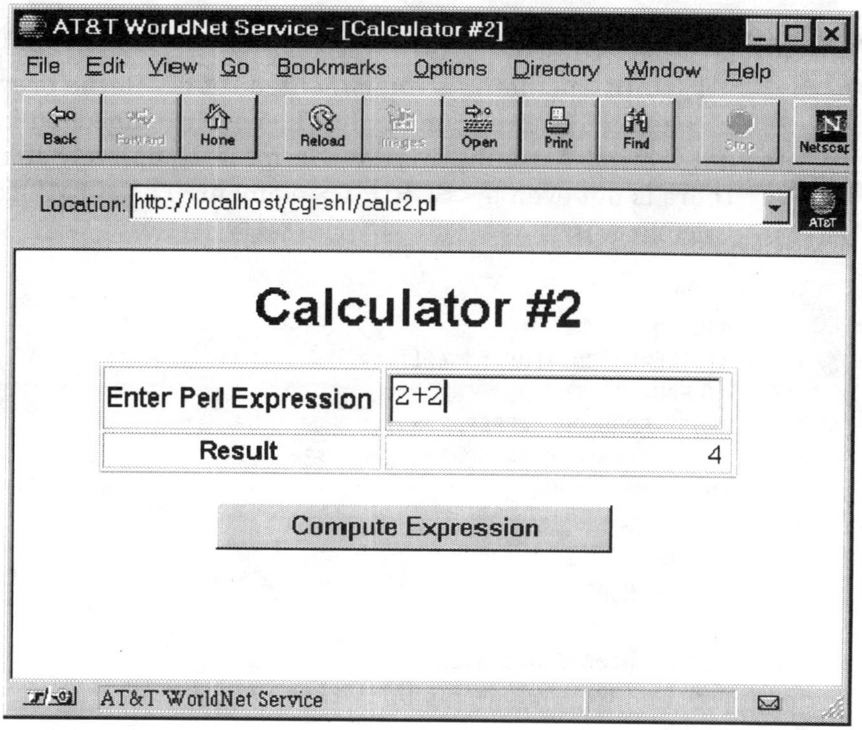

The calculator application operation is relatively straightforward:

1. The user enters an expression in the dialog box, such as "2+2," then clicks Compute Expression.
2. The browser sends the form data, EXPR, via the CGI string to the Web server specifying the program /cgi-bin/calc2.pl be run.
3. The Web server executes calc2.pl, passing the CGI string via POST because POST was specified in the **<FORM>** element.
4. Calc2.pl executes, performing the calculation.
5. Calc2.pl writes the HTML code back to the browser while substituting the result of the operation for the **$TOTAL** marker.
6. The browser receives the HTML code from the server and paints the screen.
7. The browser then waits for the next user action.

Calculator 2 is also a simple CGI-only application that illustrates dynamically generating HTML.

Calculator 3

The third calculator is implemented totally in the browser. That means no CGI program at all. The code is embedded in the HTML as JavaScript. Actually, this JavaScript is deceptively simple because there is not even a <SCRIPT> element. The HTML code for calc3.htm is:

```
<HTML>
<HEAD>
<TITLE>Calculator #3</TITLE>
</HEAD>
<BODY BGCOLOR="#FFFFFF">
<H1 ALIGN="CENTER">Calculator #3</H1>
<P>
<CENTER>
<FORM>
<TABLE BORDER>
<TR>
  <TH>Enter Expression
  <TD><INPUT ALIGN="RIGHT" TYPE="TEXT" NAME="EXPR">
</TR>
<TR>
  <TH>Result
  <TD ALIGN="RIGHT"><INPUT TYPE="TEXT" NAME="TOTAL">
</TR>
</TABLE>
<P>
<INPUT TYPE="BUTTON" VALUE="Compute Expression"
  ONCLICK="this.form.TOTAL.value = eval(this.form.EXPR.value)">
</FORM>
</BODY>
</HTML>
```

The display generated is identical to that of Calculator 2:

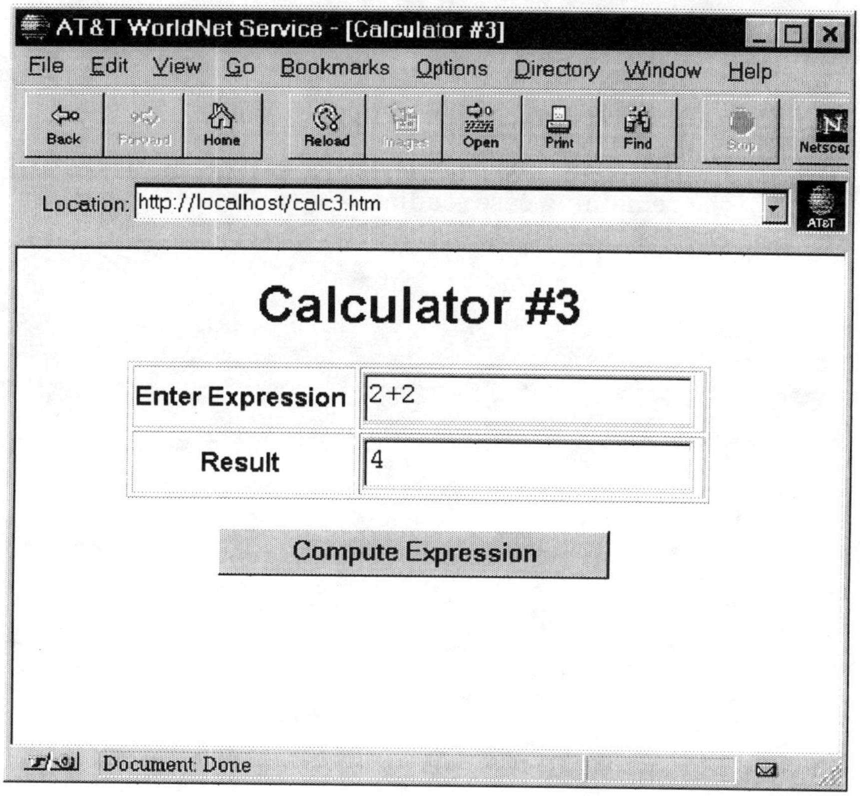

The expression typed into the Expression input box is computed by the "eval(this.form.EXPR.value)" code in the <BUTTON> element.

Calculator 3 is not typical but demonstrates the potential for limited complete client side programs.

Summary

This chapter presents three different ways to implement essentially the same application. Each way presents a different aspect of Web client-server application development. Areas touched on include:

- Using HTML tables and forms to build the user interface
- Using CGI programs to process data entered on forms
- Using HTML template files

- Dynamically generating HTML pages
- Techniques for using Data Flow Diagrams to map the processing of a Web application

Each of these basic areas will be expanded upon at various points in the remaining case studies.

Chapter 15

Case Study 2: Command Line Application

Introduction

Most command line based applications benefit from a Web front end. Unix utilities, such as RCS, are prime candidates. RCS, or the Revision Control System, is a GNU application that implements a super set of the Unix Source Code Control System (SCCS). It is a configuration management system that is flexible enough to manage everything from source code to HTML code and just about everything in between. RCS is made up of several stand-alone programs. Each RCS program has a long list of command line options. In short, this case study is an almost classic example of bringing a legacy application up to date without rewriting it from scratch.

The RCS application was chosen because it illustrates a legacy application that has multiple parts; there are about half a dozen or so stand-alone programs in the RCS package. Putting a front end on a single program does not cover the design and development aspects of a Web application the way a multiprogram application, such as RCS, does.

Problem Statement

The assignment for this case study is to put a Web front end on the basic RCS capabilities. These are defined as:

- Adding a new file to RCS
- Checking in a file
- Checking out a file, both locked and unlocked
- Listing the currently locked files

In addition, the program should include a "File Installation" capability that checks a file into RCS and moves the file to a user specified destination directory. The final capability necessary is user logon.

The implementation may use JavaScript, Perl CGI scripts, and HTML forms.

Approach

The development takes a multistep approach. The problem statement defines the basic requirements. The basic requirements are reinforced by preparing demo HTML screens to work out the user interface design. The screens are shown in the design section. The user reviews the screens and the requirements, looking for comments before the design proceeds. The demo screens for this application are:

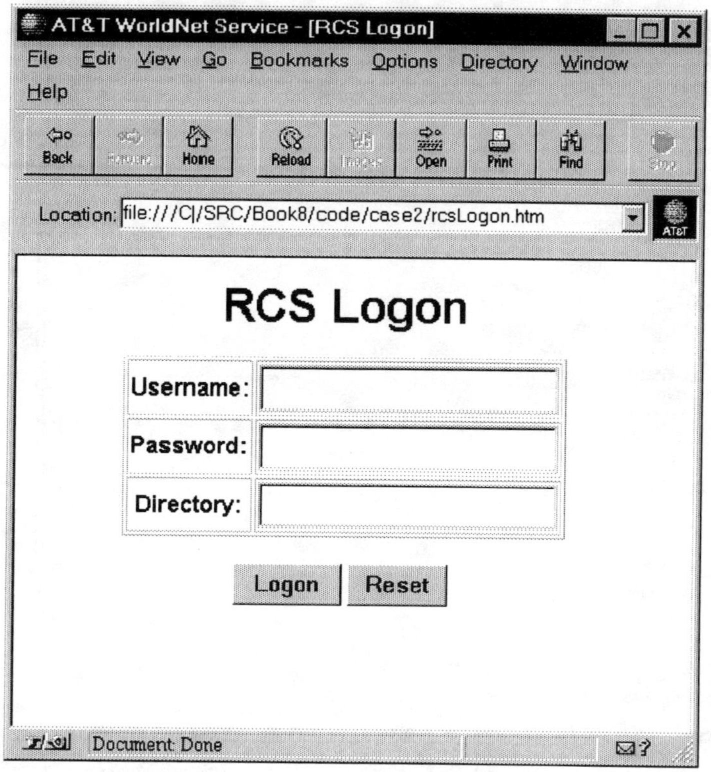
AT&T WorldNet Service - [RCS Logon]
File Edit View Go Bookmarks Options Directory Window Help
Back
Forward
Home
Reload
Images
Open
Print
Find
Stop
Location: file:///C|/SRC/Book8/code/case2/rcsLogon.htm
RCS Logon
Username:
Password:
Directory:
Logon
Reset
Document: Done

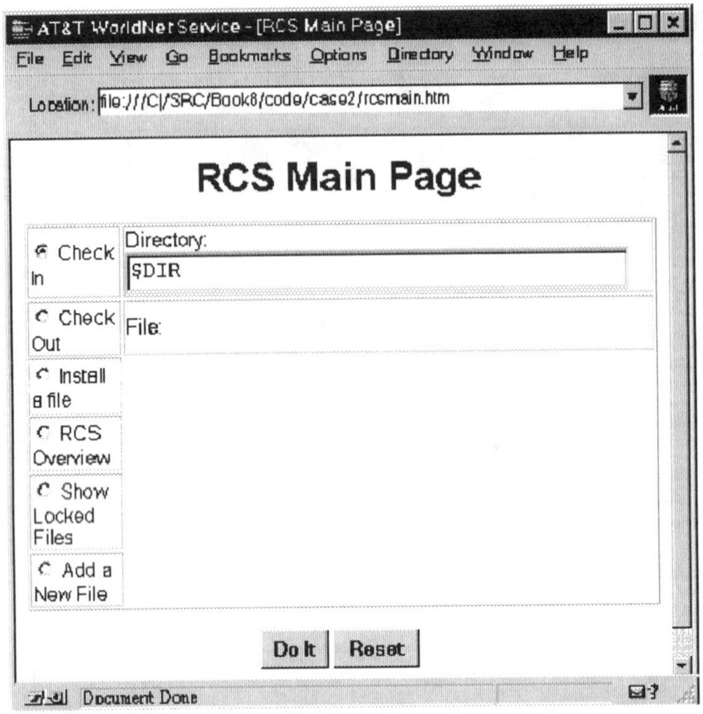
AT&T WorldNet Service - [RCS Main Page]
File Edit View Go Bookmarks Options Directory Window Help
Location: file:///C|/SRC/Book8/code/case2/rcsmain.htm
RCS Main Page
Check In
Directory:
$DIR
Check Out
File:
Install a file
RCS Overview
Show Locked Files
Add a New File
Do It
Reset
Document: Done

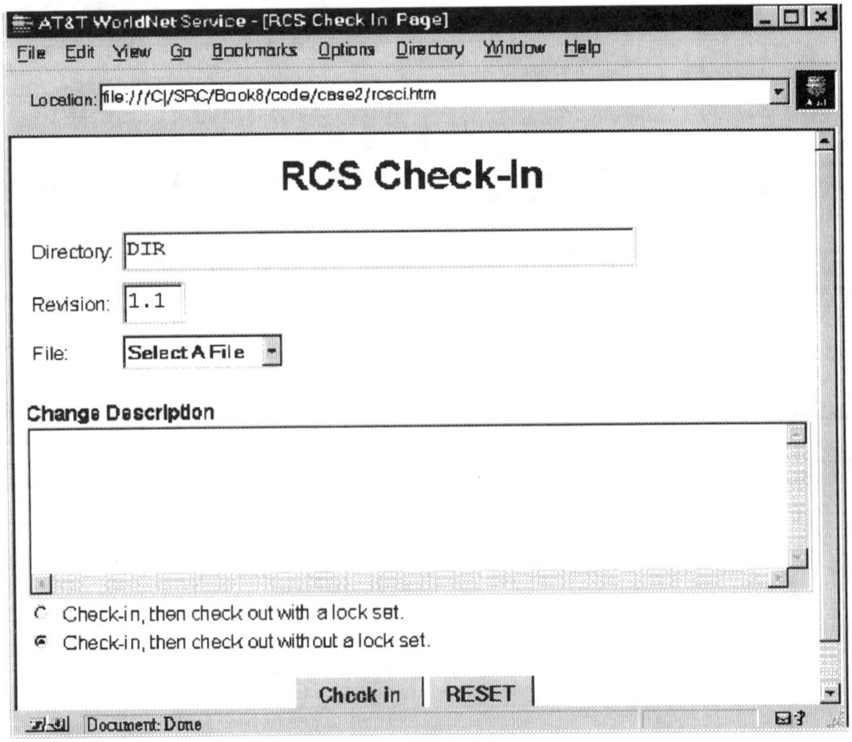
AT&T WorldNet Service - [RCS Check In Page]
File Edit View Go Bookmarks Options Directory Window Help
Location: file:///C|/SRC/Book8/code/case2/rcsci.htm
RCS Check-In
Directory: DIR
Revision: 1.1
File: Select A File
Change Description
Check-in, then check out with a lock set.
Check-in, then check out without a lock set.
Check in
RESET
Document: Done

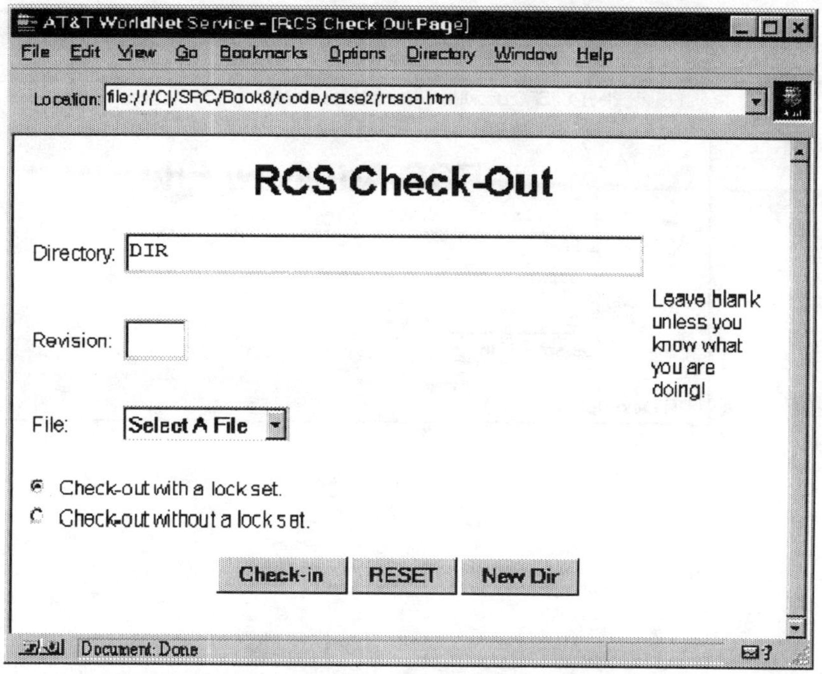
AT&T WorldNet Service - [RCS Check Out Page]
File Edit View Go Bookmarks Options Directory Window Help
Location: file:///C|/SRC/Book8/code/case2/rcsco.htm
RCS Check-Out
Directory: DIR
Revision:
Leave blank unless you know what you are doing!
File: Select A File
Check-out with a lock set.
Check-out without a lock set.
Check-in
RESET
New Dir
Document: Done

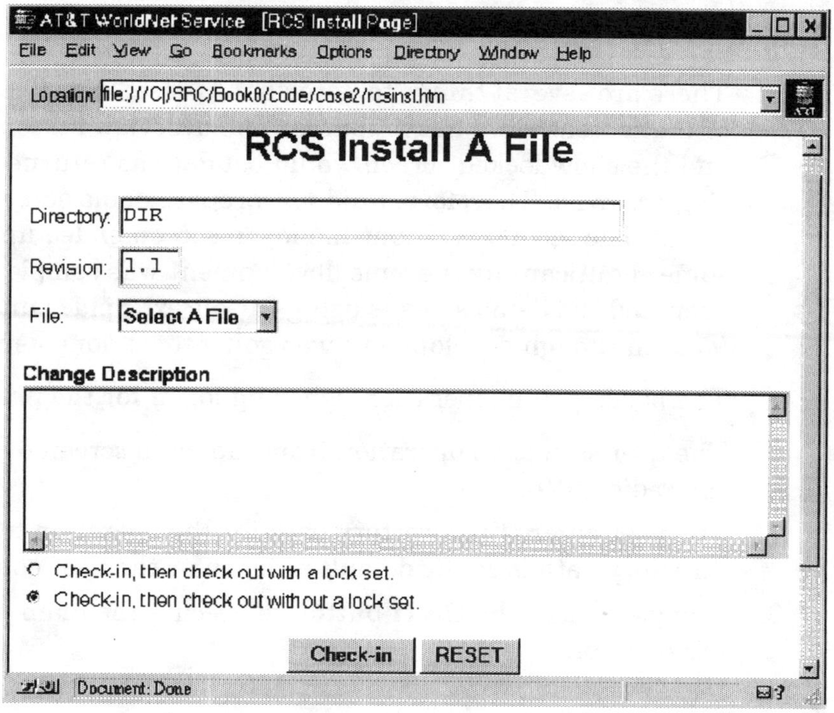
AT&T WorldNet Service [RCS Install Page]
File Edit View Go Bookmarks Options Directory Window Help
Location: file:///C|/SRC/Book8/code/case2/rcsinst.htm
RCS Install A File
Directory: DIR
Revision: 1.1
File: Select A File
Change Description
Check-in, then check out with a lock set.
Check-in, then check out without a lock set.
Check-in
RESET
Document: Done

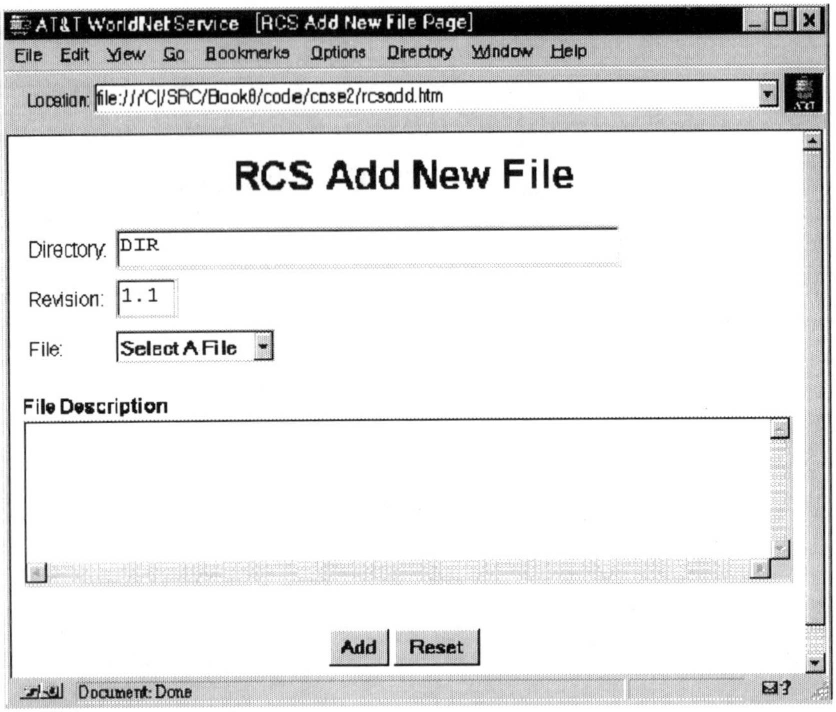

There are several things to note about these "demo" pages. First, all of the screens were not prepared. The overview screen was to be text and the show locked screen would list data as returned by the RCS rlog program. Therefore, I did not prepare demo screens for those pages. The second is all but the logon screen ended up with changes, some significant by the time development was completed. Finally, I prepared the demo screens using InContext Spider under Windows 95 even though development was going to be done using Linux.

The basic system operation, ignoring logon for the present, is:

1. The user selects an operation from the main screen by clicking one of the radio buttons.
2. The user enters the directory path for the operation to occur in. The directory path is set by default at logon or the user changes it.
3. The user clicks the **Do It** button to execute the main program (rcsmain.pl).

4. rcsmain.pl displays the operation screen to the browser by writing the HTML code to STDOUT.

   The basic way most of the operations (check-in, check-out, etc.) work is:

1. The directory path cannot be changed. The path specified on the Main Page is used.
2. The filename is selected via a pull down list.
3. Any data, such as a change description for check-in, is entered.
4. Options are selected by clicking radio buttons.
5. The operation is executed by clicking the button with the operation label. Click **Check In** on the Check In Page to execute the check-in process.

   The same operation screen is displayed after the operation completes. Error messages are presented via JavaScript pop-up Alert boxes.

   The next step was preparing a data flow diagram (DFD) for the application operation. This is also included in the design section. The DFD is shown in a later section.

   Design is normally finished quickly when putting a Web front end on an existing legacy application. There is no design necessary for the application since is already exists. The design focuses solely on the user interface and the "glue" code it takes to tie the pieces together.

   Implementation and testing are the final steps. The application is built interactively one screen at a time. A screen here implies an HTML page with some JavaScript and a CGI Perl program. The HTML page is a form for data collection and an HTML table for formatting. The JavaScript code is embedded in the HTML code. It performs data entry validation and displays error messages for the server Perl program. The Perl program builds the command line for the specified RCS operation, executes the RCS program, and displays the next HTML page.

Some of the development techniques illustrated include:

- Passing arguments from Perl to JavaScript
- Using JavaScript to control execution flow of the overall system
- Performing tasks such as loading a file list into a pull down menu
- Using JavaScript to display error messages for the server program

The emphasis is on creating a working program that shows as many facets of Web client-server development as practical.

Tools Used

RCS is primarily a Unix application, although MS-DOS and VMS versions also exist. Therefore, a Unix implementation via Linux is featured. The PC and software used is:

- 166mz Pentium
- Red Hat 4.0 Linux
- Apache Web Server
- Netscape Navigator 3.0 for Linux
- RCS Version 5.7
- Perl 5.002

In addition, InContext Spider was used under Windows 95 to construct the demo pages.

This was the first full application that I have done with Linux. I generally use a Sun SparcServer running Solaris at work. I was very pleased with the development environment provided by Linux. It is easy to see why the majority of Web servers on the WWW are running Linux.

Design

The design for this case study is driven by the screens. The demo screens represent the starting point for the design. The Main Screen is central to the user interface and therefore central to the operation. It quickly becomes the main processing point. It's hard to say which is the central program because the pieces are spread between HTML screens with JavaScript and Perl programs on the server.

Based on the problem statement and the demo screens, the following operations are necessary for this applications:

- Logon
- Main Page to launch other RCS operations
- Add a new file to RCS (ci)
- Check out an RCS file (co)
- Check in an existing RCS file (ci)
- Display an overview
- Show the files that are checked out as locked (rlog)
- Install an RCS file (ci, co, and cp)

The majority of the operations correspond to executing a single RCS program.

The following Data Flow Diagram describes the RCS Web front-end application:

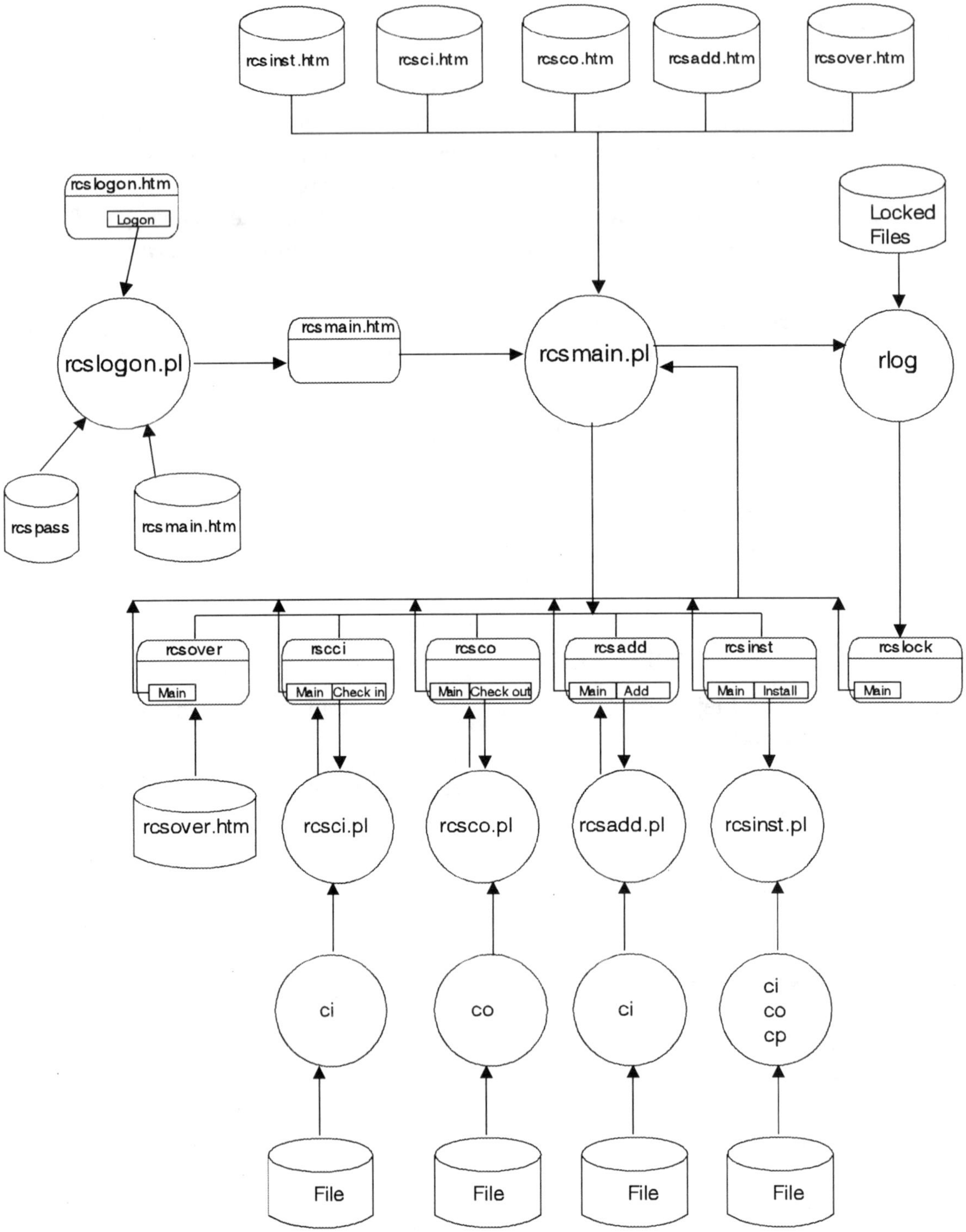
rcsinst.htm
rcsci.htm
rcsco.htm
rcsadd.htm
rcsover.htm
rcslogon.htm
Logon
Locked Files
rcslogon.pl
rcsmain.htm
rcsmain.pl
rlog
rcspass
rcsmain.htm
rcsover
Main
rscci
Main
Check in
rcsco
Main
Check out
rcsadd
Main
Add
rcsinst
Main
Install
rcslock
Main
rcsover.htm
rcsci.pl
rcsco.pl
rcsadd.pl
rcsinst.pl
ci
co
ci
ci
co
cp
File
File
File
File

The circles represent processes or programs. The rectangles with rounded corners are HTML pages, most of which contain some JavaScript processing. The rectangles with text on the HTML page represent buttons, Main, for example. The following sections describe the processing performed by each of the "operations" in the application.

Error Reporting

The error reporting technique used in this case study is a combination of JavaScript and HTML hidden fields. Error reporting is important in any GUI application. Error reporting here means displaying an error message to the user for an error detected in the server code. Errors are presented to the user via JavaScript pop-up Alert boxes.

Each HTML template file contains a hidden field named ErrorFlag with a value of 0:

```
<INPUT TYPE="HIDDEN" NAME="ErrorFlag" VALUE="$ErrorFlag">
```

The server Perl program substitutes an error value for $ErrorFlag when writing the HTML file to the browser. "0" is used to indicate no errors.

The JavaScript code in the HTML document tests the value of ErrorFlag at startup and pops up the appropriate dialog box. The things to remember about using JavaScript for error reporting are:

- Be sure to include the *NAME* attribute on the <FORM> tag.
- The name value must match the Form name used in the JavaScript object reference for the hidden value.
- The hidden field name must be used in object reference as well.

The following HTML/JavaScript code segment illustrates the above items:


```
<SCRIPT>
function ProcessErrorFlag(){
        if(document.RCSADD.ErrorFlag.value == "0"){
                alert("File Added to RCS!");
                return;
```

```
        }
        if(document.RCSADD.ErrorFlag.value == "256"){
                alert("File already in RCS!");
                return;
        }
}
</SCRIPT>
<BODY onLoad="ProcessErrorFlag()">
<FORM NAME="RCSADD" METHOD="POST" ACTION="/cgi-bin/rcsadd.pl">
<INPUT TYPE="HIDDEN" NAME="ErrorFlag" VALUE="0">
```

When the HTML file loads, it calls ProcessErrorFlag() via the *onLoad="ProcessErrorFlag()"* command in the <BODY> element. The JavaScript code executes and tests the error flag with:

```
        if(document.RCSADD.ErrorFlag.value == "0"){
                alert("File Added to RCS!");
                return;
        }
```

You can see the use of RCSADD and ErrorFlag in the JavaScript.

HINT: Hidden fields are a convenient way to pass data from the server CGI program to JavaScript.

Local Validation

Error reporting from local form validation is a little simpler since the error message can be displayed as soon as it is detected. The Alert box is the most common form of JavaScript error reporting.

rcslogon

This program verifies the user is allowed to use the application and optionally allows entry of the directory path to start RCS operations from. Default paths are supplied for the starting directory path. (There is no code in the application that validates logon in the later programs, although it is possible.)

HINT: There are several ways to implement login security within a Web application. The server security can be used to require access to the server. Server access can be limited to just computers with particular internet addresses. The user name and password or a user id can be passed as hidden fields between programs. Cookies can be used to keep the user password. It's a good idea to encrypt any logon information passed around a system.

rcsmain

The primary control point for the entire system is the RCS Main Page. It allows selection of the RCS operation to perform along with the option to modify the directory path.

rcsadd

The RCS Add Page adds a new file to RCS. The user selects the file to be added. The Perl portion:

- Makes sure an RCS directory exists
- Runs ci with the -i flag to mark a new file being inserted. An error is generated if the file already exists in RCS.
- Checks out the file after it is checked in

rcsci

An existing RCS file is checked back into RCS. The file must have been previously checked out with lock. The user selects the filename to check in from a pull down menu. The RCS ci program performs the actual check-in process.

rcsco

Files are checked out of RCS by the check-out operation. The file must have already been checked into RCS. A file must be checked out with lock before it can be checked in again.

rcsinst

This operation represents a real-world extension to the basic RCS system. Software development areas should be separated from production areas. A typical system might have the production programs in a /application/bin directory. The baseline source code would be in /application/src. Development should be done in yet a third directory, /application/dev/user. The typical sequence for modifying a program is:

- Check out the file with a lock set
- Copy the file to a development directory
- Copy the modified file back to the baseline directory
- Make modifications to the file
- Check the file into RCS clearing the lock
- Check the file back out of RCS without a lock set
- Copy the file to the production area

Applications may require additional steps if the source file needs compilation.

The Install Page and program perform most of the steps described above. This is an example of increased functionality that can be built using command line programs with a Web front end.

rcsover

This operation simply displays a short overview of the system and provides a button to return to the Main Page.

Implementation

If you understand the data flow diagram, then the implementation is relatively straightforward. I started implementation with the Logon Page, then rcslogon.pl and went from there. This section describes the implementation of each program more or less in the order they were developed.

Security Considerations

I did a couple of things during development that you should never do and a few things that could be done much safer from a security standpoint! The items discussed in this section are:

- Running the Web server as ROOT
- User authentication
- Encryption

Security is even more critical with intranet applications compared to the average Internet applications. Commerce applications with credit card numbers, etc., are an Internet application where security is also critical. Most Internet applications do not require a high level of security because their whole reason for existence is allowing public access. Most larger companies also run Web servers on dedicated machines to further minimize potential threats. Intranet applications are different because they often access sensitive data and systems which must be protected even more than normal Internet Web servers.

The security differences can be thought of this way; an Internet Web server allows anyone access, but it should have access only to public data, and an intranet Web server restricts user access but can access nonpublic data. This different mission makes the security requirements different for Internet and intranet Web applications.

Running As ROOT

The Web server actually runs the CGI Perl scripts. The scripts may read and write files outside the HTTPD tree. That means that the account that runs the Web server, Apache in this case, is effectively the user that executes CGI scripts. Apache runs as user NOBODY by default, which is the proper thing to do. I modified the configuration file, to run as ROOT because of my schedule crunch for completing the case studies for the book. [Note: Development of this case study took one evening working out the screen flows waiting for my daughter at ballet class. I started the code on a Friday night after work and finished it Sunday night about 8PM.] In my case where my Web server is not connected to a network, running as ROOT has few security impacts. Running your Web server connected to the

Internet or even a local LAN is very dangerous from a security perspective and should be avoided!

The right way to approach an application like the RCS Front End is running a dedicated server on a different port as the user who owns the files to be manipulated. You have been warned!

User Authentication

There are two forms of user authentication possible in Web applications. The first is via the Web server itself. There are several things that can be done via the server:

- The server can be set up to accept connections from specific IP addresses. Restricting IP addresses may or may not be practical if user connections are via PPP where the IP address changes every time the user starts his computer. Users coming in from a location with a firewall all appear to the Web server as a single IP address.
- Use the Secure Socket Layer (SSL) protocol.
- Restrict access to servers via Server level password.
- Make sure proper permissions are set up in the server to restrict file access according to need.
- Make sure all security patches for the host operating system and Web server are installed.
- Use a firewall. A firewall can be set up to prevent external access to Web servers running intranet applications.

The second is at the application level. This is a bit more tricky because there is no authentication beyond the SSL that most browsers support. The application must totally supply the capability beyond that. It's relatively easy to display a logon screen, validate the username and password, and allow processing accordingly. The problem comes from passing either username/password or user ID around a system unprotected. A Web system can be compromised by simply reading over a user's shoulder unless the system is implemented properly. Several things can be done with user authentication at the application level to enhance security:

- Avoid Form method of GET when possible. GET displays the CGI string in the URL window in the browser.
- Encrypt CGI data.
- Use pre-expired HTML cookies. These are normally not visible to the user and never get written to the client computer system.
- Make sure every program in the application verifies that a valid user ID or username/password combination accompanies the request.

Web applications can be built to be very secure. The catch is it must be done on purpose from the beginning.

Encryption

The previous section mentioned encryption several times. There are two areas where encryption applies: data and control information. Data is any data that is exchanged between the Web server and browser. The simplest and most practical way to encrypt that data is using SSL that is built into most servers today. If data is encrypted at the application level, then decryption code must be sent to the browser. This can potentially defeat the encryption by providing the mechanism to decrypt it.

Control information includes username, passwords, user Ids, and any other data that is restricted. One system I developed required URLs be encrypted because users had different access profiles. Encrypting URLs prevented a user from copying a URL over another user's shoulder and accessing data they did not have access to.

There are at least two publicly available encryption algorithms available. Perl implementations of DES are available on the Internet in as few as four or five lines of code. A very simple XOR algorithm was published in *Software Tools* by Kernighan and Plauger, which was published in 1976.

HINT: Pass control information via pre-expired cookies, whether encrypted or not! This makes it harder for users to access the information.

HINT: Use a runtime encryption key. This prevents a single key being used for all users. It also prevents the key from being hard coded in programs.

Require Files

A couple of source files that are not documented separately in the design need to be discussed. Files included in Perl source via the require statement are generally termed "require files." Require files are a Perl mechanism similar to C's #include statement. The general form is:

```
require "filename";
```

If *filename* does not include the full directory path, Perl looks in the Perl library directory (usually /perl/lib), then in the current directory. This is one of those places where being explicit is the safe thing to do!

HINT: Always specify the full directory path when including a file in Perl via the require statement!

The two require files used in this case study are tools.req and vars.req.

tools.req contains general CGI "tools" that are used in multiple programs with no changes. There are two user level subroutines in tools.req, dump_QS() and parse_CGI(). dump_QS() prints the contents of all the key/value pairs in the %QS associative array. dump_QS() is important during debugging because it prints the CGI arguments passed from HTML forms to the screen. parse_CGI() retrieves the CGI string passed from an HTML form, parses it, and stores each in the %QS associative array for later processing. This subroutine automatically handles data both passed via the GET and POST form methods, which is very convenient for times when a program may be called with GET in some cases and POST in others. The source code for tools.req is:

```
#
# FILE: tools.req
########################+---------+
#                       | dump_QS |
#                       +---------+
sub dump_QS{
	foreach $key (keys(%QS)){
		print "QS{'$key'}: $QS{$key}<BR>\n";
	}
}
########################+-----------+
#                       | parse_cgi |
#                       +-----------+
sub parse_cgi{
	local($i);
	local($key);
	local($val);
	local($QString);

	if($ENV{'REQUEST_METHOD'} eq "GET"){
		$QString = $ENV{'QUERY_STRING'};
	}else{
		$LEN = $ENV{'CONTENT_LENGTH'};
		read(STDIN,$QString,$LEN);
	}

	@QS = split(/&/,$QString);

	foreach $i (0 .. $#QS){
		$QS[$i] =~ s/\+/ /g;
		($key,$val) = split(/=/,$QS[$i],2);

		$key =~ s/%(..)/pack("c",hex($1))/ge;
		$val =~ s/%(..)/pack("c",hex($1))/ge;

		$QS{$key} .= "\0" if (defined($QS{$key}));
```

```
                $QS{$key} .= $val;
        }
}
return 1;
```

The second require file is vars.req. It is a convenient repository for system wide variables. The file contains full path constants for commonly used files. The advantage is the require file alone has to be changed if HTML file were moved to a new directory for example.

```
#
# FILE: vars.req
#
$PASS_DIR     = "/home/httpd/cgi-bin";
$HTML_DIR     = "/home/httpd/html";
$TEMPLATE_DIR = "/home/httpd/html/template";
return 1;
```

HINT: Although I did not do it here, it's a good idea to include the full path of program names in the global variables require file to prevent path problems. Linux stores the RCS programs in /usr/bin, which is generally in the default path. On Solaris, the RCS programs are generally in /usr/local/bin, which is not in the default path. Not specifying the full path is usually the problem when the Perl program works when run from the command line but not when run from the Web server.

RCS Logon

The user begins using the RCS front end by logging on via the RCS Logon Page. This section discusses the HTML/JavaScript source file for the page and the Perl program that processes the logon when the Logon button is clicked.

The HTML file is actually a client side program in addition to the HTML it contains. There is JavaScript code that performs simple form validation and error reporting. The HTML code provides the user interface via a fill-in-the-blank HTML form and that contains an embedded HTML table for formatting.

The user loads rcslogon.htm to start a session. The following browser display is generated:

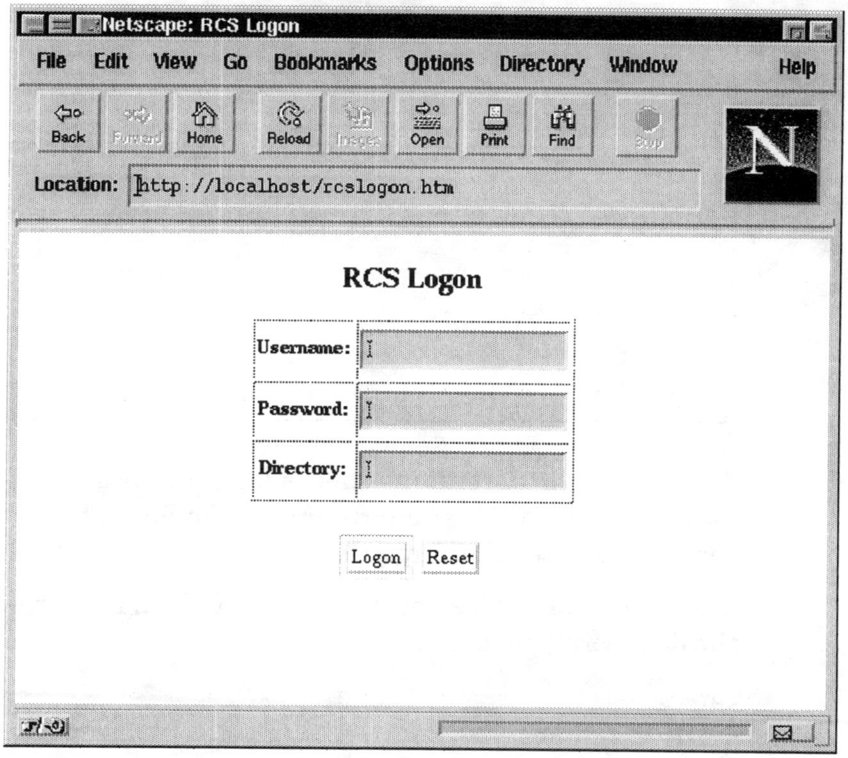

Assume the user leaves out the password. The JavaScript validation code generates an Alert box with the error message when the Logon button is clicked:

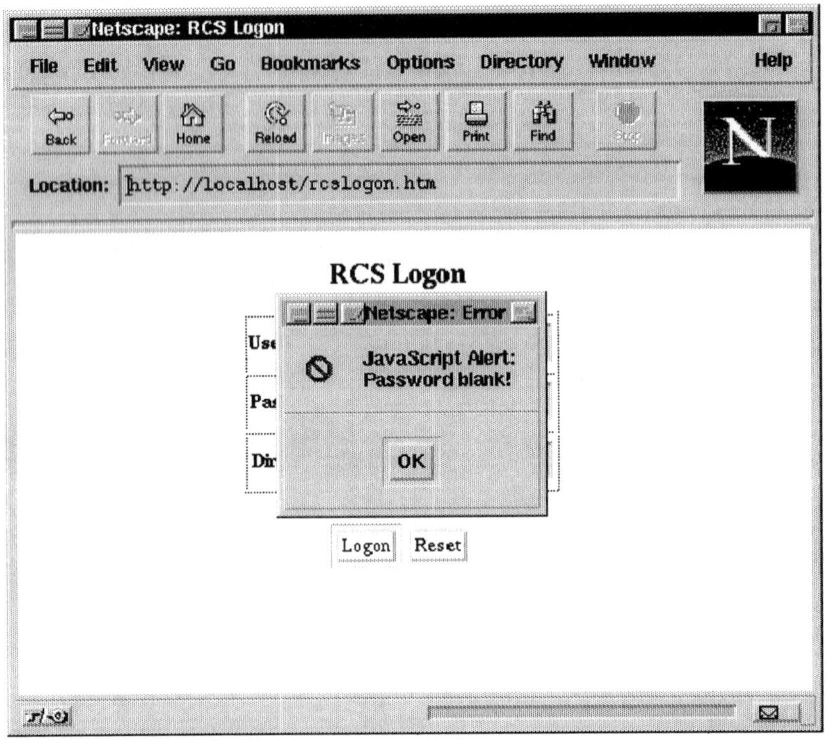

The rcslogon.htm contains checks for both missing username and password. The browser short-circuits the Submit process, allowing the user to enter the empty field.

The rcslogon.htm file begins with the HTML header, which contains the JavaScript code:

```
<HTML>
<HEAD>
<TITLE>RCS Logon</TITLE>
<!--rcslogon.htm-->
<SCRIPT LANGUAGE="JAVASCRIPT">
function validate(){
        if(document.logon.USER.value == ""){
                alert("Username blank!");
                return false;
        }
        if(document.logon.PASS.value == ""){
                alert("Password blank!");
                return false;
```

```
        }
        return true;
}
function CheckErrorFlag(){
        if(document.logon.ErrorFlag.value != "0"){
                alert("Login failed. Invalid User Name or Password!");
        }
}
</SCRIPT>
```

The validate() function makes sure that there is something in both the username and password fields. It pops up an Alert box if either is blank. validate() returns true when no error is detected and false when an error is detected. validate() is called by the browser when the Logon button is clicked.

The second function, CheckErrorFlag(), examines the *ErrorFlag* hidden field on the form. If its value is nonzero, an Alert box is displayed. CheckErrorFlag() is called automatically after the document is loaded by specifying the *onClick* event in the <BODY> element.

HINT: Use hidden fields to pass parameters from the CGI program to JavaScript. Then specify a function to execute via the *onload* event.

The remainder of rcslogon.htm is the normal HTML to generate the RCS Logon Page:

```
</HEAD>
<BODY onLoad="CheckErrorFlag()" BGCOLOR="#FFFFFF">
<H1 ALIGN="CENTER">RCS Logon</H1>
<CENTER>
<FORM NAME="logon" METHOD="POST" ACTION="/cgi-bin/rcslogon.pl"
onSubmit="return validate();">
<!-- ErrorFlag is used to pass info to JavaScript -->
<INPUT TYPE="HIDDEN" NAME="ErrorFlag" VALUE="0">
<TABLE BORDER>
<TR>
  <TH>Username:</TH>
```

```
  <TD><INPUT TYPE="TEXT" NAME="USER"></TD>
</TR>
<TR>
  <TH>Password:</TH>
  <TD><INPUT TYPE="PASSWORD" NAME="PASS"></TD>
</TR>
<TR>
  <TH>Directory:</TH>
  <TD><INPUT TYPE="TEXT" NAME="DIR"></TD>
</TR>
</TABLE>
<br>
<INPUT TYPE="SUBMIT" VALUE="Logon">
<INPUT TYPE="RESET" VALUE="Reset">
</CENTER>
</FORM>
</BODY>
</HTML>
```

Clicking the Logon button causes rcslogon.pl to execute. rcslogon.pl consists of a short "main" section and two subroutines. The main portion of the code extracts the CGI string by calling &parse_cgi(). It sets key/value pairs in the %QS associative array. The CGI string is a series of *key=value* pairs which map well into Perl's associative arrays. The subroutine is contained in tools.req.

The call to &dump_QS() is a debugging aid. It dumps the contents of the %QS associative array.

```
#!/usr/local/bin/perl
######################################################################
# FILE: rcslogon.pl
####################################
$TOOL_DIR     = "/home/httpd/cgi-bin";

require "$TOOL_DIR/tools.req";
require "$TOOL_DIR/vars.req";
        #
        # Global stuff
        #
&parse_cgi();          # Get data passed in from the HTML form
        #
```

```
        # The following two lines used for debugging
        #
#print "Content-type: text/html\n\n";
#&dump_QS();
```

The following section of code validates the username/password combination. The password file, rcspass, separates each field with a ":". Therefore, a single string can be built in the form:

```
        username:password:
```

to search for a match. The entire password file is loaded into memory and the memory array searched. This technique works well with small files but would not be practical if the system has thousands of users.

```
        #
        # Build parameter string to pass to look up
        #
$user_pw = "$QS{'USER'}:$QS{'PASS'}:";
        #
        # Load password file into memory
        #
open(PWD,"$PASS_DIR/rcspass")
        || die "Can't open Password file!\n";
while(<PWD>){
        chop;
        push(@data,$_);
}
close(PWD);
        #
        # search the password for name and password
        #
$success = 0;
foreach $passwd (@data){
        if($passwd =~ /^$user_pw/){
                $success = 1;
                &successful_logon($passwd);
                last;
        }
}
```

```
if($success == 0){
        &invalid_user();     # No data means logon failed.
}
exit;
```

$success is "0" when there is no match or "1" when there is a match. A "successful" logon causes the subroutine successful_logon() to be called. An unsuccessful logon executes invalid_user(). The primary difference between the actions of the two subroutines is the substitution of variable values. &successful_logon() returns several field values in rcsmain.htm and &invalid_user() only the *ErrorFlag* value in rcslogon.htm.

```
#######################+------------------+
#                      | successful_logon |
#                      +------------------+
# The format for the password file is:
#       username:password:real name:default check in dir:default
sub successful_logon{
        @db = split(/:/,$passwd);
        if($QS{'DIR'} eq ""){
                $QS{'DIR'}  = $db[3];
        }
        $QS{'DIR'} =~ s/\/\//\//g;
        $QS{'DEST'} = $db[4];
        $QS{'DEST'} =~ s/\/\//\//g;
        print "Content-type:  text/html\n\n";
        open (HTML,"$HTML_DIR//rcsmain.htm")
                || die "Can't open rcsmain.htm\n";

        while(<HTML>){
                if(/\$DIR/){
                        s/\$DIR/$QS{'DIR'}/e;
                }
                if(/\$DEST/){
                        s/\$DEST/$QS{'DEST'}/e;
                }
                if(/\$REV/){
                        s/\$REV/$QS{'REV'}/e;
                }
```

```
                if(/\$USER/){
                        s/\$USER/$QS{'USER'}/e;
                }
                if(/\$PASS/){
                        s/\$PASS/$QS{'PASS'}/e;
                }
                print "$_";
        }
        close(HTML);

        return;
}
########################+--------------+
#                       | invalid_user |
#                       +--------------+
sub invalid_user{
        print "Content-type:  text/html\n\n";
        open (HTML,"$HTML_DIR/rcslogon.htm")
                || die "Can't open rcslogon.htm\n";

        while(<HTML>){
                s/NAME=\"ErrorFlag\" VALUE=\"0\"/NAME=\"ErrorFlag\"
VALUE=\"1\"/;
                print "$_";
        }
        close(HTML);

        return;
}
```

The following listing is the contents of rcspass used for testing.

```
smith:norm:Norman Smith:/home/smithn/src:/home/httpd/cgi-bin
jones:john:John Jones:/home/jones:/home/httpd/cgi-bin
doe:john:John Doe:/home/doe:/home/httpd/cgi-bin
```

Assuming a successful logon, the user is presented with the RCS Main Page:

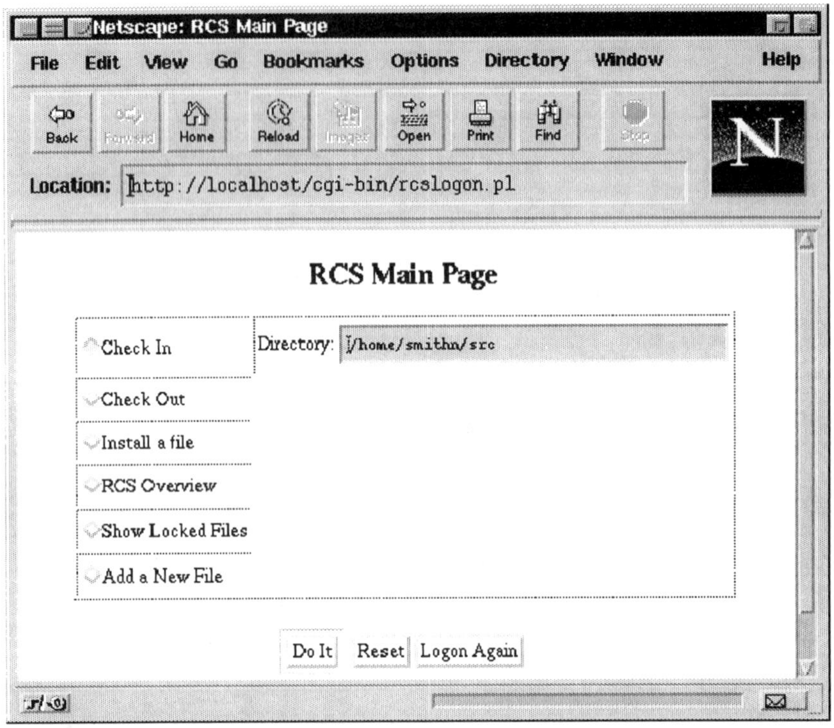

RCS is essentially controlled from this page for the case study. The current directory is displayed in the Directory text box. The initial value is the default value from the rcspass file.

There is a very small amount of JavaScript in the HTML <HEADER>. There are two functions, check_dir() and logon(). The check_dir() function is executed when the Do It button is clicked to make sure that the directory string contains text. It pops up an Alert box when DIR is empty. The logon() is tied to the Logon Again button. It brings up the RCS Logon Page to allow the user to log on again. The rest of the HTML file generates the display. The listing for rcsmain.htm is:

```
<HTML>
<!--rcsmain.htm-->
<!--03/01/97    -->
<HEAD>
<TITLE>RCS Main Page</TITLE>
<SCRIPT LANGUAGE="JAVASCRIPT">
<!-- Hide JavaScript from old browsers
```

```
function check_dir(){
        if(document.RCSMAIN.DIR.value == ""){
                alert("Directory Blank!");
                return false;
        }
}
function logon(){
        window.location.href = "../rcslogon.htm";
}
//      -->
</SCRIPT>
</HEAD>
<BODY BGCOLOR="#FFFFFF">
<H1 ALIGN="CENTER">RCS Main Page</H1>
<CENTER>
<FORM METHOD="POST" NAME="RCSMAIN" onSubmit="return check_dir();"
ACTION="/cgi-bin/rcsmain.pl">
<INPUT TYPE="HIDDEN" NAME="USER" VALUE="$USER">
<INPUT TYPE="HIDDEN" NAME="PASS" VALUE="$PASS">
<INPUT TYPE="HIDDEN" NAME="DEST" VALUE="$DEST">
<TABLE BORDER>
<TR>
  <TD><INPUT TYPE="RADIO" NAME="OPR" VALUE="CI" CHECKED>Check In</TD>
  <TD>Directory: <INPUT TYPE="TEXT" NAME="DIR" VALUE="$DIR"
SIZE="40"></TD>
</TR>
<TR>
  <TD><INPUT TYPE="RADIO" NAME="OPR" VALUE="CO">Check Out</TD>
</TR>
<TR>
  <TD><INPUT TYPE="RADIO" NAME="OPR" VALUE="INSTALL">Install a
file</TD>
  <TD></TD>
</TR>
<TR>
  <TD><INPUT TYPE="RADIO" NAME="OPR" VALUE="OVER">RCS Overview</TD>
  <TD></TD>
</TR>
<TR>
  <TD><INPUT TYPE="RADIO" NAME="OPR" VALUE="LOCK">Show Locked
Files</TD>
  <TD></TD>
</TR>
```

```
<TR>
  <TD><INPUT TYPE="RADIO" NAME="OPR" VALUE="ADD">Add a New File</TD>
  <TD></TD>
</TR>
</TABLE>
<BR>
<INPUT TYPE="SUBMIT" VALUE="Do It">
<INPUT TYPE="RESET"  VALUE="Reset">
<INPUT TYPE="BUTTON" VALUE="Logon Again" onClick="logon()">
</FORM>
</BODY>
</HTML>
```

The code for rcsmain.pl is next. It starts processing by extracting the CGI variables into %QS by calling &parse_cgi(). The bulk of the remainder of the main code section (the source to the *exit;* command) sets $template to the HTML template file associated with the specified RCS operation. The RCS operation is passed from rcsmain.htm in the *OPR* key. The subroutine &load_next_page() is called to write the template HTML file to the browser. Displaying the locked files is the only exception. The listing for rcsmain.pl is:

```
#!/usr/local/bin/perl
##################################################################
# FILE: rcsmain.pl
##################################
$TOOL_DIR     = "/home/httpd/cgi-bin";

require "$TOOL_DIR/tools.req";
require "$TOOL_DIR/vars.req";
        #
        # Global stuff
        #

&parse_cgi();          # Get data passed in from the HTML form
        #
        # Validate data...
        #
if($QS{'OPR'} eq "CI"){
        $template = "rcsci.htm";
}
if($QS{'OPR'} eq "CO"){
```

```
        $template   = "rcsco.htm";
        $QS{'DIR'} =~ s/\/RCS//g;
        $QS{'DIR'} .= "/RCS";
}
if($QS{'OPR'} eq "COO"){
        $template   = "rcsco.htm";
        $QS{'DIR'} =~ s/\/RCS//g;
}
if($QS{'OPR'} eq "LOCK"){
        $template = "rcslock.htm";
        &process_LOCK();
        exit;
}
if($QS{'OPR'} eq "INSTALL"){
        $template = "rcsinst.htm";
}
if($QS{'OPR'} eq "ADD"){
        $template = "rcsadd.htm";
}
if($QS{'OPR'} eq "OVER"){
        $template = "rcsover.htm";
}
if($template eq ""){
        print "Content-type: text/html\n\n";
        print "Invalid option! QS{'OPR'} = $QS{'OPR'}\n";
        exit;
}
&load_next_page();
exit;
########################+----------------+
#                       | load_next_page |
#                       +----------------+
sub load_next_page{
        $QS{'DIR'} =~ s/\/\/+/\//g;
        print "Content-type:  text/html\n\n";
        open (HTML,"$HTML_DIR/$template")
                || die "Can't open rcsmain.htm\n";

        while(<HTML>){
                if(/\$DIR/){
                        s/\$DIR/$QS{'DIR'}/e;
                }
                if(/\$dir/){
```

15

```
                        s/\$dir/$QS{'DIR'}/e;
                }
                if(/\$REV/){
                        s/\$REV/$QS{'REV'}/e;
                }
                if(/\$DEST/){
                        s/\$DEST/$QS{'DEST'}/e;
                }
                if(/\$PASS/){
                        s/\$PASS/$QS{'PASS'}/e;
                }
                if(/\$USER/){
                        s/\$USER/$QS{'USER'}/e;
                }
                print "$_";
                if(/<SELECT NAME=\"FILE\"/){
                        &insert_files();
                }
        }
        close(HTML);

        return;
}
#######################+--------------+
#                      | insert_files |
#                      +--------------+
sub insert_files{
        local($files);
        local($selected);

        $selected = "";
        $files    = 0;
        print "     <OPTION VALUE=\"\*\*NONE\*\*\" SELECTED>";
        print "Select A File</OPTION>\n";

        open(DIR,"ls -1F $QS{'DIR'} |")
                || die "Can't list files!\n";
        while(<DIR>){
                if(/\//){      next;   }
                s/\*//g;
                chop;                   # delete "\n"
                print "<OPTION VALUE=\"$_\">$_</OPTION>";
                $files++;
```

```
        }
}
#######################+--------------+
#                      | process_LOCK |
#                      +--------------+
sub process_LOCK{

        chdir("$QS{'DIR'}");

        print "Content-type:  text/html\n\n";
        print "<HTML>\n";
        print "<HEAD>\n";
        print "<TITLE>RCS Show Locked Page</TITLE>\n";
        print "</HEAD>\n";
        print "<BODY BGCOLOR=\"#FFFFFF\">\n";
        print "<H1 ALIGN=\"CENTER\">RCS Show Locked</H1>\n";
        print "<FORM NAME=\"RCSLOCK\" METHOD=\"POST\" ";
        print " ACTION=\"/cgi-bin/rcslock.pl\">\n";
        print "<B>Directory:</B> $QS{'DIR'}\n";
        print "<BR><BR>\n";
        print "<B>Locked Files:</B> <BR>\n";

        open(LOCK,"rlog -R -L RCS/* |")
                || die "Can't generate Lock List!\n";
        while(<LOCK>){
                print "$_<BR>";
        }
        close(LOCK);

        print "<HR>\n";
        print "<BR>\n";
        print "<B>Detailed Listing</B><BR>\n";
        print "<BR><PRE>\n";
        open(LOCK,"rlog -L -h RCS/* |")
                || die "Can't generate Lock List!\n";
        while(<LOCK>){
                print "$_";
        }
        close(LOCK);

        print "</PRE><BR>\n";
        print "<HR>\n";
        print "<CENTER>\n";
```

```
        print "<INPUT TYPE=\"BUTTON\" VALUE=\"BACK\"";
        print "onClick=\"history.back()\">\n";
        print "</CENTER>\n";
        print "<BR>\n";
        print "</FORM>\n";
        print "</BODY>\n";
        print "</HTML>\n";

}
```

The process for displaying locked files is simple enough that the code is contained within rcsmain.pl in subroutine &process_LOCK(). This subroutine executes the RCS rlog program to generate the listing in the body of the generated page.

HINT: Make sure any external program run in a CGI script is in the execution path. In this example, rlog is in /usr/bin, which is in the default path. On Solaris, rlog is in /usr/local/bin which is not in the default path. The safe thing to do is always include full execution paths when running an external program.

The screen generated by &process_LOCK() is:

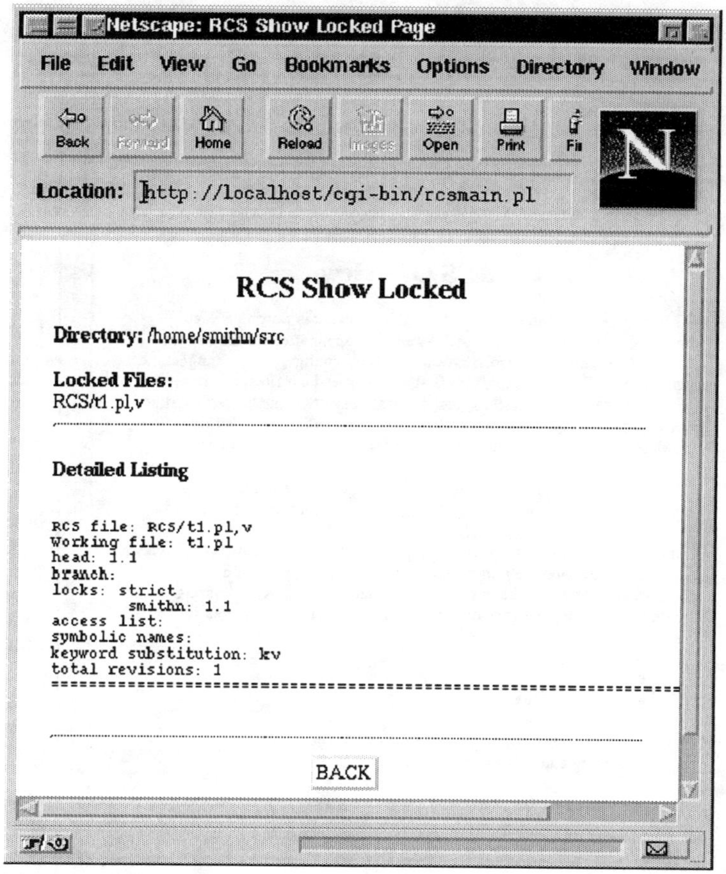

A second option on the RCS Main Page that generates a screen but has no code is the RCS Overview; it is simply an HTML page. When the user selects "RCS Overview," then clicks Do It, the following page is displayed:

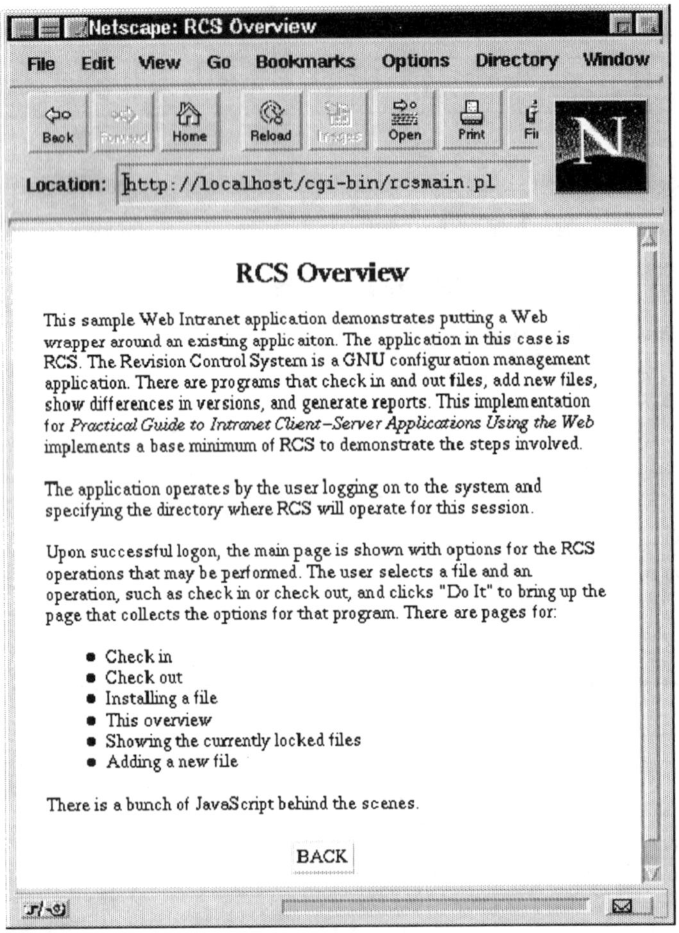

The HTML file for the overview is rcsover.htm:

```
<HTML>
<!-- rcsover.htm -->
<HEAD>
<TITLE>RCS Overview</TITLE>
<SCRIPT>

</SCRIPT>
</HEAD>
<BODY BGCOLOR="#FFFFFF">
<H1 ALIGN="CENTER">RCS Overview</H1>
<P>
```

```
This sample Web intranet application demonstrates putting
a Web wrapper around an existing application. The application
in this case is RCS. The Revision Control System is a GNU
configuration management application. There are programs that
check in and out files, add new files, show differences in
versions, and generate reports. This implementation for
<I>Practical Guide to Intranet Client-Server Applications
Using the Web</I> implements a base minimum of RCS to
demonstrate the steps involved.
<P>
The application operates by the user logging on to the
system and specifying the directory where RCS will operate
for this session.
<P>
Upon successful logon, the main page is shown with options
for the RCS operations that may be performed. The user
selects a file and an operation, such as check in or
check out, and clicks "Do It" to bring up the page that
collects the options for that program. There are pages for:
<UL>
<LI>Adding a new file
<LI>Check out
<LI>Installing a file
<LI>Check in
<LI>This overview
<LI>Showing the currently locked files
</UL>
<P>
There is a bunch of JavaScript behind the scenes.
<P>
This application breaks some security rules and should
not be used for real work!
<CENTER>
<FORM NAME="RCSOVER">
<INPUT TYPE="BUTTON" VALUE="BACK" onClick="history.back()">
</CENTER>
</BODY>
</HTML>
```

The user can click the Back button to return to the RCS Main Page.

RCSADD

The RCS Add Page is accessed by the user clicking on Add a New File on the RCS Main Page. The rcsmain.pl script copies the rcsadd.htm file to the browser. rcsadd.htm generates the following display:

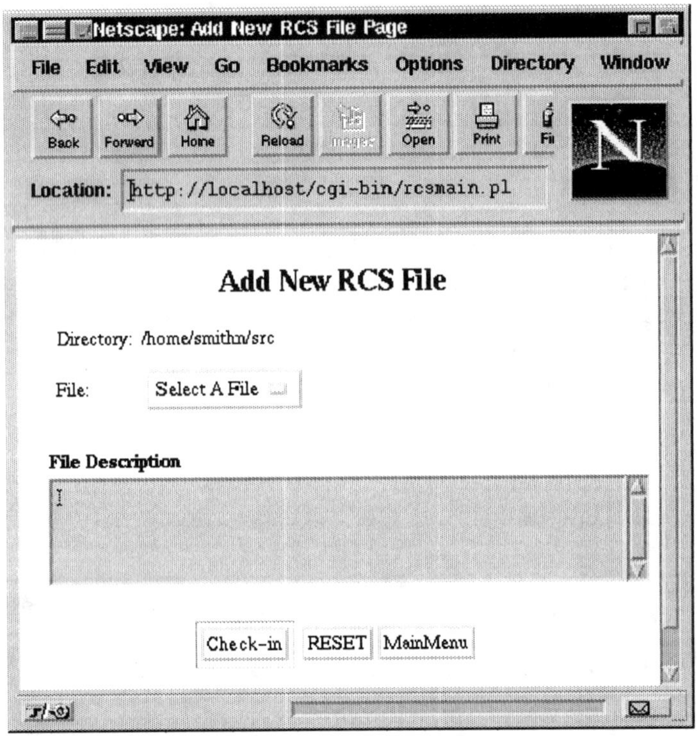

The user selects a file from the pull down menu, enters a description of the file, then clicks Check-in. Adding a new file to RCS is a special case of the RCS ci program. The program description rather than the change description is used, and an error is generated if the file already exists in RCS.

The following display is generated to add the file t3.pl to RCS:

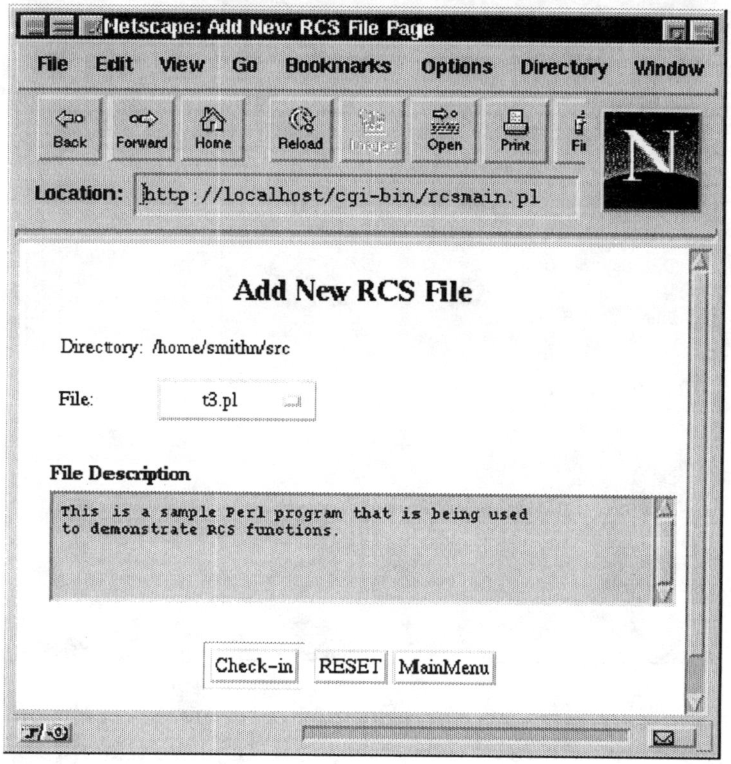

The user clicks Check-in to execute rcsadd.pl to execute the actual RCS ci program. Successfully adding the file results in the following display:

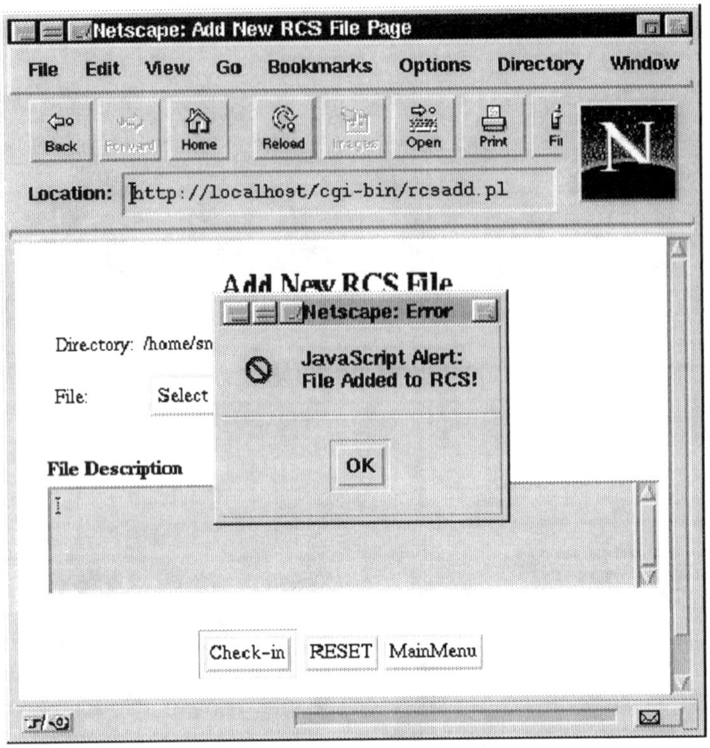

rcsadd.htm has two JavaScript functions. One, ProcessErrorFlag(), checks the value of *ErrorFlag* and displays the appropriate Alert box. "File Added to RCS!" or "File already in RCS!" is displayed in the Alert box depending on the *ErrorFlag* value.

The second JavaScript function is reload_main(). It builds the URL and loads the RCS Main Page.

The HTML portion of the file generates the Add New File Page. The code for rcsadd.htm is:

```
<HTML>
<!-- rcsadd.htm -->
<HEAD>
<TITLE>Add New RCS File Page</TITLE>
</HEAD>
<SCRIPT>
<!--
function ProcessErrorFlag(){
        if(document.RCSADD.ErrorFlag.value == "0"){
```

```
            alert("File Added to RCS!");
            return;
        }
        if(document.RCSADD.ErrorFlag.value == "256"){
            alert("File already in RCS!");
            return;
        }
}
function reload_main(){
        var url;

        url = "/cgi-bin/rcslogon.pl?DIR=" +
                document.RCSADD.DIR.value +
                "&OPR=CI" +
                "&USER=" + document.RCSADD.USER.value +
                "&PASS=" + document.RCSADD.PASS.value;
        window.location.href=url;
}
//      -->
</SCRIPT>
<BODY NAME="RCSADD" onLoad="ProcessErrorFlag()" BGCOLOR="#FFFFFF">
<H1 ALIGN="CENTER">Add New RCS File</H1>
<FORM NAME="RCSADD" METHOD="POST" ACTION="/cgi-bin/rcsadd.pl">
<INPUT TYPE="HIDDEN" NAME="ErrorFlag" VALUE="$ErrorFlag">
<INPUT TYPE="HIDDEN" NAME="DIR"       VALUE="$DIR">
<INPUT TYPE="HIDDEN" NAME="USER"      VALUE="$USER">
<INPUT TYPE="HIDDEN" NAME="PASS"      VALUE="$PASS">
<INPUT TYPE="HIDDEN" NAME="OPR"       VALUE="CI">
<TABLE>
  <TR>
    <TD>Directory:</TD>
    <TD>$DIR</TD>
  </TR>
  <TR>
    <TD>File:</TD>
    <TD><SELECT NAME="FILE" SIZE=1>
        </SELECT>
    </TD>
  </TR>
</TABLE>
<BR>
<B>File Description</B>
<BR>
```

```
<TEXTAREA NAME="DESC" ROWS=5 COLS=60 MAXLEN=1000
WRAP="PHYSICAL"></TEXTAREA>
<BR>
<CENTER>
<INPUT TYPE="SUBMIT" VALUE="Check-in">
<INPUT TYPE="RESET"  VALUE="RESET">
<INPUT TYPE="BUTTON" VALUE="MainMenu" onClick="reload_main()">
</CENTER>
<BR>
</FORM>
</BODY>
</HTML>
```

The Perl script rcsadd.pl executes when the Check-in button is clicked. It takes the filename and description, builds the appropriate ci command line, executes the command, and writes the rcsadd.htm template back to the browser.

The structure of the program is similar to the other programs described so far. The main portion extracts the arguments from the CGI string by calling &parse_cgi(). The lines from the description text box are concatenated into a single string named $DESC. The program changes directory to the correct directory, because the Web server runs it from cgi-bin and executes the ci command via system() command.

```
#!/usr/local/bin/perl
######################################################################
# FILE: rcsadd.pl
####################################
$TOOL_DIR     = "/home/httpd/cgi-bin";

require "$TOOL_DIR/tools.req";
require "$TOOL_DIR/vars.req";
        #
        # Global stuff
        #
&parse_cgi();         # Get data passed in from the HTML form
        #
        # Make sure that the File Description ends with a "."
        # on a line by itself. This is required by RCS.
        #
```

```
@desc = split(/\n/,$QS{'DESC'});
if($desc[$#desc] ne "."){
        push(@desc,".");
}
        #
        # Put the description back together into a single
        # string for passing to ci.
        #
$DESC = "";
foreach $line (@desc){
        $DESC .= "$line";
}
        #
        # Make sure there is an RCS directory
        #
chdir("$QS{'DIR'}");
system("mkdir RCS");

$status = system("ci -q -i -t-\"$DESC\" $QS{'FILE'}");
&good_add();
exit;
########################+----------+
#                       | good_add |
#                       +----------+
sub good_add{
        print "Content-type:  text/html\n\n";
        open (HTML,"$HTML_DIR//rcsadd.htm")
                || die "Can't open rcsadd.htm\n";

        while(<HTML>){
                if(/\$ErrorFlag/){
                        s/\$ErrorFlag/$status/e;
                }
                if(/\$DIR/){
                        s/\$DIR/$QS{'DIR'}/e;
                }
                if(/\$REV/){
                        s/\$REV/$QS{'REV'}/e;
                }
                if(/\$USER/){
                        s/\$USER/$QS{'USER'}/e;
                }
                if(/\$PASS/){
```

```
                        s/\$PASS/$QS{'PASS'}/e;
                }
                print "$_";
                if(/<SELECT NAME=\"FILE\"/){
                        &insert_files();
                }
        }
        close(HTML);

        return;
}
########################+--------------+
#                       | insert_files |
#                       +--------------+
sub insert_files{
        print "     <OPTION VALUE=\"\*\*NONE\*\*\" SELECTED>";
        print "Select A File</option>";
        open(DIR,"ls -1F $QS{'DIR'} |");
        while(<DIR>){
                if(/\//){       next;   }
                s/\*//g;
                print "<OPTION VALUE=\"$_\">$_</option>";
        }
}
```

The function good_add() is executed upon return from the ci operation. It repaints the Add RCS File Page allowing the user to add more than one file at a time. good_add() returns the status of the ci operation in *ErrorFlag* for the JavaScript code to use.

There are a couple of obvious enhancements that could be made to this example. Probably the easiest is listing only those files not already in RCS in the Select A File pull down menu. Collecting a few additional data items would allow automatic creation of a descriptive program header block. This could be important if consistent program headers are required in your organization as part of the software development process.

RCSCO

The second logical RCS operation is checking out an existing RCS file. The check-out operation is invoked by the user selecting the Check-Out radio button and clicking Do It on the RCS Main Page. The RCS Check-Out Page is displayed:

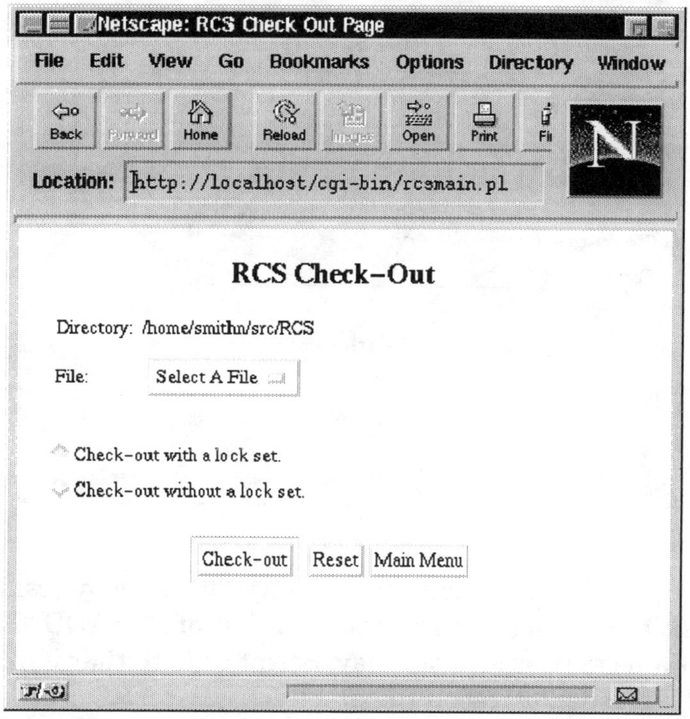

The user selects the file to check out and clicks Check-Out to run rcsco.pl. Assuming that the check-out operation was successful, the Check-Out Page is repainted and an Alert box pops up to provide the status of the check-out operation. The display for a successful check-out is:

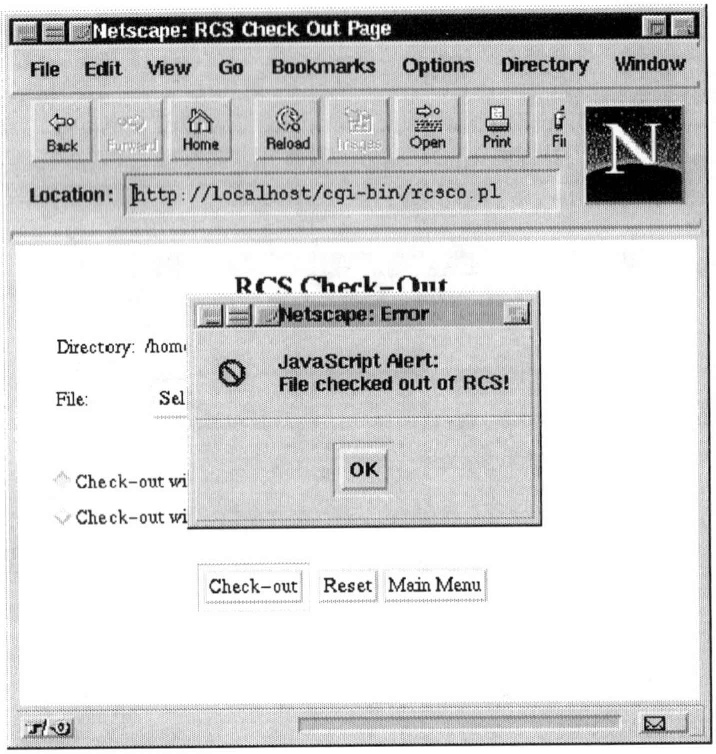

The HTML file, rcsco.htm, is painted initially by rcsmain.pl. The basic processing is very similar to that of RCSADD. The rcsco.htm contains almost identical JavaScript code to that in rcsadd.htm. The HTML code for rcsco.htm is:

```
<HTML>
<!-- rcsco.htm -->
<HEAD>
<TITLE>RCS Check Out Page</TITLE>
<SCRIPT>
<!--
function ProcessErrorFlag(){
        if(document.RCSCO.ErrorFlag.value == "0"){
                alert("File checked out of RCS!");
                return;
        }
        if(document.RCSCO.ErrorFlag.value == "256"){
                alert("File already checked out! No Action Taken!");
                return;
```

```
        }
}
function reload_main(){
        var url;

        url = "/cgi-bin/rcslogon.pl?DIR=" +
                document.RCSCO.DIR.value +
                &OPR=COO" +
                "&USER=" + document.RCSCO.USER.value +
                "&PASS=" + document.RCSCO.PASS.value;
        window.location.href=url;
}
//      -->
</SCRIPT>
</HEAD>
<BODY onLoad="ProcessErrorFlag()" BGCOLOR="#FFFFFF">
<H1 ALIGN="CENTER">RCS Check-Out</H1>
<FORM NAME="RCSCO" METHOD="POST" ACTION="/cgi-bin/rcsco.pl">
<INPUT TYPE="HIDDEN" NAME="ErrorFlag" VALUE="$ErrorFlag">
<INPUT TYPE="HIDDEN" NAME="DIR"       VALUE="$DIR">
<INPUT TYPE="HIDDEN" NAME="USER"      VALUE="$USER">
<INPUT TYPE="HIDDEN" NAME="PASS"      VALUE="$PASS">
<INPUT TYPE="HIDDEN" NAME="OPR"       VALUE="COO">
<TABLE>
  <TR>
    <TD>Directory:</TD>
    <TD>$dir</TD>
  </TR>
  <TR>
    <TD>File:</TD>
    <TD><SELECT NAME="FILE" SIZE=1>
        </SELECT>
    </TD>
  </TR>
</TABLE>
<BR>
<INPUT TYPE="RADIO" CHECKED NAME="LOCK" VALUE="-l">
  Check-out with a lock set.
<BR>
<INPUT TYPE="RADIO" NAME="LOCK" VALUE="-u">
  Check-out without a lock set.
<BR>
<BR>
```

```
<CENTER>
<INPUT TYPE="SUBMIT" VALUE="Check-out">
<INPUT TYPE="RESET" VALUE="Reset">
<INPUT TYPE="BUTTON" VALUE="Main Menu" onClick="reload_main()">
</CENTER>
<BR>
</FORM>
</BODY>
</HTML>
```

The Perl script rcsco.pl executes when the Check-Out button is clicked by the user. The filename selected is checked out of RCS by running the RCS co program. The rcsco.htm template file is written back to the browser with the appropriate *ErrorFlag* value. The only portion of the HTML page that is dynamically created is the list of filenames in the pull down menu.

HINT: The values used in the LOCK radio button in rcsco.htm are the actual command line values that the programs use. Using actual values simplifies code in the CGI script because no translation has to be done in building the command line. You simply use the value that shows up in the CGI string.

```
#!/usr/local/bin/perl
###############################################################
# FILE: rcsco.pl
###################################
$TOOL_DIR     = "/home/httpd/cgi-bin";

require "$TOOL_DIR/tools.req";
require "$TOOL_DIR/vars.req";
       #
       # Global stuff
       #
&parse_cgi();          # Get data passed in from the HTML form
       #
       # Make sure there is an RCS directory
       #
```

```
$dir  =  $QS{'DIR'};
$dir  =~ s/\/RCS//;          # Take off "/RCS" from dir string
$QS{'DIR'}  =~ s/\/RCS//;    # Take off "/RCS" from dir string
$QS{'FILE'} =~ s/,v//;              # Remove trailing ",v" from
filename

chdir("$dir");

$status = system("co -q $QS{'LOCK'} $QS{'FILE'}");
&good_co();
exit;
########################+---------+
#                       | good_co |
#                       +---------+
sub good_co{
       print "Content-type:  text/html\n\n";
       open (HTML,"$HTML_DIR/rcsco.htm")
              || die "Can't open rcsco.htm\n";

       while(<HTML>){
              if(/\$ErrorFlag/){
                     s/\$ErrorFlag/$status/e;
              }
              if(/\$DIR/){
                     $dir = "$QS{'DIR'}/RCS";
                     s/\$DIR/$QS{'DIR'}/e;
              }
              if(/\$dir/){
                      $QS{'DIR'} =~ s/\/RCS//g;
                     $dir = "$QS{'DIR'}/RCS";
                     s/\$dir/$dir/e;
              }
              if(/\$REV/){
                     s/\$REV/$QS{'REV'}/e;
              }
              if(/\$USER/){
                     s/\$USER/$QS{'USER'}/e;
              }
              if(/\$PASS/){
                     s/\$PASS/$QS{'PASS'}/e;
              }
              print "$_";
              if(/<SELECT NAME=\"FILE\"/){
```

15

```
                        &insert_files();
                }
        }
        close(HTML);

        return;
}
########################+--------------+
#                       | insert_files |
#                       +--------------+
sub insert_files{
        print "    <OPTION VALUE=\"\*\*NONE\*\*\""
        print "SELECTED>Select A File</option>";
        open(DIR,"ls -1F $QS{'DIR'}/RCS |");
        while(<DIR>){
                if(/\//){    next;  }     # skip Directories
                s/\*//g;
                print "<OPTION VALUE=\"$_\">$_</option>";
        }
}
```

A good enhancement to rcsco.pl would be only listing RCS files that are not already checked out in the file selection pull down list.

HINT: Under the lessons learned category, it's a bad habit to modify values passed from the form. Copy the value to a local variable and manipulate the local variable if necessary. I modified $QS{'DIR'} in my first pass at coding rcsco.pl. After an hour of frustration, I copied it to $DIR, did the modification, and had the bug fixed in 10 minutes. I would change $QS{'DIR'} to generate the correct value in one place and it would break in another.

RCSCI

A file is typically checked back into RCS after checking it out with a lock set, modifying the file, testing the changes, and generally being finished with the changes. Therefore, the next RCS operation discussed is checking a file back into RCS. The check-in process begins with the user selecting the Check-in operation and clicking Do It on the RCS Main Page. The RCS Check-In Page is displayed:

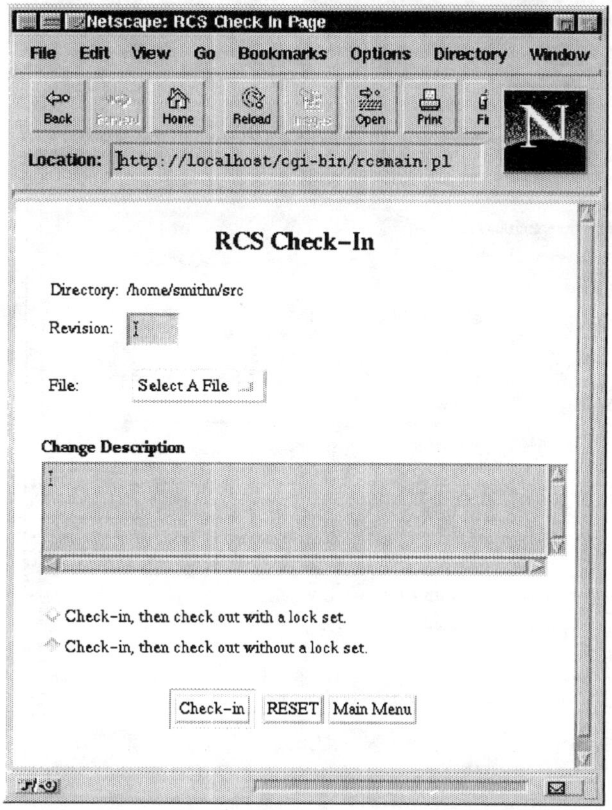

The user selects a file from the Select A File pull down menu, enters a change description, selects the type of automatic check-out to do, and clicks Check-in to actually check in the selected file.

The reason for checking out a file immediately after check-in is that the RCS deletes the file after checking it in. Unix Make program has no capability to automatically check out a file. Thus, immediately checking the file back out with no lock set makes other installation processes built around Make much more convenient to the point that it is common practice.

An example of the RCS Check-In Page ready for submission is:

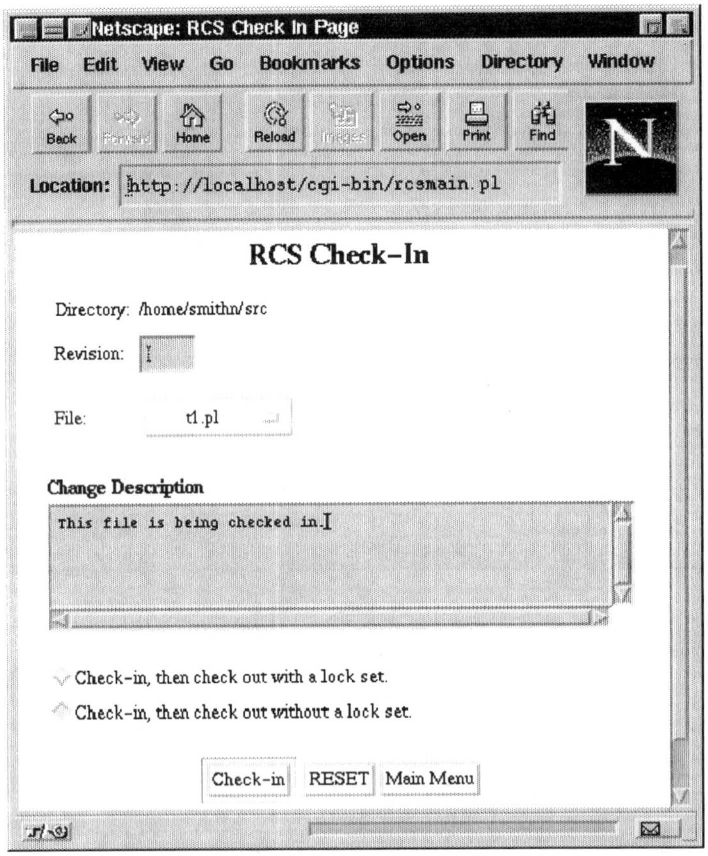

Assuming the file check-in is successful, the page is repainted and a dialog box pops up with a success/fail message. Thus, the user is given explicit feedback on the operation. The following display is created after a successful check-in:

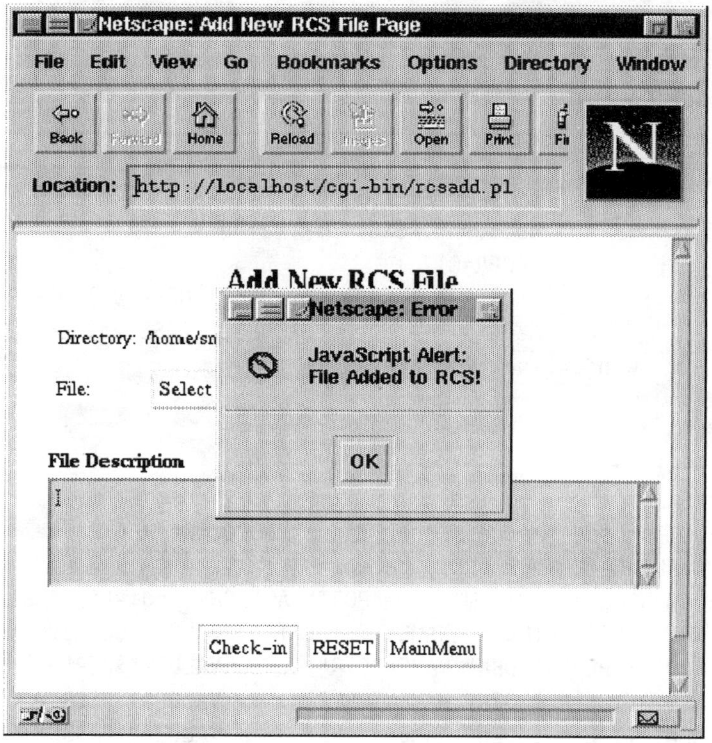

rcsci.htm contains the now familiar ProcessErrorFlag() and reload_main() JavaScript functions.

The listing for rcsci.htm is:

```
<HTML>
<!-- rcsci.htm -->
<HEAD>
<TITLE>RCS Check In Page</TITLE>
<SCRIPT>
<!--
function ProcessErrorFlag(){
        if(document.RCSCI.ErrorFlag.value == "0"){
                alert("File checked into RCS!");
                return;
        }
        if(document.RCSCI.ErrorFlag.value == "256"){
                alert("File already checked into RCS! No action
Taken!");
                return;
```

```
        }
}
function reload_main(){
        var url;

        url = "/cgi-bin/rcslogon.pl?DIR=" +
               document.RCSCI.DIR.value +
               "&OPR=CI" +
               "&USER=" + document.RCSCI.USER.value +
               "&PASS=" + document.RCSCI.PASS.value;
        window.location.href=url;
}
//      -->
</SCRIPT>
</HEAD>
<BODY onLoad="ProcessErrorFlag()" BGCOLOR="#FFFFFF">
<H1 ALIGN="CENTER">RCS Check-In</H1>
<FORM NAME="RCSCI" METHOD="POST" ACTION="/cgi-bin/rcsci.pl">
<INPUT TYPE="HIDDEN" NAME="ErrorFlag" VALUE="$ErrorFlag">
<INPUT TYPE="HIDDEN" NAME="DIR"       VALUE="$DIR">
<INPUT TYPE="HIDDEN" NAME="USER"      VALUE="$USER">
<INPUT TYPE="HIDDEN" NAME="PASS"      VALUE="$PASS">
<INPUT TYPE="HIDDEN" NAME="OPR"       VALUE="CI">
<TABLE>
  <TR>
    <TD>Directory:</TD>
    <TD>$DIR</TD>
  </TR>
  <TR>
    <TD>Revision:</TD>
    <TD><INPUT TYPE="TEXT" NAME="REV" SIZE=4 VALUE="$REV"></TD>
  </TR>
  <TR>
    <TD>File:</TD>
    <TD><SELECT NAME="FILE" SIZE=1>
        </SELECT>
    </TD>
  </TR>
</TABLE>
<BR>
<B>Change Description</B>
<BR>
<TEXTAREA NAME="DESC" ROWS=5 COLS=60></TEXTAREA>
```

```
<BR>
<INPUT TYPE="RADIO" NAME="LOCK" VALUE="-l">
  Check-in, then check out with a lock set.
<BR>
<INPUT TYPE="RADIO" NAME="LOCK" VALUE="-u" CHECKED>
  Check-in, then check out without a lock set.
<BR>
<BR>
<CENTER>
<INPUT TYPE="SUBMIT" VALUE="Check-in">
<INPUT TYPE="RESET"  VALUE="RESET">
<INPUT TYPE="BUTTON" VALUE="Main Menu" onClick="reload_main()">
</CENTER>
<BR>
</FORM>
</BODY>
</HTML>
```

The rcsci.pl Perl script executes when the user clicks the Check-in button. The code is similar to that of rcsadd.htm. The command line constructed in the program is the main difference. The listing for rcsci.pl is:

```
#!/usr/local/bin/perl
##################################################################
# FILE: rcsci.pl
##################################
$TOOL_DIR     = "/home/httpd/cgi-bin";

require "$TOOL_DIR/tools.req";
require "$TOOL_DIR/vars.req";
       #
       # Global stuff
       #
&parse_cgi();         # Get data passed in from the HTML form
       #
       # Make sure that the File Description ends with a "."
       # on a line by itself. This is required by RCS.
       #
@desc = split(/\n/,$QS{'DESC'});
if($desc[$#desc] ne "."){
       push(@desc,".");
```

15

```
}
        #
        # Put the description back together into a single
        # string for passing to ci.
        #
$DESC = "";
foreach $line (@desc){
        $DESC .= "$line";
}
        #
        # Make sure there is an RCS directory
        #
chdir("$QS{'DIR'}");
system("mkdir RCS");

$status = system("ci -q -m\"$DESC\" $QS{'FILE'}");
&good_add();
exit;
########################+----------+
#                       | good_add |
#                       +----------+
sub good_add{
        print "Content-type:  text/html\n\n";
        open (HTML,"$HTML_DIR//rcsci.htm")
                || die "Can't open rcsadd.htm\n";

        while(<HTML>){
                if(/\$ErrorFlag/){
                        s/\$ErrorFlag/$status/e;
                }
                if(/\$DIR/){
                        s/\$DIR/$QS{'DIR'}/e;
                }
                if(/\$REV/){
                        s/\$REV/$QS{'REV'}/e;
                }
                if(/\$USER/){
                        s/\$USER/$QS{'USER'}/e;
                }
                if(/\$PASS/){
                        s/\$PASS/$QS{'PASS'}/e;
                }
                print "$_";
```

```
                if(/<SELECT NAME=\"FILE\"/){
                        &insert_files();
                }
        }
        close(HTML);

        return;
}
###########################+--------------+
#                          | insert_files |
#                          +--------------+
sub insert_files{
        print "      <OPTION VALUE=\"\*\*NONE\*\*\" SELECTED>";
        print "Select A File</option>";
        open(DIR,"ls -1F $QS{'DIR'} |");
        while(<DIR>){
                if(/\//){      next;  }
                s/\*//g;
                print "<OPTION VALUE=\"$_\">$_</option>";
        }
}
```

The two programs were kept separate on purpose to allow for potential enhancements to each that might not be compatible. There are several obvious enhancements that could be made to RCSCI:

- Additional JavaScript error checking in the HTML file
- List only files that already exist in RCS in the pull down list
- List only files already checked with a lock set out of RCS
- Require a change description contain some text
- Validate the revision number if the user enters one

RCSCI is functional as is but not quite ready for production.

RCSINST

The final operation in this case study is "installing" a file. This is not a simple RCS operation but an RCS operation with additional processing necessary to install the file. The installation details probably differ for your site than the ones implemented here.

The user begins the file installation process by clicking the Install A File radio button, then clicking Do It on the RCS Main Page. The following page is displayed:

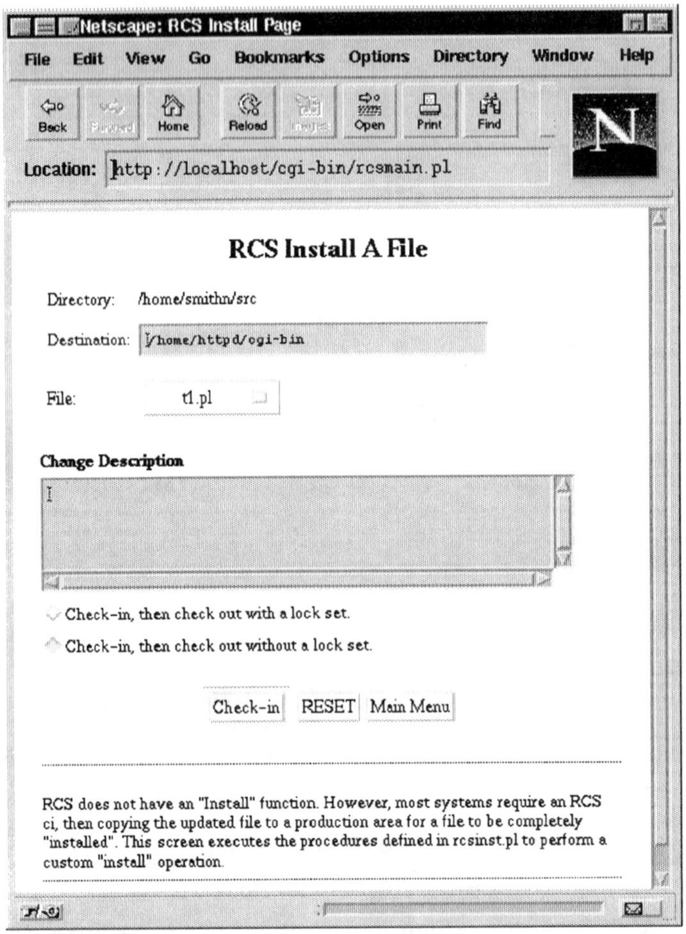

The resemblance to check-in is there. Both have a file selection pull down menu, a text box to type a change description, and radio buttons for check-out with or without a lock set. The difference is a destination box. The destination text box contains the directory path to copy the file to after check-in has successfully completed.

A JavaScript dialog box is displayed after the install operation is completed. The following display shows the result of an unsuccessful installation.

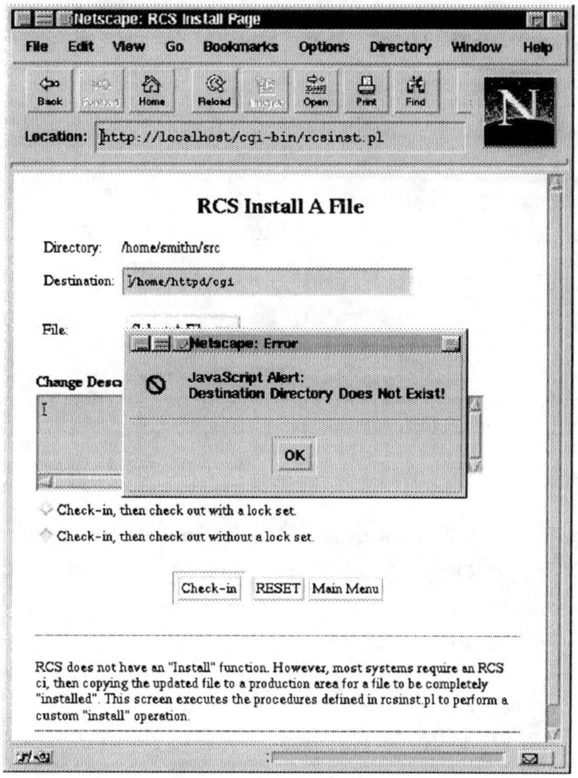

The HTML file, rcsinst.htm, is:

```
<HTML>
<!-- rcsinst.htm -->
<HEAD>
<TITLE>RCS Install Page</TITLE>
<SCRIPT LANGUAGE="JAVASCRIPT">
<!--
function validate(){
        if(document.RCSINST.DEST.value == ""){
                alert("Destination Directory Blank!!");
                return false;
        }
}
function reload_main(){
        var url;

url = "/cgi-bin/rcslogon.pl?DIR=" +
                document.RCSINST.DIR.value +
```

15

```
                "&OPR=INST" +
                "&USER=" + document.RCSINST.USER.value +
                "&PASS=" + document.RCSINST.PASS.value;
        window.location.href=url;
}
function ProcessErrorFlag(){
        if(document.RCSINST.ErrorFlag.value == "0"){
                alert("File checked into RCS and installed");
                return;
        }
        if(document.RCSINST.ErrorFlag.value == "2"){
        alert("File checked into RCS, Check-out failed, installation
failed!");
                return;
        }
        if(document.RCSINST.ErrorFlag.value == "4"){
        alert("File checked into and out of RCS, copy to dest dir
failed! ");
                return;
        }
        if(document.RCSINST.ErrorFlag.value == "5"){
                alert("Destination Directory Does Not Exist!");
                return;
        }
        if(document.RCSINST.ErrorFlag.value == "256"){
alert("File already checked into RCS! Installation Aborted!");
                return;
        }
}
//      -->
</SCRIPT>
</HEAD>
<BODY onLoad="ProcessErrorFlag()" BGCOLOR="#FFFFFF">
<H1 ALIGN="CENTER">RCS Install A File</H1>
<FORM NAME="RCSINST" METHOD="POST" onSubmit="return validate()"
ACTION="/cgi-bin/rcsinst.pl">
<INPUT TYPE="HIDDEN" NAME="ErrorFlag" VALUE="$ErrorFlag">
<INPUT TYPE="HIDDEN" NAME="DIR"       VALUE="$DIR">
<INPUT TYPE="HIDDEN" NAME="USER"      VALUE="$USER">
<INPUT TYPE="HIDDEN" NAME="PASS"      VALUE="$PASS">
<TABLE>
  <TR>
    <TD>Directory:</TD>
```

```
      <TD>$DIR
    </TR>
    <TR>
      <TD>Destination:</TD>
      <TD><INPUT TYPE="TEXT" NAME="DEST" SIZE=40 onChange="validate()"
VALUE="$DEST"></TD>
    </TR>
    <TR>
      <TD>File:</TD>
      <TD><SELECT NAME="FILE" SIZE=1>
          </SELECT>
      </TD>
    </TR>
</TABLE>
<BR>
<B>Change Description</B>
<BR>
<TEXTAREA NAME="DESC" ROWS=5 COLS=60></TEXTAREA>
<BR>
<INPUT TYPE="RADIO" NAME="LOCK" VALUE="-l">
  Check-in, then check out with a lock set.
<BR>
<INPUT TYPE="RADIO" NAME="LOCK" VALUE="-u" CHECKED>
  Check-in, then check out without a lock set.
<BR>
<BR>
<CENTER>
<INPUT TYPE="SUBMIT" VALUE="Check-in">
<INPUT TYPE="RESET" VALUE="RESET">
<INPUT TYPE="BUTTON" VALUE="Main Menu" onClick="reload_main()">
</CENTER>
<BR>
</FORM>
<HR>
<P>
RCS does not have an "Install" function. However, most
systems require an RCS ci, then copying the updated file to
a production area for a file to be completely "installed."
This screen executes the procedures defined in rcsinst.pl
to perform a custom "install" operation.
<HR>
</BODY>
</HTML>
```

15

The user initiates the file install process, rcsinst.pl, by clicking the Install button. The structure of the program is similar to the previous "operation" program. The main portion of the code gets the CGI string and breaks it out into the %QS associative array. There is code to handle the case where the file is checked out with a lock set (&file_is_locked()) and when there is no lock set (&file_not_locked()). The final portion of the main code is copying the install HTML template file back to the browser. *ErrorFlag* is used to return a success code to the JavaScript error reporting code.

The code for rcsinst.pl is:

```
#!/usr/local/bin/perl
##################################################################
# FILE: rcsinst.pl
##################################
$TOOL_DIR     = "/home/httpd/cgi-bin";

require "$TOOL_DIR/tools.req";
require "$TOOL_DIR/vars.req";
        #
        # Global stuff
        #
&parse_cgi();          # Get data passed in from the HTML form
        #
        # Make sure that the File Description ends with a "."
        # on a line by itself. This is required by RCS.
        #
@desc = split(/\n/,$QS{'DESC'});
if($desc[$#desc] ne "."){
        push(@desc,".");
}
        #
        # Put the description back together into a single
        # string for passing to ci.
        #
$DESC = "";
foreach $line (@desc){
        $DESC .= "$line";
}
        #
        # Make sure there is an RCS directory
```

```
        #
chdir("$QS{'DIR'}");

$file_match = 0;
open(LOCK,"rlog -R -L RCS/* |");
while(<LOCK>){
        s/RCS\///;                      # Remove "RCS/" from name string
        s/,v//;                         # Remove ",v" from name string
        if(/$QS{'FILE'}/){
                $file_match = 1;        # There is a locked file
                last;
        }
}
close(LOCK);
if($file_match > 0){
        &file_is_locked();
}else{
        &file_not_locked();
}
&copy_file_to_dest();
&good_add();
exit;
#######################+----------------+
#                      | file_is_locked |
#                      +----------------+
sub file_is_locked{
        system("mkdir RCS");
        $status = system("ci -q $QS{'LOCK'} -m\"$DESC\" $QS{'FILE'}");
        if($status != 0){
                &good_add();
                exit;
        }
}
#######################+-----------------+
#                      | file_not_locked |
#                      +-----------------+
sub file_not_locked{

        $status = system("co -q $QS{'LOCK'} $QS{'FILE'}");
        if($status != 0){
                $status = 2;
                &good_add();
                exit;
```

15

```
        }
}
########################+-------------------+
#                       | copy_file_to_dest |
#                       +-------------------+
sub copy_file_to_dest{
        $status = opendir(DESTDIR,"$QS{'DEST'}");
        closedir(DESTDIR);
        if($status != 1){
                $status = 5;
                &good_add();
                exit;
        }
        $status = open(FILE,">$QS{'DEST'}/$QS{'FILE'}");
        if($status != 1){
                $status = 4;
                &good_add();
                exit;
        }
        $status = 0;
        open(SOURCE,"$QS{'FILE'}");
        while(<SOURCE>){
                print FILE "$_";
        }
        close(FILE);
        close(SOURCE);
        return;
}
########################+----------+
#                       | good_add |
#                       +----------+
sub good_add{
        print "Content-type:  text/html\n\n";
        open (HTML,"$HTML_DIR//rcsinst.htm")
                || die "Can't open rcsinst.htm\n";

        while(<HTML>){
                if(/\$ErrorFlag/){
                        s/\$ErrorFlag/$status/e;
                }
                if(/\$DIR/){
                        s/\$DIR/$QS{'DIR'}/e;
                }
```

```
                if(/\$REV/){
                        s/\$REV/$QS{'REV'}/e;
                }
                if(/\$DEST/){
                        s/\$DEST/$QS{'DEST'}/e;
                }
                if(/\$USER/){
                        s/\$USER/$QS{'USER'}/e;
                }
                if(/\$PASS/){
                        s/\$PASS/$QS{'PASS'}/e;
                }
                print "$_";
                if(/<SELECT NAME=\"FILE\"/){
                        &insert_files();
                }
        }
        close(HTML);

        return;
}
#######################+--------------+
#                      | insert_files |
#                      +--------------+
sub insert_files{
        print "     <OPTION VALUE=\"\*\*NONE\*\*\" SELECTED>";
        print " Select A File</option>";
        open(DIR,"ls -1F $QS{'DIR'} |");
        while(<DIR>){
                if(/\//){     next;  }
                s/\*//g;
                print "<OPTION VALUE=\"$_\">$_</option>";
        }
}
```

The file install process for a real system is likely to be much more complicated than the process implemented here. A real system probably has a Make procedure and programs to compile, send e-mail, or any of a dozen other things that must be performed when “installing” a file. It is also not uncommon for files to be installed in groups rather than singly as shown here.

Summary

This chapter presents a typical example of adding a Web front end on a command line application. The application is the GNU Revision Control System (RCS). The general approach to the application operation is:

- Present the user with the operations that can be performed.
- Display a page specific to the operation after the user selects the operation.
- Collect the information necessary to construct the command line via an HTML form.
- Execute the operation via Perl CGI script.
- Provide feedback on the success/failure of the operation via JavaScript Alert boxes.

This implementation uses JavaScript on the client side for simple form validation and error reporting and Perl on the server side to build the command lines, execute them, and return processing results to the client. Hidden HTML form fields are used to pass information to the client JavaScript code.

The techniques presented in this chapter can be applied to almost any command line based program or application.

Chapter 16

Case Study 3: Data Entry

Introduction

The primary intranet application is data entry; updating a database of some sort. The advantages of building this type of application using Web tools on an intranet have been discussed in detail in earlier chapters of this book. The case study in this chapter is a simple data entry application. It maintains a simple flat file database describing image files. Retrieving data from and updating Oracle databases is also covered but not actually used in the case study.

The case study is organized as the previous case studies. The problem statement is given, along with the approach, the tools used, the design, and finally the implementation.

Problem Statement

Write an intranet system to maintain a simple database about graphic images. The sample data includes several Wordware book covers. The system requirements are:

- Provide user logon
- Include the ability to load a new database
- Provide a simple search mechanism
- Provide the ability to select a particular record number
- Provide the ability to add a new record to an existing database
- Provide the ability to display images with the data
- Provide the ability to edit existing database records

- Generate a report of the database with and without images
- Provide the ability to set options
- Provide the ability to logon as another user
- Provide the ability to view an existing record

The implementation should use cookies to pass parameters from JavaScript code to Perl CGI scripts.

Approach

The general approach taken in the development of this case study is similar to that used in Case 2. The requirements drive the overall design. Demo screens are proposed, based on the problem statement. The flow of the system is defined by the demo screens. I call them demo screens because their purpose is to provide a feel for the system and to use as a starting point for development. Screen details are expected to evolve as system development progresses. The demo screens for this case study follow:

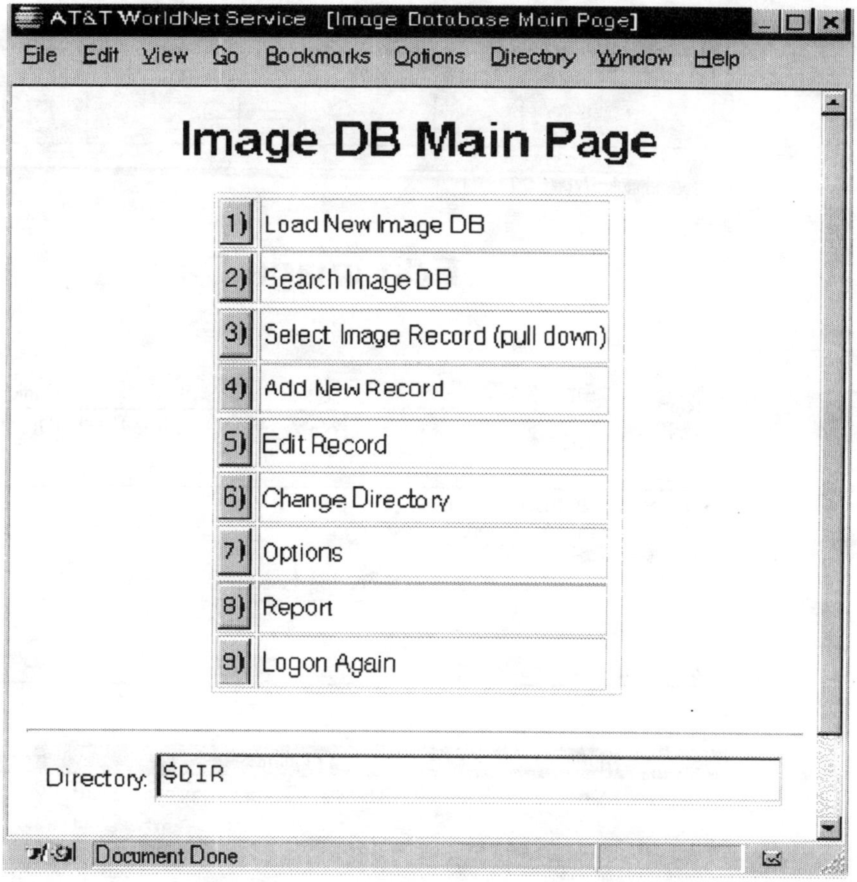

If you skip ahead to the implementation screens, the Main Page layout is rearranged into a two-column format and has an additional button selection. The page layout was changed because the screen frequently did not fit without scrolling unless the browser was sized to full screen. This was especially annoying during development when there were always several windows open on the screen.

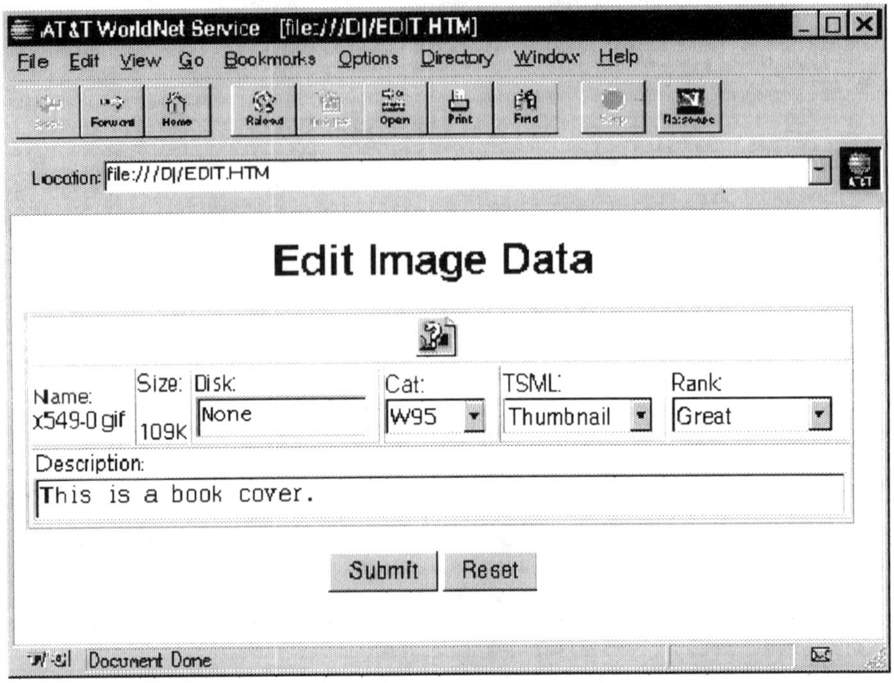
AT&T WorldNet Service [file:///D|/EDIT.HTM]
File Edit View Go Bookmarks Options Directory Window Help
Location: file:///D|/EDIT.HTM
Edit Image Data
Name: x549-0.gif
Size: 109K
Disk: None
Cat: W95
TSML: Thumbnail
Rank: Great
Description:
This is a book cover.
Submit
Reset
Document Done

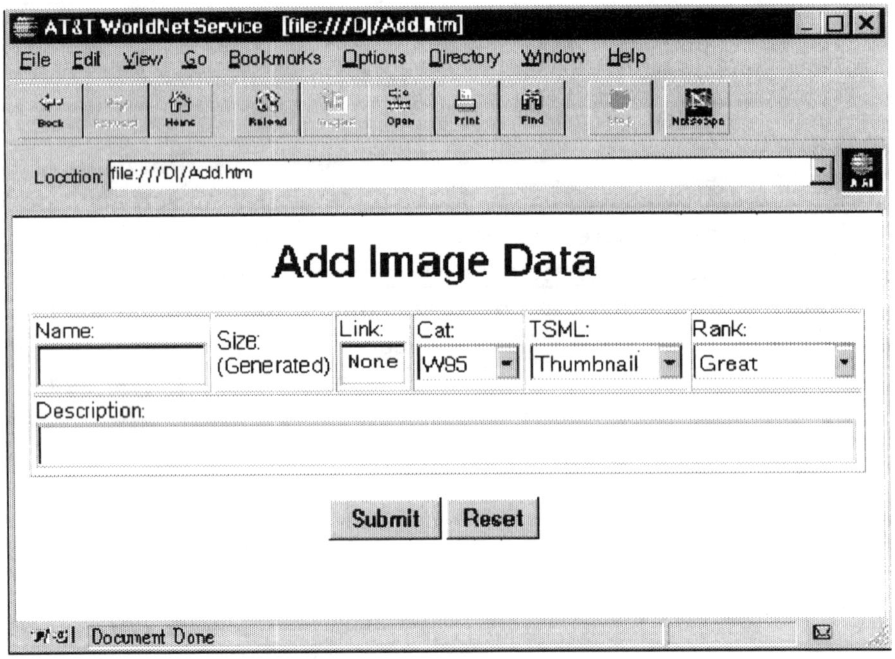
AT&T WorldNet Service [file:///D|/Add.htm]
File Edit View Go Bookmarks Options Directory Window Help
Location: file:///D|/Add.htm
Add Image Data
Name:
Size: (Generated)
Link: None
Cat: W95
TSML: Thumbnail
Rank: Great
Description:
Submit
Reset
Document Done

The Add and Edit Pages evolved as well. The TSML (Thumbnail, Small, Medium, and Large) field changed from a pull down menu to radio buttons. There are only four possible choices and listing the TSML selections as radio buttons horizontally did not widen the display significantly.

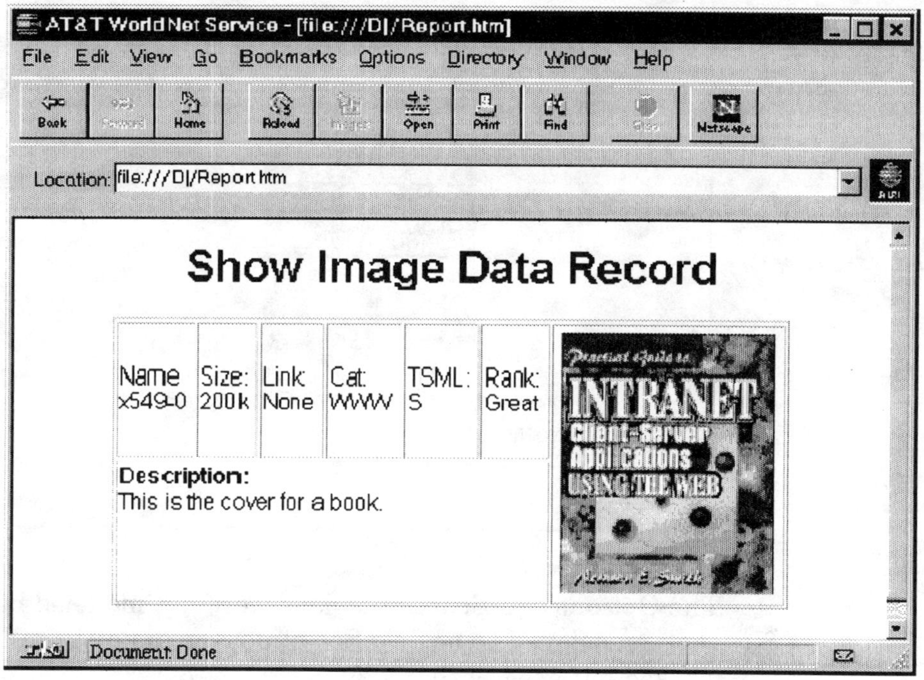

There were two versions of the Show Page, which became the View and Report Pages. The above image beside the record format was abandoned after using life-size book covers in the test data. The side-by-side format works well with small images but not for large images. The image is displayed on top of the data in the final version.

The Options and Search displays were not modeled because they were envisioned to be JavaScript pop-up dialog boxes. Neither worked out exactly that way.

The next development step is preparing the Data Flow Diagram (DFD) for the system. The DFD provides a map for implementation. Remember that DFDs for a web application must contain both server programs and HTML pages to represent all of the code. The DFD for the Image Database is presented in the Design section later in this chapter.

The operation of the system is described in the following paragraphs. The design uses cookies to pass data from the browser to the server and hidden fields to pass data from the server to JavaScript code running in the browser. This approach to passing data between the client and server is simply a design decision. The RCS application in Case 2 uses hidden fields completely. You could just as easily use cookies for all data passing. Parsing cookies to extract data adds more complexity to the JavaScript code. The hidden field/cookie combination provides good functionality for a minimum programming hassle.

HINT: Choose the combination of cookies and hidden fields to pass data between client and server on a case-by-case basis.

The user begins by logging onto the application. A valid username/password combination is required. The Main Page is presented upon successful logon. The Main Page has buttons that are clicked to initiate specific functions. The application assumes that the database describes images in a particular directory. The current directory is specified in a text box at the bottom of the page.

The first time the system is used, the user chooses Load New Image DB by clicking the 1) button. This builds a skeleton database of the GIF files in the directory. The user may edit or view an image record. Each is a two-step process. A record is selected, then the display function is initiated. Selecting a record is done by either specifying the image number or searching the database. A new record may be manually added by clicking the Add New Record button. Additional functions are generating a report, setting display and report options, and changing the current working directory.

The techniques used in this case study include:

- Using cookies to pass data between client and server
- Storing global data in cookies
- Data entry via HTML forms without submit buttons
- Programs totally implemented in the client
- Using JavaScript for form validation

There are a couple of topics, not covered in detail elsewhere in this book in this case study, that need to be touched on before getting into the design. Cookies have been mentioned but not in detail. Manipulating a real database such as Oracle in an intranet application is mentioned as a big part of intranet applications. This case study implements its database as a simple flat ASCII file so a separate database discussion is in order. The next two sections describe cookies in some detail and discuss using Oracle.

Cookies

Cookies are a Netscape invention to store information in the client that is automatically passed from the client to the server as part of a client request. Cookies are easy to use; they are also easy to abuse. Cookies may be set and read by both the client and the server.

Much of the initial use of cookies was to "track" site access. This is easy to do by simply assigning an identifier cookie with a very long expiration date. Each time the browser accesses a specific page or pages, the cookie is passed to the server. The server CGI program can save the identifier along with time and date. The net effect is the server can track access by browser with very little effort. Many people consider this usage tracking an invasion of privacy because it can be done without the user's knowledge or consent.

The flip side of the cookie coin is that cookies can be used to record transaction state, which saves a lot of programming effort and can make Web applications much more responsive to the user.

Cookie usage in intranet applications takes a little different view of how long to maintain state. There is rarely reason to save state past the current session. In many cases, you do not want information saved on the client computer. "Pre-expired" cookies are used to prevent state being saved. Cookies with no expiration date automatically expire at the end of the current browser session. Netscape Navigator in particular does not write the cookie buffers to disk until it exits. Thus, information in a pre-expired cookie is never saved on the client's system.

HINT: Pre-expired cookies are an important cog in the security of intranet applications. Although, there are ways for the user to view the contents of a pre-expired cookie, not writing the cookie to disk lessens the risk of a user collecting information and using it improperly.

The limitations on size and number of active cookies must be taken into account during design. Cookie size limitations are:

- 300 total cookies
- 20 cookies per domain or server
- 4k characters per cookie

The Image Database actually uses more cookies than necessary for illustration purposes.

HINT: The number of cookies can be minimized by building a CGI-like string for a cookie with multiple values. Then the cookie string can be passed through the CGI parsing code to extract the "key=value" pairs.

HINT: Structure cookie contents functionally. That is, put related data in the same cookie. This reduces both the total number of cookies and the number of cookies that an application may need to process.

Setting up a cookie in the CGI program on the server is relatively straightforward. The cookie command is part of the MIME header for sending an HTML file to the browser. The header is normally a single line followed by a blank line. In Perl, this would be written:

```
print "Content-type = TEXT/HTML\n\n";
```

Thus the MIME content is output first, followed by a blank line. The <HTML> tag normally follows the "Content-type" line. The following lines set a cookie named TEST to XXX:

```
Content-type = TEXT/HTML
Set-Cookie: TEST=XXX;

<HTML>
...
</HTML>
```

Don't forget to include the blank line between the last cookie and the <HTML> tag.

HINT: The easiest way to tell whether a cookie is actually set is to turn on the "Show Alert before accepting a cookie" option in the browser. An alert box pops up containing the cookie contents each time a cookie is set.

There are several additional fields that may be specified when setting a cookie. The cookie fields are:

- NAME
- EXPIRES
- PATH
- DOMAIN
- SECURE

The format for NAME is "NAME=VALUE" where NAME is the name of the cookie and VALUE is the cookie value. The CGI string content rules apply. In other words, a number of characters including blank, "%", ";", "=", etc. must be quoted. CGI strings are discussed in Chapter 5.

Cookies are automatically deleted after they expire. The expiration date is set via the EXPIRES keyword. Setting an expiration date of March 21, 1997, is:

```
Set-Cookie: MYNAME=XXX; EXPIRES=FRI, 21-MAR-1997 00:00:00 GMT;
```

The DOMAIN keyword specifies the Internet Domain Name of computer(s) that will receive the cookie. Specify:

```
Set-Cookie: MYNAME=XXX; DOMAIN=.WORDWARE.COM;
```

and the MYNAME cookie will be sent to any server in the WORDWARE.COM domain that the browser accesses. Leaving off DOMAIN only returns the cookie to the computer that set it.

Use the PATH keyword to specify the URL directory tree for which this cookie is valid. Specifying a path of:

```
Set-Cookie: YYY=ABC; PATH=/xxxx;
```

will only pass cookie YYY to URLs with a path that start with "/xxxx."

The final cookie field is SECURE. When a cookie is specified as secure, it will only be passed to the server when there is a secure connection (SSL).

Cookies may be added, changed, or deleted. Adding and changing a cookie is done by simply writing it again. Deleting a cookie is done by writing the cookie with an expired date.

Cookies are a very useful tool in developing client-server intranet applications. The up side is they provide an easy way for the server to store information (state) in the client which can simplify the server code a great deal. The down side of cookies is they are easy to abuse. Use cookies responsibly. You will benefit from the code simplification, and your users will benefit from more efficient applications.

Using Real Databases

This type of application normally would be built using a commercial database system such as Oracle, Informix, Sybase, or Ingres. There are other noncommercial databases in the Unix world, such as DBM (usually available with Perl) and Postgres, which may also be suitable.

There are almost too many options for ways to access a database, which vary depending on platform, Web server, and application language. Some of the practical ways include:

- ODBC
- Language specific interfaces
- Third-party packages
- Command line interface

The Open DataBase Connectivity (ODBC) defines a generic standard interface for SQL-based databases. It is used by most current commercial databases. ODBC is usually implemented as an API with associated middleware drivers for actually connecting to the database.

ODBC drivers for PCs are available from a number of vendors. Microsoft even includes Windows 95 ODBC drivers with most of its current programming language compilers.

Language specific database interfaces have faded as the more generic ODBC interface has gained in popularity. Notable languages with database interfaces include:

- Perl
- Java
- JavaScript
- Pro C

Perl has specific versions for most major database systems. Examples include Oraperl for Oracle and Sybperl for SyBase. These database specific versions have been replaced recently with a more generic package called dbperl which provides the same external interface to multiple database systems. Check out ftp.demon.co.uk/pub/perl/db for the latest information on dbperl.

Java has JDBC, or Java DataBase Connectivity, which can be described as ODBC for Java. JDBC has growing support within both the Java and database communities.

JavaScript in the form of Netscape LiveWire Pro also contains direct Oracle connectivity. Oracle Corp. includes ProC, a C preprocessor, with Oracle 7. It can be used to build application specific interface programs by embedding a form of SQL statement in the code. ProC can also be used to build fairly generic programs that accept basic SQL commands directly.

Third-party packages such as NeXT WebObjects, Cold Fusion, and Sapphire/Web all provide some level of database connectivity. If you use a current commercial database, the vendor probably already has a package to support access through the Web.

The final way to interface WWW applications to database systems is the most generic: the good old command line interface. A command line interface requires two things: a database with a command line interface (Oracle SQLPlus is used for these discussions) and a way to execute the command line. Interfacing databases via a command line interface works well with Unix Web servers. It may or may not work well when the server is Windows or Macintosh based.

The general operation of interfacing Oracle to the Web is doing the following steps in a Perl CGI program:

1. Execute SQLPlus, passing the SQL commands to perform.
2. Either read the output of the SQL execution as a named pipe or redirect the SQL output to a temporary file.
3. Dynamically generate the HTML output from SQL to pass back to the browser.

There are several ways to do each of the three steps. Executing SQL commands can be done by:

- ProC program
- Passing parameters to an SQLPlus shell script
- Dynamically generating a temporary SQLPlus shell script

Over the years, I have written Web applications that use each of the three ways to execute SQL and have gravitated to dynamically generating temporary SQLPlus shell script files. One reason is hassles in passing large numbers of command line arguments while making sure the correct number of quote marks get passed down the call tree so each argument is surrounded by exactly a single pair of quote characters when SQLPlus is called. The second reason is fewer shell script files to keep track of and maintain in the application.

The rest of this section provides an example of accessing an Oracle database via dynamically generated SQL shell scripts in Unix.

First, let's look at a stand-alone shell script to retrieve a list of names and phone numbers from a database. Here is the code for sample.sql:

```
#!/bin/ksh
ORACLE_HOME=/home/oracle
ORACLE_TERM=xsun5
ORA_NLS=$ORACLE_HOME/ocommon/nls/admin/data
ORACLE_SID=sid1
ORACLE_DOC=$ORACLE_HOME/odoc
LD_LIBRARY_PATH=$ORACLE_HOME/lib:$LD_LIBRARY_PATH
```

```
PATH=$ORACLE_HOME/bin:$PATH
TMPDIR=/tmp
export ORACLE_HOME ORACLE_TERM ORA_NLS ORACLE_SID ORACLE_DOC
LD_LIBRARY_PATH
export PATH TMPDIR
MENU5PATH=$ORACLE_HOME/forms30/admin/resource
export MENU5PATH
ORATERMPATH=$ORACLE_HOME/forms30/admin/resource
export ORATERMPATH
ORAENV_ASK=NO
. $ORACLE_HOME/bin/oraenv
sqlplus -s user/password << END
whenever sqlerror exit 1 rollback;
whenever oserror exit 1 rollback
set feedback off
set trim off
set tab off
set pagesize 0
set echo off
set heading off
set spa 0
set term off
set linesize 2500

spool $out

SELECT userid, "|",
       firstname, "|",
       lastname
FROM   MYTABLE;

QUIT;
END

spool off
END
if [ $? -ne 0 ]; then
 echo **ERROR**\n
 echo Error in updating profile info.
 echo Script file is sample.sql.
 rm -f /tmp/$$.errors $$.out $$.output
 exit
else
```

```
 cat $out
 rm -f /tmp/$$.errors $$.out $$.output
 exit
fi
```

Most of this script is generic SQLPlus/Unix shell script code. The username/password will have to be modified for each database as will the SQL commands. The SQL commands in sample.sql start with SELECT and end with QUIT;.

The list of SET commands is the secret in this script. The magic combination of commands turns off normal SQLPlus page headings, column headings, and such, making it possible to extract records in a delimited format. sample.sql uses "|" to delimit fields, putting the data in a form easily processed by Perl. Each record in MYTABLE is output as a single line separated by a "|". For example:

```
1|Norman      |Smith        |555-1234
2|John        |Doe          |555-1235
3|Roger       |Jones        |555-1236
```

Notice the extra white space between fields. SQLPlus pads all fields to their defined lengths. Assuming the processing program is written in Perl, removing the extra blanks is only a couple of lines of code. If an SQL error occurs during the execution of sample.sql, the script outputs **ERROR** followed by the SQL error message, which is also easy to detect and process in Perl.

HINT: The primary consideration when retrieving data from any database is returning the data and error messages in a form that is easy to process. The default SQLPlus format is hard to process. The "|" delimited format is easy to process.

The first step in creating a dynamically generated SQLPlus file is taking our sample.sql file and looking for logical breaks. There are three:

- The "header" portion down to the SPOOL $OUT statement
- The SQL code to execute, which is from the end of the header to the END statement
- The "footer" portion, which is after the END statement until the end of the script

My dynamic script implementation takes the "header" portion and places it in the file sql.hdr:

```
#!/bin/ksh
# FILE: sql.hdr
#
ORACLE_HOME=/home/oracle
ORACLE_TERM=xsun5
ORA_NLS=$ORACLE_HOME/ocommon/nls/admin/data
ORACLE_SID=sid1
ORACLE_DOC=$ORACLE_HOME/odoc
LD_LIBRARY_PATH=$ORACLE_HOME/lib:$LD_LIBRARY_PATH
PATH=$ORACLE_HOME/bin:$PATH
TMPDIR=/tmp

export ORACLE_HOME ORACLE_TERM ORA_NLS ORACLE_SID ORACLE_DOC
LD_LIBRARY_PATH
export PATH TMPDIR

MENU5PATH=$ORACLE_HOME/forms30/admin/resource
export MENU5PATH
ORATERMPATH=$ORACLE_HOME/forms30/admin/resource
export ORATERMPATH

ORAENV_ASK=NO
. $ORACLE_HOME/bin/oraenv

out=/tmp/$$.out

sqlplus -s dds/ut48nw28 << END > /tmp/$$.errors
whenever sqlerror exit 1 rollback;
whenever oserror exit 1 rollback;
set feedback off
set trim off
set tab off
set pagesize 0
```

```
set echo off
set heading off
set spa 0
set term off
set linesize 2500

spool $out
```

The "footer" portion goes in sql.ftr:

```
# FILE: sql.ftr
#
spool off
END
if [ $? -ne 0 ]; then
 echo **ERROR**\n
 echo Error in updating profile info.
 echo Script file is $$.sql.
 rm -f /tmp/$$.errors $$.out $$.output
 exit
else
 cat $out
 rm -f /tmp/$$.errors $$.out $$.output
 exit
fi
```

The SQL in the middle is dynamically created for each database access, whether it be simple retrieval or updating multiple records.

Let's put this all together in a program. sample.pl retrieves a single record from an Oracle database and substitutes the returned values into an HTML template. The code for sample.pl is:

```
#!/usr/local/bin/perl
#
# FILE: sample.pl
#

# Require files go here

require "/cgi-bin/tools.require";
```

```
@SQL_cmds = "";

&retrieve_data();

exit;
########################+---------------+
#                       | retrieve_data |
#                       +---------------+
sub retrieve_data{
            # Collect SQL commands
      push(@SQL_cmd,"select USERID, \'|\', ");
      push(@SQL_cmd,"FIRSTNAME,\'|\', LASTNAME, \'|\',");
      push(@SQL_cmd," PHONE");
      push(@SQL_cmd,"from MYTABLE;");
            # Create temporary SQL script
      &gen_SQL_proc();
      $recs = 0;
            # Execute SQL script file & process results
      open(SQL,"ksh /tmp/$$.sql |")
            || die "Can't run Query!\n";

      while(<SQL>){
            chop;
            $_ =~ s/  //g;
            $_ =~ s/ \|/\|/g;
            $_ =~ s/\| /\|/g;
            $_ =~ s/[ ]+$//g;
            if($_ =~ /\*\*ERROR\*\*/){
                  print "Content-type:  text/html\n\n";
                  print "ERROR retrieving data!\n";
                  print "$$.sql!\n";
                  $recs = -1;   #flag the error
                  last;
            }
            ($USERID, $USERNAME, $MIDDLENAME, $PHONE) =
                  split(/\|/,$_);
            $recs++;
      }
      close(SQL);
      unlink("/tmp/$$.sql");      # delete temporary file
      if($recs == 0){
            # put error handling here
      }
```

```
}
########################+--------------+
#                       | gen_SQL_proc |
#                       +--------------+
# Note this subroutine uses a global array named SQL_cmds
#
sub gen_SQL_proc{

       open(SQL,">/tmp/$$.sql")
              || die "Can't create SQL script\n";

       open(HDR,"$SQL_hdr");
       while(<HDR>){
              print SQL "$_";
       }
       close(HDR);

       foreach $cmd (@SQL_cmd){
              print SQL "$cmd\n";
       }

       open(FTR,"$SQL_footer");
       while(<FTR>){
              print SQL "$_";
       }
       close(FTR);
       close(SQL);
       @SQL_cmds = "";
}
########################+------------+
#                       | paint_form |
#                       +------------+
# Usage:
#      &paint_form(filename);
#
sub paint_form{
       $template = $_[0];

       open(FILE,"$HTML_dir/$template")
              or die "Can't open $template\n";

       print "Content-type:  text/html\n\n";
       while(<FILE>){
```

16

```
                $_ =~ s/\$TTITLE/$QS{'Profile'}/e;
                $_ =~ s/\$USER/$USERNAME/e;
                $_ =~ s/\$PHONE/$PHONE/e;
                print $_;
        }
}
```

There is a minimum amount of SQL knowledge required for any method of database access through an SQL interface. That knowledge consists of basic retrieval, updating a record, and deleting a record. The following table shows the SQL for each of the basic operations:

Operation	Select	Example
Retrieval, all records	SELECT	SELECT NAME FROM EMPLOYEE;
Retrieval, specific record	SELECT	SELECT NAME FROM EMPLOYEE WHERE EMPID = '1';
Delete all records in a table	DELETE	DELETE EMPLOYEE;
Delete a specific record from a table	DELETE	DELETE EMPLOYEE WHERE EMPID = '1';
Add new record	INSERT	INSERT INTO EMPLOYEE (NAME, PHONE) VALUES ("Norman Smith","555-1234");
Update a record	UPDATE	UPDATE EMPLOYEE SET PHONE = "555-4321" WHERE EMPID = '1';
Apply table changes	COMMIT	COMMIT;
Exit SQLPlus	QUIT	QUIT;
List fields in a table	DESCRIBE	DESCRIBE EMPLOYEE;

HINT: Be sure to test all SQL commands interactively before putting the SQL commands in a program or SQL script, especially if the SQL modifies the database. Otherwise, the database may be damaged.

There are whole books written on SQL. Get one if you plan to use SQL in real applications. The example code in these examples will not work without modifications because of system specific data.

Template files and database names are unique to each application and database.

Tools Used

The Case 3 solution is again a Unix implementation via Linux. The PC and software used are:

- 166mz Pentium
- Red Hat 4.0 Linux
- Apache Web Server
- Netscape Navigator 3.0 for Linux
- Perl 5.002

InContext Spider was used under Windows 95 to construct the demo pages.

Design

Most client-server applications are largely driven by the user interface. That means the application is controlled by the user selecting options and entering data in screens. The same comments about the difficulty in defining programs for specific functions made in Case 2 also apply to the Image Database Case. The processing normally associated with a traditional program is split across JavaScript in the client and Perl on the server.

Since the screens pretty much drive the design, here is the final list of screens identified during design:

- Logon
- Main page where the user selects actions to perform on the database
- Hit list screen for searches
- Add a new record
- Edit an existing record
- Set processing options

- A report of records in the database
- Log on again as a different user
- View a record

In addition, there are database actions that have dialog boxes instead of separate screens. These are:

- Search the database
- Select a database record

One final action, loading a new database, has no screen associated with it at all. All in all, there is quite a variety of implementation details that are different from function to function. There is no reason to make every action call up another screen; many actions can be handled effectively by popping up a dialog box instead. The following Data Flow Diagram describes the layout of the Image Database System implemented for Case 3.

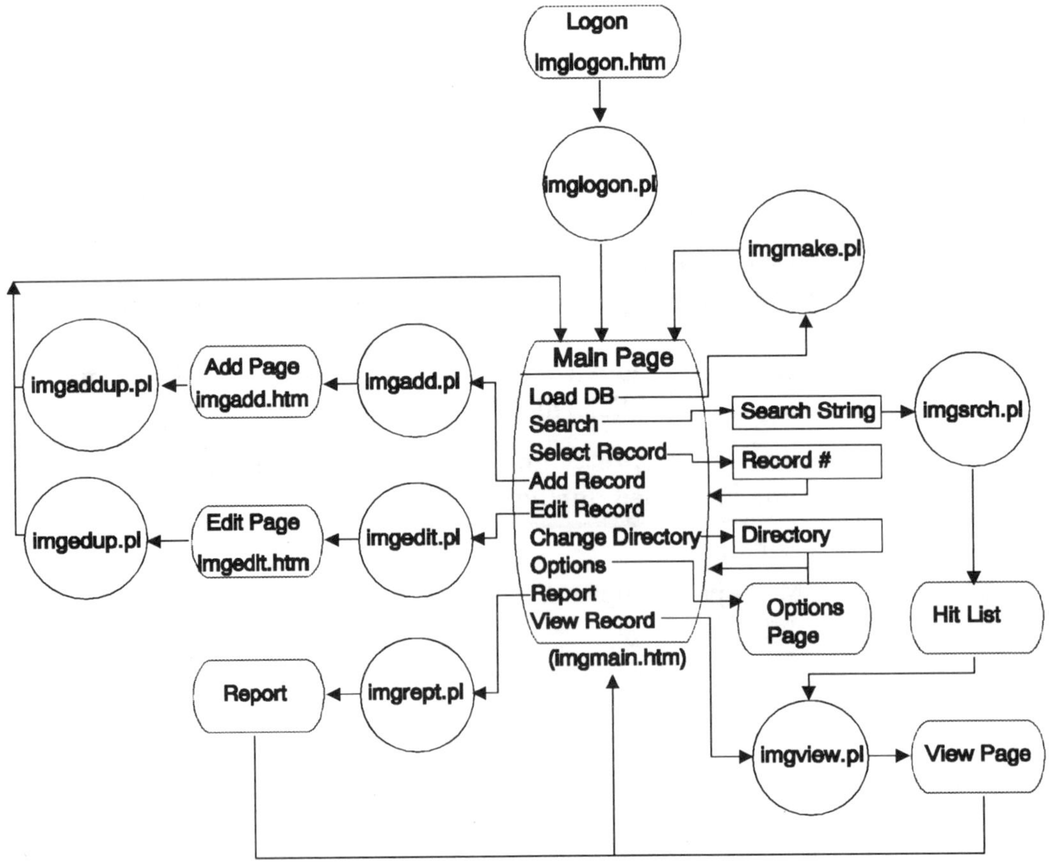

The symbols on the DFD have the same meaning as those in the DFD for Case 2. The circles represent processes or programs. The rectangles with rounded corners are HTML pages, most of which contain some JavaScript processing. The rectangles represent JavaScript dialog boxes. The filenames are listed on the HTML page or process symbols instead of including a separate disk symbol for each file. This bad DFD practice was done in an effort to get the DFD to fit on the page. In real life, this DFD should be broken down a further level with each action a separate DFD with all the detail shown.

Logon

The logon operation uses the HTML file imglogon.htm to display the logon form. The user types a username, a password, and optionally, the image directory. Each user account has a default directory that will be used if none is specified.

HINT: In a production system, the logon screen should be set up as a secure page via SSL or HTTPS.

Search Image DB

Searching the Image Database is accomplished in several stages. JavaScript code in imgmain.htm pops up a dialog box that the search string is typed into. When the user clicks the Done button, the JavaScript code builds a URL and executes imgsrch.pl passing the search string. The search implemented in this case study is a simple string search using built-in Perl capabilities. The entire record is searched, but implementing a fielded search would not be difficult.

The records that contain the search string are displayed as a separate screen called a "hit list." The record number, filename, and description fields are displayed with the record number being a hyperlink. Click on the record number to display the record via the imgview.pl program.

This is the point that interfacing with a real DBMS such as Oracle or Sybase would be done when using a database system.

Select Image

Selecting an image is done by image number. A JavaScript dialog box pops up where the record number of the image record is entered. Record numbers are zero indexed, meaning that the first record number is zero, not one. The Edit and View options use the image number to select the image to display. The image number is stored in a cookie.

Add New Record

Adding a new record starts with executing imgadd.pl when the Add New Record button is clicked. The program creates the HTML display directly; no HTML template is used. After the user enters the new data, clicking Add Record causes imgaddup.pl to run, which appends the new record to the end of the current database.

Edit Record

The record to be edited is chosen by selecting an image number via the Select Image operation above. The Perl script imgedit.pl dynamically generates the HTML page. This approach allows the values in the database to be included on the form for editing.

After the user completes editing the record, the Update Record button is clicked to execute imgedup.pl to actually update the image record.

Change Directory

Changing the current image directory is done completely within the Main Page imgmain.htm via JavaScript. A dialog box pops up; the user types the new directory and clicks Done. The JavaScript code also changes the value in the directory box at the bottom of the Main Page.

Options

The options processing is a little different than the rest of the system. It is implemented totally in JavaScript. Clicking the options button causes imgopt.htm, which contains the JavaScript, to load. The option data is collected via a normal HTML form. When the Update Options button is clicked, JavaScript code runs to set an "options" cookie and return to the Main Page.

HINT: Global values can be collected and stored as cookies totally on the client side via JavaScript.

Report

The report generated for this application is basically an HTML report of all the image records in the database. It uses one of the options stored in a cookie to determine whether or not to display the image with the record.

Logon Again

There may be times when logging on again as a different user may be necessary. The Logon Again option is simply a hyperlink to the Logon Page.

View Record

The record to view is selected via the Select Image operation described above. The CGI program imgview.pl is called to display the selected record. The record is selected using the Select Record option described above.

Implementation

The implementation phase of this case study is similar to the implementation phase of the RCS application in Case 2. Both use HTML, Perl, and JavaScript to implement the application described in the design. The remainder of this chapter describes the implementation details of the Image Database Application.

Security Considerations

The same security considerations apply that were discussed in Chapter 15. The code described here was implemented with the Web server running as ROOT, which is a bad practice in a production environment attached to a network. My Linux system is stand-alone, not attached to a network.

Even though there is a logon screen, the code in the applications does not check to make sure that the program is being run by a valid user. The hooks are all there because the User ID is stored in a cookie that can be easily accessed and checked. Always add this extra little bit of code in a real application!

Require Files

This case study uses require files to include commonly used code in the Perl programs. The files are imgvars.req and imgtools.req. It turns out that imgvars.req is almost identical to vars.req from Case 2. imgtools.req extends the original tools.req with code to parse a cookie string into an associative array named %cookie. The listing for imgvars.req is:

```
#
# FILE: imgvars.req
#
$PASS_DIR     = "/home/httpd/cgi-bin";
$HTML_DIR     = "/home/httpd/html";
$TEMPLATE_DIR = "/home/httpd/html/template";
$IMAGE_DIR    = "/home/httpd/html/images";
return 1;
```

The new subroutines in imgtools.req are &parse_cookie() and &dump_cookie(). &parse_cookie() accepts a cookie string and extracts each "key=value" pair and places them in %cookie. Thus referring to a cookie named XXX would be:

```
$value = $cookie{'XXX'};
```

in Perl. &dump_cookie() is a debugging routine that prints out all of the current entries in %cookie.

The listing for imgtools.req is:

```
# FILE: imgtools.req
########################+---------+
#                       | dump_QS |
#                       +---------+
sub dump_QS{
        foreach $key (keys(%QS)){
                print "QS{'$key'}: $QS{$key}<BR>\n";
        }
}
########################+-----------+
#                       | parse_cgi |
#                       +-----------+
sub parse_cgi{
        local($i);
        local($key);
        local($val);
        local($QString);

        if($ENV{'REQUEST_METHOD'} eq "GET"){
                $QString = $ENV{'QUERY_STRING'};
        }else{
                $LEN = $ENV{'CONTENT_LENGTH'};
                read(STDIN,$QString,$LEN);
        }
        &parse_string("$QString");
}
########################+--------------+
#                       | parse_string |
#                       +--------------+
# Usage:
#       &parse_string("string");
#
sub parse_string{
        local($QString);

        $QString = $_[0];
        @QS = split(/&/,$QString);
```

```
        foreach $i (0 .. $#QS){
                $QS[$i] =~ s/\+/ /g;
                ($key,$val) = split(/=/,$QS[$i],2);
                $key =~ s/%(..)/pack("c",hex($1))/ge;
                $val =~ s/%(..)/pack("c",hex($1))/ge;
                $QS{$key} .= "\0" if (defined($QS{$key}));
                $QS{$key} .= $val;
        }
}
########################+-------------+
#                       | dump_cookie |
#                       +-------------+
sub dump_cookie{
        foreach $key (keys(%cookie)){
                print "cookie{'$key'}: $cookie{$key}<BR>\n";
        }
}
########################+--------------+
#                       | parse_cookie |
#                       +--------------+
# This subroutine accepts a cookie string and
# splits it into the associative array %cookie.
#
sub parse_cookie{
        local(@cookies);
        local($key);
        local($val);
        local($c);

        @cookies = split(/;/,$_[0]);
        foreach $c (@cookies){
                ($key,$val)    =  split(/=/,$c);
                $key       =~ s/ //g;
                $cookie{$key} =  $val;
        }
}

return 1;
```

The more intranet applications you do, the larger the tools file will grow up to a point. Code that you discover being used over and over belongs in a require file.

Image Logon

The user starts by logging onto the Image Database. A username and password are required and an optional directory path. The logon process consists of an HTML file that contains some JavaScript, a Perl CGI script, and the password file. The initial logon display is:

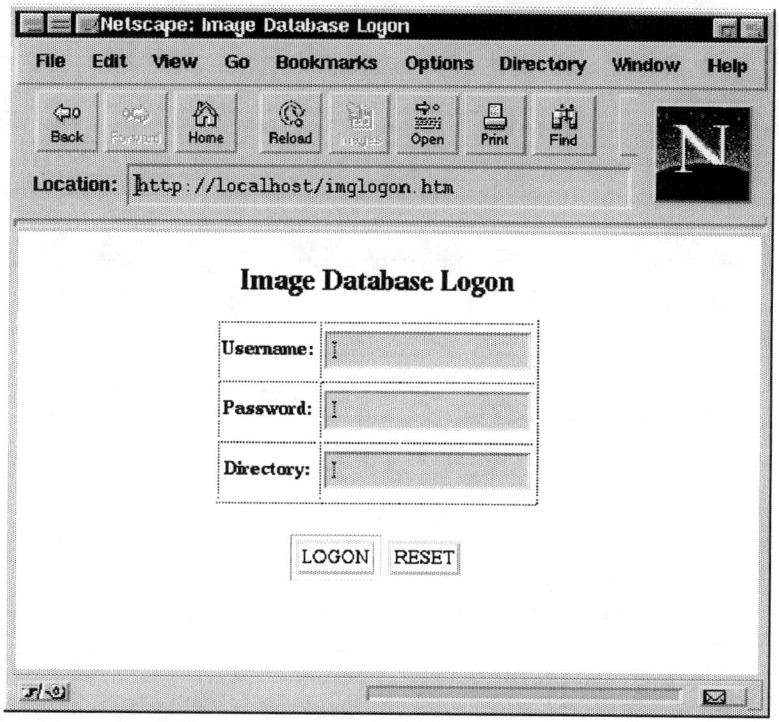

The JavaScript code in imglogon.htm does simple field validation by making sure that both the username and password fields contain text. The following display is generated when the password field is left blank.

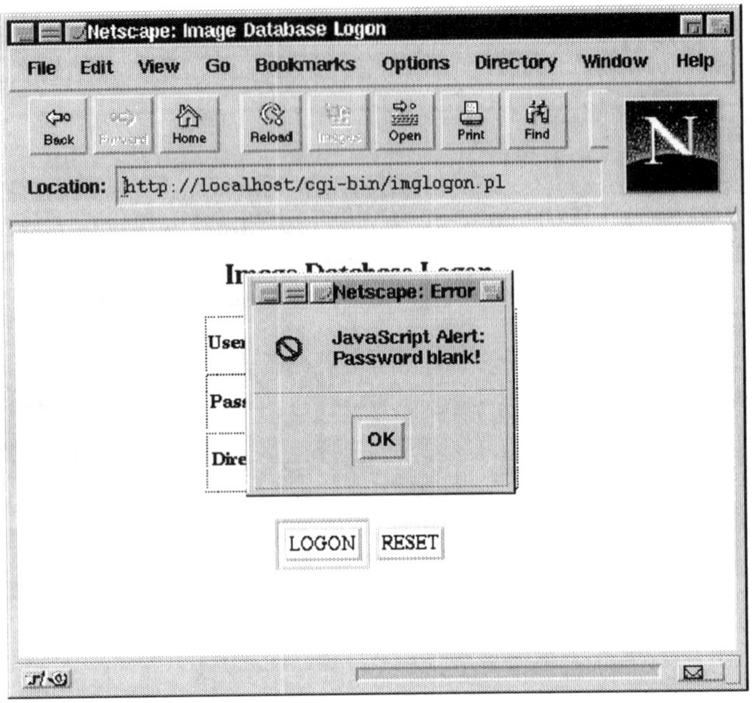

The HTML code for imglogon.htm is:

```
<HTML>
<HEAD>
<TITLE>Image Database Logon</TITLE>
<SCRIPT LANGUAGE="JAVASCRIPT">
function validate(){
        if(document.LOGON.USER.value == ""){
                alert("Username blank!");
                return false;
        }
        if(document.LOGON.PASS.value == ""){
                alert("Password blank!");
                return false;
        }
        return true;
}
function CheckErrorFlag(){
        if(document.LOGON.ErrorFlag.value != "0"){
                alert("Login failed. Invalid User Name or Password!");
        }
```

```
        document.LOGON.USER.focus();
}
</SCRIPT>
</HEAD>
<BODY BGCOLOR="#FFFFFF" onLoad="CheckErrorFlag();">
<H1 ALIGN="CENTER">Image Database Logon</H1>
<CENTER>
<FORM NAME="LOGON" METHOD="POST" ACTION="/cgi-bin/imglogon.pl"
onSubmit="return validate();">
<!-- ErrorFlag is used to pass info to JavaScript -->
<INPUT TYPE="HIDDEN" NAME="ErrorFlag" VALUE="0">
<TABLE BORDER>
<TR>
  <TH>Username:</TH>
  <TD><INPUT TYPE="TEXT" NAME="USER"></TD>
</TR>
<TR>
  <TH>Password:</TH>
  <TD><INPUT TYPE="PASSWORD" NAME="PASS"></TD>
</TR>
<TR>
  <TH>Directory:</TH>
  <TD><INPUT TYPE="TEXT" NAME="DIR"></TD>
</TR>
</TABLE>
<br>
<INPUT TYPE="SUBMIT" VALUE="LOGON">
<INPUT TYPE="RESET" VALUE="RESET">
</CENTER>
</FORM>
</BODY>
</HTML>
```

The Perl program, imglogon.pl, is executed when the user clicks Logon. The program looks up the username and password in the password file imgpass and sets the *ErrorFlag* accordingly.

```
#!/usr/local/bin/perl
###############################################################
# FILE: imglogon.pl
##################################
$TOOL_DIR      = "/home/httpd/cgi-bin";
```

```
require "$TOOL_DIR/tools.req";
require "$TOOL_DIR/vars.req";
        #
        # Global stuff
        #
        # Get data passed in from the HTML form
&parse_cgi();           #
        # The following two lines used for debugging
        #
#print "Content-type: text/html\n\n";
#&dump_QS();
        #
        # Build parameter string to pass to look up
        #
$user_pw = "$QS{'USER'}:$QS{'PASS'}:";
        #
        # Load password file into memory
        #
open(PWD,"$PASS_DIR/imgpass") || die "Can't open Password file!\n";
while(<PWD>){
        chop;
        push(@data,$_);
}
close(PWD);
        #
        # search the password for name and password
        #
$success = 0;
foreach $passwd (@data){
        if($passwd =~ /^$user_pw/){
                $success = 1;
                &successful_logon($passwd);
                last;
        }
}
if($success == 0){ # No data means logon failed.
        &invalid_user();
}
exit;
########################+------------------+
#                       | successful_logon |
#                       +------------------+
sub successful_logon{
```

```
        $pw_dir  = 4;
        $pw_uid  = 2;
        $pw_dest = 5;

        @db = split(/:/,$passwd);
        if($QS{'DIR'} eq ""){
                $QS{'DIR'}  = $db[$pw_dir];
        }
        $QS{'DIR'} =~ s/\/\//\//g;
        $QS{'DEST'} = $db[$pw_dest];
        $QS{'DEST'} =~ s/\/\//\//g;
        print "Content-type:  text/html\n";
        print "Set-Cookie: USER=$db[$pw_uid]; path=/cgi-bin;\n";
        print "Set-Cookie: IMG=0; path=/cgi-bin;\n";
        print "Set-Cookie: DIR=$db[$pw_dir]; path=/cgi-bin;\n";
        print "\n\n";
                #
                # Set up Cookie
                #
        open (HTML,"$HTML_DIR//imgmain.htm")
                || die "Can't open imgmain.htm\n";

        while(<HTML>){
                if(/\$DIR/){
                        s/\$DIR/$QS{'DIR'}/e;
                }
                print "$_";
        }
        close(HTML);

        return;
}
#########################+--------------+
#                        | insert_files |
#                        +--------------+
sub insert_files{
        print "      <OPTION VALUE=\"\*\*NONE\*\*\" SELECTED>Select A
File</option>";
        open(DIR,"ls -1F $QS{'DIR'} |");
        while(<DIR>){
                if(/\//){       next;  }
                s/\*//g;
                print "<OPTION VALUE=\"$_\">$_</option>";
```

16

```
        }
}
#######################+--------------+
#                       | invalid_user |
#                       +--------------+
sub invalid_user{
        print "Content-type:  text/html\n\n";
        open (HTML,"$HTML_DIR/imglogon.htm")
                || die "Can't open imglogon.htm\n";

        while(<HTML>){
                s/NAME=\"ErrorFlag\" VALUE=\"0\"/NAME=\"ErrorFlag\"
VALUE=\"1\"/;
                print "$_";
        }
        close(HTML);

        return;
}
```

Note that multiple cookies are set in the subroutine &successful_logon(). The cookie values used here, user ID and such, are normally single word phrases with no embedded spaces.

HINT: If the cookie values contain any of the special CGI characters such as blank, "%", ";", "+", etc, the characters must be encoded. For example, blanks must be translated to a "+".

The contents of the password file for this case study is:

```
smith:norm:1:Norman Smith:/home/httpd/html/images
jones:john:2:John Jones:/home/html/images
doe:john:3:John Doe:/home/doe:/home/httpd/cgi-bin
```

The password file is ":" delimited, which is a convenient form for Perl to process.

Image Main Page

The Image Database application is controlled from the Main Page. It is accessed from several places including the Logon Page. The Image Database Main Page is:

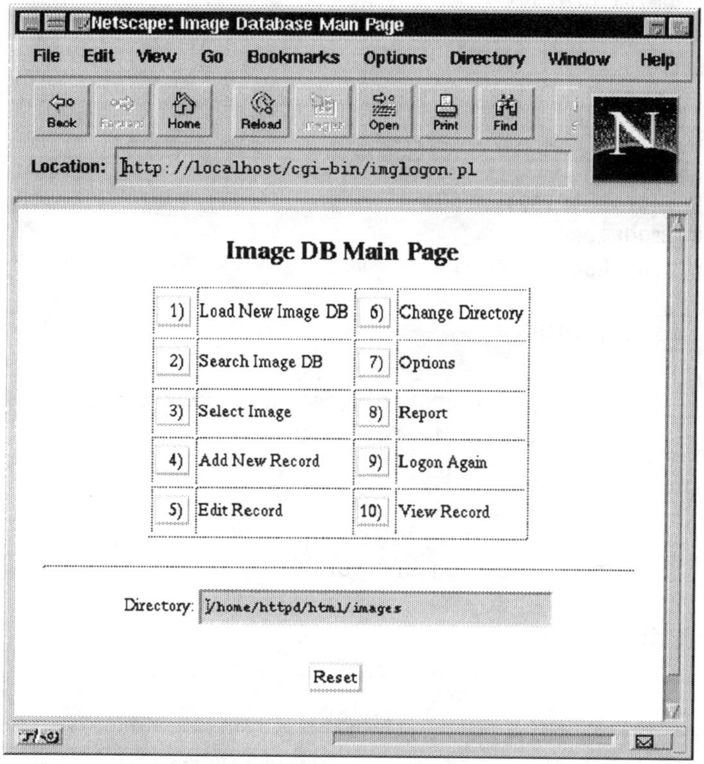

The screen is relatively straightforward. Notice that there is no Submit button. All of the numbers are generic buttons that execute JavaScript functions when clicked.

HINT: The primary disadvantage of using buttons from an aesthetic point of view is the buttons' size to hold their text. Using blanks in the button value will often work to make the buttons the same size. That is the approach used here.

Since the application is operated from this screen, we'll go through the code in detail. External programs will be discussed separately. The HTML code for imgmain.htm is:

```
<HTML>
<!--imgmain.htm-->
<!--03/09/97   -->
<HEAD>
<TITLE>Image Database Main Page</TITLE>
<SCRIPT LANGUAGE="JAVASCRIPT">
<!--
var SearchString;
var ImgNumber;
function LoadNewDB(){
        var url;
        var DIR;

        DIR = window.prompt("Load New Image DB: Enter Directory",
                document.IMGMAIN.DIR.value);
        if(!DIR){ return; }   // Exit if cancel clicked

        url = "/cgi-bin/imgmake.pl?DIR=" + DIR;
        window.location.href=url;
}
function logon(){
        window.location.href = "../imglogon.htm";
}
function initvars(){
        ImgNumber    = document.IMGMAIN.IMGNUM.value;
        SearchString = "";
}
function changeDir(){
        var oldDir;
        var DIR;
        oldDir = document.IMGMAIN.DIR.value;
        DIR    =
window.prompt("Enter New Directory",document.IMGMAIN.DIR.value);
        if(!DIR){ return; }   // Exit if cancel clicked
        if(document.IMGMAIN.DIR.value == ""){
                alert("Directory Blank!");
                document.IMGMAIN.DIR.value = oldDIR;
        }
```

```
        document.IMGMAIN.DIR.value = DIR;
}
function searchDB(){
        var oldSearch;
        var DIR;
        oldSearch    = SearchString;
        SearchString =
                window.prompt("Enter Search String",SearchString);
        if(!SearchString){ return; } // Exit if cancel clicked
        url = "/cgi-bin/imgsrch.pl?SRCH=" + SearchString;
        window.location.href = url;
}
function setOptions(){
        window.location.href = "../imgopt.htm";
}
function report(){
        window.location.href = "/cgi-bin/imgrept.pl";
}
function addRec(){
        window.location.href = "/cgi-bin/imgadd.pl";
}
function editRec(){
        window.location.href = "/cgi-bin/imgedit.pl";
}
function viewRec(){
        window.location.href = "/cgi-bin/imgview.pl";
}
function setImg(){
        var oldImg;
        var IMG;
        oldImg    = ImgNumber;
        ImgNumber = window.prompt("Enter Image Number",ImgNumber);
        if(!ImgNumber){ return; }    // Exit if cancel clicked
        document.cookie="IMG=" + ImgNumber;
}
// -->
</SCRIPT>
</HEAD>
<BODY BGCOLOR="#FFFFFF" onLoad="initvars()">
<H1 ALIGN="CENTER">Image DB Main Page</H1>
<CENTER>
<FORM METHOD="POST" NAME="IMGMAIN" onSubmit="return check_dir();"
ACTION="/cgi-bin/imgmain.pl">
```

```
<INPUT TYPE="HIDDEN" NAME="IMGNUM" VALUE="0">
<TABLE BORDER ALIGN="CENTER">
<TR>
  <TD><INPUT TYPE="BUTTON" NAME="OPR" VALUE="  1)"
onClick="LoadNewDB()"></TD>
  <TD>Load New Image DB</TD>
  <TD><INPUT TYPE="BUTTON" NAME="OPR" VALUE="  6)"
onClick="changeDir();"></TD>
  <TD>Change Directory</TD>
</TR>
<TR>
  <TD><INPUT TYPE="BUTTON" NAME="OPR" VALUE="  2)"
onClick="searchDB();"></TD>
  <TD>Search Image DB</TD>
  <TD><INPUT TYPE="BUTTON" NAME="OPS" VALUE="  7)"
onClick="setOptions();"></TD>
  <TD>Options</TD>
</TR>
<TR>
  <TD><INPUT TYPE="BUTTON" NAME="OPR" VALUE="  3)"
onClick="setImg();"></TD>
  <TD>Select Image</TD>
  <TD><INPUT TYPE="BUTTON" NAME="OPR" VALUE="  8)"
onClick="report();"></TD>
  <TD>Report</TD>
</TR>
<TR>
  <TD><INPUT TYPE="BUTTON" NAME="OPR" VALUE="  4)"
onClick="addRec();"></TD>
  <TD>Add New Record</TD>
  <TD><INPUT TYPE="BUTTON" NAME="OPR" VALUE="  9)"
onClick="logon()"></TD>
  <TD>Logon Again</TD>
</TR>
<TR>
  <TD><INPUT TYPE="BUTTON" VALUE="  5)" onClick="editRec();"></TD>
  <TD>Edit Record</TD>
  <TD><INPUT TYPE="BUTTON" VALUE="10)" onClick="viewRec();"></TD>
  <TD>View Record</TD>
</TABLE>
<BR>
<HR>
<TABLE ALIGN="CENTER">
```

```
<TR>
  <TD>Directory: <INPUT TYPE="TEXT" NAME="DIR" VALUE="$DIR"
SIZE="40"></TD>
</TR>
</TABLE>
<BR>
<INPUT TYPE="RESET"  VALUE="Reset">
<BR>
</FORM>
</BODY>
</HTML>
```

The HTML portion of imgmain.htm is relatively normal HTML with a table in a form to format the display. The main body is physically four columns wide but logically only two columns wide. Each logical column consists of a button with a number and a text phrase describing the action associated with the button. Thus you click 10), to View Record.

The first action on the menu is Load New Image DB. The LoadNewDB() JavaScript function is executed by clicking the 1) button. LoadNewDB() pops up a dialog box to type the directory path into. The directory listed in the text box at the bottom of the HTML page is used as the default. LoadNewDB() builds a URL string that includes the directory path and executes imgmake.pl.

Make a New Image Database

The process of creating a skeleton image database is done by imgmake.pl. The program reads the DIR CGI value, changes directory to that path, performs a directory listing for all files that have a ".gif" or ".jpg" extension, and builds default records for each GIF/JPG file found. The database name is imagedat. The code for imgmake.pl is:

```
#!/usr/local/bin/perl
#
# FILE: imgmake.pl
#
$TOOL_DIR     = "/home/httpd/cgi-bin";
```

```
require "$TOOL_DIR/tools.req";
require "$TOOL_DIR/vars.req";

&parse_cgi();

chdir("$QS{'DIR'}");

$i = 0;
open(DB,">imagedat") || die "Can't open imagedat!\n";
open(DIR,"ls -1 -s |");
<DIR>;                  # trash the "total" line
while(<DIR>){
        chop;
        ($blank,$size,$file,$trash) = split(/ +/,$_);
        ($trash,$ext)               = split(/\./,$file);
        if(($ext ne "gif") && ($ext ne "jpg")){ next;  }
        if($size < 4){
                $tsml = "T";
        }elsif($size < 16){
                $tsml = "S";
        }elsif($size < 50){
                $tsml = "M";
        }elsif($size < 1000){
                $tsml = "L";
        }
        print DB "$file|$i|$size|$tsml|1||1|No Description\n";
        $i++;
}
close(DIR);

print "Content-type:  text/html\n\n";

open(HTML,"$HTML_DIR/imgmain.htm")
        || die "Can't Open imgmain.htm!\n";

while(<HTML>){
        if(/\$DIR/){
                s/\$DIR/$QS{'DIR'}/e;
        }
        print "$_";
}
close(HTML);
```

The record layout for the image database is:

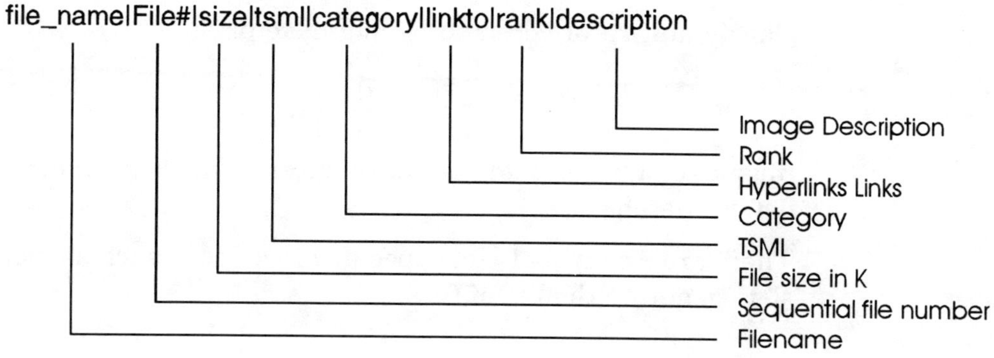

The values used for Category are:

Value	Meaning
1	Unknown
2	SGML
3	Windows 95
4	Forth
5	Perl

The values used for Rank are:

Value	Meaning
1	Great!
2	Excellent
3	Good
4	OK
5	No Interest

The TSML values are:

Value	Meaning
T	Thumbnail
S	Small
M	Medium
L	Large

These values are important because the software must translate the values to the text meaning for display.

The default record created by imgmake.pl is:

```
file|filenum|size|T|1||1|No Description
```

imgmake.pl reloads imgmain.htm after it finishes building the default database.

There are a couple of Unix specific bits of code such as using "ls -1 -s" to generate the list of files.

HINT: Put operating specific commands, such as the "ls -1 -s", into a variable in a require file if the server portion of an application must run on multiple platforms. That way supplying a different version of the require file is all that is necessary to port the code.

Search Image DB

The second action on the Image Main Page is searching an image database. The 2) button is tied to the searchDB() JavaScript function in imgmain.htm. It pops up a dialog box for the search string, then builds a URL string to execute imgsrch.pl with the search string and current image directory as arguments. The following display shows the search string dialog box:

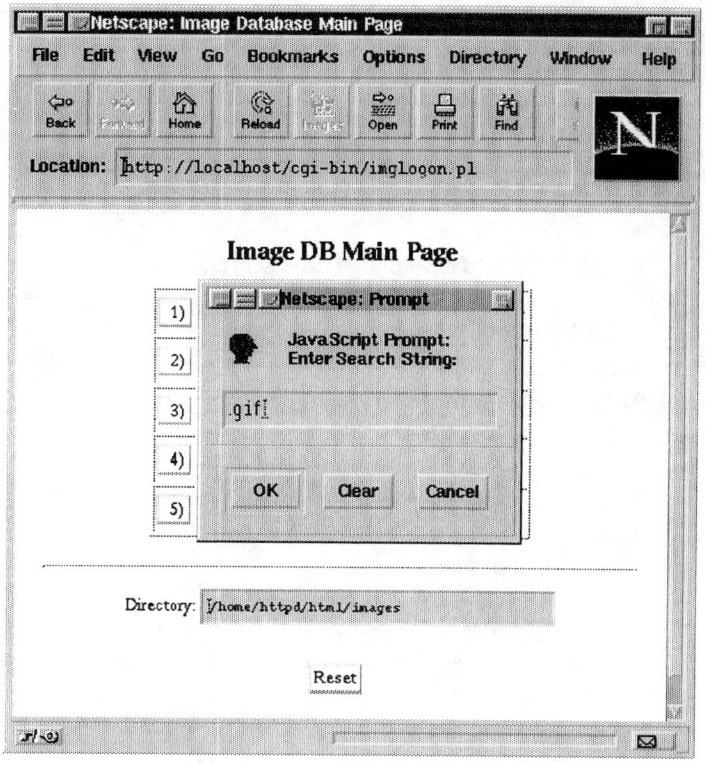

The code for imgsrch.pl is:

```
#!/usr/local/bin/perl
#
# FILE: imgsrch.pl
#

$TOOL_DIR     = "/home/httpd/cgi-bin";

require "$TOOL_DIR/imgtools.req";
require "$TOOL_DIR/imgvars.req";

print "Content-type:  text/html\n\n";
```

```
&parse_cgi();
&parse_cookie($ENV{'HTTP_COOKIE'});
        #
        # Generate the start of the Hit List Page
        #
&display_start();
        #
        # Search for the record specified.
        #
$srch  = $QS{'SRCH'};
$count = 0;
open(DIR,"$cookie{'DIR'}/imagedat");
while(<DIR>){
        chop;
        $rec = $_;
        if($rec =~ /$srch/){
                $count++;
                @fld = split(/\|/,$_);
                print "<TR>\n<TD ALIGN=\"RIGHT\">";
                print "<A HREF=\"/cgi-bin/imgview.pl?IMG=$fld[1]\">"
                Print " $fld[1]</A></TD>\n";
                print "<TD>$fld[0]</TD>\n";
                print "<TD>$fld[7]</TD>\n";
                print "</TR>\n";
        }
}
close(DIR);
if($count == 0){
        print "<TR><TH COLSPAN=3>No Hits!</TH></TR>\n";
}
&display_end();
exit;
########################+---------------+
#                       | display_start |
#                       +---------------+
sub display_start{
        print "<HTML>\n";
        print "<HEAD>\n";
        print "<SCRIPT LANGUAGE=\"JAVASCRIPT\">\n";
        print "function MainMenu(){\n";
        print "window.location.href=\"/cgi-bin/imgmain.pl\";\n";
        print "}\n";
        print "</SCRIPT>\n";
```

```
        print "</HEAD>\n";
        print "<BODY BGCOLOR=\"#FFFFFF\">\n";
        print "<H1 ALIGN=\"CENTER\">Image Database Hit List</H1>\n";
        print "<CENTER>\n";
        print "<TABLE BORDER>\n";
        print "<TR>\n";
        print "  <TH>Rec#</TH>\n";
        print "  <TH>File</TH>\n";
        print "  <TH>Description</TH>\n";
        print "</TR>\n";
}
########################+-------------+
#                       | display_end |
#                       +-------------+
sub display_end{
        print "</TABLE>\n";
        print "<BR>\n";
        print "<HR>\n";
        print "<FORM>\n";
        print "<INPUT TYPE=\"BUTTON\" VALUE=\"Main Page\"";
        print " onClick=\"MainMenu()\">\n";
        print "</FORM>\n";
        print "</CENTER>\n";
        print "</BODY>\n";
        print "</HEAD>\n";
        print "</HTML>\n";
}
```

The code has a couple of items worth noting. The program generates what is commonly termed a "Hit List" of records that match the search. The following display is a Hit List Page for the ".gif" search:

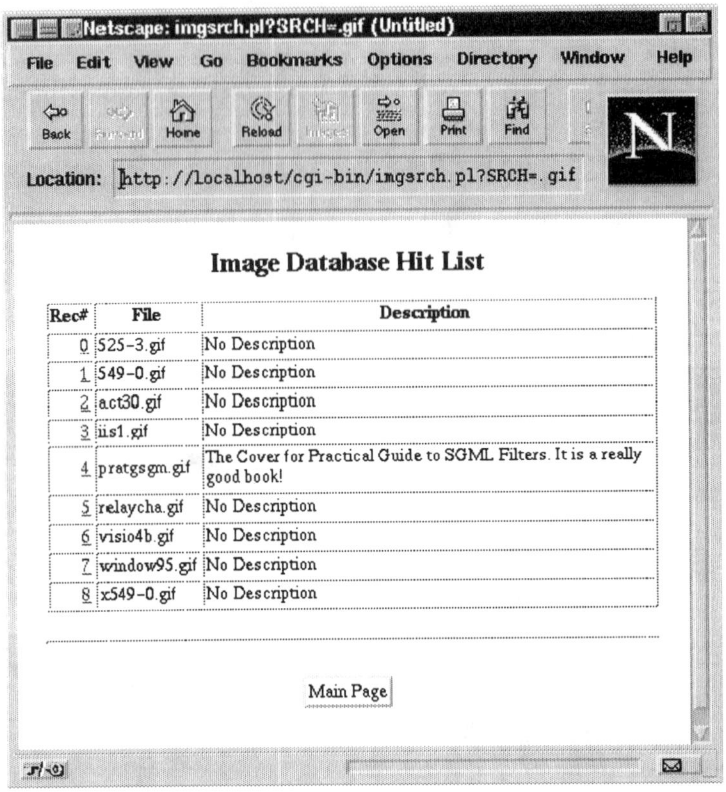

The main section of the code outputs the top portion of the HTML page, then outputs each detail line as records match the search string. Finally, the bottom portion is generated to close the page. The display is totally generated within imgsrch.pl based on data at run time.

The "hits" all include the record number, the filename, and the description field. The record number is set up as a hyperlink. Simply clicking on a record number will display that record. The following display results from clicking on record 8:

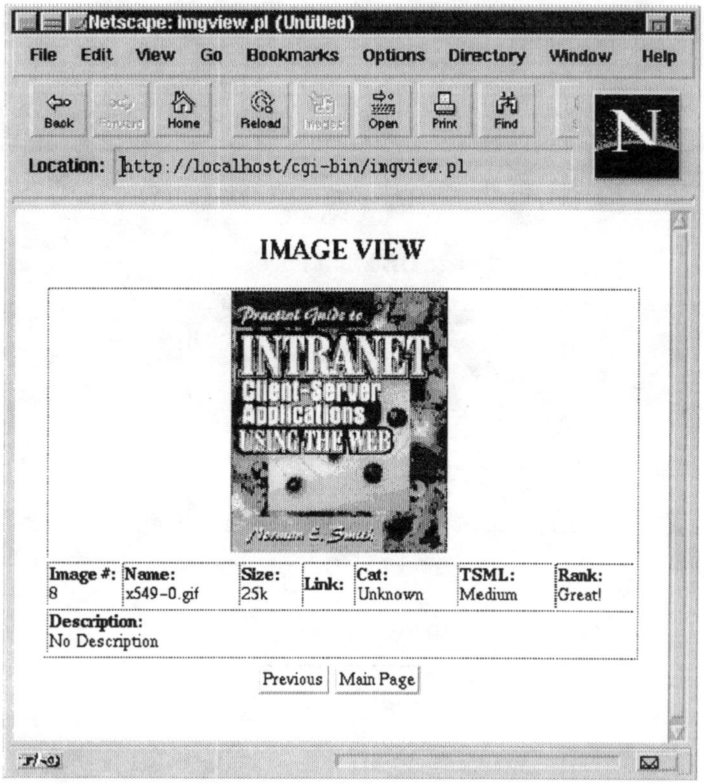

The display is created by imgview.pl, which is discussed below. Returning to the Main Page is accomplished by clicking on the Main Page button.

Select an Image Record

A record must be selected before it can be viewed or edited. Selecting an image is done totally within imgmain.htm. When the 3) button is clicked, the browser calls setImg(). A dialog box pops up to key the record number into:

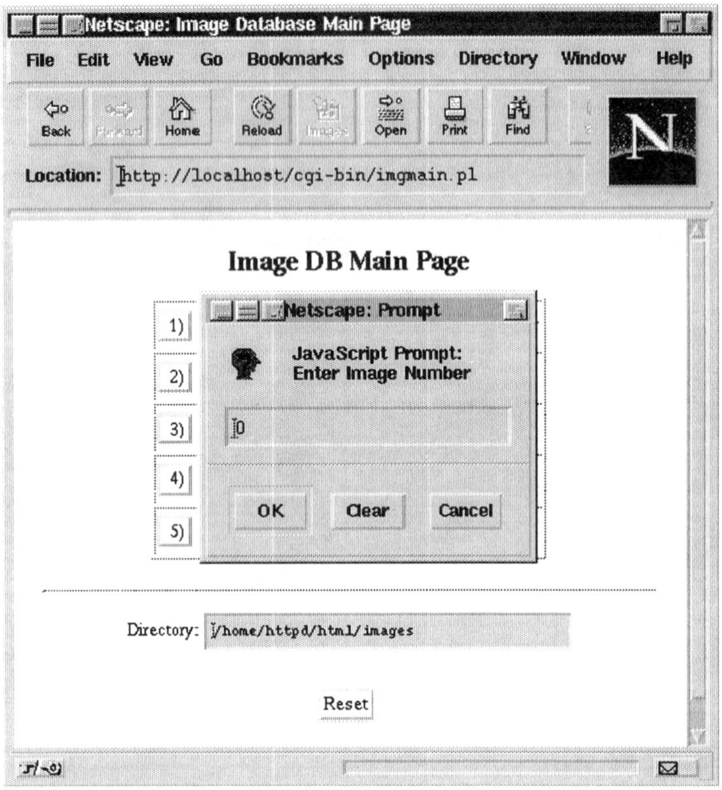

setImg() sets the *IMG* cookie to the value entered. The edit and view actions use the cookie to determine the record number to process.

Add New Record

Use Add New Record to add a new record to the image database after the initial load process. Click button 4) to execute imgadd.pl, which generates the following display:

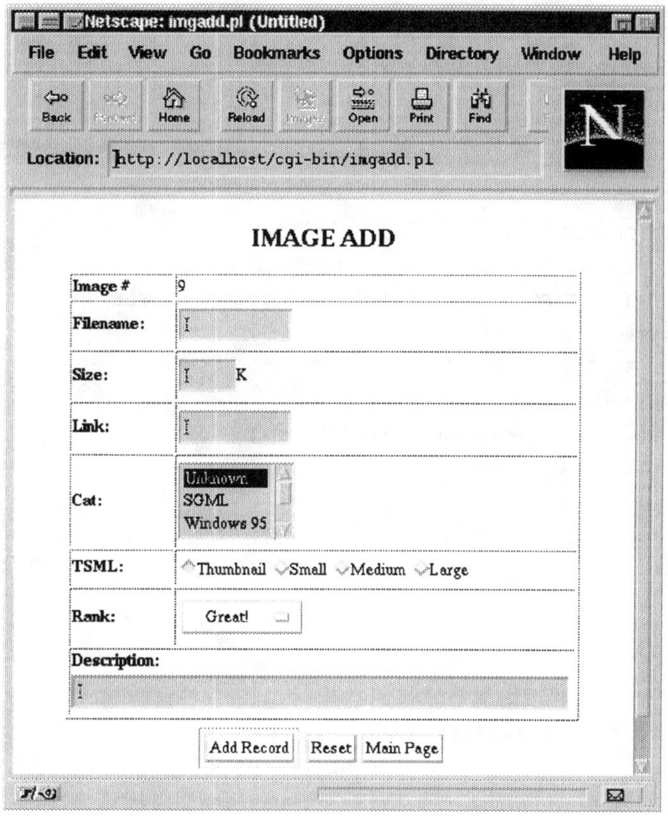

HINT: Flat file databases, such as the one used here, have some pretty major limitations. Always use a multiuser database such as Oracle when more than one user may be updating the database at any given time. Using a flat file for a database is practical when the database is read only and when the database size is small.

The code for imgadd.pl is:

```
#!/usr/local/bin/perl
#
# FILE: imgadd.pl
#

$TOOL_DIR     = "/home/httpd/cgi-bin";
```

```
require "$TOOL_DIR/imgtools.req";
require "$TOOL_DIR/imgvars.req";

print "Content-type:  text/html\n\n";

&parse_cgi();
&parse_cookie($ENV{'HTTP_COOKIE'});
        #
        # Figure out what the last record number is
        #
$rec   = "";
$count = 0;
open(DIR,"$cookie{'DIR'}/imagedat");
while(<DIR>){
        $count++;
}
close(DIR);

&display_rec();

exit;
########################+-------------+
#                       | display_rec |
#                       +-------------+
sub display_rec{
        print "<HTML>\n";
        print "<HEAD>\n";
        print "<SCRIPT LANGUAGE=\"JAVASCRIPT\">\n";
        print "function MainMenu(){\n";
        print "window.location.href=\"/cgi-bin/imgmain.pl\";\n";
        print "}\n";
        print "function SetTSML(){\n";
        print "var value = parseInt(document.ADD.SIZE.value);\n";
        print "}\n";
        print "</SCRIPT>\n";
        print "</HEAD>\n";
        print "<BODY BGCOLOR=\"#FFFFFF\">\n";
        print "<H1 ALIGN=\"CENTER\">IMAGE ADD</H1>\n";
print "<FORM NAME=\"ADD\"";
        print " ACTION=\"/cgi-bin/imgaddup.pl\">\n";
        print "<CENTER>\n";
        print "<TABLE BORDER>\n";
```

```
        &display_form();

        print "<INPUT TYPE=\"SUBMIT\" VALUE=\"Add Record\">\n";
        print "<INPUT TYPE=\"RESET\"  VALUE=\"Reset\">\n";
        print "<INPUT TYPE=\"BUTTON\" VALUE=\"Main Page\"";
        print " onClick=\"MainMenu()\">\n";
        print "</CENTER>\n";
        print "</FORM>\n";
        print "</BODY>\n";
        print "</HEAD>\n";
        print "</HTML>\n";
}
########################+--------------+
#                       | display_form |
#                       +--------------+
sub display_form{
        local($TSML);
        local($Rank);

        print "<TR>\n";
        print "<TD><B>Image #<B></TD><TD>$count</TD>\n";
        print "</TR>\n";

        print "<TR>\n";
        print "<TD><B>Filename:</B></TD>\n";
        print "<TD><INPUT TYPE=TEXT NAME=\"NAME\" SIZE=12";
        print " MAXLENGTH=32></TD>\n";
        print "</TR>\n";
        print "<TR>\n";
        print "<TD><B>Size:</B></TD>\n";
        print "<TD><INPUT TYPE=TEXT NAME=\"SIZE\" SIZE=5";
        print " MAXLENGTH=32 onChange=\"SetTSML()\">K</TD>\n";
        print "</TR>\n";
        print "<TR>\n";
        print "<TD><B>Link:</B></TD>\n";
        print "<TD><INPUT TYPE=TEXT NAME=\"LINK\" SIZE=12";
        print " MAXLENGTH=32></TD>\n";
        print "</TR>\n";
        print "<TR>\n";
        print "<TD><B>Cat:</B></TD>\n";
        print "<TD>\n";
        print "<SELECT NAME=\"CAT\" SIZE=3>\n";
        print "<OPTION VALUE=\"1\" SELECTED>Unknown</OPTION>\n";
```

```
        print "<OPTION VALUE=\"2\">SGML</OPTION>\n";
        print "<OPTION VALUE=\"3\">Windows 95</OPTION>\n";
        print "<OPTION VALUE=\"4\">Forth</OPTION>\n";
        print "<OPTION VALUE=\"5\">Perl</OPTION>\n";
        print "</SELECT>\n";
        print "</TD>\n";
        print "</TR>\n";
        print "<TR>\n";
        print "<TD><B>TSML:</B></TD>\n";
        print "<TD>\n";
        print "<INPUT TYPE=\"RADIO\" NAME=\"TSML\" VALUE=\"T\"";
        print " CHECKED>Thumbnail\n";
        print "<INPUT TYPE=\"RADIO\" NAME=\"TSML\"";
        print " VALUE=\"S\">Small\n";
        print "<INPUT TYPE=\"RADIO\" NAME=\"TSML\" VALUE=\"M";
        print " \">Medium\n";
        print "<INPUT TYPE=\"RADIO\" NAME=\"TSML\"";
        print " VALUE=\"L\">Large\n";
        print "</TD>\n";
        print "</TR>\n";
        print "<TR>\n";
        print "<TD><B>Rank:</B></TD>\n";
        print "<TD>\n";
        print "<SELECT NAME=\"RANK\" SIZE=1>\n";
        print "<OPTION VALUE=\"1\" SELECTED>Great!</OPTION>\n";
        print "<OPTION VALUE=\"2\">Excellent</OPTION>\n";
        print "<OPTION VALUE=\"3\">Good</OPTION>\n";
        print "<OPTION VALUE=\"4\">OK</OPTION>\n";
        print "<OPTION VALUE=\"5\">No Interest</OPTION>\n";
        print "</SELECT>\n";
        print "</TD>\n";
        print "</TR>\n";
        print "<TR>\n";
        print "<TD COLSPAN=\"2\"><B>Description:</B><BR>\n";
        print "<INPUT TYPE=TEXT NAME=\"DESC\" SIZE=60";
        print " MAXLENGTH=80>\n";
        print "</TR>\n";
        print "</TABLE>\n";
}
```

The user fills in the blanks and clicks the Add Record button to add the record to the database by imgaddup.pl. The record is automatically added to the end of the database. The code for imgadd.pl is:

```
#!/usr/local/bin/perl
#
# FILE: imgaddup.pl
#

$TOOL_DIR     = "/home/httpd/cgi-bin";

require "$TOOL_DIR/imgtools.req";
require "$TOOL_DIR/imgvars.req";

#print "Content-type:  text/html\n\n";

&parse_cgi();
&parse_cookie($ENV{'HTTP_COOKIE'});
        #
        # Figure out what the last record number is
        #
$rec   = "";
$count = 0;
open(DIR,"$cookie{'DIR'}/imagedat");
while(<DIR>){
        $count++;
}
close(DIR);

open(DB,">>$cookie{'DIR'}/imagedat");
print DB "$QS{'NAME'}|$count|$QS{'SIZE'}|$QS{'TSML'}|";
print DB "$QS{'CAT'}|$QS{'LINK'}|$QS{'RANK'}|$QS{'DESC'}\n";
close(DB);
system("/home/httpd/cgi-bin/imgadd.pl");

exit;
```

16

The Add Page menu is redisplayed by running imgadd.pl, allowing the user to add multiple records before going back to the Main Page.

Edit an Existing Record

The next action on the Main Menu is *Edit Record*. The user clicks the 5) button to run the JavaScript function editRec() in imgmain.htm. EditRec() then runs imgedit.pl to generate and edit an existing record display:

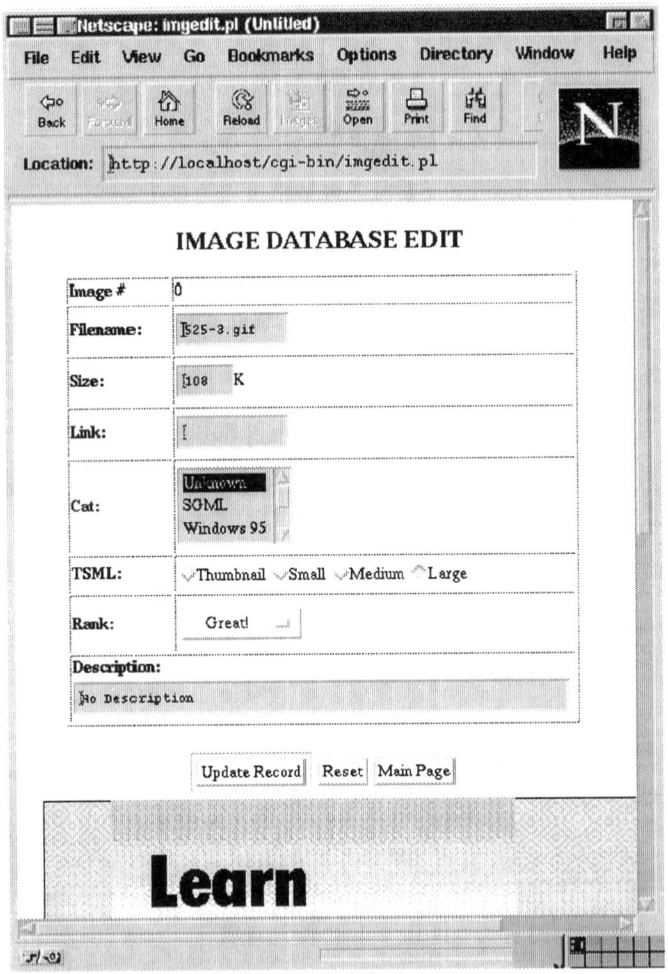

imgedit.pl uses the contents of cookie IMG as the image record number to display. This screen is different from other record displays so far, because it displays the actual image file after the data entry form. The code for imgedit.pl is:

```
#!/usr/local/bin/perl
#
# FILE: imgedit.pl
#

$TOOL_DIR     = "/home/httpd/cgi-bin";

require "$TOOL_DIR/imgtools.req";
require "$TOOL_DIR/imgvars.req";

print "Content-type:  text/html\n\n";

&parse_cgi();
&parse_cookie($ENV{'HTTP_COOKIE'});


$rec   = "";
$count = 0;
open(DIR,"$cookie{'DIR'}/imagedat");
while(<DIR>){
       $count++;
       chop;
       @fld = split(/\|/,$_);
       if($fld[1] eq $cookie{'IMG'}){
              $rec = $_;
              next;
       }
       $prev_rec = $_;
}
$count--;
if($count < $cookie{'IMG'}){
       $cookie{'IMG'}    = $count;
       $cookie{'MAXIMG'} = $count;
       $rec = $prev_rec;
}
close(DIR);

@fld = split(/\|/,$rec);
&display_rec();

exit;
```

```
########################+-------------+
#                       | display_rec |
#                       +-------------+
sub display_rec{
        print "<HTML>\n";
        print "<HEAD>\n";
        print "<SCRIPT LANGUAGE=\"JAVASCRIPT\">\n";
        print "function MainMenu(){\n";
        print "window.location.href=\"/cgi-bin/imgmain.pl\";\n";
        print "}\n";
        print "function SetTSML(){\n";
        print "var value = parseInt(document.ADD.SIZE.value);\n";
        print "}\n";
        print "</SCRIPT>\n";
        print "</HEAD>\n";
        print "<BODY BGCOLOR=\"#FFFFFF\"";
        print " onLoad=\"document.EDIT.NAME.focus();\">\n";
        print "<H1 ALIGN=\"CENTER\">IMAGE DATABASE EDIT</H1>\n";
        print "<FORM NAME=\"EDIT\"";
        print " ACTION=\"/cgi-bin/imgedup.pl\">\n";
        print "<CENTER>\n";
        print "<TABLE BORDER>\n";

        &display_form();

        print "<BR>\n";
        print "<INPUT TYPE=\"SUBMIT\" VALUE=\"Update Record\">\n";
        print "<INPUT TYPE=\"RESET\"  VALUE=\"Reset\">\n";
        print "<INPUT TYPE=\"BUTTON\" VALUE=\"Main Page\"";
        print " onClick=\"MainMenu()\">\n";
        print "<BR>\n";
        print "<img src=\"/images/$fld[0]\"><BR>\n";
        print "</CENTER>\n";
        print "</FORM>\n";
        print "</BODY>\n";
        print "</HEAD>\n";
        print "</HTML>\n";
}
########################+--------------+
#                       | display_form |
#                       +--------------+
sub display_form{
        local($TSML);
```

```
local($Rank);

print "<TR>\n";
print "<TD><B>Image #<B></TD><TD>$cookie{'IMG'}</TD>\n";
print "</TR>\n";

print "<TR>\n";
print "<TD><B>Filename:</B></TD>\n";
print "<TD><INPUT TYPE=\"TEXT\" NAME=\"NAME\"";
print " VALUE=\"$fld[0]\" SIZE=12 MAXLENGTH=32></TD>\n";
print "</TR>\n";
print "<TR>\n";
print "<TD><B>Size:</B></TD>\n";
print "<TD><INPUT TYPE=TEXT NAME=\"SIZE\" ";
print " VALUE=\"$fld[2]\" SIZE=5 MAXLENGTH=32";
print " onChange=\"SetTSML()\">K</TD>\n";
print "</TR>\n";
print "<TR>\n";
print "<TD><B>Link:</B></TD>\n";
print "<TD><INPUT TYPE=TEXT NAME=\"LINK\" ";
print " VALUE=\"$fld[5]\" SIZE=12 MAXLENGTH=32></TD>\n";
print "</TR>\n";
print "<TR>\n";
print "<TD><B>Cat:</B></TD>\n";
print "<TD>\n";
print "<SELECT NAME=\"CAT\" SIZE=3>\n";
$selected ="";
if($fld[4] eq "1"){
        $selected = " SELECTED";
}
print "<OPTION VALUE=\"1\"$selected>Unknown</OPTION>\n";
$selected ="";
if($fld[4] eq "2"){
        $selected = " SELECTED";
}
print "<OPTION VALUE=\"2\"$selected>SGML</OPTION>\n";
$selected ="";
if($fld[4] eq "3"){
        $selected = " SELECTED";
}
print "<OPTION VALUE=\"3\"$selected>Windows 95</OPTION>\n";
$selected ="";
if($fld[4] eq "4"){
```

```
        $selected = " SELECTED";
}
print "<OPTION VALUE=\"4\"$selected>Forth</OPTION>\n";
$selected ="";
if($fld[4] eq "5"){
        $selected = " SELECTED";
}
print "<OPTION VALUE=\"5\"$selected>Perl</OPTION>\n";
print "</SELECT>\n";

print "</TD>\n";
print "</TR>\n";
print "<TR>\n";
print "<TD><B>TSML:</B></TD>\n";
print "<TD>\n";
$selected ="";
if($fld[3] eq "T"){
        $selected = " CHECKED";
}
print "<INPUT TYPE=\"RADIO\" NAME=\"TSML\"";
print " VALUE=\"T\"$selected>Thumbnail\n";
$selected ="";
if($fld[3] eq "S"){
        $selected = " CHECKED";
}
print "<INPUT TYPE=\"RADIO\" NAME=\"TSML\"";
print " VALUE=\"S\"$selected>Small\n";
$selected ="";
if($fld[3] eq "M"){
        $selected = " CHECKED";
}
print "<INPUT TYPE=\"RADIO\" NAME=\"TSML\" VALUE=\"M\"";
print " $selected>Medium\n";
$selected ="";
if($fld[3] eq "L"){
        $selected = " CHECKED";
}
print "<INPUT TYPE=\"RADIO\" NAME=\"TSML\"";
print " VALUE=\"L\"$selected>Large\n";
print "</SELECT>\n";

print "</TD>\n";
print "</TR>\n";
```

```
        print "<TR>\n";
        print "<TD><B>Rank:</B></TD>\n";
        print "<TD>\n";
        print "<SELECT NAME=\"RANK\" SIZE=1>\n";
        $selected ="";
        if($fld[6] eq "1"){
              $selected = " SELECTED";
        }
        print "<OPTION VALUE=\"1\"$selected>Great!</OPTION>\n";
        $selected ="";
        if($fld[6] eq "2"){
              $selected = " SELECTED";
        }
        print "<OPTION VALUE=\"2\"$selected>Excellent</OPTION>\n";
        $selected ="";
        if($fld[6] eq "3"){
              $selected = " SELECTED";
        }
        print "<OPTION VALUE=\"3\"$selected>Good</OPTION>\n";
        $selected ="";
        if($fld[6] eq "4"){
              $selected = " SELECTED";
        }
        print "<OPTION VALUE=\"4\"$selected>OK</OPTION>\n";
        $selected ="";
        if($fld[6] eq "5"){
              $selected = " SELECTED";
        }
        print "<OPTION VALUE=\"5\"$selected>No Interest</OPTION>\n";
        print "</SELECT>\n";
        print "</TD>\n";
        print "</TR>\n";
        print "<TR>\n";
        print "<TD COLSPAN=\"2\"><B>Description:</B><BR>\n";
        print "<INPUT TYPE=TEXT NAME=\"DESC\" VALUE=\"$fld[7]\"";
        print " SIZE=60 MAXLENGTH=80>\n";
        print "</TR>\n";
        print "</TABLE>\n";
}
```


The record is actually replaced by imgedup.pl when the Update Record button is clicked. The code for imgedup.pl is:

```
#!/usr/local/bin/perl
#
# FILE: imgaddup.pl
#

$TOOL_DIR     = "/home/httpd/cgi-bin";

require "$TOOL_DIR/imgtools.req";
require "$TOOL_DIR/imgvars.req";

&parse_cgi();
&parse_cookie($ENV{'HTTP_COOKIE'});
        #
        # Figure out what the last record number is and
        # load the whole file into memory...
        #
$rec   = "";
$count = 0;
open(DIR,"$cookie{'DIR'}/imagedat");
while(<DIR>){
        $count++;
        push(@recs,$_);
}
close(DIR);
        #       Replace the record number with the updated one
$recs[$cookie{'IMG'}]  = "$QS{'NAME'}|$cookie{'IMG'}";
$recs[$cookie{'IMG'}] .= "|$QS{'SIZE'}|$QS{'TSML'}|$QS{'CAT'}|";
$recs[$cookie{'IMG'}] .= "$QS{'LINK'}|$QS{'RANK'}|$QS{'DESC'}\n";
        #       Dump database back to disk
open(DB,">$cookie{'DIR'}/imagedat");
foreach $rec (@recs){
        print DB "$rec";
}
close(DB);
system("/home/httpd/cgi-bin/imgedit.pl");

exit;
```

imgedup.pl uses the same technique of running the original program to generate the display for the user. It runs imgedit.pl.

Change Image Directory

The next action on the Main Page is *Change Directory*. There are actually two ways to change the image database directory. The first is modifying the directory path in the text box at the bottom of the Main Page, and the second is clicking button 6). Clicking 6) causes the JavaScript changeDir() function in imgmain.htm to execute. changeDir() pops up a dialog box containing the current directory path. The user edits the path and clicks Done. The following display shows the Change Directory dialog box open:

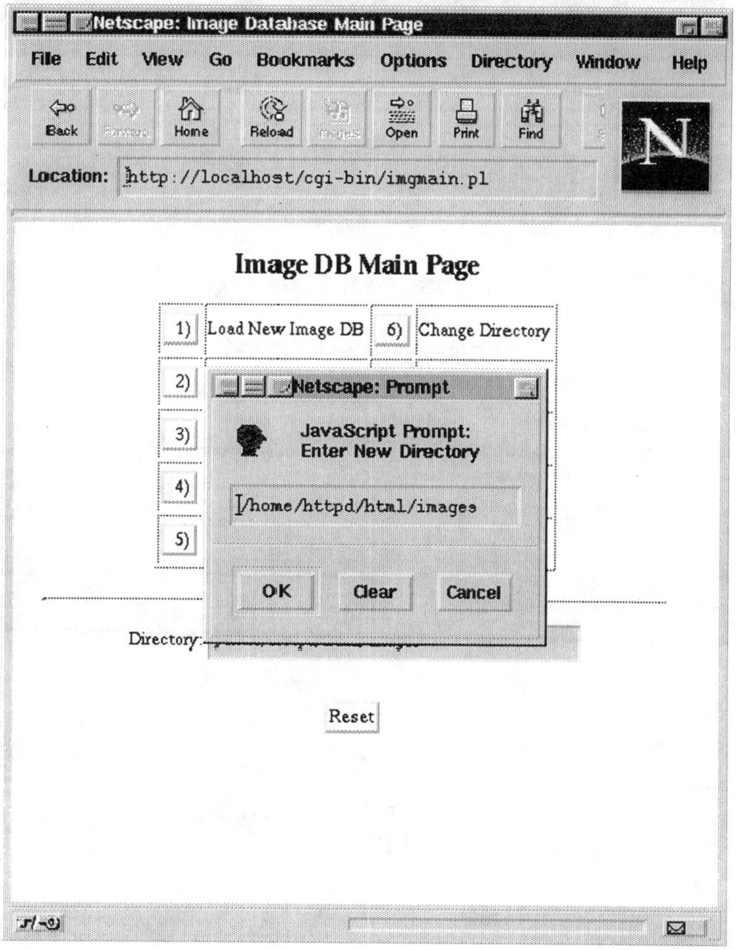

The directory value is stored for later use in the DIR text box.

Options

Setting options is unique within this application because it is done totally in JavaScript on the client. When the user clicks the 7) button, the setOptions() JavaScript function in imgmain.htm executes, which loads imgopt.htm. imgopt.htm contains not only the HTML for the data entry form but the JavaScript to process it. The Options Page display is:

The listing for imgopt.htm is:

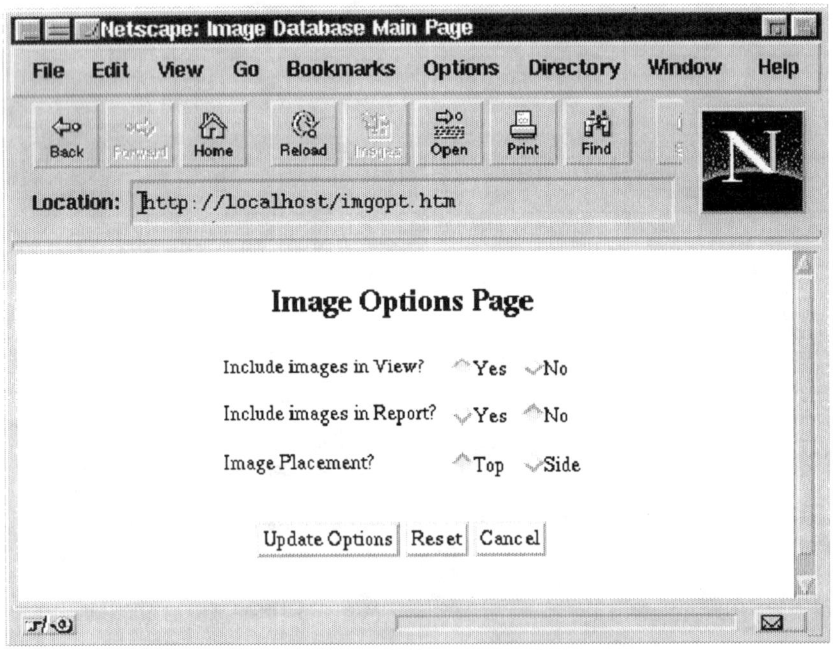


```
<HTML>
<!--imgopt.htm-->
<HEAD>
<TITLE>Image Database Main Page</TITLE>
<SCRIPT LANGUAGE="JAVASCRIPT">
<!--
function SetOpts(){
        var value;
        value = document.OPT.VIMG[0].checked;
        if(document.OPT.VIMG[0].checked){
                value = "Y";
```

```
        }else{
                value = "N";
        }
        document.cookie = "VIMG=" + value + ";";

        value = document.OPT.RIMG[0].checked;
        if(document.OPT.RIMG[0].checked){
                value = "Y";
        }else{
                value = "N";
        }
        document.cookie = "RIMG=" + value + ";";

        value = document.OPT.PIMG[0].checked;
        if(document.OPT.PIMG[0].checked){
                value = "Y";
        }else{
                value = "N";
        }
        document.cookie = "PIMG=" + value + ";";
        window.location = "/cgi-bin/imgmain.pl";
}
function MainMenu(){
         window.location = "/cgi-bin/imgmain.pl";
}
// -->
</SCRIPT>
</HEAD>
<BODY BGCOLOR="#FFFFFF">
<H1 ALIGN="CENTER">Image Options Page</H1>
<CENTER>
<FORM NAME="OPT">
<TABLE ALIGN="CENTER">
<TR>
  <TD>Include images in View?</TD>
  <TD><INPUT TYPE="RADIO" NAME="VIMG" VALUE="Y" CHECKED>Yes</TD>
  <TD><INPUT TYPE="RADIO" NAME="VIMG" VALUE="N">No</TD>
</TR>
<TR>
  <TD>Include images in Report?</TD>
  <TD><INPUT TYPE="RADIO" NAME="RIMG" VALUE="Y">Yes</TD>
  <TD><INPUT TYPE="RADIO" NAME="RIMG" VALUE="N" CHECKED>No</TD>
</TR>
```

```
<TR>
  <TD>Image Placement?</TD>
  <TD><INPUT TYPE="RADIO" NAME="PIMG" VALUE="T" CHECKED>Top</TD>
  <TD><INPUT TYPE="RADIO" NAME="PIMG" VALUE="S">Side</TD>
</TR>
</TABLE>
<BR>
<INPUT TYPE="BUTTON" VALUE="Update Options" onClick="SetOpts();">
<INPUT TYPE="RESET"  VALUE="Reset">
<INPUT TYPE="BUTTON" VALUE="Cancel" onClick="MainMenu();">
<BR>
</FORM>
</BODY>
</HTML>
```

The JavaScript code in imgopt.htm processes the form data when the Update Options button is clicked. The function SetOpts() reads the form data and constructs a cookie string for each of the three options and reloads the Main Page.

Report Generation

The report generation is very limited in this application. When the 8) button is clicked on the Main Page, the JavaScript function report() in imgmain.htm is executed. report() executes imgrept.pl on the server, which generates the "report" display. The report may take either of two formats depending on the value of the "Include images in report" option. The following display is generated when the option is set to no:

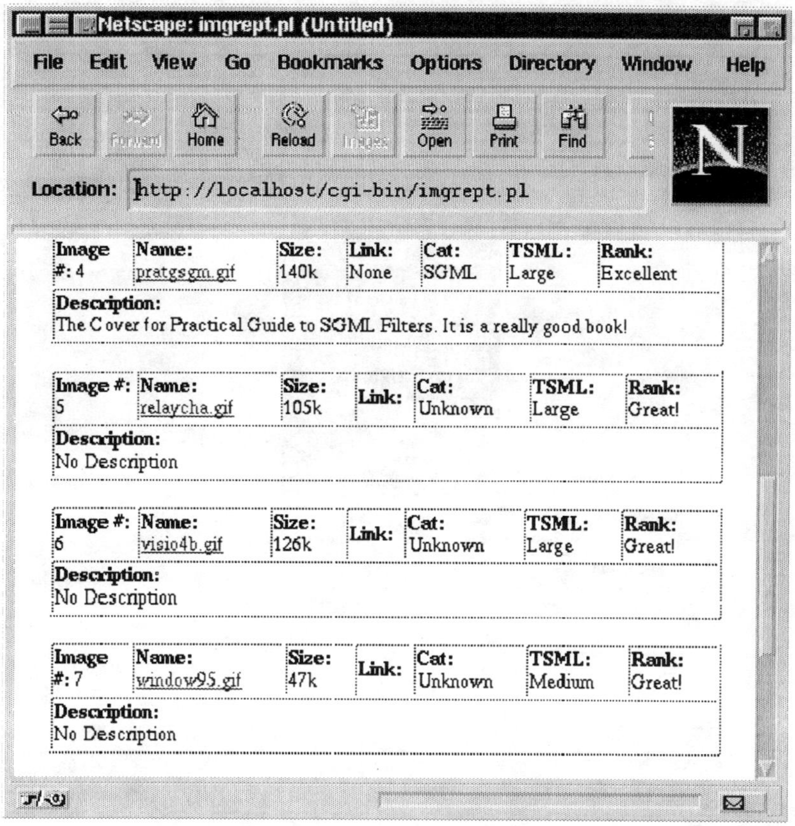

Notice that the filename is a hyperlink that can be clicked to display the image. When the image option is set to yes, the following display is created for the report:

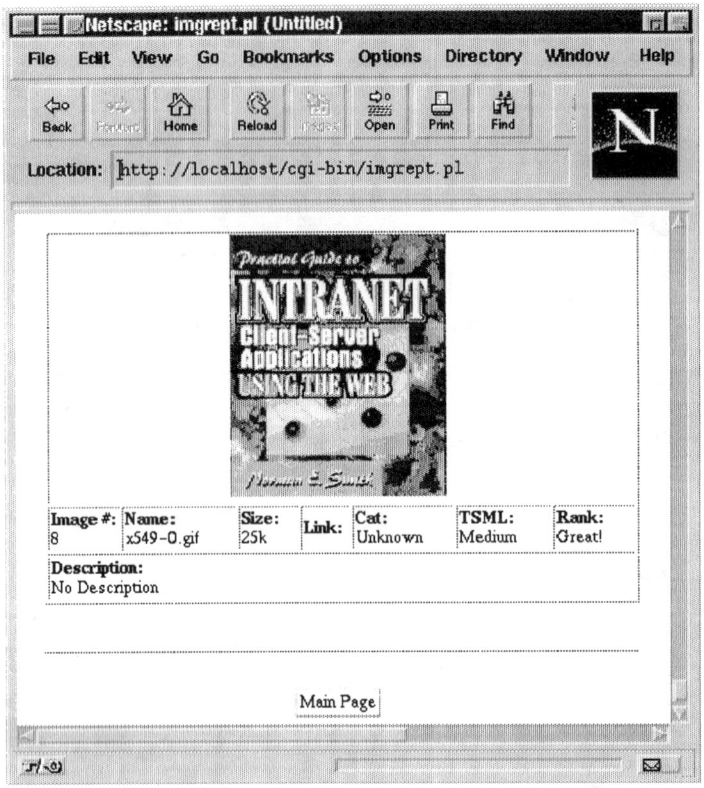

The report in this display is for every record in the file. This time the filename is not a hyperlink because the image is already on the screen. The code for imgrept.pl is:

```
#!/usr/local/bin/perl
#
# FILE: imgview.pl
#
$TOOL_DIR     = "/home/httpd/cgi-bin";

require "$TOOL_DIR/imgtools.req";
require "$TOOL_DIR/imgvars.req";


print "Content-type:  text/html\n\n";

&parse_cgi();
&parse_cookie($ENV{'HTTP_COOKIE'});
```

```
if($cookie{'RIMG'} ne "Y"){
        $Image = "N";
}else{
        $Image = "Y";
}
        #
        # Display the start of the HTML display
        #
&display_start();

$rec   = "";
$count = 0;
open(DIR,"$cookie{'DIR'}/imagedat");
while(<DIR>){
        $count++;
        chop;
        &display_rec();
}
close(DIR);

&display_end();

exit;
########################+-------------+
#                       | display_rec |
#                       +-------------+
sub display_rec{
        local($TSML);
        local($Rank);

        @fld = split(/\|/,$_);

        print "<TABLE WIDTH=\"100%\" BORDER>\n";
        if($Image eq "Y"){
                print "<TR>\n";
                print "<TD COLSPAN=\"7\" ALIGN=\"CENTER\">";
                print "<img src=\"/images/$fld[0]\">\n";
                print "</TR>\n";
        }
        print "<TR>\n";
        print "<TD><B>Image #:</B> $fld[1]\n";
        if($Image eq "Y"){
                print "<TD><B>Name:</B> $fld[0]\n";
```

```
}else{
        print "<TD><B>Name:</B> ";
        print "<A HREF=\"/images/$fld[0]\">$fld[0]</A>\n";
}
print "<TD><B>Size:</B> $fld[2]k\n";
print "<TD><B>Link:</B> $fld[5]\n";
print "<TD><B>Cat:</B>  ";
        #
        # Generate the Category field
        #
$selected ="";
if($fld[4] eq "1"){
        $selected = " Unknown";
}
if($fld[4] eq "2"){
        $selected = " SGML";
}
if($fld[4] eq "3"){
        $selected = " W95";
}
if($fld[4] eq "4"){
        $selected = " Forth";
}
if($fld[4] eq "5"){
        $selected = " Perl";
}
print "$selected\n";
        #
        # Generate TSML field
        #
print "<TD><B>TSML:</B> ";
$TMSL ="";
if($fld[3] eq "T"){
        $TMSL = " Thumbnail";
}
if($fld[3] eq "S"){
        $TMSL = " Small";
}
if($fld[3] eq "M"){
        $TMSL = " Medium";
}
if($fld[3] eq "L"){
        $TMSL = " Large";
```

```
        }
        print "$TMSL\n";
        print "</TD>\n";
              #
              # Generate Rand field display
              #
        print "<TD><B>Rank:</B>  \n";
        $Rank ="";
        if($fld[6] eq "1"){
              $Rank = " Great!";
        }
        if($fld[6] eq "2"){
              $Rank = " Excellent";
        }
        if($fld[6] eq "3"){
              $Rank = " Good";
        }
        if($fld[6] eq "4"){
              $Rank = " OK";
        }
        if($fld[6] eq "5"){
              $Rank = " No Interest";
        }
        print "$Rank\n";
        print "</TR>\n";
        print "<TR>\n";
        print "<TD COLSPAN=\"7\"><B>Description:</B><BR>\n";
        print "$fld[7]\n";
        print "</TR>\n";
        print "</TABLE>\n";
        print "<BR>\n";
}
########################+---------------+
#                       | display_start |
#                       +---------------+
sub display_start{
        print "<HTML>\n";
        print "<HEAD>\n";
        print "<SCRIPT LANGUAGE=\"JAVASCRIPT\">\n";
        print "function MainMenu(){\n";
        print "window.location.href=\"/cgi-bin/imgmain.pl\";\n";
        print "}\n";
        print "</SCRIPT>\n";
```

```
        print "</HEAD>\n";
        print "<BODY BGCOLOR=\"#FFFFFF\">\n";
        print "<H1 ALIGN=\"CENTER\">Image Database Hit List</H1>\n";
        print "<CENTER>\n";
}
########################+-------------+
#                       | display_end |
#                       +-------------+
sub display_end{
#       print "</TABLE>\n";
        print "<BR>\n";
        print "<HR>\n";
        print "<FORM>\n";
        print "<INPUT TYPE=\"BUTTON\" VALUE=\"Main Page\"";
        print " onClick=\"MainMenu()\">\n";
        print "</FORM>\n";
        print "</CENTER>\n";
        print "</BODY>\n";
        print "</HEAD>\n";
        print "</HTML>\n";
}
```

There is nothing significant in imgrept.pl that has not already been pointed out in previous scripts.

Logon Again

There are times in most data entry systems where the user needs to log on again without having to get completely out of the system. The *Logon Again* option allows the user to do this. The processing is completely contained within imgmain.htm. The JavaScript function logon() loads imglogon.htm when button 9) is clicked to redisplay the Logon Page.

View Record

The final action on the Main Page is *View Record*. It is activated by clicking on button 10). viewRec() in imgmain.htm is executed which builds a URL to run imgview.pl on the server. imgview.pl uses the value stored in the IMG cookie to specify the record number to display. The following display is generated:

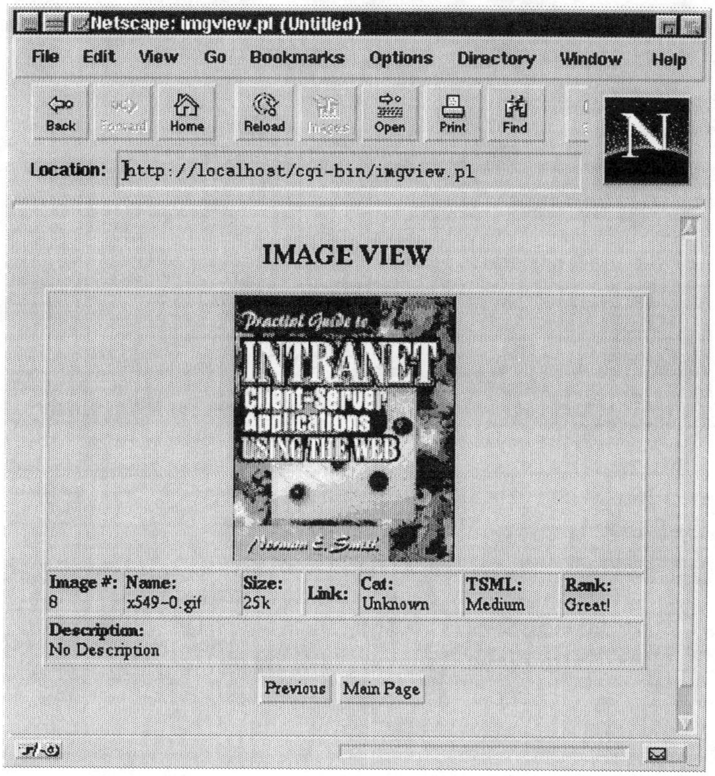

Notice that there is a Previous button to go to the previous page. This example happens to be the last page in the database, otherwise there would also be a Next button. The code for imgview.pl is:

```
#!/usr/local/bin/perl
#
# FILE: imgview.pl
#
$TOOL_DIR     = "/home/httpd/cgi-bin";

require "$TOOL_DIR/imgtools.req";
require "$TOOL_DIR/imgvars.req";

print "Content-type:  text/html\n\n";

&parse_cgi();
&parse_cookie($ENV{'HTTP_COOKIE'});
        #
        # This is a kludge to let imgview.pl work with the Search
```

```
        # hit list as well as the Main Menu with a minimum
        # number of changes.
        #
if($QS{'IMG'} ne ""){
        $cookie{'IMG'} = $QS{'IMG'};
}
        #
        # End Kludge...
        #
        #
        # Search for the record specified.
        #
$rec   = "";
$count = 0;
open(DIR,"$cookie{'DIR'}/imagedat");
while(<DIR>){
        $count++;
        chop;
        @fld = split(/\|/,$_);
        if($fld[1] eq $cookie{'IMG'}){
                $rec = $_;
                next;
        }
        $prev_rec = $_;
}
$count--;
if($count < $cookie{'IMG'}){
        $cookie{'IMG'}    = $count;
        $cookie{'MAXIMG'} = $count;
        $rec = $prev_rec;
}
close(DIR);

&display_rec();

exit;
#######################+-------------+
#                      | display_rec |
#                      +-------------+
sub display_rec{
        print "<HTML>\n";
        print "<HEAD>\n";
        print "<SCRIPT LANGUAGE=\"JAVASCRIPT\">\n";
```

```
print "function NextImage(){\n";
print "var newIMG = parseInt(document.IMAGE.IMG.value)";
print " + 1;\n";
print "if(newIMG >";
print " parseInt(document.IMAGE.MAXIMG.value)){ \n";
print "        newIMG = document.IMAGE.MAXIMG.value;\n";
print "        alert(\"This is the last record.\") \n";
print "}\n";
print "document.cookie=\"IMG=\" + newIMG + \";\"\n";
print "window.location.href=\"/cgi-bin/imgview.pl\"\n";
print "}\n";
print "function PrevImage(){\n";
print "var newIMG = parseInt(document.IMAGE.IMG.value)";
print " - 1;\n";
print "if(newIMG < 0){        newIMG = 0; }\n";
print "document.cookie=\"IMG=\" + newIMG + \";\"\n";
print "window.location.href=\"/cgi-bin/imgview.pl\"\n";
print "}\n";
print "function MainMenu(){\n";
print "window.location.href=\"/cgi-bin/imgmain.pl\";\n";
print "}\n";
print "</SCRIPT>\n";
print "</HEAD>\n";
print "<BODY BGCOLOR=\"#FFFFFF\">\n";
print "<H1 ALIGN=\"CENTER\">IMAGE VIEW</H1>\n";
print "<FORM NAME=\"IMAGE\">\n";
print "<CENTER>\n";
print "<TABLE BORDER>\n";

print "<INPUT TYPE=\"HIDDEN\" NAME=\"MAXIMG\"";
print " VALUE=\"$count\">\n";
print "<INPUT TYPE=\"HIDDEN\" NAME=\"IMG\"";
print " VALUE=\"$cookie{'IMG'}\">\n";
if($rec ne ""){
        @fld = split(/\|/,$rec);
        &display_form();
}
print "<INPUT TYPE=\"BUTTON\" VALUE=\"Previous\" ";
print " onClick=\"PrevImage();\">\n";
if($count > $cookie{'IMG'}){
        print "       <INPUT TYPE=\"BUTTON\" VALUE=\"Next\" ";
        print "       onClick=\"NextImage();\">\n";
}
```

```
        print "<INPUT TYPE=\"BUTTON\" VALUE=\"Main Page\"";
        print " onClick=\"MainMenu()\">\n";
        print "</CENTER>\n";
        print "</FORM>\n";
        print "</BODY>\n";
        print "</HEAD>\n";
        print "</HTML>\n";
}
#######################+--------------+
#                      | display_form |
#                      +--------------+
sub display_form{
        local($TSML);
        local($Rank);

        print "<TR>\n";
        print "<TD COLSPAN=\"7\" ALIGN=\"CENTER\">";
        print "<img src=\"/images/$fld[0]\">\n";
        print "</TR>\n";
        print "<TR>\n";
        print "<TD><B>Image #:</B> $cookie{'IMG'}\n";
        print "<TD><B>Name:</B> $fld[0]\n";
        print "<TD><B>Size:</B> $fld[2]k\n";
        print "<TD><B>Link:</B> $fld[5]\n";
        print "<TD><B>Cat:</B>  ";
        $selected ="";
        if($fld[4] eq "1"){
                $selected = " Unknown";
        }
        if($fld[4] eq "2"){
                $selected = " SGML";
        }
        if($fld[4] eq "3"){
                $selected = " W95";
        }
        if($fld[4] eq "4"){
                $selected = " Forth";
        }
        if($fld[4] eq "5"){
                $selected = " Perl";
        }
        print "$selected\n";
        print "<TD><B>TSML:</B> ";
```

```
        $TMSL ="";
        if($fld[3] eq "T"){
              $TMSL = " Thumbnail";
        }
        if($fld[3] eq "S"){
              $TMSL = " Small";
        }
        if($fld[3] eq "M"){
              $TMSL = " Medium";
        }
        if($fld[3] eq "L"){
              $TMSL = " Large";
        }
        print "$TMSL\n";
        print "</TD>\n";
        print "<TD><B>Rank:</B>  \n";
        $Rank ="";
        if($fld[6] eq "1"){
              $Rank = " Great!";
        }
        if($fld[6] eq "2"){
              $Rank = " Excellent";
        }
        if($fld[6] eq "3"){
              $Rank = " Good";
        }
        if($fld[6] eq "4"){
              $Rank = " OK";
        }
        if($fld[6] eq "5"){
              $Rank = " No Interest";
        }
        print "$Rank\n";
        print "</TR>\n";
        print "<TR>\n";
        print "<TD COLSPAN=\"7\"><B>Description:</B><BR>\n";
        print "$fld[7]\n";
        print "</TR>\n";
        print "</TABLE>\n";

}
```

The code for imgview.pl looks a lot like imgedit.pl except for the HTML generated.

Enhancements

There are a whole bunch of enhancements that could make the Image Database a useful system. These include:

- Using a real database such as Oracle
- Verifying the User ID is valid in every server side program
- Adding a delete record action to the Main Page
- Adding image manipulation functions that automatically rescale the image to fit the screen better

None of these is hard to do. In particular using a real database and adding image manipulation imply commercial software in addition to the base Web server/HTML/JavaScript/Perl development software.

Summary

There you have a sample database oriented application. The Image Database is a single-user application. It uses flat ASCII files rather than a database system to store the database. A database system automatically handles record locking to prevent two users from trying to modify the data at the same time. All of the other aspects of a client-server intranet application are included in this case study.

Chapter 17

Conclusion

Introduction

This book covers a lot of territory. It provides a general background on client-server computing, identifying a number of ways to approach client-server applications. The main thrust of the book is developing Intranet based client-server applications. The groundwork information on Intra/Internet technologies is laid out with the discussions of Web tools including languages, browsers, servers, and HTML. Candidate applications are identified; the two main categories of which are command line applications and data entry applications.

A large portion of the book covers the "practical" aspects of client-server Web applications via several large case studies. The case studies assume a knowledge of HTML and Perl. The JavaScript used in the examples is simple enough that anyone with a C or Perl background should have little trouble figuring out what's going on.

The primary advantages of the client-server development techniques described in this book are:

- They used an open approach that can be used effectively on almost any platform.
- The pieces necessary for use in a production environment exist today.
- Application development is significantly less expensive than traditional client-server applications.
- Development tools for Web client-server applications are maturing rapidly.

The future looks very bright for Web-based Intranet client-server applications. Don't wait too long to climb aboard the train!

Appendix A

HTML 2.0 Document Type Definition

Introduction

HTML 2.0 was the first HTML DTD officially published by W3C (http://www.w3c.org). It added Forms to the basic HTML tag set. HTML 2.0 opened up the Web to client-server computing because data could be entered and passed back to the server and processed via CGI scripts. This appendix contains the HTML 2.0 Document Type Definition.

```
<!--    html.dtd

         Document Type Definition for the HyperText Markup Language (HTML DTD)

        $Id: html.dtd,v 1.22 1994/11/30 23:45:40 connolly Exp $

        Author: Daniel W. Connolly <connolly@hal.com>
        See Also: html.decl, html-0.dtd, html-1.dtd
                  http://www.hal.com/%7Econnolly/html-spec/index.html
                  http://info.cern.ch/hypertext/WWW/MarkUp2/MarkUp.html
-->

<!ENTITY % HTML.Version
        "-//IETF//DTD HTML 2.0//EN"

         -- Typical usage:

            <!DOCTYPE HTML PUBLIC "-//IETF//DTD HTML//EN">
```

```
            <html>
            ...
            </html>
        --
        >

<!--=================== Feature Test Entities ================================-->

<!ENTITY % HTML.Recommended "IGNORE"
        -- Certain features of the language are necessary for compatibility
           with widespread usage, but they may compromise the structural
           integrity of a document. This feature test entity enables
           a more prescriptive document type definition that eliminates
           those features.
        -->

<![ %HTML.Recommended [
        <!ENTITY % HTML.Deprecated "IGNORE">
]]>

<!ENTITY % HTML.Deprecated "INCLUDE"
        -- Certain features of the language are necessary for compatibility
           with earlier versions of the specification, but they tend
           to be used an implemented inconsistently, and their use is
           deprecated. This feature test entity enables a document type
           definition that eliminates these features.
        -->

<!ENTITY % HTML.Highlighting "INCLUDE"
        -- Use this feature test entity to validate that a document
           uses no highlighting tags, which may be ignored on minimal
           implementations.
        -->

<!ENTITY % HTML.Forms "INCLUDE"
        -- Use this feature test entity to validate that a document
           contains no forms, which may not be supported in minimal
           implementations
        -->

<!--=================== Imported Names ========================================-->

<!ENTITY % Content-Type "CDATA"
```

```
        -- meaning an internet media type
           (aka MIME content type, as per RFC1521)
        -->

<!ENTITY % HTTP-Method "GET | POST"
        -- as per HTTP specification, in progress
        -->

<!ENTITY % URI "CDATA"
         -- The term URI means a CDATA attribute
            whose value is a Uniform Resource Identifier,
            as defined by
        "Universal Resource Identifiers" by Tim Berners-Lee
        aka http://info.cern.ch/hypertext/WWW/Addressing/URL/URI_Overview.html
        aka RFC 1630

        Note that CDATA attributes are limited by the LITLEN
        capacity (1024 in the current version of html.decl),
        so that URIs in HTML have a bounded length.

         -->

<!--================== DTD "Macros" =========================================-->

<!ENTITY % heading "H1|H2|H3|H4|H5|H6">

<!ENTITY % list " UL | OL | DIR | MENU " >

<!--================= Character mnemonic entities ============================-->

<!ENTITY % ISOlat1 PUBLIC
  "ISO 8879-1986//ENTITIES Added Latin 1//EN//HTML">
%ISOlat1;

<!ENTITY amp CDATA "&#38;"     -- ampersand          -->
<!ENTITY gt CDATA "&#62;"      -- greater than       -->
<!ENTITY lt CDATA "&#60;"      -- less than          -->
<!ENTITY quot CDATA "&#34;"    -- double quote       -->

<!--================== SGML Document Access (SDA) Parameter Entities =====-->

<!-- HTML 2.0 contains SGML Document Access (SDA) fixed attributes in
support of easy transformation to the International Committee for
```

```
Accessible Document Design (ICADD) DTD "-//EC-USA-CDA/ICADD//DTD
ICADD22//EN". ICADD applications are designed to support usable access
to structured information by print-impaired individuals through Braille,
large print and voice synthesis. For more information on SDA & ICADD:
        - ISO 12083:1993, Annex A.8, Facilities for Braille, large print
          and computer voice
        - ICADD ListServ <ICADD%ASUACAD.BITNET@ARIZVM1.ccit.arizona.edu>
        - Usenet news group bit.listserv.easi
        - Recording for the Blind, +1 800 221 4792
-->

<!ENTITY % SDAFORM  "SDAFORM  CDATA  #FIXED"  -- one to one mapping        -->
<!ENTITY % SDARULE  "SDARULE  CDATA  #FIXED"  -- context-sensitive mapping -->
<!ENTITY % SDAPREF  "SDAPREF  CDATA  #FIXED"  -- generated text prefix     -->
<!ENTITY % SDASUFF  "SDASUFF  CDATA  #FIXED"  -- generated text suffix     -->
<!ENTITY % SDASUSP  "SDASUSP  NAME   #FIXED"  -- suspend transform process -->

<!--=================== Text Markup =====================================-->

<![ %HTML.Highlighting [

<!ENTITY % font " TT | B | I ">

<!ENTITY % phrase "EM | STRONG | CODE | SAMP | KBD | VAR | CITE ">

<!ENTITY % text "#PCDATA | A | IMG | BR | %phrase | %font">

<!ELEMENT (%font;|%phrase) - - (%text)*>
<!ATTLIST ( TT | CODE | SAMP | KBD | VAR )
        %SDAFORM; "Lit"
        >
<!ATTLIST ( B | STRONG )
        %SDAFORM; "B"
        >
<!ATTLIST ( I | EM | CITE )
        %SDAFORM; "It"
        >
<!-- <TT>     Typewriter text                  -->
<!-- <B>      Bold text                        -->
<!-- <I>      Italic text                      -->

<!-- <EM>     Emphasized phrase                -->
<!-- <STRONG> Strong emphais                   -->
```

```
<!-- <CODE>    Source code phrase                    -->
<!-- <SAMP>    Sample text or characters             -->
<!-- <KBD>     Keyboard phrase, e.g. user input      -->
<!-- <VAR>     Variable phrase or substituable       -->
<!-- <CITE>    Name or title of cited work           -->

<!ENTITY % pre.content "#PCDATA | A | HR | BR | %font | %phrase">

]]>

<!ENTITY % text "#PCDATA | A | IMG | BR">

<!ELEMENT BR    - O EMPTY>
<!ATTLIST BR
        %SDAPREF; "&#RE;"
        >

<!-- <BR>      Line break    -->

<!--================== Link Markup =======================================-->

<![ %HTML.Recommended [
       <!ENTITY % linkName "ID">
]]>

<!ENTITY % linkName "CDATA">

<!ENTITY % linkType "NAME"
       -- a list of these will be specified at a later date -->

<!ENTITY % linkExtraAttributes
        "REL %linkType #IMPLIED
        REV %linkType #IMPLIED
        URN CDATA #IMPLIED
        TITLE CDATA #IMPLIED
        METHODS NAMES #IMPLIED
        ">

<![ %HTML.Recommended [
       <!ENTITY % A.content   "(%text)*"
       -- <H1><a name="xxx">Heading</a></H1>
              is preferred to
          <a name="xxx"><H1>Heading</H1></a>
```

```
        -->
]]>

<!ENTITY % A.content   "(%heading|%text)*">

<!ELEMENT A       - - %A.content -(A)>
<!ATTLIST A
        HREF %URI #IMPLIED
        NAME %linkName #IMPLIED
         %linkExtraAttributes;
         %SDAPREF; "<?SDATrans A: #AttList>"
         >
<!-- <A>              Anchor; source and/or destination of a link-->
<!-- <A NAME="...">   Name of this anchor                        -->
<!-- <A HREF="...">   Address of link destination                -->
<!-- <A URN="...">    Permanent address of destination           -->
<!-- <A REL=...>      Relationship of this anchor to destination -->
<!-- <A REV=...>      Relationship of destination to this anchor -->
<!-- <A TITLE="..."> Title of destination (advisory)                -->
<!-- <A METHODS="..."> Operations allowed on destination (advisory)    -->

<!--==================== Images ==========================================-->

<!ELEMENT IMG     - O EMPTY>
<!ATTLIST IMG
         SRC %URI;  #REQUIRED
        ALT CDATA #IMPLIED
        ALIGN (top|middle|bottom) #IMPLIED
        ISMAP (ISMAP) #IMPLIED
         %SDAPREF; "<Fig><?SDATrans Img: #AttList>#AttVal(Alt)</Fig>"
         >

<!-- <IMG>            Image; icon, glyph or illustration  -->
<!-- <IMG SRC="..."> Address of image object             -->
<!-- <IMG ALT="..."> Textual alternative                 -->
<!-- <IMG ALIGN=...> Position relative to text           -->
<!-- <IMG ISMAP>      Each pixel can be a link            -->

<!--==================== Paragraphs=======================================-->

<!ELEMENT P      - O (%text)*>
<!ATTLIST P
         %SDAFORM; "Para"
```

```
        >

<!-- <P>       Paragraph      -->

<!--=================== Headings, Titles, Sections =========================-->

<!ELEMENT HR     - O EMPTY>
<!ATTLIST HR
        %SDAPREF; "<Para><?SDATrans HR: #AttList></Para>"
        >

<!-- <HR>      Horizontal rule -->

<!ELEMENT ( %heading )  - -  (%text;)*>
<!ATTLIST H1
        %SDAFORM; "H1"
        >
<!ATTLIST H2
        %SDAFORM; "H2"
        >
<!ATTLIST H3
        %SDAFORM; "H3"
        >
<!ATTLIST H4
        %SDAFORM; "H4"
        >
<!ATTLIST H5
        %SDAFORM; "H5"
        >
<!ATTLIST H6
        %SDAFORM; "H6"
        >

<!-- <H1>      Heading, level 1 -->
<!-- <H2>      Heading, level 2 -->
<!-- <H3>      Heading, level 3 -->
<!-- <H4>      Heading, level 4 -->
<!-- <H5>      Heading, level 5 -->
<!-- <H6>      Heading, level 6 -->

<!--=================== Text Flows ======================================-->

<![ %HTML.Forms [
```

```
        <!ENTITY % block.forms "BLOCKQUOTE | FORM | ISINDEX">
]]>

<!ENTITY % block.forms "BLOCKQUOTE">

<![ %HTML.Deprecated [
        <!ENTITY % preformatted "PRE | XMP | LISTING">
]]>

<!ENTITY % preformatted "PRE">

<!ENTITY % block "P | %list | DL
        | %preformatted
        | %block.forms">

<!ENTITY % flow "(%text|%block)*">

<!ENTITY % pre.content "#PCDATA | A | HR | BR">
<!ELEMENT PRE - - (%pre.content)*>
<!ATTLIST PRE
        WIDTH NUMBER #implied
        %SDAFORM; "Lit"
        %SDAPREF; "<?SDATrans Pre: #AttList>"
        >

<!-- <PRE>           Preformatted text              -->
<!-- <PRE WIDTH=...> Maximum characters per line    -->

<![ %HTML.Deprecated [

<!ENTITY % literal "CDATA"
        -- historical, non-conforming parsing mode where
           the only markup signal is the end tag
           in full
        -->

<!ELEMENT (XMP|LISTING) - -  %literal>
<!ATTLIST XMP
        %SDAFORM; "Lit"
        %SDAPREF; "Example:&#RE;"
        >
<!ATTLIST LISTING
        %SDAFORM; "Lit"
```

```
        %SDAPREF; "Listing:&#RE;"
        >

<!-- <XMP>              Example section        -->
<!-- <LISTING>          Computer listing       -->

<!ELEMENT PLAINTEXT - O %literal>
<!-- <PLAINTEXT>        Plain text passage     -->

<!ATTLIST PLAINTEXT
        %SDAFORM; "Lit"
        >
]]>

<!--=================== Lists ============================================-->

<!ELEMENT DL    - -  (DT | DD)+>
<!ATTLIST DL
       COMPACT (COMPACT) #IMPLIED
        %SDAFORM; "List"
        %SDAPREF; "<?SDATrans DL: #AttList>"
       >

<!ELEMENT DT    - O (%text)*>
<!ATTLIST DT
        %SDAFORM; "Term"
        >

<!ELEMENT DD    - O %flow>
<!ATTLIST DD
        %SDAFORM; "LItem"
        >

<!-- <DL>               Definition list, or glossary -->
<!-- <DL COMPACT>       Compact style list           -->
<!-- <DT>               Term in definition list      -->
<!-- <DD>               Definition of term           -->
<!ELEMENT (OL|UL) - -  (LI)+>
<!ATTLIST OL
        COMPACT (COMPACT) #IMPLIED
        %SDAFORM; "List"
        %SDAPREF; "<?SDATrans OL: #AttList>"
        >
```

```
<!ATTLIST UL
        COMPACT (COMPACT) #IMPLIED
        %SDAFORM; "List"
        %SDAPREF; "<?SDATrans UL: #AttList>"
        >
<!-- <UL>             Unordered list               -->
<!-- <UL COMPACT>     Compact list style           -->
<!-- <OL>             Ordered, or numbered list    -->
<!-- <OL COMPACT>     Compact list style           -->


<!ELEMENT (DIR|MENU) - -  (LI)+ -(%block)>
<!ATTLIST DIR
        COMPACT (COMPACT) #IMPLIED
        %SDAFORM; "List"
        %SDAPREF; "<?SDATrans Dir: #AttList><LHead>Directory</LHead>"
        >
<!ATTLIST MENU
        COMPACT (COMPACT) #IMPLIED
        %SDAFORM; "List"
        %SDAPREF; "<?SDATrans Menu: #AttList><LHead>Menu</LHead>"
        >

<!-- <DIR>            Directory list               -->
<!-- <DIR COMPACT>    Compact list style           -->
<!-- <MENU>           Menu list                    -->
<!-- <MENU COMPACT>   Compact list style           -->

<!ELEMENT LI    - O %flow>
<!ATTLIST LI
        %SDAFORM; "LItem"
        >

<!-- <LI>             List item                    -->

<!--=================== Document Body ========================================-->

<![ %HTML.Recommended [
        <!ENTITY % body.content "(%heading|%block|HR|ADDRESS)*"
        -- <h1>Heading</h1>
           <p>Text ...
               is preferred to
           <h1>Heading</h1>
```

```
        Text ...
      -->
]]>

<!ENTITY % body.content "(%heading | %text | %block | HR | ADDRESS)*">

<!ELEMENT BODY O O  %body.content>
<!ATTLIST BODY
        %SDAPREF; "<?SDATrans Body: #AttList>"
        >

<!-- <BODY>   Document body -->

<!ELEMENT BLOCKQUOTE - - %body.content>
<!ATTLIST BLOCKQUOTE
        %SDAFORM; "BQ"
        >

<!-- <BLOCKQUOTE>    Quoted passage -->

<!ELEMENT ADDRESS - - (%text|P)*>
<!ATTLIST  ADDRESS
        %SDAFORM; "Lit"
        %SDAPREF; "Address:&#RE;"
        >

<!-- <ADDRESS>Address, signature, or byline for document or passage    -->

<!--================ Forms ===============================================-->

<![ %HTML.Forms [

<!ELEMENT FORM - - %body.content -(FORM) +(INPUT|SELECT|TEXTAREA)>
<!ATTLIST FORM
       ACTION %URI #IMPLIED
       METHOD (%HTTP-Method) GET
       ENCTYPE %Content-Type; "application/x-www-form-urlencoded"
        %SDAPREF; "<Para><?SDATrans Form: #AttList>Form:</Para>"
        %SDASUFF; "<Para><?SDATrans Form: #End>Form End.</Para>"
       >

<!-- <FORM>                    Fill-out or data-entry form  -->
<!-- <FORM ACTION="...">       Address for completed form   -->
```

```
<!-- <FORM METHOD=...>       Method of submitting form    -->
<!-- <FORM ENCTYPE="...">    Representation of form data  -->

<!ENTITY % InputType "(TEXT | PASSWORD | CHECKBOX |
                     RADIO | SUBMIT | RESET |
                     IMAGE | HIDDEN )">
<!ELEMENT INPUT - O EMPTY>
<!ATTLIST INPUT
       TYPE %InputType TEXT
       NAME CDATA #IMPLIED
       VALUE CDATA #IMPLIED
       SRC %URI #IMPLIED
       CHECKED (CHECKED) #IMPLIED
       SIZE CDATA #IMPLIED
       MAXLENGTH NUMBER #IMPLIED
       ALIGN (top|middle|bottom) #IMPLIED
        %SDAPREF; "<?SDATrans Input: #AttList>"
       >

<!-- <INPUT>                 Form input datum                 -->
<!-- <INPUT TYPE=...>        Type of input interaction        -->
<!-- <INPUT TYPE=...>        Name of form datum               -->
<!-- <INPUT VALUE="...">     Default/initial/selected value   -->
<!-- <INPUT SRC="...">       Address of image                 -->
<!-- <INPUT CHECKED>         Initial state is "on"            -->
<!-- <INPUT SIZE=...>        Field size hint                  -->
<!-- <INPUT MAXLENGTH=...>   Data length maximum              -->
<!-- <INPUT ALIGN=...>       Image alignment                  -->

<!ELEMENT SELECT - - (OPTION+)>
<!ATTLIST SELECT
       NAME CDATA #REQUIRED
       SIZE NUMBER #IMPLIED
       MULTIPLE (MULTIPLE) #IMPLIED
        %SDAFORM; "List"
        %SDAPREF;
        "<?SDATrans Select: #AttList><LHead>Select #AttVal(Multiple)</LHead>"
       >

<!-- <SELECT>                Selection of option(s)                  -->
<!-- <SELECT NAME=...>       Name of form datum                      -->
<!-- <SELECT SIZE=...>       Number of options displayed at a time   -->
```

```
<!-- <SELECT MULTIPLE>       Multiple selections allowed              -->

<!ELEMENT OPTION - O (#PCDATA)*>
<!ATTLIST OPTION
        SELECTED (SELECTED) #IMPLIED
        VALUE CDATA #IMPLIED
         %SDAFORM; "LItem"
         %SDAPREF;
         "<?SDATrans Option: #AttList>#AttVal(Value) #AttVal(Selected)"
        >

<!-- <OPTION>                A selection option                 -->
<!-- <OPTION SELECTED>       Initial state                      -->
<!-- <OPTION VALUE="...">    Form datum value for this option   -->

<!ELEMENT TEXTAREA - - (#PCDATA)*>
<!ATTLIST TEXTAREA
        NAME CDATA #REQUIRED
        ROWS NUMBER #REQUIRED
        COLS NUMBER #REQUIRED
         %SDAFORM; "Para"
         %SDAPREF; "<?SDATrans TextArea: #AttList>#AttVal(Name): "
        >

<!-- <TEXTAREA>              An area for text input             -->
<!-- <TEXTAREA NAME=...>     Name of form datum                 -->
<!-- <TEXTAREA ROWS=...>     Height of area                     -->
<!-- <TEXTAREA COLS=...>     Width of area                      -->

]]>

<!--================= Document Head =========================================-->

<!ENTITY % head.link "& LINK*">

<![ %HTML.Recommended [
        <!ENTITY % head.nextid "">
]]>
<!ENTITY % head.nextid "& NEXTID?">

<!ENTITY % head.content "TITLE & ISINDEX? & BASE? & META*
                          %head.nextid
```

```
                    %head.link">

<!ELEMENT HEAD O O  (%head.content)>
<!ATTLIST HEAD
        %SDAPREF; "<?SDATrans Head: #AttList>"
      >

<!-- <HEAD>   Document head -->

<!ELEMENT TITLE - -  (#PCDATA)*>
<!ATTLIST TITLE
        %SDAFORM; "Ti"
      >

<!-- <TITLE>  Title of document -->

<!ELEMENT LINK - O EMPTY>
<!ATTLIST LINK
       HREF %URI #REQUIRED
        %linkExtraAttributes;
        %SDAPREF; "<?SDATrans Link: #AttList>"
        >

<!-- <LINK>                Link from this document                          -->
<!-- <LINK HREF="...">     Address of link destination                      -->
<!-- <LINK URN="...">      Lasting name of destination                      -->
<!-- <LINK REL=...>        Relationship of this document to destination     -->
<!-- <LINK REV=...>        Relationship of destination to this document     -->
<!-- <LINK TITLE="...">    Title of destination (advisory)                  -->
<!-- <LINK METHODS="...">  Operations allowed on destination (advisory)     -->

<!ELEMENT ISINDEX - O EMPTY>
<!ATTLIST ISINDEX
        %SDAPREF;
   "<Para><?SDATrans IsIndex: #AttList>[Document indexed/searchable.]</Para>">

<!-- <ISINDEX>             Document is a searchable index                   -->

<!ELEMENT BASE - O EMPTY>
<!ATTLIST BASE
        HREF %URI; #REQUIRED
        %SDAPREF; "<?SDATrans Base: #AttList>"
        >
```

```
<!-- <BASE>                   Base context document              -->
<!-- <BASE HREF="...">        Address for this document          -->

<!ELEMENT NEXTID - O EMPTY>
<!ATTLIST NEXTID
        N %linkName #REQUIRED
        %SDAPREF; "<?SDATrans NextID: #AttList>"
        >

<!-- <NEXTID>          Next ID to use for link name              -->
<!-- <NEXTID N=...>    Next ID to use for link name              -->

<!ELEMENT META - O EMPTY>
<!ATTLIST META
        HTTP-EQUIV  NAME    #IMPLIED
        NAME        NAME    #IMPLIED
        CONTENT     CDATA   #REQUIRED
        %SDAPREF; "<?SDATrans Meta: #AttList>"
        >

<!-- <META>                   Generic Metainformation            -->
<!-- <META HTTP-EQUIV=...>    HTTP response header name          -->
<!-- <META HTTP-EQUIV=...>    Metainformation name               -->
<!-- <META CONTENT="...">     Associated information             -->

<!--================ Document Structure ==================================-->

<![ %HTML.Deprecated [
       <!ENTITY % html.content "HEAD, BODY, PLAINTEXT?">
]]>
<!ENTITY % html.content "HEAD, BODY">

<!ELEMENT HTML O O  (%html.content)>
<!ENTITY % version.attr "VERSION CDATA #FIXED '%HTML.Version;'">

<!ATTLIST HTML
       %version.attr;
        %SDAFORM; "Book"
        %SDAPREF; "<?SDATrans HTML: #AttList>"
       >

<!-- <HTML>                   HyperText Markup Language Document  -->
```

Appendix B

HTML 3.0 Document Type Definition

Introduction

HTML Version 3.0 adds Tables to the basic HTML tag set. Presentation could be spruced up using tables. A combination of Forms and Tables allow professional-looking data entry screens. The HTML 3.0 DTD follows and is available on the Web at http://www.w3c.org.

```
<!--
        html3.dtd

        Document Type Definition for the HyperText Markup Language (HTML DTD)

        Draft: Fri 24-Mar-95 09:46:33

        Author: Dave Raggett <dsr@hplb.hpl.hp.com>

        W3O is developing a testbed browser to provide practical
        experience with HTML 3.0 before it becomes a standard.
        See:  http://www.w3.org/hypertext/WWW/Arena/

        This is an open process and comments are welcomed on the
        www-html mailing list.

        Please use the following MIME content type:

              Content-Type: text/html; version=3.0
```

This will allow clients to distinguish HTML 3.0 from current HTML documents. This is most easily achieved by saving files with the extension ".html3" or ".ht3" so that servers can easily distinguish these files from HTML 2.0 files.

The entity HTML.Recommended can be used to give a more rigorous version of the DTD suitable for use with SGML authoring tools. The default version of the DTD offers a laxer interpretation, e.g. allowing authors to omit leading <P> elements. You can switch on the more rigorous version of the DTD by including the following at the start of your HTML document.

```
<!DOCTYPE HTML PUBLIC "-//IETF//DTD HTML 3.0//EN//"
   [ <!ENTITY % HTML.Recommended "INCLUDE"> ] >
```

Design Objectives:

- Backwards compatibility with 2.0
- Tightening up HTML.Recommended and moving more things to HTML.Deprecated
- Keep HTML - simple don't compete with CALS
- Make it practical for people to edit HTML 3.0 documents directly, i.e. avoid long names.
- Tables, figures and math from HTML+ with tweaks based on recent experience
- Client-side event handling for figures and graphical form selection menus
- Add limited presentational controls with a view to use of linked style sheets (style overrides are supported)
- Compatibility with ICADD as per Yuri's suggestions

HTML 3.0 relies on linked style info to give authors control over the appearence of documents. Such info is placed in a linked style sheet, or as overrides in the

```
    HTML document head, using the STYLE element. The generic
    CLASS attribute can be used to subclass elements when
    you want to use a different style from normal, e.g. you
    might use <h2 class=bigcaps> for headers with enlarged
    capital letters. Note that the class attribute has a
    wider scope than just style changes, e.g. browsers could
    provide the means for searching through documents,
    restricting search according to element class values.

    The DTD contains a small number of attributes for direct
    control of basic alignment parameters; column widths for
    tables; support for custom bullets, sequence numbering for
    lists and headers; and text flow. These attributes offer
    control over appearence which would be inconvenient to
    express exclusively via associated style sheets.

    The MD attribute for each hypertext or inline link specifies a
    message digest such as MD5 for the linked object and is needed
    to ensure someone hasn't tampered with a linked document.

History:

  24th March '95

  Changed ROLE->CLASS for HTML element
  Added dummy elements to fix problem with mixed
  content models for BODY, BLOCKQUOTE/BQ and FIG
  Dropped audio fields from FORMs
  Reinstated MIN/MAX for range fields
  Reinstated DISABLED and ERROR attributes for fields

  22nd March '95

  Changed from em to en units. The latter
  is a typographical unit = half point size
  Merged NEEDS into CLEAR for control of textflow

  21st March '95

  Added REL=Banner to LINK element
  Added BANNER element in place of <DIV CLASS=BANNER>
  Added RANGE and SPOT elements
  Added FN in place of <NOTE ROLE=FOOTNOTE>
```

```
Changed ROLE->CLASS for NOTE element

17th March '95

Fixed bug in PRE content model
Changed external references to omit trailling //
Dropped <!DOCTYPE HTML [ ... ]> wrapper to avoid problems
  with "real" sgml parsers
Added NOFLOW attribute to FIG and TABLE
Fixed typo in IMG ALIGN attribute
Made SELECT match IMG for graphic attributes
Added decimal alignment for tabs and table cells
Added ALIGN attribute to TEXTAREA for parity
  with IMG and INPUT, including ALIGN=LEFT etc.

13th March '95

Dropped MARK tag on advice from SGML Open
Allowed spaces in table colspec attribute
Changed ARRAY element
Added CHOOSE tag to BOX element
Cleaned up PRE content model
Obsoleted tags incompatible with SGML

6th March '95

Added several tags to MATH: %mathface, %mathvec
and improved ROOT, with new SQRT convience tag

1st March '95

Dropped align attribute from BR element
Added indent attribute to TAB
Added optional CREDIT to end of BQ
Changed FIG to %body.content to allow headers

22nd February '95

Added align attribute, and dropped before, after, center and right
  attributes to clean up TAB element
Added INS and DEL for legal documents
Added CREDIT to end of FIG element
Dropped FN in favor of <NOTE ROLE=FootNote>
```

```
      9th Feburuary '95

    Dropped base attribute mechanism for scoping relative URLs
    Dropped nofold attribute for disabling whitespace folding
    Dropped border width attributes for FIG (-> style sheet)
    Dropped delims attribute from math BOX element
    Dropped stylistic attributes from OL such as inherit (-> stylesheet)
    Added baseline to list of valign attribute values for tables.
    Added DIV element for generic container class and static banners
    Added MARK element for marked range class
    Added closed set of LINK REL values for toolbars
    Added numbering attributes to headers
    Added bullet attributes to headers
    Added TERM element to math for style sheet control of term rendering
    Changed to imagemap=URI for server-side event handling for FIG/OVERLAY
    Changed delimiter attributes for math arrays
    Changed ROOT element for maths to allow an arbitrary radix
    Simplified numbering attributes for ordered lists
    Simplified STYLE element to leave binding to style language
-->

<!ENTITY % HTML.Version
        "-//IETF//DTD HTML 3.0//EN"

        -- Typical usage:

            <!DOCTYPE HTML PUBLIC "-//IETF//DTD HTML 3.0//EN">
            <html>
            ...
            </html>
        --
        >

<!--================== Flags for Marked Sections ==========================-->

<!ENTITY % HTML.Recommended "IGNORE"
        -- Certain features of the language are necessary for compatibility
           with widespread usage, but they may compromise the structural
           integrity of a document. This feature test entity enables
           a more prescriptive document type definition that eliminates
           the above features.
        -->
```

```
<![ %HTML.Recommended [
        <!ENTITY % HTML.Deprecated "IGNORE">
]]>

<!ENTITY % HTML.Deprecated "INCLUDE"
        -- Certain features of the language are necessary for compatibility
           with earlier versions of the specification, but they tend
           to be used an implemented inconsistently, and their use is
           deprecated. This feature test entity enables a document type
           definition that eliminates these features.
        -->

<!ENTITY % HTML.Obsoleted "IGNORE"
        -- The XMP, LISTING and PLAINTEXT tags are incompatible with SGML
           and derive from very early versions of HTML. They require non-
           standard parsers and will cause problems for processing
           documents with standard SGML tools.
        -->

<!--================== Imported Names ====================================-->

<!ENTITY % Content-Type "CDATA"
        -- meaning a MIME content type, as per RFC1521
        -->

<!ENTITY % HTTP-Method "GET | POST"
        -- as per HTTP specification
        -->

<!ENTITY % URI "CDATA"
        -- The term URI means a CDATA attribute
           whose value is a Uniform Resource Identifier,
           as defined by
        "Uniform Resource Identifiers" by Tim Berners-Lee
        aka http://info.cern.ch/hypertext/WWW/Addressing/URL/URI_Overview.html
        aka RFC 1630

        Note that CDATA attributes are limited by the LITLEN
        capacity (1024 in the current version of html.decl),
        so that URIs in HTML have a bounded length.
        -->
```

```
<!ENTITY % REAL "CDATA" -- real numbers (not in SGML) -->

<!ENTITY % SHAPE "CDATA"
    -- Shape of hotzone in image.

       All coordinates are assumed to be numbers in the range 0 to 1
       and interpreted as fractional width/height and measured from
       the top left corner of the associated image.

       The attribute value is a string taking one of the following forms:

              "default"

       Used to define a default link for the figure background.

            "circle x, y, r"

       (x, y) define the center and r the radius.

            "rect x, y, w, h"

       (x, y) defines upper left, and w and h the width and height.

            "polygon x1, y1, x2, y2, ..."

       Given n pairs of x, y coordinates, the polygon is closed by a
       line linking the n'th point to the first. Intersecting polygons
       use the non-zero winding number rule to determine if a point lies
       inside the polygon.I
    -->

<!-- 3.0 Parameter Entities -->

<!ENTITY % heading "H1|H2|H3|H4|H5|H6">

<![ %HTML.Obsoleted [
    <!ENTITY % preformatted "PRE | XMP | LISTING">
]]>

<![ %HTML.Deprecated [
    <!ENTITY % list "UL | OL | DIR | MENU">
    <!ENTITY % blockquote "BLOCKQUOTE | BQ">
]]>
```

```
<!ENTITY % list "UL | OL">

<!ENTITY % blockquote "BQ">

<!ENTITY % preformatted "PRE">


<!-- The CLASS attribute is used to subclass HTML elements for
     rendering purposes, when used with style sheets, e.g. DSSSL lite -->

<!ENTITY % attrs  -- common attributes for elements --
       'id       ID      #IMPLIED -- as target for hrefs (link ends) --
        lang     CDATA   "en.us"  -- ISO language, country code --
        class    NAMES   #IMPLIED -- for subclassing elements --'>

<!-- SGML standard forces different NAMES for all attribute values
     in the same element, regardless of the attribute name! As a result
     CDATA is used for CLEAR attribute to avoid clash with ALIGN attribute.-->

<!--
When text flows around a figure or table in the margin, you sometimes want
to start an element like a header, paragraph or list below the figure rather
than alongside it. The CLEAR attribute allows you to move down unconditionally:

       clear=left          move down until left margin is clear
       clear=right         move down until right margin is clear
       clear=all           move down until both margins are clear

Alternatively, you can decide to place the element alongside the figure just
so long as there is enough room. The minimum width needed is specified as:
       clear="40 en"       move down until there is at least 40 en units free
       clear="100 pixels"  move down until there is at least 100 pixels free

The style sheet (or browser defaults) may provide default minimum widths for
each class of block-like elements.
-->

<!ENTITY % needs -- Attributes for controlling text flow. Used in headers
                    and other elements to guarantee sufficient room --
       'clear  CDATA #IMPLIED'>
```

```
<!--
    The following attribute may be included where ever a URL can be given:

    md      message digest e.g. md="md5:jV2OfH+nnXHU8bnkPAad/mSQlTDZ"
            where the digest is base64 encoded and preceded by a prefix
            denoting the algorithm (in this case MD5).
-->

<!ENTITY % url.link -- Attributes associated with URL based links --
        "md     CDATA  #IMPLIED  -- message digest for linked object --">

<!--================ Character mnemonic entities ===========================-->

<!-- The HTML list of Latin-1 entities includes the full range
     of characters in widely available Latin-1 fonts, and as such
     is a mixture of ISOlat1 and other ISO publishing symbols -->

<!ENTITY % HTMLlat1 PUBLIC
  "ISO 8879-1986//ENTITIES Added Latin 1//EN//HTML">
%HTMLlat1;

<!--================ Entities for special symbols =========================-->

<!ENTITY emsp   SDATA "[emsp  ]" -- em space -->
<!ENTITY ensp   SDATA "[ensp  ]" -- en space (1/2-em) -->
<!ENTITY mdash  SDATA "U+1420" --[mdash ] em dash -->
<!ENTITY ndash  SDATA "U+1320" --[ndash ] en dash (1/2-em) -->
<!ENTITY nbsp   SDATA "U+2000" -- non breaking space -->
<!ENTITY shy    SDATA "U+AD00" -- soft hyphen -->
<!ENTITY copy   SDATA "U+00A9" --[copy  ] copyright sign -->
<!ENTITY trade  SDATA "U+2122" --[trade ] trade mark sign -->
<!ENTITY reg    SDATA "U+00AD" --[reg   ] registered sign -->

<!ENTITY amp    SDATA "U+0026" -- ampersand          -->
<!ENTITY gt     SDATA "U+003E" -- greater than       -->
<!ENTITY lt     SDATA "U+003C" -- less than          -->
<!ENTITY quot   SDATA "U+0022" -- double quote       -->

<!--================ Entities for standard icons ==========================-->

<!-- a range of standard icons such as &folder; for use
     in speeding up display of directory listings etc. -->
```

```
<!-- Not available yet
<!ENTITY % HTMLicons PUBLIC
  "-//IETF//ENTITIES icons for HTML//EN">
%HTMLicons;
-->

<!--================= Entities for math symbols ================================-->

<!-- ISO subset chosen for use with the widely available Adobe math font -->

<!-- Not available yet
<!ENTITY % HTMLmath PUBLIC
  "-//IETF//ENTITIES Math and Greek for HTML//EN">
%HTMLmath;
-->

<!--==================== Text Markup ==========================================-->

<!ENTITY % font " U | S | TT | I | BIG | SMALL">

<!ENTITY % phrase "EM | STRONG | CODE | SAMP | KBD | VAR | CITE">

<!ENTITY % misc "Q | LANG | AU | DFN | PERSON | ACRONYM | ABBREV | INS | DEL">

<!ENTITY % special "TAB | MATH | A | IMG | BR">

<!ENTITY % notmath "%font | %phrase | %special | %misc">

<!ENTITY % text "#PCDATA | SUB | SUP | B | %notmath">


<!ENTITY % pre.exclusion "TAB|MATH|IMG|BIG|SMALL|SUB|SUP">

<!ELEMENT (%font|B|%phrase|%misc) - - (%text)+>
<!ATTLIST (%font|B|%phrase|%misc) %attrs;>

<!-- Subscripts and superscripts. The ALIGN attribute is only used for math -->

<!ELEMENT (SUB|SUP) - - (%text)+>
<!ATTLIST (SUB|SUP)
        %attrs;
        align (left|center|right) #IMPLIED
        >
```

```
<!-- Forced line break -->

<!ELEMENT BR    - O EMPTY>
<!ATTLIST BR
        %attrs;
        %needs; -- for control of text flow --
        >

<!-- Named left, center and right tab stops (independent of '\t' char) -->

<!ELEMENT TAB - O EMPTY>
<!ATTLIST TAB
        id        ID        #IMPLIED  -- defines named tab stop --
        indent    NUMBER    0         -- en units before new tab stop --
        to        IDREF     #IMPLIED  -- jump to named tab stop --
        align   (left|center|right|decimal) left
        dp       CDATA      #IMPLIED  -- decimal point e.g. dp="," --
        >

<!--================== Link Markup ==========================================-->

<!--
    With HTML 3.0 you can use ID attributes on most elements for named
    link ends. The use of the NAME attribute on anchors is deprecated.

    Do we want to support arbitrary elements for link starts? This would
    involve adding HREF and related attributes to most elements.
-->

<![ %HTML.Deprecated [
    <!ENTITY % linkName "name CDATA #IMPLIED -- named link end --">
]]>

<!ENTITY % linkName "">


<!ENTITY % ToolBar "home|toc|index|glossary|copyright|
                    up|previous|next|help|bookmark"

        -- LINK RELationship values which are used to create toolbar
           buttons or menu items for navigation, where toc stands
           for table of contents and bookmark provides for an open
           ended set of links, i.e. you can use multiple bookmarks
```

```
          for key entry points. Use the optional TITLE attribute
          to override default names.
      -->

<!ENTITY % linkType "NAME"
      -- A definitive list will be specified at a later date.

          They are used

                a) by stylesheets to control how collections of
                   html nodes are rendered into printed documents

                b) for document specific toolbars/menus when used
                   with the LINK element in document head:

                    "home|toc|index|glossary|copyright|
                           up|previous|next|help|bookmark"

                   where toc stands for table of contents and
                   bookmark provides for an open ended set of links,
                   i.e. you can use several bookmarks for key entry
                   points. Use the optional TITLE attribute to
                   override default names.
                c) for hypertext paths or guided tours,
                   with REL=NODE and REL=PATH.

                d) to make a link to a style sheet, e.g. rel=stylesheet
                   (used only with the LINK element).

                e) to make a link to a separate banner, e.g. rel=banner
                   (used only with the LINK element).
      -->


<!ENTITY % linkExtraAttributes -- URN moved to %url.link --
      "rel %linkType #IMPLIED -- forward relationship type --
       rev %linkType #IMPLIED -- reversed relationship type
                                 to referent data --
       title   CDATA #IMPLIED -- advisory only --
       methods NAMES #IMPLIED -- supported public methods of the object:
                                        TEXTSEARCH, GET, HEAD, ... --
       ">
```

```
<![ %HTML.Deprecated [
    <!ENTITY % A.content "(%heading|%text)+">
]]>

<!ENTITY % A.content   "(%text)+">

<!ELEMENT A     - - %A.content -(A)>

<!ATTLIST A
        %attrs;
        href   %URI;  #IMPLIED
        %url.link;     -- standard link attributes --
        %linkName;     -- name attribute is deprecated; use ID instead --
        shape %SHAPE; #IMPLIED -- for shaped hotzones in FIGs --
        %linkExtraAttributes;
        >

<!--=================== Images ==========================================-->

<!-- Desired widths are used for negotiating image size
     with the module responsible for painting the image.
     align=left or right cause image to float to margin
     and for subsequent text to wrap around image -->

<!ELEMENT IMG    - O EMPTY --  Embedded image -->
<!ATTLIST IMG
        %attrs;
        src  %URI;  #REQUIRED  -- URI of image to embed --
        %url.link;             -- standard link attributes --
        alt CDATA   #IMPLIED   -- for display in place of image --
        align  (top|middle|bottom|left|right) top -- relative to baseline
        --          width  NUMBER #IMPLIED -- desired width in en's or pixels --
        height NUMBER #IMPLIED -- desired height in en's or pixels --
        units  (en|pixels) pixels -- units for width and height --
        ismap (ismap) #IMPLIED -- pass clicks to server --
        >

<!--=================== Paragraphs==========================================-->

<!ELEMENT P     - O (%text)+>
<!ATTLIST P
        %attrs;
        align  (left|center|right|justify) #IMPLIED
```

```
        %needs; -- for control of text flow --
        nowrap (nowrap) #IMPLIED -- disable wordwrap --
        >

<!--=================== Headings, Titles, Sections ========================-->

<!ELEMENT HR    - O EMPTY -- customizable horizontal rule -->
<!ATTLIST HR
        %attrs;
        src     %URI;   #IMPLIED -- URI of custom rule graphic --
        %url.link;               -- standard link attributes --
        %needs; -- for control of text flow --
        >

<!--
  Headers can be numbered, although this is a matter for style sheets.
  The style sheet controls the numbering style:

     a) whether the parent numbering is inherited, e.g.  5.i.c
        where 5 is the current sequence number for H1 headers, and
        1 is the number for H2 headers and 3 for H3 headers.

     b) what style is used for current sequence number
        e.g. arabic, upperalpha, loweralpha, upperroman, lowerroman
        or a numbering scheme appropriate for the current language

  The skip attribute is used to skip over sequence numbers for items
  which have been left out of the list, e.g. skip=3 advances the
  sequence number past 3 omitted items. The seqnum sets the sequence
  number to a specified value. Note that the style sheet may take
  advantage of the sequence number for higher level headers.

  The dingbat or src attributes may be used to specify a bullet like
  image to be placed adjacent to the header. Defining this in the
  header element simplifies the document markup and avoids the need
  to use the clear or needs attribute in the following element to
  prevent it flowing around this image.
-->

<!ELEMENT ( %heading )  - -  (%text;)+>
<!ATTLIST ( %heading )
        %attrs;
        align  (left|center|right|justify) #IMPLIED
```

```
        %needs; -- for control of text flow --
        seqnum   NUMBER   #IMPLIED  -- starting sequence number --
        skip     NUMBER   0         -- skip seq nums for missing items --
        dingbat  ENTITY   #IMPLIED  -- dingbat entity from HTMLicons --
        src      (%URI;)  #IMPLIED  -- bullet defined by graphic --
        %url.link;                  -- standard link attributes --
        nowrap   (nowrap)  #IMPLIED -- disable wordwrap --
        >

<!ELEMENT TITLE - -  (#PCDATA)
          -- The TITLE element is not considered part of the flow of text.
             It should be displayed, for example as the page header or
             window title.
          -->

<!-=================== Text Flows ==========================================->

<!ENTITY % block
     "P | %list | DL
        | %preformatted
        | %blockquote
        | FORM | ISINDEX | FN
        | TABLE | FIG | NOTE">

<!--
  ((%block)* | (%text)*) would be much nicer as it would avoid the need
  for a <P> tag when all you want is a few words of text. The problem
  is that it also prevents: "<LI> <P>some text" since it forbids PCDATA
  and hence the white space between the <LI> and the <P>.
-->

<![ %HTML.Recommended [
    <!ENTITY % flow "(%block)*">
]]>

<!ENTITY % flow "(%text | %block)*">

<!ELEMENT PRE - - (%text)* -(%pre.exclusion)>

<!ATTLIST PRE
        %attrs;
        width NUMBER #implied
        %needs; -- for control of text flow --
```

```
        >

<![ %HTML.Obsoleted [

<!ENTITY % literal "CDATA"
        -- special non-conforming parsing mode where
           the only markup signal is the end tag
           in full. This will cause problems for
           standard SGML tools!
        -->

<!ELEMENT XMP - -  %literal>
<!ELEMENT LISTING - -  %literal>
<!ELEMENT PLAINTEXT - O %literal>

]]>

<!--=================== Lists ============================================-->

<!ELEMENT DL    - -  (LH?, (DT|DD)+) -- this is perhaps too lax? -->
<!ATTLIST DL
        %attrs;
        %needs; -- for control of text flow --
        compact (compact) #IMPLIED -- more compact style --
        >

<!ELEMENT DT    - O  (%text)+>
<!ELEMENT DD    - O  %flow;>
<!ATTLIST (DT|DD)
        %attrs;
        %needs; -- for control of text flow --
                       >


              <!ELEMENT (OL|UL) - -  (LH?, LI+) -- should we allow a list header ?
              -->

              <!-- style sheet controls numbering style
                  a) whether the parent numbering is inherited, e.g.  5.1.c
    b) what style is used for current sequence number
        e.g. arabic, upperalpha, loweralpha, upperroman, lowerroman
        or a numbering scheme for the current language
-->
```

```
<!ATTLIST OL
        %attrs;
        %needs; -- for control of text flow --
        continue (continue)  #IMPLIED   -- don't restart sequence number --
        seqnum    NUMBER     #IMPLIED   -- starting sequence number --
        compact (compact)    #IMPLIED   -- reduced interitem spacing --
        >

<!-- Unordered lists:

    o   single or multicolumn with
        horizontal or vertical wrapping

    o   plain or bulletted list items

    o   bullets can be customised via:
            - entities (dingbats in HTMLicons)
            - external graphic via URL
            - individual attributes on LI tags
-->
<!ATTLIST UL
        %attrs;
        %needs; -- for control of text flow --
        wrap (vert|horiz|none) none -- multicolumn list style --
        plain   (plain)  #IMPLIED   -- suppress bullets --
        dingbat  ENTITY  #IMPLIED   -- dingbat entity from HTMLicons --
        src     (%URI;)  #IMPLIED   -- bullet defined by graphic --
        %url.link;                  -- standard link attributes --
        compact (compact) #IMPLIED  -- reduced interitem spacing --
        >
<!ELEMENT LH - O (%text;)+ -- list header -->
<!ATTLIST LH %attrs;>

<!--
    For unordered lists, you can override the standard bullet with
    a custom graphic specified via a URI e.g. src="splash.gif" or
    a reference to one of the HTMLicons graphics e.g. dingbat=folder

    The skip attribute is used with ordered lists to skip over sequence
    numbers for items which have been left out of the list, e.g. skip=3
    advances the sequence number past 3 omitted items.
-->
```

```
<!ELEMENT LI - O %flow; -- list item -->
<!ATTLIST LI
        %attrs;
        %needs; -- for control of text flow --
        dingbat ENTITY #IMPLIED -- dingbat entity from HTMLicons --
        src  (%URI;) #IMPLIED   -- custom bullet graphic --
        %url.link;              -- standard link attributes --
        skip NUMBER 0           -- skip seq nums for missing items --
        >

<!-- DIR and MENU are now subsumed by UL with type=plain. Use the
     wrap attribute to control wrapping style for multicolumn lists -->

<![ %HTML.Deprecated [
    <!ELEMENT (DIR|MENU) - - (LI)+ -(%block)>
    <!ATTLIST (DIR|MENU)
        compact (compact) #IMPLIED>
]]>

<!--=================== Document Body =====================================-->

<![ %HTML.Recommended [
        <!ENTITY % body.content "(DIV|%heading|%block|HR|ADDRESS)*"
        -- <h1>Heading</h1>
           <p>Text ...
                is preferred to
           <h1>Heading</h1>
           Text ...
        -->
]]>

<!ENTITY % body.content "(DIV | %heading | %text | %block | HR | ADDRESS)*">

<!ELEMENT BODY O O  (BANNER?, BODYTEXT) +(SPOT)>
<!ATTLIST BODY
        %attrs;
        background %URI; #IMPLIED  -- texture tile for document background --
        >

<!ELEMENT BODYTEXT O O %body.content -- dummy element -->

<!--
  The BANNER element is used for a banner section which appears at
```

```
  the top of the window and doesn't scroll with window contents.
  This can be used for corporate logos, copyright statements and
  disclaimers, as well as customized navigation/search controls.
-->
<!ELEMENT BANNER - - %body.content>
<!ATTLIST BANNER %attrs; >

<!-- SPOT is used to insert IDs at arbitrary places
     e.g. for end points of a marked range (see RANGE) -->
<!ELEMENT SPOT - O EMPTY>
<!ATTLIST SPOT id ID #REQUIRED>

<!ELEMENT (%blockquote) - - (BODYTEXT, CREDIT?)>
<!ATTLIST (%blockquote)
        %attrs;
        %needs; -- for control of text flow --
        nowrap   (nowrap)  #IMPLIED -- disable wordwrap --
        >

<!ENTITY % address.content "((%text;)* | P*)">

<!ELEMENT ADDRESS - - %address.content>
<!ATTLIST ADDRESS
        %attrs;
        %needs; -- for control of text flow --
        >

<!--
  DIV can be used with the CLASS attribute to represent different
  kinds of container, e.g. chapter, section, abstract, appendix.
-->

<!ELEMENT DIV - - %body.content>
<!ATTLIST DIV
        %attrs;
        %needs; -- for control of text flow --
        align   (left|center|right) left -- alignment of following text --
        nowrap   (nowrap)  #IMPLIED -- disable wordwrap --
                      >

<!--================ Forms ============================================-->

<!--
```

```
    As HTML 2.0 plus a few extensions:

        a)  A RANGE control which varies between pair of values
            specified with the size attribute, e.g. SIZE="1, 10"

        b)  FILE widget for uploading one or more files to a server

        c)  SCRIBBLE on image widget that sends the "ink" to the server

        d)  SUBMIT/RESET buttons can now be customised with an image.
            This subsumes the IMAGE type which is now deprecated.

        e)  Graphical SELECTion menus are now supported, using
            the new SHAPE attribute on OPTION elements.

    Further extensions are in the pipeline (e.g. table entry,
    multiple data formats for textarea fields and client-side
    scripts with custom widgets) but will have to wait until
    the backlog of implementation work diminishes.
-->

<!ELEMENT FORM - - %body.content -(FORM) +(INPUT|SELECT|TEXTAREA)>
<!ATTLIST FORM
        action %URI #REQUIRED -- server-side form handler --
        method (%HTTP-Method) GET -- see HTTP specification --
        enctype %Content-Type; "application/x-www-form-urlencoded"
        script %URI #IMPLIED -- link to client-side script --
        >

<![ %HTML.Deprecated [
    <!ENTITY % InputType "(TEXT | PASSWORD | CHECKBOX | RADIO | SUBMIT
                | RESET | RANGE | FILE | SCRIBBLE | HIDDEN | IMAGE)">
]]>

<!ENTITY % InputType "(TEXT | PASSWORD | CHECKBOX | RADIO | SUBMIT
                | RESET | RANGE | FILE | SCRIBBLE | HIDDEN)">

<!ELEMENT INPUT - O EMPTY>
<!ATTLIST INPUT
        %attrs;
        type %InputType TEXT
        name  NAME  #IMPLIED      -- required for all but submit and reset --
        value CDATA #IMPLIED      -- required for radio buttons & checkboxes --
```

```
        disabled (disabled) #IMPLIED -- read-only fields --
        error CDATA #IMPLIED        -- why field is in error --
        checked (checked) #IMPLIED -- for radio buttons and check boxes --
        size NUMBER #IMPLIED        -- visible width of TEXT fields --
        maxlength NUMBER #IMPLIED   -- max number of chars for TEXT fields --
        min %REAL #IMPLIED          -- lower limit for RANGE fields --
        max %REAL #IMPLIED          -- upper limit for RANGE fields --
        accept CDATA #IMPLIED       -- list of MIME types for file fields --
        src   %URI  #IMPLIED        -- for fields with background images --
        %url.link;                  -- standard link attributes --
        align  (top|middle|bottom|left|right) top
        >

<!--
  SRC attribute added for graphical selection menus
  The WIDTH, HEIGHT and UNITS attributes apply to the
  image specified by the SRC attribute.
 -->

<!ELEMENT SELECT - - (OPTION+) -(INPUT|TEXTAREA|SELECT)>
<!ATTLIST SELECT
        %attrs;
        name CDATA #REQUIRED
        multiple (multiple) #IMPLIED
        disabled (disabled) #IMPLIED -- read-only menu --
        error CDATA #IMPLIED    -- why selections are in error --
        src  %URI  #IMPLIED     -- for graphical selection menus --
        %url.link;              -- standard link attributes --
        width  NUMBER #IMPLIED -- desired width of in en's or pixels --
        height NUMBER #IMPLIED -- desired height in en's or pixels --
        units  (en|pixels) pixels -- units for width and height --
        align  (top|middle|bottom|left|right) top
        >

<!ELEMENT OPTION - O (#PCDATA)>
<!ATTLIST OPTION
        %attrs;
        selected (selected) #IMPLIED
        value  CDATA  #IMPLIED -- default to element content --
        shape %SHAPE; #IMPLIED -- for graphical selection menus --
        disabled (disabled) #IMPLIED -- unselectable option --
        error CDATA #IMPLIED   -- why this choice is in error --
        >
```

```
<!--
  Multi-line text input field. align=left or right
  causes the field to float to margin and for
  subsequent text to wrap around the field.
-->

<!ELEMENT TEXTAREA - - (#PCDATA) -(INPUT|TEXTAREA|SELECT)>
<!ATTLIST TEXTAREA
        %attrs;
        name CDATA #REQUIRED
        rows NUMBER #REQUIRED
        cols NUMBER #REQUIRED
        disabled (disabled) #IMPLIED -- read-only field --
        error CDATA #IMPLIED         -- why field is in error --
        align  (top|middle|bottom|left|right) top
        >

<!--======================= Captions ======================================-->

<!ELEMENT CAPTION - - (%text;)+ -- table or figure caption -->
<!ATTLIST CAPTION
        %attrs;
        align (top|bottom|left|right) #IMPLIED
        >
<!--======================= Tables ========================================-->

<!--
    Tables and figures can be aligned in several ways:

    bleedleft   flush left with the left (window) border
    left        flush left with the left text margin
    center      centered (text flow is disabled for this mode)
    right       flush right with the right text margin
    bleedright  flush right with the right (window) border
    justify     when applicable the table/figure should stretch
                to fill space between the text margins

    Note: text will flow around the table or figure if the browser
    judges there is enough room and the alignment is not centered
    or justified. The table or figure may itself be part of the
    text flow around some earlier figure. You can in this case use
    the clear or needs attributes to move the new table or figure
    down the page beyond the obstructing earlier figure. Similarly,
```

```
    you can use the clear or needs attributes with other elements
    such as headers and lists to move them further down the page.
-->

<!ENTITY % block.align
        "align  (bleedleft|left|center|right|bleedright|justify) center">

<!--
    The HTML 3.0 table model has been chosen for its simplicity
    and the ease in writing filters from common DTP packages.

    By default the table is automatically sized according to the
    cell contents and the current window size. Specifying the columns
    widths using the colspec attribute allows browsers to start
    displaying the table without having to wait for last row.

    The colspec attribute is a list of column widths and alignment
    specifications. The columns are listed from left to right with
    a capital letter followed by a number, e.g. COLSPEC="L20 C8 L40".
    The letter is L for left, C for center, R for right alignment of
    cell contents. J is for justification, when feasible, otherwise
    this is treated in the same way as L for left alignment.
    Column entries are delimited by one or more space characters.

    The number specifies the width in en's, pixels or as a
    fractional value of the table width, as according to the
    associated units attribute. This approach is more compact
    than used with most SGML table models and chosen to simplify
    hand entry. The width attribute allows you to specify the
    width of the table in pixels, en units or as a percentage
    of the space between the current left and right margins.

    To assist with rendering to speech, row and column headers
    can be given short names using the AXIS attribute. The AXES
    attribute is used to explicitly specify the row and column
    names for use with each cell. Otherwise browsers can follow
    up columns and left along rows (right for some languages)
    to find the corresponding header cells.

    Table content model: Braille limits the width of tables,
    placing severe limits on column widths. User agents need
    to render big cells by moving the content to a note placed
```

```
    before the table. The cell is then rendered as a link to
    the corresponding note.

    To assist with formatting tables to paged media, authors
    can differentiate leading and trailing rows that are to
    be duplicated when splitting tables across page boundaries.
    The recommended way is to subclass rows with the CLASS attribute
    For example: <TR CLASS=Header>, <TR CLASS=Footer> are used for
    header and footer rows. Paged browsers insert footer rows at
    the bottom of the current page and header rows at the top of
    the new page, followed by the remaining body rows.
-->

<!ELEMENT TABLE - - (CAPTION?, TR*) -- mixed headers and data -->
<!ATTLIST TABLE
        %attrs;
        %needs; -- for control of text flow --
        border (border) #IMPLIED -- draw borders --
        colspec CDATA   #IMPLIED -- column widths and alignment --
        units  (en|pixels|relative) en -- units for column widths --
        dp      CDATA   #IMPLIED -- decimal point e.g. dp="," --
        width NUMBER    #IMPLIED -- absolute or percentage width --
        %block.align;  -- horizontal alignment --
        noflow (noflow) #IMPLIED -- noflow around table --
        nowrap (nowrap) #IMPLIED -- don't wrap words --
        >

<!ENTITY % cell "TH | TD">
<!ENTITY % horiz.align "left|center|right|justify">
<!ENTITY % vert.align  "top|middle|bottom|baseline">

<!--
    Browsers should tolerate an omission of the first <TR>
    tag as it is implied by the context. Missing trailing
    <TR>s implied by rowspans should be ignored.

    The alignment attributes act as defaults for rows
    overriding the colspec attribute and being in turn
    overridden by alignment attributes on cell elements.
    Use valign=baseline when you want to ensure that text
    in different cells on the same row is aligned on the
    same baseline regardless of fonts. It only applies
    when the cells contain a single line of text.
```

```
-->

<!ELEMENT TR - O (%cell)* -- row container -->
<!ATTLIST TR
        %attrs;
        align  (%horiz.align) #IMPLIED -- horizontal alignment --
        valign (%vert.align)  top  -- vertical alignment --
        dp     CDATA     #IMPLIED  -- decimal point e.g. dp="," --
        nowrap (nowrap)  #IMPLIED  -- don't wrap words --
        >

<!--
    Note that table cells can include nested tables.
    Missing cells are considered to be empty, while
    missing rows should be ignored, i.e. if a cell
    spans a row and there are no further TR elements
    then the implied row should be ignored.
-->

<!ELEMENT (%cell) - O %body.content>
<!ATTLIST (%cell)
        %attrs;
        colspan NUMBER    1      -- columns spanned --
        rowspan NUMBER    1      -- rows spanned --
        align  (%horiz.align) #IMPLIED -- horizontal alignment --
        valign (%vert.align) top -- vertical alignment --
        dp      CDATA    #IMPLIED  -- decimal point e.g. dp="," --
        nowrap (nowrap)  #IMPLIED  -- don't wrap words --
        axis CDATA #IMPLIED -- axis name, defaults to element content --
        axes CDATA #IMPLIED -- comma separated list of axis names --
        >

<!--====================== Figures ========================================-->

<!--
  The element contains text for use in non-graphical displays. Note that
  you can use the shape attribute in anchors to specify hotzones on images.
  This provides for local processing of pointer clicks and a unified method
  for dealing with graphical and non-graphical displays.

  Text is flowed around figures when the figure is left or right aligned.
  You can request the browser to move down until there is enough room for
```

```
  the next element, see the CLEAR and NEED attributes (in %needs)

  Figures offer a path towards embedding arbitrary information formats
  via some kind of OLE/OpenDoc mechanism.
-->

<!ELEMENT FIG - - (OVERLAY*, CAPTION?, FIGTEXT, CREDIT?) -(FIG|IMG)>
<!ATTLIST FIG
        %attrs;
        %needs;                    -- for control of text flow --
        src  %URI;  #REQUIRED      -- URI of document to embed --
        %url.link;                 -- standard link attributes --
        %block.align;              -- horizontal alignment --
        noflow (noflow) #IMPLIED -- noflow around figure --
        width  NUMBER #IMPLIED     -- desired width in units --
        height NUMBER #IMPLIED     -- desired height in units --
        units (en|pixels) pixels -- specifies units as en's or pixels --
        imagemap (%URI) #IMPLIED -- pass background clicks to server --
        >

<!ELEMENT FIGTEXT O O %body.content -- dummy element -->

<!--
   Figure overlays. When combined with local caching, overlays
   provide a cheap way of modifying a larger base image sent as
   part of a previous page.
-->

<!ELEMENT OVERLAY - O EMPTY -- image overlay -->
<!ATTLIST OVERLAY
        src  %URI;  #REQUIRED      -- URI of image overlay --
        %url.link;                 -- standard link attributes --
        units (en|pixels) pixels -- specifies units as en's or pixels --
        x      NUMBER   0          -- offset from left in units --
        y      NUMBER   0          -- offset from top in units --
        width  NUMBER #IMPLIED     -- desired width in units --
        height NUMBER #IMPLIED     -- desired height in units --
        imagemap (%URI) #IMPLIED -- pass background clicks to server --
        >

<!ELEMENT CREDIT - - (%text;)* -- source of image -->
<!ATTLIST CREDIT
        %attrs;
```

```
        >

<!--======================== Notes =======================================-->

<!--
The NOTE element is used for admonishments. The CLASS attribute
is used to differentiate NOTE's, e.g. Note, Caution or Warning.
-->

<!ELEMENT NOTE - - %body.content; -- admonishment -->
<!ATTLIST NOTE
        %attrs;
        src %URI;   #IMPLIED  -- URI of custom graphic --
        %url.link;            -- standard link attributes --
        %needs;               -- for control of text flow --
        >

<!--======================== Footnotes ===================================-->

<!--
Typically rendered as popup note. These elements are referenced
by hypertext links specified with the anchor element.
-->
<!ELEMENT FN - - %body.content;>
<!ATTLIST FN %attrs;>

<!--======================== Math  =======================================-->

<!-- Use     etc for greater control of spacing. -->

<!-- Subscripts and Superscripts

  <SUB> and <SUP> are used for subscripts and superscripts.

                                         i j
    X <SUP>i</SUP>Y<SUP>j</SUP>  is   X  Y

  i.e. the space following the X disambiguates the binding.
  The align attribute can be used for horizontal alignment,
  e.g. to explicitly place an index above an element:
                                            i
      X<sup align=center>i</sup>  produces  X
```

```
Short references are defined for superscripts, subscripts and boxes
to save typing when manually editing HTML math, e.g.

      x^2^    is mapped to   x<sup>2</sup>
      y_z_    is mapped to   y<sub>z</sub>
      {a+b}   is mapped to   <box>a + b</box>

Note that these only apply within the MATH element and can't be
used in normal text!
-->
<!ENTITY REF1   STARTTAG   "SUP">
<!ENTITY REF2   ENDTAG     "SUP">
<!ENTITY REF3   STARTTAG   "SUB">
<!ENTITY REF4   ENDTAG     "SUB">
<!ENTITY REF5   STARTTAG   "BOX">
<!ENTITY REF6   ENDTAG     "BOX">

<!USEMAP MAP1   MATH>
<!USEMAP MAP2   SUP>
<!USEMAP MAP3   SUB>
<!USEMAP MAP4   BOX>

<!SHORTREF MAP1 "^" REF1
                "_" REF3
                "{" REF5 >

<!SHORTREF MAP2 "^" REF2
                "_" REF3
                "{" REF5 >

<!SHORTREF MAP3 "_" REF4
                "^" REF1
                "{" REF5 >

<!SHORTREF MAP4 "}" REF6
                "^" REF1
                "_" REF3
                "{" REF5 >

<!--
 The inclusion of %math and exclusion of %notmath is used here
 to alter the content model for the B, SUB and SUP elements,
 to limit them to formulae rather than general text elements.
```

```
-->

<!ENTITY % mathvec "VEC|BAR|DOT|DDOT|HAT|TILDE" -- common accents -->
<!ENTITY % mathface "B|T|BT" -- control of font face -->
<!ENTITY % math "BOX|ABOVE|BELOW|%mathvec|ROOT|SQRT|ARRAY|SUB|SUP|%mathface">
<!ENTITY % formula "#PCDATA|%math">

<!ELEMENT MATH - - (#PCDATA)* -(%notmath) +(%math)>
<!ATTLIST MATH
        id      ID      #IMPLIED
        class    NAMES   #IMPLIED -- e.g. class=chem -->

<!-- The BOX element acts as brackets. Delimiters are optional and
     stretch to match the height of the box. The OVER element is used
     when you want a line between numerator and denominator. This line
     is suppressed with the alternative ATOP element. CHOOSE acts like
     ATOP but adds enclosing round brackets as a convenience for binomial
     coefficients. Note the use of { and } as shorthand for <BOX> and
     </BOX> respectively:

                               1 + X
     {1 + X<OVER>Y}  is      -------
                                 Y

                                   a + b
     {a + b<ATOP>c - d} is
                                   c - d

     The delimiters are represented using the LEFT and RIGHT
     elements as in:

     {[<LEFT>x + y<RIGHT>]}    is   [ x + y ]
     {(<LEFT>a<RIGHT>]}        is   (a]
     {||<LEFT>a<RIGHT>||}      is   || a ||

     Use &lbrace; and &rbrace; for "{" and "}" respectively as
     these symbols are used as shorthand for BOX, e.g.

     {&lbrace;<LEFT>a+b<RIGHT>&rbrace;}  is  {a+b}

     You can stretch definite integrals to match the integrand, e.g.
```

```
     {&int;<SUB>a</SUB><SUP>b</SUP><LEFT>{f(x)<over>1+x} dx}

            b
            /  f(x)
            | ----- dx
            / 1 + x
            a

     Note the complex content model for BOX is a work around
     for the absence of support for infix operators in SGML.

     You can get oversize delimiters with the SIZE attribute,
     for example <BOX SIZE=large>(<LEFT>...<RIGHT>)</BOX>

     Note that the names of common functions are recognized
     by the parser without the need to use "&" and ";" around
     them, e.g. int, sum, sin, cos, tan, ...
-->

<!ELEMENT BOX - - ((%formula)*, (LEFT, (%formula)*)?,
                   ((OVER|ATOP|CHOOSE), (%formula)*)?,
                   (RIGHT, (%formula)*)?)>
<!ATTLIST BOX
        size  (normal|medium|large|huge) normal -- oversize delims -->

<!ELEMENT (OVER|ATOP|CHOOSE|LEFT|RIGHT) - O EMPTY>

<!-- Horizontal line drawn ABOVE contents
     The symbol attribute allows authors to supply
     an entity name for an accent, arrow symbol etc.
     Generalisation of LaTeX's overline command.

     e.g. <above sym=ssmile>x</above>
     places an upwardly turning curve above the "x"
 -->

<!ELEMENT ABOVE - - (%formula)+>
<!ATTLIST ABOVE sym ENTITY #IMPLIED>

<!-- Horizontal line drawn BELOW contents
     The symbol attribute allows authors to
     supply an entity name for an arrow symbol etc.
     Generalisation of LaTeX's underline command.
```

```
 -->

<!ELEMENT BELOW - - (%formula)+>
<!ATTLIST BELOW sym ENTITY #IMPLIED>

<!-- Convenience tags for common accents:
     vec, bar, dot, ddot, hat and tilde
-->

<!ELEMENT (%mathvec) - - (%formula)+>

<!--
  T and BT are used to designate terms which should
  be rendered in an upright font (& bold face for BT)
-->

<!ELEMENT (T|BT) - - (%formula)+>
<!ATTLIST (T|BT) class NAMES #IMPLIED>

<!-- Roots  e.g. <ROOT>3<OF>1+x</ROOT> -->

<!ELEMENT ROOT - - ((%formula)+, OF, (%formula)+)>
<!ELEMENT OF - O (%formula)* -- what the root applies to -->

<!ELEMENT SQRT - - (%formula)* -- square root convenience tag -->

<!-- LaTeX like arrays. The COLDEF attribute specifies
     a single capital letter for each column determining
     how the column should be aligned, e.g. coldef="CCC"

        "L"     left
        "C"     center
        "R"     right

     An optional separator letter can occur between columns
     and should be one of + - or =, e.g. "C+C+C+C=C".
     Whitespace within coldef is ignored. By default, the
     columns are all centered.

     The ALIGN attribute alters the vertical position of the
     array as compared with preceding and following expressions.

     Use LDELIM and RDELIM attributes for delimiter entities.
```

```
     When the LABELS attribute is present, the array is
     displayed with the first row and the first column as
     labels displaced from the other elements. In this case,
     the first element of the first row should normally be
     left blank.

     Use &vdots; &cdots; and &ddots; for vertical, horizontal
     and diagonal ellipsis dots. Use &dotfill; to fill an array
     cell with horizontal dots (e.g. for a full row).
     Note &ldots; places the dots on the baseline, while &cdots;
     places them higher up.
-->

<!ELEMENT ARRAY - - (ROW)+>
<!ATTLIST ARRAY
        align (top|middle|bottom) middle -- vertical alignment --
        coldef  CDATA   #IMPLIED  -- column alignment and separator --
        ldelim  CDATA   #IMPLIED  -- stretchy left delimiter --
        rdelim  CDATA   #IMPLIED  -- stretchy right delimiter --
        labels (labels) #IMPLIED  -- TeX's \bordermatrix style -->

<!ELEMENT ROW - O (ITEM)*>
<!ELEMENT ITEM - O (%formula)*>
<!ATTLIST ITEM
        align   CDATA  #IMPLIED  -- override coldef alignment --
        colspan NUMBER 1         -- merge columns as per TABLE --
        rowspan NUMBER 1         -- merge rows as per TABLE -->

<!--================= Document Head ==========================================-->

<![ %HTML.Deprecated [
    <!ENTITY % head.content "TITLE & ISINDEX? & BASE? & STYLE?
                             & META* & LINK* & RANGE* & NEXTID?">
]]>

<!ENTITY % head.nextid "">

<!ENTITY % head.content "TITLE & ISINDEX? & BASE? & STYLE?
                         & META* & LINK* & RANGE*">

<!ELEMENT HEAD O O  (%head.content)>

<!ELEMENT LINK - O EMPTY>
```

```
<!ATTLIST LINK
        href %URI #REQUIRED
        %linkExtraAttributes; >

<!ELEMENT RANGE - O EMPTY>
<!ATTLIST RANGE
        id    ID    #IMPLIED  -- for naming marked range --
        class NAMES #IMPLIED  -- for subclassing --
        from  IDREF #REQUIRED -- start of marked range --
        until IDREF #REQUIRED -- end of marked range --
        >

<!ELEMENT ISINDEX - O EMPTY>
<!ATTLIST ISINDEX
        href   %URI  #IMPLIED -- server handling queries --
        prompt CDATA #IMPLIED -- prompt message -->

<!--
    The BASE element gives the base URL for
    dereferencing relative URLs, e.g.

         <BASE href="http://foo.com/images">
         ...
         <IMG SRC="bar.gif">

    The image is deferenced to

         http://foo.com/images/bar.gif
-->

<!ELEMENT BASE - O EMPTY>
<!ATTLIST BASE
        id   ID    #IMPLIED
        href %URI; #REQUIRED
        >

<![ %HTML.Deprecated [
    <!ELEMENT NEXTID - O EMPTY>
    <!ATTLIST NEXTID N CDATA #REQUIRED>
]]>

<!ELEMENT META - O EMPTY    -- Generic Metainformation -->
<!ATTLIST META
```

```
    http-equiv  NAME    #IMPLIED  -- HTTP response header name  --
    name        NAME    #IMPLIED  -- metainformation name       --
    content     CDATA   #REQUIRED -- associated information     --
    >

<!--
  A style sheet can be associated with the document using the
  LINK element, e.g. <LINK rel=style href="housestyle.dsssl">.
  Style overrides can be placed in the document head using the
  STYLE element, e.g.

    <style notation=dsssl-lite>
      dsss-lite stuff
    </style>

  Later on in the document you can use:
    <h2 class=bigcaps>Header with bigger than normal capitals</h2>
    <p class=abstract>A paragraph with a unique style of its own
    ...

  Statements in the given style notation

  The tag names, class and id attributes are used in the style sheet
  notation to describe how to render matching elements.
-->

<!ENTITY % style-notations "dsssl-lite | w3c-style">
<!NOTATION dsssl-lite PUBLIC
     "ISO/IEC 10179:1995//NOTATION DSSSL Style Language//EN">

<!NOTATION w3c-style PUBLIC "IETF/RFC nnn/W3C Style Language//EN">

<!ELEMENT STYLE - O (#PCDATA)>
<!ATTLIST STYLE
  notation NOTATION (%style-notations;) #REQUIRED
>

<!--================ Document Structure ===================================-->

<!ENTITY % html.content "HEAD, BODY">

<!ELEMENT HTML O O  (%html.content)>
```

```
<!ENTITY % version.attr "VERSION CDATA #FIXED '%HTML.Version;'">

<!-- suggested roles are: TOC, DOC, DOCPART, HITLIST, DIALOG -->

<!ATTLIST HTML
        %version.attr;        -- report DTD version to application --
        urn   CDATA #IMPLIED -- universal resource name for this document --
        class NAMES #IMPLIED -- role of this document, eg table of contents --
        >

<!-- The END -->
```

Appendix C

HTML 3.2 Document Type Definition

Introduction

HTML 3.2 is the current HTML specification as this is being written. Its features include:

- Basic HTML
- Tables
- Forms
- Scripting language support
- Style sheets

The new tags, <SCRIPT> and <STYLE>, support client side scripting languages and style sheets, respectively. The HTML 3.2 DTD follows and is available on the Web at http://www.w3c.org.

```
<!--
        W3C Document Type Definition for the HyperText Markup Language
        This version is code named Wilbur, and also as "HTML 3.2".

        Draft: Tuesday August 21st 1996

        Author: Dave Raggett <dsr@w3.org>

        This is subject to change, pending final approval by the W3C
        member companies.
```

```
        HTML 3.2 aims to capture recommended practice as of early '96
        and as such to be used as a replacement for HTML 2.0 (RFC 1866).
        Widely deployed rendering attributes are included where they
        have been shown to be interoperable. SCRIPT and STYLE are
        included to smooth the introduction of client-side scripts
        and style sheets. Browsers must avoid showing the contents
        of these element Otherwise support for them is not required.
        ID, CLASS and STYLE attributes are not included in this version
        of HTML.

        The next version of HTML after Wilbur is code named Cougar and
        will add support for <OBJECT>, client-side scripting, style
        sheets, and extensions to fill-out forms.
-->

<!ENTITY % HTML.Version
        "-//W3C//DTD HTML 3.2 Draft 19960821//EN"

        -- Typical usage:

            <!DOCTYPE HTML PUBLIC "-//W3C//DTD HTML 3.2 Draft 19960821//EN">
            <html>
            ...
            </html>
        --
        >

<!--================== Deprecated Features Switch =========================-->

<!ENTITY % HTML.Deprecated "INCLUDE">

<!--================== Imported Names =====================================-->

<!ENTITY % Content-Type "CDATA"
        -- meaning a MIME content type, as per RFC1521
        -->

<!ENTITY % HTTP-Method "GET | POST"
        -- as per HTTP specification
        -->

<!ENTITY % URL "CDATA"
        -- The term URL means a CDATA attribute
```

```
        whose value is a Uniform Resource Locator,
        See RFC1808 (June 95) and RFC1738 (Dec 94).
    -->

<!-- Parameter Entities -->

<!ENTITY % head.misc "SCRIPT|STYLE|META|LINK" -- repeatable head elements -->

<!ENTITY % heading "H1|H2|H3|H4|H5|H6">

<!ENTITY % list "UL | OL |  DIR | MENU">

<![ %HTML.Deprecated [
    <!ENTITY % preformatted "PRE | XMP | LISTING">
]]>

<!ENTITY % preformatted "PRE">

<!--================= Character mnemonic entities ==========================-->

<!ENTITY % ISOlat1 PUBLIC
       "ISO 8879-1986//ENTITIES Added Latin 1//EN//HTML">
%ISOlat1;

<!--================= Entities for special symbols =========================-->
<!-- &trade &shy and &cbsp are not widely deployed and so not included here -->

<!ENTITY copy   CDATA "&#169"   -- copyright sign     -->
<!ENTITY reg    CDATA "&#174"   -- registered sign    -->
<!ENTITY amp    CDATA "&#38;"   -- ampersand          -->
<!ENTITY gt     CDATA "&#62;"   -- greater than       -->
<!ENTITY lt     CDATA "&#60;"   -- less than          -->
<!ENTITY quot   CDATA "&#34;"   -- double quote       -->
<!ENTITY nbsp   CDATA " "  -- non breaking space -->

<!--=================== Text Markup ======================================-->

<!ENTITY % font "TT | I | B  | U | STRIKE | BIG | SMALL | SUB | SUP">

<!ENTITY % phrase "EM | STRONG | DFN | CODE | SAMP | KBD | VAR | CITE">

<!ENTITY % special "A | IMG | APPLET | FONT | BASEFONT | BR | SCRIPT | MAP">
```

```
<!ENTITY % form "INPUT | SELECT | TEXTAREA">

<!ENTITY % text "#PCDATA | %font | %phrase | %special | %form">

<!ELEMENT (%font|%phrase) - - (%text)*>

<!-- there are also 16 widely known color names although
  the resulting colors are implementation dependent:

   aqua, black, blue, fuchsia, gray, green, lime, maroon,
   navy, olive, purple, red, silver, teal, white, and yellow

 These colors were originally picked as being the standard
 16 colors supported with the Windows VGA palette.
 -->

<!ELEMENT FONT - - (%text)*      -- local change to font -->
<!ATTLIST FONT
    size    CDATA   #IMPLIED    -- [+]nn e.g. size="+1", size=4 --
    color   CDATA   #IMPLIED    -- #RRGGBB in hex, e.g. red: color="#FF0000" --
    >

<!ELEMENT BASEFONT - O EMPTY    -- base font size (1 to 7)-->
<!ATTLIST BASEFONT
    size    CDATA   #IMPLIED    -- e.g. size=3 --
    >

<!ELEMENT BR    - O EMPTY    -- forced line break -->
<!ATTLIST BR
        clear (left|all|right|none) none -- control of text flow --
        >

<!--================== HTML content models ===================================-->
<!--
    HTML has three basic content models:

        %text       character level elements and text strings
        %flow       block-like elements e.g. paragraphs and lists
        %bodytext   as (b) plus headers and ADDRESS
-->

<!ENTITY % block
     "P | %list | %preformatted | DL | DIV | CENTER |
```

```
    BLOCKQUOTE | FORM | ISINDEX | HR | TABLE">

<!-- %flow is used for DD and LI -->

<!ENTITY % flow "(%text | %block)*">

<!--==================== Document Body ======================================-->

<!ENTITY % body.content "(%heading | %text | %block | ADDRESS)*">

<!ENTITY % color "CDATA" -- a color specification: #HHHHHH @@ details? -->

<!ENTITY % body-color-attrs "
        bgcolor %color #IMPLIED
        text %color #IMPLIED
        link %color #IMPLIED
        vlink %color #IMPLIED
        alink %color #IMPLIED
        ">

<!ELEMENT BODY O O  %body.content>
<!ATTLIST BODY
        background %URL #IMPLIED  -- texture tile for document background --
        %body-color-attrs;        -- bgcolor, text, link, vlink, alink --
        >

<!ENTITY % address.content "((%text;) | P)*">

<!ELEMENT ADDRESS -- %address.content>

<!ELEMENT DIV -- %body.content>
<!ATTLIST DIV
        align   (left|center|right) #IMPLIED -- alignment of following text --
        >

<!-- CENTER is a shorthand for DIV with ALIGN=CENTER -->
<!ELEMENT center -- %body.content>

<!--=================== The Anchor Element ==================================-->

<!ELEMENT A - - (%text)* -(A)>
<!ATTLIST A
        name    CDATA   #IMPLIED    -- named link end --
```

```
        href    %URL    #IMPLIED    -- URL for linked resource --
        rel     CDATA   #IMPLIED    -- forward link types --
        rev     CDATA   #IMPLIED    -- reverse link types --
        title   CDATA   #IMPLIED    -- advisory title string --
        >

<!--================== Client-side image maps ============================-->

<!-- These can be placed in the same document or grouped in a
     separate document although this isn't yet widely supported -->
<!ENTITY % SHAPE "(rect|circle|poly|default)">
<!ENTITY % COORDS "CDATA" -- comma separated list of numbers -->

<!ELEMENT MAP - - (AREA)*>
<!ATTLIST MAP
    name    CDATA   #IMPLIED
    >

<!ELEMENT AREA - O EMPTY>
<!ATTLIST AREA
    shape   %SHAPE  rect
    coords  %COORDS #IMPLIED  -- always needed except for shape=default --
    href    %URL    #IMPLIED  -- this region acts as hypertext link --
    nohref (nohref) #IMPLIED  -- this region has no action --
    alt     CDATA   #REQUIRED
    >

<!--================== The LINK Element ==================================-->

<!ENTITY % Types "CDATA"
        -- See Internet Draft: draft-ietf-html-relrev-00.txt
           LINK has been part of HTML since the early days
           although few browsers as yet take advantage of it.

           Relationship values can be used in principle:

                a) for document specific toolbars/menus when used
                   with the LINK element in document head:
                b) to link to a separate style sheet (rel=stylesheet)
                c) to make a link to a script (rel=script)
                d) by stylesheets to control how collections of
                   html nodes are rendered into printed documents
                e) to make a link to a printable version of this document
```

```
                 e.g. a postscript or pdf version (rel=print)
-->

<!ELEMENT LINK - O EMPTY>
<!ATTLIST LINK
        id      ID      #IMPLIED    -- SGML ID attribute --
        href    %URL    #IMPLIED    -- URL for linked resource --
        rel     %Types  #IMPLIED    -- forward link types --
        rev     %Types  #IMPLIED    -- reverse link types --
        title   CDATA   #IMPLIED    -- advisory title string --
        >

<!--=================== Images ============================================-->

<!ENTITY % Length "CDATA" -- nn for pixels or nn% for percentage length -->
<!ENTITY % Pixels "CDATA" -- integer representing length in pixels -->

<!-- Suggested widths are used for negotiating image size
     with the module responsible for painting the image.
     align=left or right cause image to float to margin
     and for subsequent text to wrap around image -->

<!ENTITY % IAlign "(top|middle|bottom|left|right)">

<!ELEMENT IMG    - O EMPTY --  Embedded image -->
<!ATTLIST IMG
        src     %URL     #REQUIRED  -- URL of image to embed --
        alt     CDATA    #IMPLIED   -- for display in place of image --
        align   %IAlign  #IMPLIED   -- vertical or horizontal alignment --
        height  %Pixels  #IMPLIED   -- suggested height in pixels --
        width   %Pixels  #IMPLIED   -- suggested width in pixels --
        border  %Pixels  #IMPLIED   -- suggested link border width --
        hspace  %Pixels  #IMPLIED   -- suggested horizontal gutter --
        vspace  %Pixels  #IMPLIED   -- suggested vertical gutter --
        usemap  %URL     #IMPLIED   -- use client-side image map --
        ismap   (ismap)  #IMPLIED   -- use server image map --
        >

<!-- USEMAP points to a MAP element which may be in this document
  or an external document, although the latter is not widely supported -->

<!--=================== Java APPLET tag ===================================-->
<!--
```

```
  This tag is supported by all java enabled browsers. Applet resources
  (including their classes) are normally loaded relative to the document
  URL (or <BASE> element if it is defined). The CODEBASE attribute is used
  to change this default behavior. If the CODEBASE attribute is defined then
  it specifies a different location to find applet resources. The value
  can be an absolute URL or a relative URL. The absolute URL is used as is
  without modification and is not effected by the documents <BASE> element.
  When the codebase attribute is relative, then it is relative to the
  document URL (or <BASE> tag if defined).
-->
<!ELEMENT APPLET - - (%text)* +(PARAM)>
<!ATTLIST APPLET
        codebase %URL      #IMPLIED   -- code base --
        code     CDATA     #REQUIRED  -- class file --
        alt      CDATA     #IMPLIED   -- for display in place of applet --
        name     CDATA     #IMPLIED   -- applet name --
        width    %Pixels   #REQUIRED  -- suggested width in pixels --
        height   %Pixels   #REQUIRED  -- suggested height in pixels --
        align    %IAlign   #IMPLIED   -- vertical or horizontal alignment --
        hspace   %Pixels   #IMPLIED   -- suggested horizontal gutter --
        vspace   %Pixels   #IMPLIED   -- suggested vertical gutter --
        >

<!ELEMENT PARAM - O EMPTY>
<!ATTLIST PARAM
        name     NAME      #REQUIRED  -- The name of the parameter --
        value    CDATA     #IMPLIED   -- The value of the parameter --
        >

<!--
Here is an example:

    <applet codebase="applets/NervousText"
        code=NervousText.class
        width=300
        height=50>
    <param name=text value="Java is Cool!">
    <img src=sorry.gif alt="This looks better with Java support">
    </applet>
-->

<!--=================== Horizontal Rule ==================================-->
```

```
<!ELEMENT HR    - O EMPTY>
<!ATTLIST HR
        align (left|right|center) #IMPLIED
        noshade (noshade) #IMPLIED
        size  %Pixels #IMPLIED
        width %Length #IMPLIED
        >
<!--=================== Paragraphs=========================================-->

<!ELEMENT P     - O (%text)*>
<!ATTLIST P
        align  (left|center|right) #IMPLIED
        >

<!--=================== Headings =========================================-->

<!--
  There are six levels of headers from H1 (the most important)
  to H6 (the least important).
-->

<!ELEMENT ( %heading )  - -  (%text;)*>
<!ATTLIST ( %heading )
        align  (left|center|right) #IMPLIED
        >

<!--=================== Preformatted Text ==================================-->

<!-- excludes images and changes in font size -->

<!ENTITY % pre.exclusion "IMG|BIG|SMALL|SUB|SUP|FONT">

<!ELEMENT PRE - - (%text)* -(%pre.exclusion)>
<!ATTLIST PRE
        width NUMBER #implied -- is this widely supported? --
        >

<![ %HTML.Deprecated [

<!ENTITY % literal "CDATA"
        -- historical, non-conforming parsing mode where
           the only markup signal is the end tag
           in full
```

```
    -->

<!ELEMENT (XMP|LISTING) - -  %literal>
<!ELEMENT PLAINTEXT - O %literal>

]]>

<!--=================== Block-like Quotes ================================-->

<!ELEMENT BLOCKQUOTE - - %body.content>

<!--=================== Lists ============================================-->

<!--
   HTML 3.2 allows you to control the sequence number for ordered lists.
   You can set the sequence number with the START and VALUE attributes.
   The TYPE attribute may be used to specify the rendering of ordered
   and unordered lists.
-->

<!-- definition lists - DT for term, DD for its definition -->

<!ELEMENT DL    - -  (DT|DD)*>
<!ATTLIST DL
      compact (compact) #IMPLIED -- more compact style --
      >

<!ELEMENT DT - O  (%text)*>
<!ELEMENT DD - O  %flow;>

<!-- Ordered lists OL, and unordered lists UL -->
<!ELEMENT (OL|UL) - -  (LI)*>

<!--
      Numbering style
   1  arabic numbers     1, 2, 3, ...
   a  lower alpha        a, b, c, ...
   A  upper alpha        A, B, C, ...
   i  lower roman        i, ii, iii, ...
   I  upper roman        I, II, III, ...
```

```
    The style is applied to the sequence number which by default
    is reset to 1 for the first list item in an ordered list.

    This can't be expressed directly in SGML due to case folding.
-->

<!ENTITY % OLStyle "CDATA" -- constrained to: [1|a|A|i|I] -->

<!ATTLIST OL -- ordered lists --
        type      %OLStyle   #IMPLIED   -- numbering style --
        start     NUMBER     #IMPLIED   -- starting sequence number --
        compact  (compact)   #IMPLIED   -- reduced interitem spacing --
        >

<!-- bullet styles -->

<!ENTITY % ULStyle "disc|square|circle">
<!ATTLIST UL -- unordered lists --
        type    (%ULStyle)   #IMPLIED   -- bullet style --
        compact (compact)    #IMPLIED   -- reduced interitem spacing --
        >

<!ELEMENT (DIR|MENU) - -  (LI)* -(%block)>
<!ATTLIST DIR
        compact (compact) #IMPLIED
        >
<!ATTLIST MENU
        compact (compact) #IMPLIED
        >

<!-- <DIR>              Directory list                  -->
<!-- <DIR COMPACT>      Compact list style              -->
<!-- <MENU>             Menu list                       -->
<!-- <MENU COMPACT>     Compact list style              -->

<!-- The type attribute can be used to change the bullet style
     in unordered lists and the numbering style in ordered lists -->

<!ENTITY % LIStyle "CDATA" -- constrained to: "(%ULStyle|%OLStyle)" -->
```

```
<!ELEMENT LI - O %flow -- list item -->
<!ATTLIST LI
        type    %LIStyle     #IMPLIED   -- list item style --
        value    NUMBER      #IMPLIED   -- reset sequence number --
        >

<!--================ Forms ===============================================-->

<!ELEMENT FORM - - %body.content -(FORM)>
<!ATTLIST FORM
        action %URL #IMPLIED  -- server-side form handler --
        method (%HTTP-Method) GET -- see HTTP specification --
        enctype %Content-Type; "application/x-www-form-urlencoded"
        >

<!ENTITY % InputType
        "(TEXT | PASSWORD | CHECKBOX | RADIO | SUBMIT
            | RESET | FILE | HIDDEN | IMAGE)">

<!ELEMENT INPUT - O EMPTY>
<!ATTLIST INPUT
        type %InputType TEXT     -- what kind of widget is needed --
        name  CDATA #IMPLIED     -- required for all but submit and reset --
        value CDATA #IMPLIED     -- required for radio and checkboxes --
        checked (checked) #IMPLIED -- for radio buttons and check boxes --
        size CDATA  #IMPLIED     -- specific to each type of field --
        maxlength NUMBER #IMPLIED
        src   %URL  #IMPLIED     -- for fields with background images --
        align  (top|middle|bottom|left|right) top -- image alignment --
        >

<!ELEMENT SELECT - - (OPTION+)>
<!ATTLIST SELECT
        name CDATA #REQUIRED
        size NUMBER #IMPLIED
        multiple (multiple) #IMPLIED
        >

<!ELEMENT OPTION - O (#PCDATA)*>
<!ATTLIST OPTION
        selected (selected) #IMPLIED
        value  CDATA  #IMPLIED -- defaults to element content --
        >
```

```
<!-- Multi-line text input field. -->

<!ELEMENT TEXTAREA - - (#PCDATA)*>
<!ATTLIST TEXTAREA
        name CDATA #REQUIRED
        rows NUMBER #REQUIRED
        cols NUMBER #REQUIRED
        >

<!--======================== Tables ==========================================-->

<!-- Widely deployed subset of the full table standard, see RFC 1942
     e.g. at http://www.ics.uci.edu/pub/ietf/html/rfc1942.txt -->

<!-- horizontal placement of table relative to window -->
<!ENTITY % Where "(left|center|right)">

<!-- horizontal alignment attributes for cell contents -->
<!ENTITY % cell.halign
        "align  (left|center|right) #IMPLIED"
        >

<!-- vertical alignment attributes for cell contents -->
<!ENTITY % cell.valign
        "valign  (top|middle|bottom|baseline)  #IMPLIED"
        >

<!ELEMENT table - - (caption?, tr+)>
<!ELEMENT tr - O (th|td)*>
<!ELEMENT (th|td) - O %body.content>

<!ATTLIST table                          -- table element --
        align     %Where;    #IMPLIED  -- table position relative to window --
        width     %Length    #IMPLIED  -- table width relative to window --
        border    %Pixels    #IMPLIED  -- controls frame width around table --
        dummy     (border)   #IMPLIED  -- fixes SGML error for border w/o value --
        cellspacing %Pixels #IMPLIED  -- spacing between cells --
        cellpadding %Pixels #IMPLIED  -- spacing within cells --
        >

<!ELEMENT CAPTION - - (%text;)* -- table or figure caption -->
<!ATTLIST CAPTION
        align (top|bottom) #IMPLIED
```

```
       >

<!ATTLIST tr                        -- table row --
       %cell.halign;                -- horizontal alignment in cells --
       %cell.valign;                -- vertical alignment in cells --
       >

<!ATTLIST (th|td)                   -- header or data cell --
       nowrap (nowrap)  #IMPLIED    -- suppress word wrap --
       rowspan NUMBER   1           -- number of rows spanned by cell --
       colspan NUMBER   1           -- number of cols spanned by cell --
       %cell.halign;                -- horizontal alignment in cell --
       %cell.valign;                -- vertical alignment in cell --
       width   %Pixels  #IMPLIED    -- suggested width for cell --
       height  %Pixels  #IMPLIED    -- suggested height for cell --
       >

<!--================ Document Head ========================================-->

<!-- %head.misc defined earlier on as "SCRIPT|STYLE|META|LINK" -->

<!ENTITY % head.content "TITLE & ISINDEX? & BASE?">

<!ELEMENT HEAD O O  (%head.content) +(%head.misc)>

<!ELEMENT TITLE - -  (#PCDATA)* -(%head.misc)
         -- The TITLE element is not considered part of the flow of text.
            It should be displayed, for example as the page header or
            window title.
         -->

<!ELEMENT ISINDEX - O EMPTY>
<!ATTLIST ISINDEX
       prompt CDATA #IMPLIED -- prompt message -->

<!--
    The BASE element gives an absolute URL for dereferencing relative
    URLs, e.g.

        <BASE href="http://foo.com/index.html">
        ...
        <IMG SRC="images/bar.gif">
```

```
    The image is deferenced to

         http://foo.com/images/bar.gif

   In the absence of a BASE element the document URL should be used.
   Note that this is not necessarily the same as the URL used to
   request the document, as the base URL may be overridden by an HTTP
   header accompanying the document.
-->

<!ELEMENT BASE - O EMPTY>
<!ATTLIST BASE
        href %URL  #REQUIRED
        >

<!ELEMENT META - O EMPTY -- Generic Metainformation -->
<!ATTLIST META
        http-equiv  NAME    #IMPLIED  -- HTTP response header name  --
        name        NAME    #IMPLIED  -- metainformation name       --
        content     CDATA   #REQUIRED -- associated information     --
        >

<!-- SCRIPT/STYLE are place holders for transition to next version of HTML -->

<!ELEMENT STYLE  - - (#PCDATA)*  -(%head.misc) -- style info -->
<!ELEMENT SCRIPT - - (#PCDATA)*  -(%head.misc) -- script statements -->

<!--================ Document Structure ==================================-->

<!ENTITY % version.attr "VERSION CDATA #FIXED '%HTML.Version;'">

<![ %HTML.Deprecated [
    <!ENTITY % html.content "HEAD, BODY, PLAINTEXT?">
]]>

<!ELEMENT HTML O O  (%html.content)>
<!ATTLIST HTML
        %version.attr;
        >
```

Index

Other Books from Wordware Publishing, Inc.

Popular Applications Series

Build Your Own Computer (2nd Ed.)
Creating Help for Windows Applications
Developing Utilities in Assembly Language
Developing Utilities in Visual Basic 4.0
Getting the Most From Your HP LaserJet
HP LaserJet Handbook
Learn AmiPro in a Day (Ver 2.0 & 3.0)
Learn AutoCAD in a Day
Learn AutoCAD 12 in a Day
Learn AutoCAD LT for Windows in a Day
Learn AutoCAD LT Rel. 2 for Windows in a Day
Learn C in Three Days
Learn CompuServe for Windows in a Day
Learn dBASE Programming in a Day (2nd Ed.)
Learn DOS 6.2 in a Day
Learn Generic CADD 6.0 in a Day
Learn Lotus 1-2-3 Rel. 4 for DOS in a Day
Learn Lotus 1-2-3 Rel. 4 for Windows in a Day
Learn Lotus 1-2-3 Rel. 5 for Windows in a Day
Learn MS Access 2.0 for Windows in a Day
Learn MS Access 7.0 for Windows 95 in a Day
Learn Microsoft Assembler in a Day
Learn MS Excel 7.0 for Windows 95 in a Day
Learn MS PowerPoint 7.0 for Windows 95 in a Day
Learn MS Publisher 2.0 for Windows in a Day
Learn MS Word 6.0 for Windows in a Day
Learn MS Word 7.0 for Windows 95 in a Day
Learn Microsoft Works in a Day (Ver 2.0)
Learn Microsoft Works 3.0 in a Day
Learn Microsoft Works 3.0 for Windows in a Day
Learn Novell NetWare Software in a Day
Learn PageMaker 5.0 in a Day
Learn PAL 4.5 in a Day
Learn PROCOMM PLUS 2.0 for Widows in a Day
Learn Quattro Pro 5.0 in a Day
Learn To Use Your Modem in a Day
Learn Turbo Assembler in a Day
Learn Visual Basic 4.0 in Three Days
Learn Visual dBASE 5.5 for Windows in a Day
Learn Windows in a Day

Popular Applications Series (Cont.)

Learn Windows 95 in a Day
Learn WordPerfect 5.2 for Windows in a Day
Learn WordPerfect 6.0 for Windows in a Day
Learn WordPerfect Presentations in a Day
Moving from WordPerfect for DOS to WordPerfect for Windows
Networks for Small Businesses
Repair and Upgrade Your Own PC (2nd Ed.)
Write TSRs Now
Write Your Own Programming Language Using C++ (2nd Ed.)

Programmer's Example Series

The Delphi 3 Example Book
The WordBasic Example Book
The Visual Basic 4.0 Example Book

At A Glance Series

ACT! 2.0 for Windows at a Glance
CorelDRAW 5.0 for Windows at a Glance
Lotus 1-2-3 Rel. 4 for Windows at a Glance
Microsoft Word 6.0 for Windows at a Glance
Paradox 5.0 for Windows at a Glance
Quattro Pro 5.0 for Windows at a Glance
WordPerfect 6.0 for Windows at a Glance

Hands-On Windows Programming Series

1: Intro To Window Programming
2: Child Windows
3: Painting the Screen
4: Transferring Data To and From Windows
5: Mouse, Timer, and Keyboard Inputs
6: Text and Special Fonts, Menus, and Printing
7: AppStudio Graphics Editor
8: C to C++ Conversion
9: Special Topics, Index for Books 1-9

Illustrated Books

Illustrated DacEasy Accounting 4.2
Illustrated UNIX System V

Call Wordware Publishing, Inc. for names of the bookstores in your area
(972) 423-0090

Other Books from Wordware Publishing, Inc.

General and Advanced Computer Books

Collaborative Computing with Delphi 3
The Complete Communication Handbook (2nd Ed.)
Delphi 3 Developer's Guide to Microsoft Windows 32 API
Demystifying SNA
Demystifying TCP/IP (2nd Ed.)
Developing Internet Information Services
Innovation, Inc.
Integrating TCP/IP into SNA
Learn ACT! 3.0 for Windows 95
Learn Advanced JavaScript Prog.
Learn AutoCAD LT for Windows 95
Learn Computers in a Day
Learn Graphics File Programming with Delphi 3
Learn Internet Publishing with Microsoft Publisher 97
Learn Internet Relay Chat
Learn Lotus Domino
Learn the MFC C++ Classes
Learn Microsoft FrontPage 97
Learn Microsoft Office 95
Learn Microsoft Office 97
Learn Microsoft Windows NT 4.0
Learn Multimedia Programming with Visual Basic
Learn Oracle 7.3 and PowerObjects 2.0
Learn P-CAD Master Designer
Learn Pascal in Three Days (2nd Ed.)
Learn Visual Basic 5.0 in 3 Days
Lotus Notes Developer's Guide
Microsoft DirectX 3 Games Programming with Delphi 3
Practical Guide to Intranet Client-Server App. Using the Web

General and Advanced Computer Books (Cont.)

Practical Guide to SGML Filters
Software and Interface Design Guide for Delphi 3
The Ultimate Computer Buyer's Guide
Visio 4 for Everyone
Windows NT 4.0 Core and Enterprise Networking Technologies

Games and Entertainment

Alliances Revealed: A Review of the Magic: The Gathering Alliances Edition
Baxter on Magic: A Guide to Proper Playing Techniques for Magic: The Gathering
Deep Magic: Advanced Strategies for Experienced Players of Magic: The Gathering
Dolan's Almanac of Magic
Dominating Dominia: A Type II Tournament Player's Guide for Magic: The Gathering
Magic Cards Simplified: For Player Parents and Beginners of Magic: The Gathering
Mastering Middle-earth: Strategies for Middle-earth: The Wizards
Mastering Netrunner
Mirage Revealed: A Review of the Mirage Edition of Magic: The Gathering
Pro Magic: The Art of Professional Deck Construction
The Tables of Magic: The Ultimate Reference Guide to Magic: The Gathering
Single Card Strategies for Magic: The Gathering
HeroZero: The Uncollectable Card Collection Game
HeroZero: The Uncollectable Card Collection Game—Box of 10
Visions Revealed: A Review of the Visions Edition of Magic: The Gathering

Call Wordware Publishing, Inc. for names of the bookstores in your area
(972) 423-0090

READER RESPONSE INFORMATION

Wordware Publishing, Inc. is interested in your feedback about our books. Please take a few minutes and fill out this brief questionnaire and mail or fax it to our attention at the address listed at the bottom of the page.

Name: ______________________________

Company/Title: ______________________________

Address: ______________________________

City/State: ______________________ Zip Code: __________

1. Book title ______________________________
2. What is the primary reason you purchased this book from Wordware?

____

3. Where did you purchase this book?
   - ❑ Bookstore (name) ______________________________
   - ❑ Software or computer game store (name) ______________________________
   - ❑ Mail order (which company) ______________________________
   - ❑ Direct advertisement (which publication) ______________________________
   - ❑ Internet ______________________________
4. Approximately how many computer books do you purchase each year?

   ❑ 1 ❑ 2-5 ❑ 6-10 ❑ more than 10
5. What software applications do you use most frequently?

____

6. How would you judge the quality of this Wordware book?

   ❑ very good ❑ good ❑ satisfactory ❑ poor
7. What chapters or sections did you find the least and most valuable and why?

____

8. If you could change anything in this book what would it be?

____

9. I am interested in either writing or reviewing computer books. Please contact me. ❑

I enjoyed using this Wordware book. By signing my name below, I give Wordware permission to use my name and quote me in advertisements about Wordware books. Please include day-time phone number.

Signature: ______________________ Phone: __________

e-mail: ______________________

Wordware Publishing, Inc.
2320 Los Rios Boulevard
Plano, Texas 75074
Fax: 972 / 881-9147
info@wordware.com

Practical Guide to Intranet Client-Server Applications Using the Web Companion CD

The companion CD contains examples and case studies, a demo version of FolkWeb Web Server, Perl 4 for DOS, Perl 5 for Windows 95, SGMLS and NSGMLS SGML parsers, HTML 3.2 DTD, and other related software. Each directory includes a README.TXT that describes the contents of that directory. In addition, an HTML version of the main readme file, README.HTM, contains hyperlinks to the other readme files on the CD as well as hyperlinks to related Web sites. Simply use your Web browser to access README.HTM as a local file.